*Treasury Management
and Finance Series*

International
Cash Management

A Practical Guide to Managing
Cash Flows, Liquidity, Working Capital
and Short-term Financial Risks

Edited by
Michiel P. Ranke
Alexander Huiskes
Anthony N. Birts
Carlo R. W. de Meijer
Petra Plompen
Gary Throup

CIP DATA KONINKLIJKE BIBLIOTHEEK, DEN HAAG
International Cash Management (fourth edition)
International Cash Management – A Practical Guide to Managing Cash Flows, Liquidity, Working Capital and Short-term Financial Risks / Ranke, Michiel P.; Huiskes, Alexander and Birts, Anthony N. (editorial board)

NUR 782
treasury, (international) cash management, working capital (management), liquidity management, foreign exchange risk, interest rate risk, cash flow management, financial risk management, short-term investments, payment processing, clearing, settlement.

ISBN 978-90-79304-04-2

Includes index

Published by Riskmatrix
Frederik Hendrikplein 16 A
2582 AV Den Haag (The Hague)
The Netherlands
www.riskmatrix.eu
info.riskmatrix.eu

Book design: Magenta Xtra, Bussum (www.magentaxtra.nl)

This fourth edition is a revised version of previous editions and was authored by an editorial board comprised of experts from ING Bank, Ernst & Young Accountants and treasury professionals. Some sections were written by guest authors, as mentioned in the list of contributors. The first and second editions were authored by a board consisting of Lex van der Wielen, Willem van Alphen, Joost Bergen and Philip Lindow (second edition only). The third edition was authored by a board consisting of Willem van Alphen, Carlo R. W. de Meijer and Steve Everett.

Although the utmost care was taken in preparing this publication, the editorial board, the authors and their employers, the sponsors and the publisher make no guarantee, representation, warranty or assurance of any kind, express or implied, as to the accuracy or completeness of the information contained herein, accept no responsibility or liability for its accuracy or completeness and have no obligation to update or correct any of the contents of this publication. This publication does not constitute advice. Further, this publication does not purport to be all-inclusive or constitute any form of recommendation or to be an analysis of all potentially material issues and is not to be taken as a substitute for readers exercising their own judgment or seeking their own advice.

Foreword

It is my pleasure to introduce the fourth edition of *International Cash Management*. The first three editions were very successful. Thousands of financial practitioners have read the book as well as many students and academicians who used it as a welcome practical supplement to their fundamental research activities.

Once again, many interesting developments in the arena of cash management provided good reason to revise the contents. In the preface to the third edition, I remarked that the banking crisis and the pressures on the euro have brought enormous changes to the world of finance and risk management. As a result of the credit crunch, the treasurer's need to make liquidity available to the company has become strategically important to its success – and possibly its survival. Although the credit crunch itself has passed, this strategic roll remains extremely important. Companies must be aware that market situations have changed and that it will no longer be as easy to obtain enough funds for investments and daily operations in the future. In addition, companies continue to operate in a world with many uncertainties in light of the changing geopolitical situation, Brexit and the general uncertainties in the eurozone.

In the meantime, developments in market infrastructure, technology and regulation continue to dramatically change the duties of the cash manager. For many international companies, it is impossible to organise the majority of their international cash management activities at one core cash management centre. Meanwhile, FinTech developments are providing challenging new opportunities, although it is not clear which techniques will survive.

In order to adequately fulfil their role, treasurers must be professionals with a thorough knowledge of the company's business. This will enable them to accurately evaluate the company's finance needs and to optimise its treasury operations. In addition, as stated in the preface of previous editions, insight into the main financial markets and treasury tools will remain key requirements. All this continues to be valid today.

In addition, this fourth printing provides an updated overview of modern international cash management. Relevant topics such as working capital, infrastructure, cash pooling techniques, payment technologies and many others are covered from the point of view of the cash manager of a non-financial international company. For completeness, we have also included several topics that may be described by some practitioners as risk management issues rather than pure cash management topics.

This edition has been edited by an editorial board consisting of Anthony Birts, Carlo de Meijer, Alexander Huiskes, Michiel Ranke, Petra Plompen and Gary Throup. Other international experts also contributed to the book as authors.

Dr. Mattheus van der Nat

Professor of Treasury Management at VU Amsterdam University
(Vrije Universiteit) in Amsterdam

Contents

Part D
Liquidity Management

Chapter 18
Short-Term Interest Risk Management

Part F
Regulations

Chapter 19
Tax Consequences of Cash Management

Chapter 20
Legal Considerations

Chapter 21
Treasury Accounting and Control

Preface

You are about to read the most comprehensive book on cash management that is available in the market. The experts who have authored and worked on this book are passionate and eager to share their knowledge and experience with you. Working with many of them over the years has taught me a simple lesson: the solutions clients use require constant reviewing, either in light of new regulations or technological developments.

At the same time, treasury departments are expected to do more with fewer (human) resources. Examples include setting up an in-house bank, optimising the cost of and managing working capital and ensuring liquidity flows through the company in the most efficient, risk-averse and beneficial way. These tasks that fall within the domain of the treasury department are increasingly complex and require more and more automation to stay efficient. What appears to be a relatively simple question – whether to use a zero-balancing cash pool or a notional pool, or do we move to instant inter-company cash concentration enabled by virtual accounts – turns out to be complex, involving discussions with the tax, legal, operational and IT departments.

A lot has changed since the previous edition of this book: the financial world has seen the advent of FinTech companies that aim to take over part of the cash management role traditionally provided by banks. These companies keep the banks alert and on their toes. Banks might have the experience and budgets but FinTechs have the unbiased views on challenges, creativity and resilience. For centuries, banks have built up and worked to foster a unique value proposition: trust. Even during and after the financial crisis, people continued to trust banks with their precious savings and investments. It could take a generation before FinTechs can compete on this front with banks, but once they do, the financial landscape will have changed for good. One thing is for sure, our clients will benefit from these developments.

Technology has made tremendous progress. New developments like blockchain, robotics and artificial intelligence, as well as the use of application programming interfaces (APIs), have had an immense impact on the financial industry. New technology gives companies instant access to millions of customers around the globe. The changes for banks have been enormous as well. Clients have gone from relying on branch opening hours to accessing the bank from their home computer, and are now able to manage their finances from their mobile phone anywhere and anytime.

New regulations have been introduced, some as the result of the financial crisis, some aimed at opening up the market to increase competition, such as PSD 2 in the European Economic Area. It is fascinating to see the resulting creativity and boost in new solutions.

Payments means data. While payments were and, to an extent, still are at the core of the business model of banks, we now realize that the data underlying the payment contain value for the company. This is even more so when it is enriched with additional and external data. While payment data in the past was primarily used to ensure the correct execution and reconciliation of a transfer, we are now shifting to using payment data to understand the behaviour of clients, to improve risk management, for marketing and many other purposes as yet to be discovered. New regulations and rapidly growing technological developments have created a combination that makes data accessible, instant and therefore highly usable. It is my firm belief that the next edition of this book will include further coverage of this phenomenon as, by then, it will have taken over as the most dominant source of income and value in cash management.

At ING, our purpose is 'empowering people to stay ahead in life and in business'. Empowerment is a feeling of self-reliance, of being confident and in control of your own future. This book will contribute to this feeling. By the time you come to the end, I am certain you will have gained additional, new insights into the complexity and dynamics that come into play when running an efficient cash management operation that serves your company.

I wish you a pleasant and informative read of this fantastic book!

Dick Oskam

Head of Transaction Services Sales, ING

About This Book

This book focuses on the cash management function of a typical multinational company. We will discuss the environment within which the cash manager operates, the tasks that must be completed, the instruments at the cash manager's disposal and the necessary day-to-day activities and objectives that allow the business to function smoothly. We will also describe some of the external factors that can cause cash managers to adapt their approach in order to ensure their operations remain competitive. Throughout the book, examples are used to highlight specific practices or scenarios.

The book consists of the following sections:

A.   *Treasury Management* (chapters 1-3)
B.   *Working Capital Management* (chapters 4-6)
C.   *Payments and Receivables* (chapters 7-11)
D   *Liquidity Management* (chapters 12-15)
E.   *Risk Management* (chapters 16-18)
F.   *Regulations* (chapters 19-22)
G.   *Innovation* (chapter 23)
H.   *Best Practices* (chapters 24-25)

A.   Treasury Management (chapters 1-3)

In the first part of the book, we describe the treasury organisation of a multinational company. We describe the treasury's place within the finance department and the role of the cash management function. We provide a higher-level overview of the cash management role and explain how it can be broken down into separate functions – each with their own policies, objectives and organisational requirements. We give special attention to fundamental changes in techniques and environment that have made transformation to a modern treasury a necessity.

B.   Working Capital Management (chapters 4-6)

In the next section, we discuss the concept of working capital and highlight its relationship to operations and profitability. We highlight how the correlation between working capital and liquidity enables a company-wide approach to improve working capital performance that can help position a business effectively in order to respond better to an economic upswing. We also discuss trade finance, the management of the capital used in international trade flows and the common challenges associated with international trade.

C.   Payments and Receivables (chapters 7-11)

Here, we provide an overview of transaction instruments and electronic interfaces. In addition, we cover the policy aspects of cash flow management and identify the essential aims and objectives that companies wish to achieve through first-class cash flow management. In particular, we focus on strategies that can reduce transaction costs and help to ensure cash flows are tightly controlled. We explain the basics of cash flow management and provide our view on the definition, objectives and relevance of cash flow management. We also discuss the options available to reduce the costs of the payments process.

Over the last few years, delivery channels – especially internet systems – have become more sophisticated through a combination of wider product ranges and stronger self-service components such as the tracking and tracing of service requests. At the same time, companies need to manage working capital effectively and incorporate delivery channels into their organisational structures and processes in a more efficient manner – while mitigating risks. In this section, we discuss such delivery channels and their importance in the world of international cash management.

It is clear that although the Single Euro Payments Area (SEPA) will help to harmonise domestic solutions and improve cross-border payment capabilities between euro countries, not all banks have access to the same routing options. As a result, their capabilities and product offerings also differ. We discuss this and focus on characteristics of the various routing options that are available.

D.   Liquidity Management (chapters 12-15)

Liquidity management can be broken down into two main activities – cash balances management and (short-term) investment management and funding. We discuss both in this section, as well as explaining the requirements needed for successful liquidity management overall. We also highlight some of the organisational aspects and key trends in cash balances management. Our focus is drawn to the basic concept of cash pooling as we discuss the different instruments in physical cash concentration and notional pooling. In addition, we provide a comprehensive overview of the cash pooling techniques provided by some of the major international cash management banks.

The content in this section includes information on the systems that are available to support a treasurer's day-to-day activities. Elsewhere in this section, we explain the investment management options that are available, as well as describing some of the cash flow forecasting methods and discussing how companies are sourcing the data needed to populate such reports.

E.   Risk Management (chapters 16-18)

This section is about risk and specifically includes content about the various FX risks that a company may incur as well as how it can deal with such risk. We also highlight potential FX management policy options alongside the various instruments available to a treasurer who wishes to hedge their FX risk.

In addition, we include content on cross-currency liquidity management best practice methods and explain how future liquidity positions generate interest risks (as well as highlighting the potential instruments that can be used to cover those risks). And we describe how interest results can be fixed or managed for future periods.

F. Regulations (chapters 19-22)

The implementation of an international cash management structure presents treasurers with many challenges. One particularly significant challenge is related to the many different tax rules across the globe. In this section, we provide a high-level overview of the potential tax consequences of international cash management structures with respect to factors such as withholding tax on interest, stamp duties, transfer pricing, thin capitalisation, controlled foreign companies and treasury centre locations.

We also discuss legal issues relevant for international cash management and treasury accounting. Later on, we describe regulatory initiatives that can affect corporates' cash and liquidity management. These include regulatory reforms such as the Payment Services Directive (PSD) and Basel III, but also anti-money laundering rules.

G. Innovation (chapter 23)

Many new techniques have been further developed since the previous edition of this book. In this section, key developments are discussed that may influence the treasury function in the future. Important examples are the developments on data in the cloud, big data and blockchain technology.

H. Best Practices (chapters 24-25)

In this section, we provide a typical roadmap for companies to rationalise and centralise their cash management operations. In addition, several case studies are given, demonstrating best practices in different regions.

Part A

Treasury
Management

Chapter 1

The Treasury Organisation

1   The Treasury Organisation

1.1
Introduction

In this chapter, we provide an overview of the treasury management function and its relationship with cash management. We will also describe the roles and responsibilities of the treasurer and how they fit with those of the corporate controller and company operations, as well as external service providers and corporate investors. In addition, we will describe how the treasury is transforming and what role technology innovations can play in that process. In general, the treasury management function consists of three main components:

- Daily cash management
- Financial risk management – identification and hedging of foreign exchange risks and interest rate risks
- Corporate finance – management of financial assets and liabilities on the balance sheet as well as long-term funding and the financial aspects of mergers and acquisitions

In addition, the treasurer may also have a responsibility to manage banking relationships and provide input or direction concerning investor relations, working capital management, pensions, tax and the monitoring of operational business risks.

Of course the full remit of the treasury management function tends to be tailored to fit the individual needs of each company. In larger companies, a number of treasury functions are often carried out by a dedicated treasury department and this is certainly the case in many multinational corporates (MNCs). In smaller companies, however, it is likely that such functions are performed by the finance team or a dedicated person within the finance team who is performing the treasury role or taking care of cash management activities.

Treasury management includes the management of:
- Liquidity and cash flows
- Financial risks
- Long-term funding and the balance sheet

In order to:
- Optimise interest results, maximise credit interest, minimise debit interest
- Minimise transaction costs
- Protect the company against financial losses due to market rate fluctuations and other credit risks
- Ensure that sufficient liquidity or credit is available for the company to conduct its core business

1.2
Treasury responsibilities

The role of the treasury function has grown significantly in recent years as companies have expanded their business operations internationally. This has resulted in many new tasks for the treasurer as well as the centralisation of local financial activities in order to optimise efficiencies.

When discussing treasury roles and responsibilities, it is important to understand the overall finance policy and to distinguish treasury tasks from the other financial functions – such as the accounting and control departments.

In many organisations, a treasurer is often responsible for the execution of treasury policy regarding financing, risk and the management of cash flows and liquidity. It is also very common for a treasurer to be involved in tasks that are designed to make a company more effective in managing its working capital. On the other hand, a treasury controller frequently undertakes to control and minimise the risks arising from the treasury activity, as well as to advise management about the status and execution of treasury activities and the degree to which they conform to regulations. There are a number of tasks on which it is common for the treasurer and controller to cooperate in order to achieve greater success. These include the management of financial and operational risks, the drafting of customer guarantees/securities and the optimisation of working capital.

Over time, the treasury function has expanded into several different fields. These are briefly summarised in figure 1.1.

FIGURE 1.1   OVERVIEW OF THE TREASURY FUNCTION

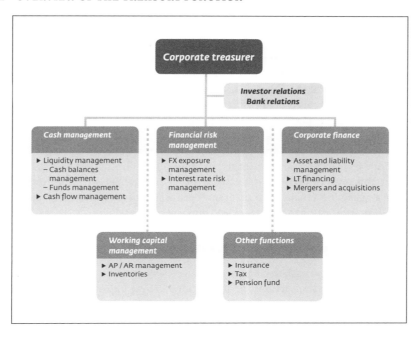

The larger the company, the more important it is for specific tasks, roles and responsibilities to be defined and clearly structured in order to ensure resources are used efficiently. This is particularly the case where significant volumes and sums of cash are managed on a daily basis. The front office executes the financial transactions, the middle office provides information and controls the way in which the transactions are executed. The back office is responsible for the accounting, administration and reporting duties of the organisation.

1.2.1   CASH MANAGEMENT

While we have included working capital management in this book, please note that it is not considered to be part of cash management in its strictest definition. However, because of its impact on liquidity, a treasurer often has a say in working capital management policies so it is relevant to the content here.

Cash management is the management of short-term liquidity, daily cash flows and (subject to the caveat above) working capital. The treasurer or cash manager seeks to optimise a company's cash position while keeping costs arising from cash flows as low as possible. This normally entails the minimisation of interest costs and bank fees, and the maximisation of interest income.

1.2.2   LIQUIDITY MANAGEMENT

Liquidity management can be divided into cash balances management and short-term investment management and funding. The former refers to the day-to-day management of the company's balances on current accounts. Every day, the cash manager seeks to control the company's cash balances in such a manner that the interest result on those balances is optimised and that the balances are allocated to the accounts targeted by the company. If the company has centralised cash management and several subsidiaries, the challenge is to move the balances to the accounts where they can be used to offset deficits.

Investment management and funding refers to the management of the company's short-term liquidity by investing excess cash and funding deficits. In contrast to cash balances management, this involves cash positions that exist for a longer period of time (for instance, longer than a week). It is crucial for the treasurer or cash manager to have accurate and appropriate cash flow forecasting to manage this as efficiently as possible.

1.2.3   CASH FLOW MANAGEMENT

Another important cash management task is to ensure there is a reliable and robust process whereby all daily transactions can be executed in time and at the lowest possible cost. This relates to external commercial transactions, such as collections from customers and payments to vendors, as well as other types of external and internal transactions.

There are various ways to improve cash flow management and reduce its operating costs. It is critical to organise an appropriate structure of cash flows. For instance, cross-border cash flows can be reduced or avoided by routing foreign cash flows through non-resident accounts in the country of destination. Rather than make multiple cross-border payments, one large cross-border payment can be made and then broken down into smaller domestic payments. Inter-company transactions can be reduced by implementing an in-house netting system. It is also critical to control the timing of transactions to make sure that each transaction takes place 'just in time'. Another way of ensuring efficiency is to integrate external and internal processing systems, avoid manual intervention and achieve straight-through processing.

1.2.4   WORKING CAPITAL MANAGEMENT

In many companies, working capital management is also one of the areas where the treasurer is involved. Working capital is the difference between current assets (cash and quickly realisable assets, including investments) and current liabilities (those repayable within one year). In general, the size and composition of working capital determines a company's liquidity.

Working capital = current assets – current liabilities

In this book, we will distinguish between working capital (which includes cash) and operating working capital (which does not). Operating working capital breaks down into:

–   Accounts receivable management
–   Accounts payable management
–   Inventory management

Many of these activities are executed by other departments or specialists. Larger companies generally have a dedicated accounts receivable department and a dedicated accounts payable department. Very often, a specialised credit manager is responsible for policies regarding credit to (potential) customers and overseeing the risks related to outstanding receivables. Inventories are usually managed by the production entities. Many different departments are involved in the daily execution of working capital management. However, the treasurer will always keep close track of all the variables that influence the daily cash flows and liquidity positions. This is natural given that the company's cash position largely depends on the type of business and the quality of its working capital management. It is an area of increasing importance, since there is considerable financial benefit to be gained from the optimisation of working capital.

1.3
Corporate finance

FIGURE 1.2
SIMPLIFIED BALANCE
SHEET STRUCTURE

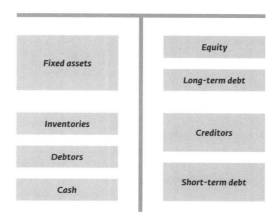

The corporate finance function has the following core roles:

–   Optimising the balance sheet structure
–   Planning and executing long-term financing
–   Managing the financial aspects of mergers and acquisitions

As is clear from the simplified balance sheet, many balance sheet components are determined by the type of core business that the company is running. Production companies will have substantial fixed assets such as production plants. Trading companies will have much smaller fixed assets but may have large trade debtors and trade creditors. It is the responsibility of the treasurer to fund the gap between assets and liabilities by attracting the optimal mix of equity and long-term debt.

The appropriate funding of the balance sheet is of utmost importance to the success of every business. The optimal mix between equity and debt should be determined. This optimum is far from stable – it will change according to the size of the organisation and its performance, as well as the cost of capital (both equity and debt). One of the key challenges facing a treasury department is finding the right level of debt at the right price and providing as little collateral as possible with a minimum of financial performance targets – known as covenants – required by the banks.

1.4
Financial risk management

Financial risk management is usually referred to as the activity dedicated to controlling the foreign exchange risks and interest rate risks of a company.

1.4.1   FOREIGN EXCHANGE RISK

Foreign exchange risk is the risk that fluctuating foreign exchange rates will have a negative effect on a company's results or value. Companies operating in several countries can be exposed to different types of foreign exchange risk. They face a 'transaction risk' when imports and exports are priced and settled in currencies that differ from that of the company's operational costs and funding. They can also be exposed to 'translation risks' when they have assets which are denominated in one currency without offsetting liabilities in another currency. The risk is that the net value of the company will decrease due to adverse fluctuations in foreign exchange rates. Another form of translation risk is that net earnings will decrease due to adverse currency fluctuations when translating earnings from foreign operations into the consolidated income statement. Finally, companies may be exposed to an 'economic risk' when they are selling products imported from a country with an appreciating currency while competitors are importing from countries with a depreciating currency.

In chapter 16 of this book, we provide a more extensive explanation of the currency risks to which companies can be exposed and we will discuss what actions may be taken by the treasurer to control those risks.

The following tasks are often assigned to the treasurer to manage foreign currency risks:

- Propose and agree foreign exchange risk strategy
- Identify and report risk exposures and potential effects on net earnings and net worth
- Deploy various instruments to reduce or avoid risks

1.4.2 INTEREST RATE RISK RELATED TO FUNDING

At its highest level, interest rate risk occurs where interest rate movements have a potential effect on operating results. It arises when future interest flows from funding and investments are not fixed and can result in both positive as well as negative effects depending on the direction in which the floating interest rates are moving.

Most companies are sensitive to fluctuations in interest rates. The treasurer's task is to reduce the potential negative effect of such fluctuations. The treasurer is expected to:

- Help prepare and agree an interest rate forecast over the short and long term
- Identify and monitor the company's interest rate exposure
- Conclude transactions in the money markets and derivatives markets to reduce exposures when appropriate

1.4.3 OTHER ACTIVITIES

In addition to the responsibilities discussed above, the treasurer may be involved in a number of other financial activities. A very important responsibility is to maintain good relationships with the company's banking partners. Such relationships are often managed centrally by the treasury department. For companies with public listings and those issuing bonds and commercial paper, it is important to maintain good relationships with (potential) investors. Larger companies will often have a dedicated investor relations manager but the treasurer may also assume that role. Investor relations tend to have a broader scope than bank relations and involve the supply of information about the company's performance to all potential suppliers of funds. In any case, the corporate treasurer is likely to have an advisory role.

Finally, there are several activities that may or may not be allocated to the treasury department. One of them is the insurance of business risks. This role has evolved over time from buying insurance policies to analysing operational business risks and, increasingly, covering certain business risks by making internal provisions. This role is increasingly performed by operational business risk managers. Treasurers may also be tasked with managing tax activities. Where the treasurer combines financing expertise with in-depth knowledge of tax affairs, it can help to create a highly tax-efficient financing structure.

A company's pension fund is often allocated to a separate entity. However, the treasurer may have an advisory role with respect to the pension fund and may leverage the knowledge in the treasury team about the financial markets.

1.5
Treasury organisation – front office, middle office and back office

As we have discussed, the larger the company, the more important it is for specific tasks, roles and responsibilities to be defined and clearly structured in order to ensure the most efficient use of resources. As illustrated by the box below, there are often clearly delineated roles for the front, middle and back office within a company.

Treasury roles: front office, middle office and back office

Front office
- Maintain contact with internal and external counterparties and banks
- Make transaction proposals based on internal requests and treasury policy
- Execute those transactions
- Always act in line with treasury policy

Middle office
- Compile the company's cash and risk position reports
- Check the deals executed by the front office (formal and material)
- After relevant controls and approval, forward the transaction to the back office for administration
- Make all required periodic and ad hoc treasury reports

Back office
- Handle administration of transactions executed
- Reconcile cash flows, transactions and bookings
- Provide input for periodic and ad hoc treasury reports
- Comply with treasury policy and accounting principles

1.5.1   RELATIONSHIP BETWEEN CONTROLLER AND TREASURER

The diagram below displays the important relationship between the roles of the corporate treasurer and corporate controller. In this example, the board is responsible for the strategic policy and will create the guidelines and framework for all parties to execute the business plan. While the treasurer takes care of the funding and manages the company's short-term and long-term financial assets and liabilities, the corporate controller is responsible for the provision of full management information to ensure the business is run in accordance with the policies and procedures of the company.

FIGURE 1.3   ROLE OF A CONTROLLER AND TREASURER

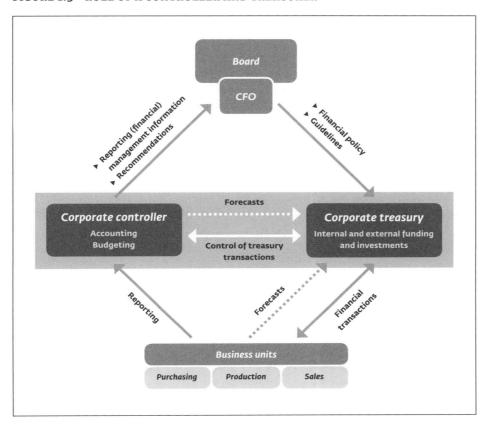

The controller also has an important role to fulfil in relation to the treasury. As we have mentioned previously, it is vital that the control of treasury activities is organisationally segregated from the execution of treasury transactions. Larger companies often appoint a dedicated treasury controller to monitor the activities of the treasury department.

Treasury controller objectives
– Controlling and minimising the risks arising from the treasury activity
– Advising management of the status and execution of the treasury activities
– Providing complete, accurate and timely reports on the treasury activities
– Frequently reviewing adherence to treasury policy / treasury regulations and reporting of findings to management

1.5.2   CONTROL FUNCTION

The control function often uses both preventive and repressive controls. Preventive controls are used to attempt to deter or prevent undesirable events from occurring. They are proactive and can help to prevent a loss. Examples include the effective segregation of duties, proper authorisation levels and passwords, adequate documentation and the physical control of financial positions and transactions. Meanwhile, repressive controls are designed to detect undesirable acts. They include a range of actions after a loss has occurred. Examples include reviews, analyses, reconciliations, physical inventories and audits.

Robust preventive controls are essential. These include limits set on transactions, on counterparts and on ratios (e.g. debt/equity) to prohibit the excessive use of certain financial instruments (such as derivatives). Repressive controls are important to ensure that the business adheres to the rules and procedures set out by management. It is also important that if deviations are detected, appropriate escalation paths are in place as well as controls to avoid similar situations in future.

In order to avoid any potential confusion, it is essential that the roles and responsibilities of both treasurer and controller are clear. The treasurer and controller often cooperate in the following areas:

- Management of financial and operational risks
- Drafting of guarantees/securities from customers
- Provision of conditions for external borrowing
- Optimisation of working capital
- Implementation of cash flow forecasting

1.6
Key areas influenced by treasury

A treasury department may have a variety of roles to play in a large international organisation. These include acting as:

- Principal
- Consultant
- Agent
- In-house bank

1.6.1   TREASURY AS PRINCIPAL

This involves the central execution of financial transactions on behalf (and on the books) of the holding company. This structure is often used for long-term financing of forecasted needs. The treasury department attracts funding from capital markets or banks based on the long-term financing of forecasted needs. The funding received is often transferred to the local entities through inter-company loans. In this case, treasury is the only party to attract funding for the company. Exceptions are local mortgages and the funding of assets in more restricted jurisdictions or in respect of assets with a complex ownership structure, such as joint ventures. It is usually also responsible for most bank activities and will service the internal units.

1.6.2   TREASURY AS CONSULTANT

This structure is very different from the role as principal. In this case, transactions are executed by local entities. The treasury acts as a knowledge centre and provides treasury advice to the operating companies without changing the responsibilities of those operating companies.

1.6.3   TREASURY AS AGENT

In this scenario, treasury is a centre of expertise and acts on behalf (and on the books) of the operating companies. For example, an operating company has an FX exposure that will be hedged by the treasury by buying a forward contract on behalf of the operating company. The settlement of this transaction will take place on the books and current accounts of the operating company rather than the treasury bank accounts.

1.6.4   TREASURY AS IN-HOUSE BANK

In this structure, there is a contractual relationship between the central treasury and the local operating company. Due to tax implications, they engage in a financial transaction as independent business partners on an arm's length basis. If we consider the example above, the operating company concludes a forward FX contract with the treasury (the in-house bank), with which it agrees on a price that is the same as it would receive from the bank in the agency model. The in-house bank will have many more internal FX contracts with operating companies and retains the foreign exchange exposure of all operating companies on its own books. This enables the in-house bank to independently determine a course of action, provided it adheres to the company policy.

The benefit of such a structure compared with the agency module is that the company will need far fewer bank accounts in foreign currencies. The main advantage is that the company has a central overview of all currency exposures and hedge transactions. In addition, there is the potential to internally offset long and short positions in one currency with the in-house bank.

In practice, we see the four different models combined in one treasury:

FIGURE 1.4
TREASURY
MODELS

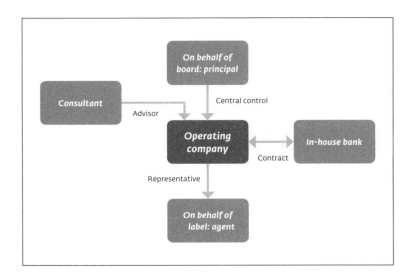

1.7
Centralisation versus decentralisation

Most multinational companies have centralised treasury and cash management activities. However, when businesses first venture into international markets, they tend to select a decentralised structure. As a result, overseas business units often have considerable autonomy.

In this phase, cash management activities are usually also decentralised. Local cash managers carry full responsibility for managing liquidity and currency positions and all transactions are settled with local banks. Over time, such companies realise there are significant potential efficiencies and financial benefits that can be achieved by centralising treasury activities.

1.7.1   ADVANTAGES OF CENTRALISATION

- Concentration of knowledge and experience – leading to improved results with fewer people and reduced risk of error
- Matching of financial positions (natural hedge) – resulting in better margins and lower costs
- Central purchasing of financial services and bank relationship management – leading to larger volumes and more competitive rates and terms and conditions
- Tighter treasury control to ensure implementation of daily processes that are aligned with the mandate of the treasury policy

1.7.2 DISADVANTAGES OF CENTRALISATION:

- Reduction of local knowledge
- Resistance from local management – may require a change in policy and responsibilities
- Complex management information system (MIS) flows and increased demands on enterprise resource planning (ERP) systems

For large companies, the advantages of centralisation often outweigh the disadvantages. However, centralisation is not necessarily suitable for all companies. Often, the centralisation of treasury goes hand-in-hand with the centralisation of core operational processes.

1.7.3 TIME ZONE RESTRICTIONS

Multinational companies with global activities often open regional treasury centres in the key time zones:

- Asia
- Europe
- US

These regional treasury centres perform the treasury operations of all subsidiaries in the relevant time zone. Though the regional treasury centres are frequently located in a different country from the holding company, they form a critical functional part of this holding company. Wherever possible, the regional treasury centres are located in a country with a conducive monetary and investment climate. In Europe, this includes cities such as Brussels, Amsterdam, Dublin and Zurich.

1.7.4 COST CENTRE VERSUS PROFIT CENTRE

Where all or some of the treasury tasks are centralised, it is necessary to determine who bears the risks of the treasury activities and how the resulting costs and revenues are distributed across the central treasury and the operating companies.

If the treasury is a profit centre, it has its own profit target. To comply with that goal, treasury is permitted to take financial positions that are not necessarily the same as the positions of the company's operating businesses. If the treasury department has no profit target of its own, it is called a cost centre. In some cases, treasury is obliged to immediately hedge all positions arising from a company's business (as a defensive strategy). In other cases, the treasury department can postpone the necessary hedge transaction or leave a part of the position open (as an offensive strategy). In the latter case, the treasury department is sometimes referred to as a service centre.

1.7.5 AUTOMATION

A comprehensive treasury information system that captures all the treasury flows is an absolute must for an effective treasurer. The core functionalities include data on the following subjects:

- Deal capture
- Cash management
- Forecasting
- In-house banking
- Debt management
- Accounting
- Risk management

In the modern trading environment, most deals are entered directly into a treasury system by the traders or uploaded automatically by a link between the dealing platform and the treasury management system (TMS). The actual execution of the settlement of the deal is performed by the back office. The treasurer or senior treasury manager often gives payment approval for each deal.

The cash management part of the system helps treasury manage all the cash in all the relevant bank accounts worldwide. The system should include the upload of electronic bank statements. All pooling and netting arrangements should be set up in the system and it should be possible to simulate a cash pool as it is operated by the bank. The more advanced systems are even able to shadow the cash pooling structure and calculate the net and individual interest results of pooled bank accounts. The forecast function of these systems helps organisations to implement a cash flow forecast separately and independently from other systems within the company. The system will facilitate the aggregation and integration of individual forecasts received from the business units.

The in-house bank structure deals with the capture and management of contractual relationships between treasury and operating companies. When treasury acts as an in-house bank, the inter-company transactions that are created must be monitored and recorded in order to keep inter-company account balances up-to-date and automatically post entries to the general ledger.

TMS systems are capable of capturing debt transactions in all shapes and forms. The system should also help to indicate when more funding is required and should automatically initiate periodic settlement of such transactions. Sometimes, accounting functions are also available in a TMS. Automatic posting of deals and other transactions can be facilitated by maintaining a set of posting rules or treasury accounts in the system, which can be mapped to the ERP system and posted into the general ledger.

The more advanced treasury systems are able to monitor financial exposures. Data from accounts payable, accounts receivable, purchases and sales can be captured to identify and evaluate exposure to foreign exchange and interest rates. That information can then be used in hedging programmes. The reporting format of the treasury system should be compatible with the general accounting standards of the company. For a more in-depth description of treasury management systems, see Chapter 10.

1.8
Corporate treasury responsibilities

The increasing importance of the benefits of a dedicated treasury organisation has gone hand in hand with growth in the areas of responsibility. It is now common for treasury to have input into the strategic development of a company from a financial and risk point of view. When a business expands in new territories, it can create more complicated trade and cash flows – such as inter-company transactions across borders. This results in greater exposure to financial and operational risk. In addition, legislative changes in a variety of different tax and regulatory regimes mean that a dedicated treasury unit can help to overcome some of the challenges this presents.

The deregulation of capital markets sparked a tremendous increase in the use of investment and financing instruments. However, the restrictive impact of Basel III on banks and IFRS and EMIR on corporates has resulted in extra compliance demands. It has also resulted in substantial work for treasury departments that must implement processes to comply with relevant regulations while offering a streamlined and efficient structure. The increasing burden of risk management and corporate governance has also added essential tasks and responsibilities to the treasury department.

Many treasurers are not only focused on the management of their company's assets and liabilities but also on the provision of liquidity. In conditions where external funding sources may be relatively restricted, the benefits of improving operational processes and reducing invested capital are great. Most dedicated treasury departments are heavily involved in areas that can affect liquidity, financial risks and future funding needs.

As a result, it's clear that many treasurers are expected to create and maintain optimal balance sheet ratios by adjusting key drivers of the debt/equity ratio and long-term/short-term debt by pursuing active working capital management. It is important that a company's management sets clear guidelines for its treasury department. While one of management's core aims may be the generation of shareholder value, it is not necessarily in the interest of the company for treasury to be a profit centre.

For example, a treasury unit that operates as a profit centre may be more motivated to undertake greater levels of risk in an effort to optimise treasury revenues. They may add costs into transactions when acting as an agent. Such actions will not necessarily support the long-term sustainability of the company or the provision of shareholder value over this period. However, the operations and the mandates of the treasury unit have to be defined within the treasury policy.

The role of the treasurer has developed significantly in recent decades. Now, many multinational corporates have well-established, formal treasury organisations. Initially, the treasury function was a very specific activity that focused on two core functions. These were acting as a control unit for short and long-term financing and the management of daily cash and currency activities within the financial markets.

As many companies have grown internationally by establishing separate operating companies, the importance of a centralised overview has become essential. Within a company, the CFO is often responsible for financial policy and corporate planning, control, accounting, treasury and consolidation while the treasurer is responsible for the execution of treasury policy concerning financing, risk and the management of cash flows and liquidity. It is also very common for a treasurer to be involved in tasks that are designed to make a company more effective in managing its working capital.

1.9
Treasury in transformation

The corporate treasury is not a static organisation. In recent years, companies have undergone many transformations in their finance and treasury organisations, triggered by innovations, regulations and changed customer behaviours. Treasurers are thereby seeking to effectively manage their cash and risk. This transformation of the corporate treasury is necessary to allow increased efficiency, enhanced visibility and reduced costs. But it is above all needed to fulfil their growing strategic role (for a more detailed description of this transformation process, see chapter 3).

Transformation in key strategic areas may lead to more streamlined systems and processes, and potentially reduce the overall costs of corporate treasury, enabling more automated processing and richer decision-making. The challenge of moving from a traditional transactional focus to a proactive, strategic resource for the whole company requires both a change in mind-set and operational change for the treasurer, the treasury team and the organisation.

1.9.1   TRIGGERS FOR TRANSFORMATION

There are various reasons why transformation is becoming such a compelling proposition for treasurers. Treasury transformation can be triggered by both internal and external events.

Internal events such as organic growth of the company or a decision to go international, or indeed event-driven such as mergers & acquisitions. In addition, transformation can be prompted by the changing role of the treasury itself with an increased focus on liquidity, risk and strategy. External events such as globalisation, the financial crisis of 2008, regulatory reforms and fuelling technology have also triggered treasury transformation. The markets in which treasurers currently operate have changed radically. The demands of globalisation were already creating a new treasury landscape, resulting in global and regional treasury centres, more sophisticated cash management structures and greater demands on treasury management and communication technology.

The financial crisis of 2008 and the resulting regulatory reform has increased the focus on liquidity management, maximising available cash across the business including unlocking 'trapped' cash in more difficult markets. It also reduced the need for high working capital levels, and for improving the factors that contribute to working capital requirements such as payments and collections.

Treasury technology innovation is another major enabler of corporate treasury transformation. These innovations have brought enormous opportunities to improve processes, increase visibility, accuracy and completeness of information and to support better decisions.

1.9.2 CHANGING TREASURY ROLE: FROM TRANSACTIONAL TO STRATEGIC

Triggered by these developments, the responsibilities and tasks of the treasury department have clearly changed. Treasuries have increasingly moved beyond their traditional transactional role to embrace new challenges including a greater focus on reducing costs, enhanced operational efficiency, financial and risk management strategies and efficient working capital management. Along with this, they are increasingly taking on an advisory and strategic role within corporations. The treasury's input into strategic decision-making will become increasingly critical to the business.

As a consequence, treasury needs to develop a broad set of skills and expertise and become more sophisticated. A new generation of integrated treasury and risk management systems (TRMs) has evolved to reflect treasury's changing role and responsibilities within the organisation. These TRMs allow CFOs and treasurers to align corporate finance, treasury and risk management functions, and to concentrate on more strategic challenges and objectives.

1.10
Treasury and innovation

Corporate treasurers are facing waves of innovation across the payments and financial technologies (fintech) areas. These are being driven by new technological capabilities and the various challenges many corporates are confronting in terms of increased need for efficiency, visibility and control over liquidity and risk.

Corporate treasurers are increasingly exposed to credit, market, and operational risks, caused by a complex and volatile market environment, globalisation, changed client behaviours, regulatory initiatives and others. These have increased the complexity of the traditional treasury management function. Existing silos of their systems further add to this complexity.

There is growing pressure for the corporate treasury to become more efficient. Pressure to use cash and liquidity efficiently and to deploy transaction banking and deal-hedging capabilities at key points in the corporate supply chain are a significant part of this dynamic. As a result, corporate treasuries are significantly increasing their spending on treasury technology and innovations.

1.10.1   OPPORTUNITIES IN INNOVATION

Corporates are looking to take advantage of opportunities in innovation, where technology can carry out existing inefficient and laborious manual processes more quickly. These innovations may bring opportunities to improve, speed up and streamline a company's cash, liquidity, risk and working capital management and allow the treasurer to better react to the company's current cash and working capital needs.

In this context, they are focusing on innovative tools that may meet the changing needs of corporate treasurers and risk managers, helping them gain greater visibility over their business critical information and greater strategic control over their cash. This, in turn, will reduce risk and strengthen internal controls.

1.10.2   KEY INNOVATIONS

There are a number of key game changing technology innovations that will greatly impact the corporate treasury, including digitalisation, the rise of cloud-based solutions, mobile, big data and analytics and blockchain or distributed ledger technology. These will be broadly discussed in chapter 23.

Banks and other service providers are working increasingly hard on developing creative solutions to bring innovations into the corporate banking sphere. The list of innovative tools that add value is clearly growing, ranging from simple bank connectivity to cash forecasting, financial analysis and information. Both banks and specialised third parties are offering a wide range of solutions such as cost-efficient core functionalities of treasury management systems (TMS). Together, these innovations will have a major impact on corporate cash management and wider operations, and may help to convert the role of the treasurer into a strategic one.

Chapter 2

Cash Management Responsibilities

2   Cash Management Responsibilities

2.1
Introduction

The core responsibilities of the corporate treasurer include cash management, the daily handling of cash and cash flows. Although it is often the case that many different people in a company are involved in executing these operations, the corporate treasurer takes ultimate responsibility for managing the 'life blood' of the company. The treasurer makes sure that cash is available where and when it is needed to meet the company's obligations and ensure that its costs and benefits are optimised. In this chapter, we will provide an overview of the cash management role, explain how it can be broken down into separate functions – each with their own policies, objectives and organisational requirements – and explore the future of cash management. As this book focuses on understanding the international cash management of a multinational company, it is critical that we use a consistent framework for defining daily activities and organisational responsibilities. Throughout this book, we will be using the cash management framework as presented in this chapter.

2.2
High-level overview of cash management

In this section, we provide a high-level overview of the cash management function, how we define corporate cash management, how it has been developed and why it is important for companies.

2.2.1   THE BASIC CONCEPT OF CASH MANAGEMENT

The core business of a company is to produce goods and services and sell them to customers. The process of producing these goods and services, and distributing them to those customers, is generally described as the company's 'supply chain' (see chapter 5). The financial counterpart of the product supply chain of the company is the financial supply chain. The product supply chain and the financial supply chain are very closely related. Each action in the supply chain generates a financial action, as can be seen in the following diagram.

FIGURE 2.1   SUPPLY CHAIN

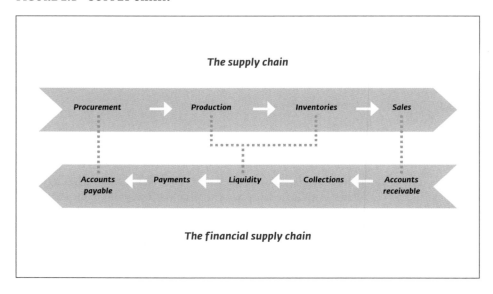

Selling goods and services creates accounts receivables positions, which lead to incoming cash flows – the collections – when customers start paying their bills. The incoming cash flows will create cash balances and these cash balances are also required for funding production activities and sourcing raw materials. This is a relatively simplistic view of a process that, in practice, is far more complex and must be managed by financial experts. One of these experts is the cash manager, who manages the financial supply chain together with the financial controller. While the financial controller oversees the accounts receivables and the accounts payables, the cash manager is the logistical manager of stocks and flows of money. The cash manager has the challenging job of effectively managing cash and cash flows in order to minimise unnecessary cash balances, reduce processing costs and avoid unnecessary cash flows while ensuring adequate access to liquidity whenever it is needed. The successful management of these criteria is critical to ensure the company operates smoothly and efficiently.

Cash management was first introduced as a dedicated corporate role in the US in the 1970s. Back then, it was typical for cash managers to be assigned to manage balances and cash flows on multiple accounts spread nationwide. Banks equipped them with electronic banking and cash pooling systems to improve control over an ever increasing number of bank accounts. Gradually, this fresh corporate cash management approach was exported. US companies adopted the new practices in their European operations and this encouraged European competitors to implement similar processes. By the 1980s, this trend had triggered the banking industry to develop improved instruments and equip their corporate clients with electronic banking systems to manage balances and payments in a much more efficient way.

Corporates in Europe faced an additional challenge because of the varied and complex requirements in the various member states. Each had different payment and banking systems that were denominated in different currencies. New structures and operating models were implemented to run cash management at a cross-border level. The introduction of the euro in 2002 prompted European banks to introduce cross-border transaction initiation systems and offer cross-border cash pooling products. Europe became a best practice area for international cash management as corporates and banks began to implement innovations such as in-house banks, multi-currency centres and centralised transaction processing centres. Banks in Europe and the US used such innovations to extend their services globally. Although cash management in other regions is often complicated by regulatory constraints, the basics of the solutions applied in regions such as Eastern Europe and Asia are still comparable to those originally developed for companies in Western Europe and the US.

2.2.2   DEFINITION AND OBJECTIVES

As we have explained previously, cash management includes the management of cash flows and short-term liquidity. In addition, we consider working capital to be a key component of cash management because working capital operations often have a significant impact on the overall liquidity position of a company.

Cash management definition and objectives
Management of:
– Working capital
– Daily cash flows
– Short-term liquidity
In order to:
– Minimise net working capital
– Minimise transaction costs
– Ensure access to liquidity
– Control short-term interest risks
– Optimise interest costs and revenues

This means that cash management can be divided into three main components:

- Working capital management
- Cash flow management
- Liquidity management

These three areas cover many different activities. In addition to the daily operational execution of transactions, they include activities such as the management of electronic interfaces with banks, cash flow forecasting, managing short-term interest rate risks and resolving tax and legal issues. The structure of this book is built around these three core components, with a complete section devoted to each. In a number of separate chapters (see chapters 16, 17 and 18), we will address financial risk management activities, including foreign exchange exposure management, short-term interest rate risk management and multi-currency liquidity management. Although the management of foreign exchange risk is not normally part of cash management, it is closely associated with the daily management of cash flows, liquidity and working capital. Many transactions of a multinational company are cross-border and they are often denominated in foreign currencies. This has resulted in an increasing need for currency hedging and foreign currency accounts. These requirements can complicate liquidity management. In this book, we will consider foreign currency hedging activities as part of foreign currency exposure management and the handling of foreign currency accounts as part of liquidity management. It is important that liquidity in foreign currencies as well as the domestic currency is actively managed. Short-term interest rate risk management is seen as an important additional activity because companies want to manage interest results on future positions as well as current liquidity positions. We will also discuss multi-currency liquidity management in chapter 17 as this requires the use of specialised instruments (such as currency swaps).

Financial accounting

So far, we have explained cash management as an operational logistical process. It is possible to take a financial accounting view and define cash management as the short-term items on the balance sheet but we feel that a pure financial accounting approach is placing too much emphasis on the administrative aspects. Cash management should be organised as a separate financial function that is distinct from financial controlling and accounting. This is because it focuses more on managing current and future positions rather than on registering and analysing positions of the past. Cash management therefore requires a different skill – a hands-on and proactive approach. Nevertheless, it is important to be aware of the balance sheet items that are affected by cash management.

	Balance sheet items affected
Short-term assets	**Short-term liabilities**
– Bank balances	– Short-term bank loans
– Receivables	– Payables
– Inventories	

2.2.3   CASH MANAGEMENT AS A STRATEGIC PRIORITY

Although cash management is often handled by very small corporate teams, the strategic impact on a company's performance cannot be underestimated. To some extent, cash management is an essential requirement to operate a company successfully since it can ensure the availability of funds and enable payments to be made on time. In addition, cash management can be an effective weapon to enhance a company's competitive position. Cost reduction is often seen as a strategic priority and, to this end, companies implement cash management structures which contribute significantly to reducing operational costs. Clear examples of this are centralised transaction processing in shared service centres (SSCs) and regional cash management centres, which provide cheap internal funding. In fact, one of the key benefits of working in a group of companies is the ability to combine cash management and implement efficient systems across the corporation.

Cash management can also be a critical instrument to measure and demonstrate improved financial performance to external analysts and the outside world in general. Generating free cash flow by reducing working capital is instrumental in the creation of shareholder value. Reducing working capital and increasing liquidity can improve financial ratios such as economic profit, gearing ratio and return on capital employed since interest results and short-term assets are included in the calculation of these ratios. Within a company, cash managers are often seen as strategic partners to the business because they help their business counterparts with funding and advice to achieve their commercial goals.

2.3
Cash management operations in more detail

In this section, we will provide an overview of the daily cash management activities in more detail. A full description can be found in the relevant sections of this book.

2.3.1   OVERVIEW OF CASH MANAGEMENT FUNCTIONS

As we have seen, we can distinguish three main cash management functions: working capital management, cash flow management and liquidity management. Within each of these three areas, we can identify different operational activities as illustrated in the diagram below.

FIGURE 2.2   OVERVIEW OF CASH MANAGEMENT FUNCTIONS

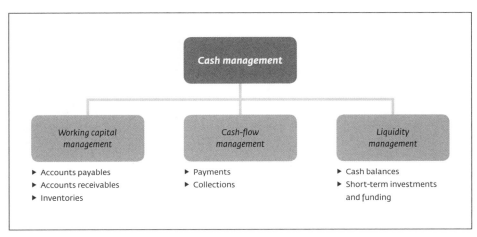

These operational activities are very much interlinked. Accounts receivables generate collections, accounts payables generate payments and these cash flows will increase or decrease liquidity. The execution of these tasks is often widespread across the company but it is the job of the cash manager to oversee the process as a whole and agree on consistent policies with the business partners involved. To this end, it is critical to have a commonly agreed set of definitions for each activity – with agreed policies and objectives as well as adequate instruments to execute such policies.

Working capital management
Financial accountants will define working capital as accounts receivables plus inventories plus cash less accounts payables. This 'Total Working Capital' approach includes all cash elements related to the product supply chain, including short-term bank debt. However, for the purpose of this book we will apply a narrower definition of working capital without these cash elements. For a more detailed definition, see Chapter 4.1.

> *Net working or operating working capital =*
> *Receivables + Inventories – Payables*

The cash components will be extensively addressed in separate sections of this book and, as we will see, they will be more broadly defined to include cash components not directly related to the product supply chain (such as treasury transactions). The working capital area can be divided into three main processes:

- *Payables* – also called *'sourcing to settle'* process: all activities from planning, ordering and invoicing up to settlement of the final invoice
- *Receivables* – also called *'customer to cash'* process: all activities from selling strategy, sales order processing and order fulfilment up to cash collection
- *Inventory* – also called *'forecast to fulfil'* process: all activities which have an impact on inventories, from customer forecasting, supply chain planning and manufacturing up to warehousing and distribution

In many companies, cash managers do not have direct responsibility for managing receivables, inventories and payables. Instead, sales teams, purchasing departments and financial controlling generally have direct responsibility for working capital. However, we increasingly see company-wide initiatives to improve working capital performance, where treasurers and cash managers are participating as advisors or managers. Sometimes, a dedicated working capital manager is appointed within or outside the corporate treasury.

Objectives	Activities
– Reduce net working capital	– Payables/sourcing-to-settle activities
– Release working capital from operations	– Receivables/customer-to-cash activities
– Balance costs, service and risks	– Inventories/forecast-to-fulfil activities

Cash flow management

It makes sense that one of the most important cash management tasks involves managing the company's cash flows. These will consist of different types of transactions, such as collecting receivables from customers, paying invoices from vendors, paying taxes and salaries, executing transactions between the company's subsidiaries and processing treasury transactions. Many of them will be processed by the company's core banks but some transactions may also be processed by the company itself and settled on internal accounts. The company will aim to operate a robust and reliable transaction process, minimise internal and external transaction costs and exercise maximum control over the timing of the transactions to ensure that each transaction happens 'just in time'. Cost savings can be achieved by reducing internal handling costs using straight-through-processing, by negotiating competitive rates for transactions, by optimising the routing of the cash flows (which is especially important for international transactions) and by organising efficient internal processing.

	Cash flow management
Objectives	**Activities**
– Control operational risks	– Manage operational risks
– Optimise cash flow structure and process	– Organise optimal routing of transactions
– Minimise internal processing costs	– Purchase transaction services from external providers
– Minimise external transaction costs	– Implement electronic interfaces
– Achieve straight-through-processing	– Process collections
	– Process payments

Liquidity management

Liquidity management can be broken down into two main activities – cash balances management and (short-term) investment management and funding.

Cash balances management is the daily activity of the cash manager who starts each morning by identifying which balances the company maintains with which banks on which accounts and in which currencies. This information – collected and reported through electronic banking systems – is then compared with the company's own expected cash position based on its internal cash flow forecast for the short and medium term. Based on these predictions, balances can be moved by manual transfer or automated cash pooling to cash concentration accounts. There, matching can be completed between surpluses and deficits. Balances can earn higher interest (or incur lower costs) and can be centrally invested or funded in the money markets.

Short-term investment and funding includes activities such as the forecasting of future liquidity positions, collecting information on interest rate developments and executing investment and funding transactions. In addition, long positions in one currency can be swapped into currencies with a short position. This is called cross-currency liquidity management.

Short-term liquidity management	
Objectives	**Activities**
– Ensure availability of liquidity	– Design and implement current account structure
– Maximise interest income	
– Minimise interest costs	– Determine investment and funding policy, including counterparty risk management
– Control interest rate risks	
	– Determine balance positions
	– Pool cash to central accounts
	– Forecast cash flows and liquidity
	– Gather information on interest rates
	– Assess interest rate risks
	– Execute investment and funding transactions
	– Swap long currencies into short currencies

2.3.2 REQUIREMENTS FOR EFFECTIVE CASH MANAGEMENT

Cash management is a dynamic area (see chapter 3, Treasury Transformation). Companies are continuously reviewing current practices and looking for improvements. Very often, treasurers and cash managers do not have the organisational levers to implement the changes across the operating business and, as a result, key opportunities for improvement are missed. It may also be that companies are looking for quick fixes without clearly defining their strategies. It is therefore imperative that consistent policies are defined, endorsed by senior management and implemented across the business. For each of the individual cash management activities, clear policies need to state clear and measurable objectives as well as provide guidelines to control operational and financial risks.

In addition, the company will need an appropriate infrastructure for its cash management in terms of organisation, banking infrastructure, current account structure and, most importantly, information systems. Effective cash management is dependent on complete and up-to-date information from internal and external sources. When discussing each cash management function in the relevant sections of this book, we will address the information requirements in more detail.

FIGURE 2.3   THE CASH MANAGEMENT TREE

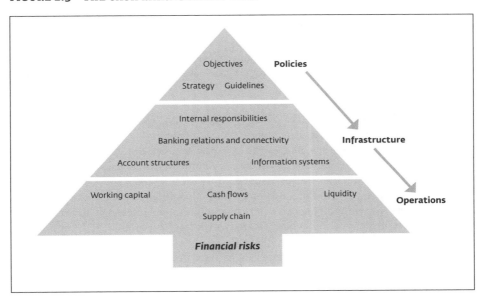

2.4
Operating cash management on an international basis

So far, we have discussed cash management mainly as an in-country activity. However, as this book is focused on international cash management, we will now explain what makes international cash management so different from domestic cash management. We will also highlight some of the key trends in the international cash management industry.

2.4.1   THE CHALLENGES OF INTERNATIONAL CASH MANAGEMENT

Operating cash management at an international level creates an additional degree of complexity which generates multiple challenges for the cash manager.

–   *International transactions:* Executing transactions in multiple countries involves different domestic and cross-border payments systems with different payment instruments, different formats and different execution times. As a result, international payments can be more expensive and may take longer to execute. The Single

Euro Payments Area (SEPA) initiative in Europe has removed these problems within the EU for payments in euros and the Payment Services Directive (PSD) standardises rules for payments to achieve uniform payment instruments across the EU.

- *Lack of standardisation:* Companies need to connect to multiple banks and clearing institutions. This will involve different message formats and security protocols and that makes straight-through-processing difficult to achieve.

- *Account complexity:* Operating accounts in multiple countries, in multiple currencies and often with multiple banks makes liquidity management a more challenging exercise. It will be more difficult to concentrate funds and use excess liquidity to fund liquidity shortfalls. Using a range of banks also requires varied electronic and employee interfaces.

- *Local regulations:* Companies will be confronted with a range of legal, tax and accounting regulations, depending on the countries in which they operate. In Central and Eastern Europe, Asia Pacific and Latin America, different exchange control regulations will apply. That can make cross-border transfers more difficult or even impossible. The latter creates 'trapped cash' – earnings that cannot be repatriated and must be reinvested in the foreign jurisdiction. Differences in tax regulations – especially in withholding taxes and 'thin capitalisation' rules – will have a strong impact on cross-border liquidity management (see Chapter 19).

- *Time zone differences:* Companies headquartered in one time zone often feel the need to hire local cash management staff in other time zones to communicate effectively with their own business colleagues and with banks to execute (financial market) transactions and fulfil any local administration or documentary requirements.

These aspects pose substantial challenges to the international cash manager. The good news is that many international companies are experiencing similar issues and that solutions can be found for many of these challenges. The challenges and appropriate solutions are discussed in more detail in the relevant sections of this book.

2.4.2 CENTRALISATION OF CASH MANAGEMENT

Initially, large companies used to operate their cash management on an in-country basis. Typically, they would use domestic banks in each country for transaction services and liquidity management. In-country cash managers would run the business. In the main countries in Western Europe, that domestic approach has been replaced by a regional approach driven by accelerated cross-border trade within the European Union and the introduction of the euro in 1999. Increasingly, companies have been centralising one or more cash management functions at a regional level. However, there are still several companies who operate cash management on an in-country basis only. Often, that is due to a decentralised management approach where local management and entrepreneurship is considered crucial to success. The in-country operating model is also common in other regions – such as Central and Eastern Europe, Latin America and Asia Pacific.

Liquidity centralisation

Most companies in Europe have centralised their liquidity operations in a phased approach where a series of treasury responsibilities are transferred to the region. The first centralised responsibilities are often long-term funding and corporate finance. These are among the minimum set of head office responsibilities, even in the most decentralised of companies. Between 1980 and 2000, companies increasingly centralised financial risk management and short-term inter-company loans. This enabled subsidiaries to place excess cash with their European treasury or borrow funds from them at 'arm's length' rates (i.e. favourable rates that are close to market levels). After the introduction of the euro, companies started to concentrate their current account balances in that currency and centralise all money market operations. This was facilitated by banks that introduced cross-border cash pooling services. There are clear benefits to be achieved from liquidity centralisation:

- Cash-poor operations can be funded internally using excess cash from cash-rich subsidiaries, resulting in lower overall funding costs
- Reduction of external debt, which improves the balance sheet
- Improved rates generated by central investments and funding due to larger amounts and centralised expertise
- Saving staff time/resources at a local level

The last step in liquidity centralisation is to pool cash in all convertible currencies into a multi-currency centre. This stage is one that several companies are currently adopting and it is likely to bring yet more benefits across many more currencies. In fact, it means that subsidiaries can outsource all liquidity operations to the regional centre.

FIGURE 2.4 CENTRALISATION STEPS

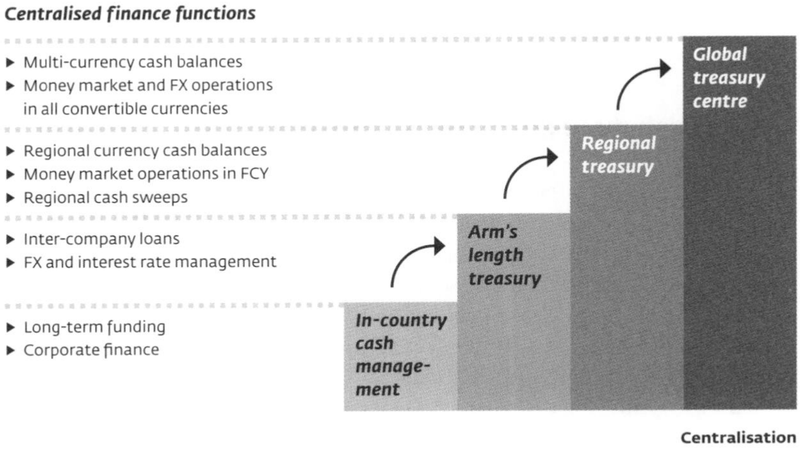

Centralised finance functions

- Multi-currency cash balances
- Money market and FX operations in all convertible currencies

- Regional currency cash balances
- Money market operations in FCY
- Regional cash sweeps

- Inter-company loans
- FX and interest rate management

- Long-term funding
- Corporate finance

Global treasury centre

Regional treasury

Arm's length treasury

In-country cash management

Centralisation

Cash flow centralisation

We have also seen companies centralising transaction processing into regional shared service centres (SSCs) or payment factories. This development was driven by US companies who were the first to establish such processing centres in their home country and have taken the approach into Europe and Asia. These regional transaction centres usually have centralised interfaces to banks in a number of countries. They exchange transaction information (such as payment orders and remittance information) with their internal clients i.e. the subsidiaries of the company. Internal transactions are settled in-house by the regional centre and external transactions are sent to the banks. The main objectives are to:

– Reduce processing costs
– Improve the quality and reliability of operations
– Free-up resources and remove non-core business from subsidiaries

In chapter 24 of this book, we will provide a more extensive overview of the different operating models used to improve cash management performance at an international level.

2.4.3 OUTSOURCING OF CASH MANAGEMENT

Another important trend has been the outsourcing of cash management operations to external service providers. Running in-house cash management is relatively expensive and companies have been looking to reduce these costs. Special vehicles were set up in countries such as Ireland (especially by US companies that wanted to outsource their European cash management operations and achieve additional tax benefits).

This trend has reversed in recent years. Many companies have been able to reduce operating costs in an alternative way using automated cash management solutions. Banks have increasingly offered automated processes for activities that were previously done manually inside the company. We have seen this happening with cash sweeps between banks, short-term investments and funding, and foreign exchange operations. As a result, companies have removed a lot of manual, daily recurring, operations from their treasury teams and this has allowed them more time to focus on the strategic management aspects of cash management.

2.5
Future cash management environment

Corporate treasury professionals are being confronted with fundamental changes. Treasurers are facing a growing number of challenges, which have led to an increasingly complex business environment. This has elevated cash and liquidity management to high priority. As a result, corporate management outside the treasury department will need a better understanding of a company's cash position and forecasts. There is a greater demand at the corporate level for advice on how to effectively move money around. Corporate treasurers have started to position themselves for changes in the way they manage their short-term cash, focusing on optimising cash management and more effective risk management.

2.5.1 COMPLEX ENVIRONMENT

Various challenges are impacting corporate cash and risk management including increased regulatory requirements as a response to the financial crisis of 2008/2009, political (geopolitical turmoil, Brexit, Trump, Ukraine, IS, terrorism, etc.) and economic uncertainty (higher volatility in financial markets, low interest rates etc.), changed client behaviours and expectations, and a growing threat of cyberattacks.

Treasurers are also facing waves of technology innovation across the payments and fintech arenas that are impacting cash management and are transforming the treasury industry. These include digitisation, cloud, blockchain, big data, etc. For a more detailed description see chapter 3, Treasury Transformation, and chapter 23, Key Developments.

2.5.2 GREATER EMPHASIS ON CASH MANAGEMENT

Treasury's enhanced role is triggered by the growing emphasis on efficient cash management and liquidity management in the current complex environment, as well as the close attention to the company's overall risk exposure. This requires a more enterprise (holistic) approach to cash and risk management.

The drying up of liquidity, the low interest rate environment and the fact that many corporates are relatively cash-rich have caused treasuries to increasingly focus on the need to strike a balance between cash concentration and accessibility as well as the crucial optimisation of working capital management. Effective management of the cash flow, making best use of cash balances and an increased speed in transferring funds between accounts is thereby crucial.

It is therefore urgent that cash managers actively track cash flows. Effective liquidity and cash forecasting is becoming a core cash management issue to identify future cash needs. Making the right decisions regarding the use of cash based on accurate data and cash (flow) forecasting is even more important.

In addition to the focus on cash, liquidity and working capital, there is a renewed focus among corporate treasuries on effective risk management to address the risks inherent in trading and implementing transactions. The traditional risk management areas (involving interest rate, currency, counterparty and commodity risk) have been supplemented by credit, insurance, concentration and liquidity risk.

2.5.3 CHALLENGES

Corporate treasuries are confronted with a number of issues that make present cash management, liquidity management and risk management a more challenging business. Alongside difficulties in obtaining short-term liquidity, many corporate treasuries are not (yet) skilled at making optimal decisions to enable an optimal use of cash. A lack of automated and standardised processes and workflows, outdated technology and limited visibility within the company may lead to inaccurate cash forecasting and non-optimal decisions.

Difficulties obtaining short-term liquidity
Corporates increasingly have difficulties obtaining short-term liquidity from their banks. As short-term liquidity has become a pressing issue, treasurers' concerns are increasingly becoming heard at board level.

Lack of automated and standardised processes
Many corporate processes and workflows are paper-based. Systems are not able to generate automated real-time data regarding a cash position, which limits forecast possibilities.

Outdated technology
Corporates also often have inadequate, outdated and fragmented IT architecture (limited technology solutions, including operational difficulties and risk). Most rely on multiple ERPs for data sources, using multiple solutions. This makes it difficult to gain a current and comprehensive (consolidated) view of a corporate's cash positions and cash requirements.

Inadequate cash forecasting methods
In many corporate treasuries, current cash forecasting methods still leave much to be desired (in terms of accuracy). They often still rely on spreadsheets (not automated), leading to inaccurate cash forecasting. This may hinder effective cash management.

2.5.4   REQUIREMENTS

Maintaining day-to-day liquidity – ensuring at the most basic level that corporates can continue to transact – is a key goal for cash management. To meet tomorrow's needs for effective cash/liquidity management and to enable the treasury to fulfil its growing responsibility role, there are a number of requirements that should be fulfilled. These include increased efficiency and simplicity, improved global cash visibility and control, accurate cash and liquidity forecasting and ensuring regulatory compliance via greater transparency. These are fundamental steps towards obtaining a clear financial picture and more accurate reporting, and towards enabling the treasury to better identify and measure financial risks.

Increased efficiency
Efficient day-to-day cash management has become the key priority within the corporate treasury. Squeezing efficiencies from the most essential processes is thereby of utmost importance. To meet these goals, cash management must be shifted to fully automated electronic formats, away from paperwork only. A high level of automation should allow optimal efficient use of resources.

Other requirements include bringing together disparate systems, integration with other businesses within the company and standardisation of strategic and tactical activities and control to cash, liquidity and risk management.

Improved global cash visibility and control

As corporates seek to minimise the amount of cash and financing required to finance the day-to-day needs of the business, making better use of working capital has become a priority in corporate treasuries. To achieve this, it is essential to know a corporate's optimal cash balance and thereby receive accurate and trusted information. That knowledge necessitates improved global cash visibility and control.

There is a need for a complete and continuous global overview of the cash and the liquidity situation at all group subsidiaries to ensure the necessary liquidity for those subsidiaries as well as for the group as a whole. This requires greater insight into all cash balances around the world and insight into all payments and collections patterns. This information should enable the cash manager to control and influence cash flow processes.

Accurate cash, analytics and forecasting

Improving the accuracy, consistency and quality of cash forecast data has become a high priority for every corporate treasury department. The pressure to provide insightful and pro-active cash reporting and forecasting is clearly growing. Treasury functions will need to find ways to provide management with information on cash positions and cash forecasts faster and with deeper insight. Decisions should be based on detailed analysis and improved forecasts of transaction flows, payables and receivables. The use of supporting technology is needed to achieve innovative cash forecasting.

Ensuring regulatory compliance

There is also the need for complete transparency to meet regulatory requirements and ensure compliance with increasing audit regulations. This requires more structured risk management solutions using technology innovations.

2.5.5 SOLUTIONS

To deal with these challenges and to meet the various requirements, corporate treasury teams are looking at how to centralise their operations, automate processes and increase efficiency.

Creation of more centralised/consolidated models

For corporate treasuries tasked with driving efficiencies and ensuring compliance, centralising the group's cash and liquidity management activities has become important (and sometimes critical) to effectively managing cash.

Centralising and streamlining workflows and business processes for cash, liquidity and risk management by integrating multiple ERP systems to collect information in a timely manner, will enable the treasurer to better identify and measure financial risk (either FX risk, interest rate risk, commodity risk and/or credit risk). Corporates are increasingly striving to bring together disparate systems, moving them away from their silos. The creation of more centralised/consolidated models for cash, liquidity and risk management may provide treasurers with an aggregated view of their cash flow and risk positions, improved data quality/consistency and visibility, and a detailed analysis of their transaction flows, payables and receivables.

Using technology to speed up the cash conversion cycle

Technology support is critical in enabling fully integrated solutions with products and value-added services that enhance cash visibility and support reconciliation. Improvements will become possible thanks to emerging technologies. Corporate treasurers are thereby increasingly focusing on new incoming tools to improve their cash, liquidity and risk management processes. Banks and other providers are now leveraging technology innovations to enhance existing systems with a view to optimising cash, liquidity and risk management and providing new services. By leveraging an innovative platform, corporates can ensure that they implement a solution that enables full integration with their ERP system in addition to shifting to fully electronic solutions.

Using advanced analytical and cash forecasting tools

There is increased demand among corporates for advanced real-time business intelligence solutions to enable cash managers to make a better, more integrated and more thorough analysis of cash, liquidity and risk exposures. Advanced data analytical tools, including advanced analytics, business intelligence and artificial intelligence (AI), are increasingly available and can be used by corporate treasuries to undertake cash management analysis, achieve innovative cash flow forecasting, simulate different cash scenarios and address shortfalls.

Treasurers will need to have access to up-to-date and reliable data at all times, be aware of everything and immediately see where risks need to be hedged. Backed by complete and up-to-date information, this should allow the corporate treasurer to focus more on its strategic advisory role.

Towards complete automation

Automation, digitisation and integration of existing siloed systems may enable easier and faster transaction and communication processes. As core business processes become automated, treasury has the resources and information to deliver information that makes it a critical source of business value. There are already tools available that can automate and deliver timely reporting. This aids in turning big data into scalable reporting and visualisation solutions, providing sophisticated analytics and insightful value for strategic decisions, including risk analytics and risk visualisation.

In-house banks and payment factories

There is also a surge in demand for solutions that make the best use of internal liquidity and transactions within a group and minimise reliance on external borrowing. Less dependence on banks for short-term lending and borrowing has stimulated a stronger trend towards internal methods, such as in-house banks, shared service centres and payments factories.

2.5.6   CHANGING BANKING RELATIONSHIPS

There is a trend towards growing disintermediation in the banking world. The funding landscape is shifting towards alternatives to bank financing. The result is increasing fragmentation in the types of financing available. Over time, independent and less-regulated companies may take over (part) of their transactional services, increasing their speed and lowering costs.

Changed banking role

Corporate banking is set to change from pure transaction servicing to a more trusted advisory role, particularly as regards risk management. This change, which was sparked by technology innovations, is leading to new global cash management solutions that are meeting client needs. These solutions relate to account management, payment & collection services, liquidity management, cross-border cash management and risk management, among others. But also big data management intelligence of banks towards corporates could become increasingly important, enabling banks to provide both day-to-day advisory services as well as strategic long-term advisory services.

Rationalise banking relationships

Corporates should reassess their relationships with their core bank. To this end, corporates should look to rationalise their existing banking relationships and bank accounts, and reduce the number of cash pools wherever possible. They are also looking to simplify their banking arrangements to give them greater oversight of liquidity and exposure.

Chapter 3

Treasury Transformation

3   Treasury Transformation

3.1
Introduction

The corporate treasury is not a static concept. In recent years, companies have undergone many transformations in their finance and treasury organisations triggered by innovations, regulations and changed customer behaviours. In this process, treasurers are seeking to effectively manage their cash and risk. This transformation of the corporate treasury is necessary to allow increased efficiency, enhanced visibility and reduced costs. But above all, to fulfil the growing strategic role of the corporate treasury.

Treasury transformation refers to defining and implementing the future status of a treasury department. It implies more than simply embracing change. It may suggest a complete rethink/review of existing policies, processes, technology and treasury relationships involving extended counterparties and the wider business. The ultimate aim is to allow the treasury to meet the challenges of today and tomorrow.

Transformation in key strategic areas may lead to more streamlined systems and processes, and potentially reduce overall costs within corporate treasury. This will enable more automated processing and richer decision-making. The challenge of moving from a traditional transactional focus to a proactive, strategic resource for the company as a whole requires a change in mindset and operational approach to the treasurer, the treasury team and the organisation.

3.2
Triggers for transformation

There are various reasons why transformation is becoming such a compelling proposition for treasurers. Treasury transformation can be triggered both by internal and external events.

- Organic growth
- Technology-driven innovation
- Event-driven: mergers & acquisitions
- External factors: changing regulations/globalisation/shifting market conditions and practices (SEPA)
- Changing role of treasury: increased focus on liquidity and risk

The financial crisis of 2008 / 2009 and the resulting regulatory reforms (See Chapter 22) have increased the focus on liquidity management, maximising available cash across the business including unlocking 'trapped' cash in more difficult markets. This also reduced the need for high working capital levels and improved the factors that contribute to working capital requirements, such as payments and collections.

Treasury technology innovation is another major enabler of corporate treasury transformation. Technology innovations have created tremendous opportunities to improve processes, increase the visibility as well as the accuracy and completeness of information, and support better decisions.

3.3
Changing treasury role: from transactional to strategic

Triggered by these developments, the responsibilities and tasks of the treasury department have changed. Treasuries have increasingly moved beyond their traditional transactional role to embrace new challenges, including a larger focus on reducing costs, enhanced operational efficiency, financial and risk management strategies and efficient working capital management. They also are increasingly taking on an advisory and strategic role within corporations. The treasury's input into strategic decision-making is becoming increasingly critical to the business.

- (Liquidity) risk management
- Steward for risk management in the company
- Leading, governing and driving working capital market improvement initiatives
- Enhanced governance and control over domestic and overseas operations
- Strategic advisor to the business
- Value-added partner to the CFO
- Access to capital markets to finance growth

As a consequence of their changing role, treasury needs to develop a broad set of skills and expertise, and must become more sophisticated. A new generation of integrated treasury and risk management systems (TRMs) has evolved to reflect treasury's changing role and responsibilities within the organisation. These allow CFOs and treasurers to align corporate finance, treasury and risk management functions and concentrate on more strategic challenges and objectives.

3.4
Treasury transformation process

The treasury is under constant pressure to operate more efficiently, and to ensure transparency for compliance reasons. It is seeking to meet these demands by automating processes and centralising the management of group cash and liquidity. By reducing transactional pressures, technological developments are allowing treasuries to focus more on providing advice to CFOs and informing strategic decisions.

Treasury transformation can only be successful when it is ensured that internal policies, processes, skills and technology are appropriate to the current and evolving needs of the company. The treasury transformation process requires a strategic review approach, whereby a company's treasury policy is regularly reviewed to take account of the key trends in the various areas that may be impacted. These areas include:

- Treasury organisation and strategy
- System infrastructure
- Treasury workflows and processes
- The banking landscape

Treasury Area	Trend	Present	Future
Organisation & strategy	Centralisation of treasury activities Virtualisation Redesign of banking and cash management strategy	Decentralised Local services	(Virtual) global organisation Centralised (in-house bank/payment factory)
System infrastructure	Automation of treasury activities System integration STP	Stand-alone systems Non-automated interfaces	One global portal Integrated best-of-breed TM5 vs full ERP solution Seamless interfaces No paper
Workflows & processes	Standardisation Simplification Enhance compliance Enhance operational processes	Many different processe; Not (very) standardised Labour intensive	Uniform processes More with less Dematerialisation of paper System-integrated controls
Banking landscape	Rationalisation – Bank partners – Bank accounts Bank agnostic Reduction number of cash pools	Multiple – Banks – Bank accounts – E-banking accounts – Single cash pools	Balanced banking wallet Simplified account structure Independent bank connectivity Multi-currency overlay cash pool

3.5
Treasury organisation & strategy

3.5.1   PRESENT STATE

Corporate treasuries are becoming increasingly centralised. In particular, corporates that have expanded their operations into multiple countries have found that their finance arrangements have become more complex and fragmented. Fragmented cash and treasury operations may lead to lack of central visibility and control over cash and risk. Because a consistent treasury policy and process cannot be enforced early in such an environment, this often leads to high costs for borrowing and foreign exchange.

3.5.2   TRANSFORMATION TRENDS

There is a long-standing transformation trend in treasury towards centralisation. Tasked with driving efficiencies and ensuring compliance, corporate treasuries are acknowledging the benefits of the centralisation of treasury. A centralised treasury may give them a better overview and control over their cash and liquidity positions as well as the related risks, and greater transparency of reporting for regulatory purposes. By leveraging a single treasury technology, infrastructure and standard interfaces to banking partners, technology efficiency could be greatly improved and costs significantly reduced.

Technical advancements such as digitalisation are facilitating increased centralisation and allowing companies to more easily set up global pooling structures, in-house banks and shared service centres, as well as payment and collection factories. These facilitate centralising the processing and implementation of payments and the implementation of payables and receivables (collections) on behalf of structures (POBs and COBs). Centralising payments and collections into regional, or even global processing centres is a growing trend amongst multinational corporations. SEPA, for example, has been a catalyst for centralisation by harmonising payment and collection instruments and legal conditions in each EU member state.

3.5.3   FUTURE ENVIRONMENT

The changing ecosystem is driving companies towards more centralised treasury models. This could take place via the setup of global or regional/local corporate treasury centres under central oversight, whereby cash, liquidity and risk are managed centrally and the treasury may act as an in-house bank for their business units.

A regional treasury structure is most suited for corporates who want to manage their cash and treasury management activities centrally, but who need to transact business across a number of time zones. Regional treasury centres usually operate according to policies and procedures determined by group treasury, and may share a common treasury management system (TMS). In some cases, back office processing may take place centrally, such as through a shared service centre (SSC).

Fragmented banking relationships, complex organisational structures, diverse tax and regulatory requirements may require corporate treasuries to choose a more hybrid model with central visibility and policy netting. At the same time, they grant limited responsibilities to local treasury centres that effectively operate as satellites of the group or regional treasury.

3.6
System infrastructure

3.6.1 PRESENT STATE

The primary challenge facing treasury groups is inadequate treasury systems. The present infrastructure is often one of stand-alone systems and non-automated interfaces.

Most corporate treasuries rely on multiple enterprise resource planning (ERP) systems for data sources and multiple solutions (some manual) to address their company needs. This may lead to operational difficulties, including a lack of efficiency, automation and visibility for sophisticated reporting and decision support.

3.6.2 TRANSFORMATION TRENDS

The role of technology and its innovations in transforming the core treasury function has increased. The changing ecosystem is driving companies towards automation of treasury activities and integration of the various systems in use towards increased straight-through processing (STP). This increasingly demands a future system infrastructure with one global portal, integrated best-of-breed TMS vs. a full ERP solution, seamless interfaces and no paper. Combining the different systems previously used by the treasury into one can reduce costs significantly.

The emergence of new (or more prevalent) technology deployment models is making it easier and more cost effective to adopt treasury technology. It also allows for the adoption and optimisation of ERP systems via the migration onto a single ERP platform that enables improved data sourcing and consolidation.

3.6.3 FUTURE ENVIRONMENT

When implementing specialist treasury management solutions, companies will have the choice of various deployment methods: hosted solutions or blockchain-based software-as-a-service (SaaS) models.

Hosted, or ASP (application service provider) solutions are hosted on a dedicated platform and managed by the vendor or a third party. These solutions not only alleviate security concerns, but also reduce the amount of IT resources required compared to maintaining the hardware and software in-house. This allows treasuries without dedicated IT resources to use sophisticated systems.

A blockchain-based SaaS model takes the concept of a hosted environment even further. The TMS is hosted in a common environment with a shared database, whereby each company only has access to its own data. Upgrades are handled by the vendor, so users have consistent access to the most current version of the software.

Links to other commonly used systems such as electronic banking, rates providers and confirmation matching can be managed automatically. This gives users access to a comprehensive treasury technology framework, without the need to manage multiple systems.

3.7
Treasury workflows & processes

3.7.1   PRESENT STATE

Existing treasury workflows & processes show many different (stand-alone) processes, most of which are not very standardised and labour intensive. A lack of straight-though processing along the financial supply chain limits the visibility to global operations, cash and financial risk exposures. The pressure on corporate treasuries to process transactions more efficiently and cost effectively is growing. Treasures are seeking to introduce leaner and more efficient operations.

3.7.2   TRANSFORMATION TRENDS

Treasury policy and organisational changes are often a trigger for reviewing, revising and automating processes and workflows to create greater efficiencies and economies of scale. As treasury functions are becoming more centralised, there is a growing need at corporate treasuries to regularly re-evaluate and integrate their workflows and processes in order to achieve their strategic and operational objectives.

Changing working practices such as automation, digitalisation and the use of electronic online platforms to execute transactions are enabling easier and faster transaction and communication processes. Although centralisation is an important trend for payments and collections, it does not necessarily lead to greater efficiency. Consequently, a related transformation initiative is to optimise payments and/or collections processing via simplification, standardisation, and reporting and enhanced compliance. Treasury increasingly needs to consider treasury processes, controls and integration across the financial supply chain as part of corporate transformation initiatives, instead of focusing solely within the treasury department. This more holistic approach is needed to test controls, measure efficiency and evaluate new technology.

3.7.3   FUTURE ENVIRONMENT

The future treasury environment will be one of uniform processes, more with less, dematerialisation of paper and system-integrated controls. However, the way in which payments/collections processing optimisation projects are conducted will vary significantly according to the industry, business model, countries and payment/collection methods in use. The concept of enterprise risk management that takes an integrated view of business, financial and market risks – as opposed to managing each type of risk individually – will gain further acceptance by more companies. Indeed, this will represent a major change to treasury's role and will place the treasury function at the heart of the business strategy. This development will be driven by changes in accounting regulations, radical shifts in market conditions and changing attitudes towards risk.

Companies may also decide to outsource all or part of their treasury processing to a third party provider (bank or independent party). This may allow them to have a more robust and extensive operational and technology infrastructure than they would be able to achieve in-house, whilst maintaining the same degree of visibility over their transactions and control over treasury policies. Outsourcing enables treasury to concentrate on policy and strategic decision-making as opposed to treasury processing.

3.8
Banking landscape

3.8.1   PRESENT STATE

These days, treasuries of large global corporates deal with multiple banks and, as a result, have multiple bank accounts. Cash management and funding are often managed locally in the various countries, where multiple banking partners are involved. This fragmented approach of cash management and funding has resulted in the use of multiple non-interoperable banking tools and a large number of single cash pools.

This creates a number of challenges for bank account management, particularly in situations where the responsibility for opening, closing and managing authorities on accounts is distributed across the business. It is not possible to concentrate cash effectively through automated pooling structures, or to include accounts in national pools. It also limits timely, accurate cash control.

There are currently various ways in which corporate treasurers communicate with their banks' proprietary systems. Large corporations often use a combination of bank communication tools (e.g. SWIFT) or host-to-host communications in group treasury, regional treasury centres and shared service centres, and web-based electronic banking systems in subsidiaries and local finance offices. This makes it difficult to integrate them effectively with their own TMS and ERP systems.

3.8.2   TRANSFORMATION TRENDS

There are a number of key elements involved in the transformation of banking relationships, bank accounts, cash and working capital solutions and bank connection tools. As their treasuries evolve, corporates are increasingly rationalising their banking relationships and bank accounts and reducing the number of cash pools. They are also looking to simplify their banking arrangements to give them greater oversight of liquidity and exposure.

While one global cash management bank may bring a number of advantages (cash is simplified and there is more opportunity to centralise cash at a global level), treasurers are more inclined to appoint regional cash management banks, potentially with an overlay structure to centralise cash globally. This avoids concentrating too much risk at a single bank. It also allows treasurers to select banks that provide the best solution and coverage in each region.

3.8.3   FUTURE LANDSCAPE

In the future environment, corporate treasury will have a more balanced banking wallet, simplified account structures, independent bank connectivity and multi-currency overlay cash pools (reduced number of cash pools). Centralising payments and collections, particularly using POBO (payments on behalf of) and COBO (collections on behalf of) may have a marked effect on the number of accounts that are required by channelling payments and/or collections through a single account. Establishing treasury as an in-house bank can help to further reduce the number of accounts.

Similarly, corporate treasuries will increasingly introduce virtual accounts, enabling sufficient granularity of information for reconciliation and account posting purposes, but without the need to hold separate bank accounts.

New technology in which treasury connects with its financial partners, particularly banks, is evolving fast. Cloud-based SaaS solutions now integrate services so that treasurers gain access to a wide range of services through a single point of access (online dealing platforms and confirmation matching systems that may be integrated into TMS and ERP). Increased standardisation for exchanging financial messages between counterparties will allow easier integration of systems and processes thanks to ISO 20022.

Corporate treasurers are becoming more bank agnostic. Reviewing or replacing bank connectivity is an important part of treasury transformation. It is becoming easier to switch or avoid cash management banks, not least thanks to the growth of SWIFT corporate access and more consistent XML breed formats. SWIFT host-to-host connectivity technology allows the use of a single communication channel across multiple banks and streamlines financial information flows.

3.9
Treasury transformation strategy

The treasury transformation process demands a structured approach. Changes to the treasury policy may have a considerable impact on the way treasury operates and its internal and external relationships. It should ensure that these policies support prevailing market and regulatory conditions, and are aligned with the evolving corporate strategy.

In many large global companies, treasury policies and organisations are already largely fit for progress and aligned with wider business strategy. Transformation may only involve operational change such as a review of processes, refreshing technology or skills and training. If transformation is more fundamental, it will also require changes on an organisational level. The centralisation of corporate treasury is a particularly major undertaking.

3.9.1 HOLISTIC APPROACH

The key to effective treasury transformation involves the following:

- Creating a clear transition process, common culture and a sense of one team and purpose
- Focussing on change management
- Understanding that one size does not fit all
- Developing a clear vision across liquidity, transactions and structure

It is important thereby to take a holistic approach, covering the organisational structure and strategy, the banking landscape, the systems infrastructure and the treasury workflows and processes.

3.9.2 TREASURY TRANSFORMATION PROJECT

Treasury transformation often requires a dedicated treasury transformation project. Such a project should be managed carefully and responsibly, with clear priorities and objectives, choosing the right internal and external partners, appropriate resources and a responsible project approach.

3.9.3 TREASURY TRANSFORMATION PLAN

Transforming and repositioning the treasury demands a well-defined and executed strategic transformation plan. The purpose of this strategic planning is to set the direction and long-range goals of the organisation with well-defined strategies, supporting tactics and aligned resources.

A phased approach is needed here as the treasury transformation plan consists of a number of key steps.

Treasury transformation plan: key steps
- Review &assessment
- Solution design
- Roadmap
- Business case
- Selection(s)
- Execution and post-execution

Review & assessment

The first step in a strategic transformation plan is review & assessment. Treasurers can achieve considerable operational and financial efficiency by reviewing/revising existing policies, processes, organisational structure and banking relationships.

The first objective is to gain in-depth understanding of the organisational structures, governance and strategy bodies, treasury system infrastructure, treasury workflows and procedures, financial risk management as well as banking infrastructure and cash management. Every treasury task should be scrutinised from the perspective of both efficiency and control. Based on the review and assessment, existing gaps can be identified along with where the treasury organisation wants to go in the future, both operationally and strategically.

Solution design

The output of this review & assessment step will be the input for step two: solution design. The key objective of this step is to establish the high-level design of the future state of the treasury organisation. During this phase, the strategic and operational options available, such as central or regional treasury organisation, in-house bank, payment factory and shared service centre will be clearly outlined. Recommendations will be made on how to achieve optimal efficiency, effectiveness and control in the areas of treasury organisation & strategy, system infrastructure, treasury workflows & processes and banking landscape.

Roadmap

The third step is to make a treasury transformation roadmap. The solution design will include several sub-projects. For the overall success of the transformation, it is important that all sub-projects are subsequently sequenced, incorporating all inter-relationships, and are managed as one coherent programme. The treasury roadmap organises the solution design into these sub-projects and prioritises each area as appropriate. The roadmap portrays the timeframe to fully complete the transformation and individually estimates the time required to fully complete each component of the treasury transformation programme.

Business case

The next step in the treasury transformation programme is to establish a business case. This is needed to gain approval from the Board for this (often costly) treasury transformation. It may be a high-level business case, or a set of multiple more detailed business cases.

Such a business case for a treasury transformation programme will include the following parts:

- *The strategic context*: identifies the business needs, scope and desired outcomes
- *The analysis and recommendation section*: concerned with understanding all of the options available, aligning them with the business requirements, weighing the costs against the benefits and providing a complete risk assessment of the project
- *The management and controlling section*: includes the planning and project governance, interdependencies and overall project management elements

- Practicalities of implementation
- Internal and external costs
- Resource requirement
- Technology implication
- Benefits to the wider organisation

Selection(s)
An important step is the selection stage. Key evaluation & selection decisions are commonly required for choosing: bank partners, bank connectivity channels, treasury systems and organisational structure. Common objectives for the selection of these items in a treasury transformation programme include: efficiency, visibility and cost reduction.

Execution and post-execution
The sixth and final step of treasury transformation is execution. In this step, the future-state treasury design will be realised. Solution design will include several sub-projects and it is important for the overall success of the transformation that the sub-projects are aligned.

The post-execution step is an important part of the treasury transformation programme as a whole. This should include an evaluation of all these steps and a check to see if the final results meet the original set goals.

Working Capital Management

Chapter 4

Working Capital Management

4   Working Capital Management

4.1
Working capital – fundamentals and principles

In this chapter, we will discuss the concept of working capital and highlight its relationship with operations and profitability. Proactive working capital management is often overshadowed by a simpler way to plug a funding gap – borrowing.

The financial crisis of 2008 and the resulting regulatory reform has increased the focus on liquidity management, maximising available cash across the business including unlocking 'trapped' cash in more difficult markets. It also reduced the need for high working capital levels and improving the factors that contribute to working capital requirements, such as payments and collections.

4.1.1   WORKING CAPITAL – DEFINITION

Financial accountants define working capital as the difference between current assets and current liabilities. Current assets include cash, inventory, accounts receivable and quickly realisable assets (including investments such as marketable securities). Current liabilities include accounts payable, wages payable, taxes payable and short-term debt (repayable within one year).

Working capital definition

Net working capital
Current assets – current liabilities

Current assets
Cash, inventory, accounts receivable and quickly realisable assets (investments such as securities)

Current liabilities
Accounts payable, wages payable, taxes payable and short-term debt (repayable within one year)

In this chapter we will focus on the non-cash components of working capital management, which are also referred to as operating working capital management.

Operating working capital or trade working capital
Accounts receivable + inventory – accounts payable

Working capital management ensures that a company has sufficient funds to continue its business and meet short-term liabilities like operational expenses and supplier payments. Positive net working capital means that the company is able to cover its short-term liabilities. In a more conservative version, the working capital ratio – sometimes called quick ratio – indicates whether short-term liabilities can be paid without selling inventory. Negative net working capital means that the company is unable to cover its short-term liabilities with current assets alone.

Current assets (e.g. receivables and inventory) represent a company's use of liquidity, because cash is invested in these assets and will only become available once the receivables are collected or the inventory is sold. Current liabilities (e.g. payables) represent a source of liquidity because, until payment occurs, the company will keep its cash. Net working capital can be seen as an investment that needs to be financed, such as by a credit facility. As such, it will lead to additional interest costs and also represents opportunity costs as the invested funds could be used for other business purposes. To optimise working capital management, treasurers need to be aware of these costs and strive to have the least amount of cash tied up in working capital without impacting business continuity.

Key metrics – definitions

Trade working capital as % of sales
The amount of working capital that is required to generate sales.

Days working capital (DWC)
Time it takes to convert resource inputs into cash flows/cash.
DWC = DSO + DIO - DPO

Days sales outstanding (DSO)
Time it takes a company to collect cash from its customers.
(Accounts receivable/sales) X 365 days

>

Days inventory outstanding (DIO)
Time it takes to sell inventory (i.e. raw materials, work in progress, finished goods).
(Inventory/cost of goods sold) X 365 days

Days payables outstanding (DPO)
Time it takes a company to pay its trade creditors.
(Accounts payable/cost of goods sold) X 365 days

4.2
Working capital metrics

Working capital is an essential part of business operations and key performance indicators (KPIs) are often used to maintain working capital at an acceptable level. The effective management of a company's working capital requires a suite of KPIs that operate at various levels. These include those that cover working capital performance across the organisation as a whole, as well as those operationally-focused KPIs that help to drive ownership at levels where performance is actually managed. Please see section 4.1 for a list and associated definitions of key metrics .

4.2.1   BUILDING THE METRICS NETWORK

The exact make-up of the metrics that are relevant for a specific company is heavily dependent on the nature of the business involved and the maturity of the organisation. It is essential that KPIs initiate appropriate action within the organisation. For example, in a manufacturing organisation, poor product quality can lead to higher levels of returns or invoice disputes, impacting DSO. At first glance, the problem may occur within the accounts receivable collection function. However, the root cause in this case appears to lie in manufacturing and this issue can only be addressed by ensuring an overall view of the process.

Similarly, the visibility and interpretation of metrics can identify approaches that may conflict across functions. In the case of suppliers, for example, if there is a lack of alignment between procurement and accounts payable, the definition of on-time payments can often lead to early payments. Ensuring that both functions are operating according to the same set of guidelines helps to not only ensure that working capital is optimised but that supplier expectations are managed effectively, relationships with suppliers are improved and processes remain efficient.

As with all metric systems, a common issue often encountered in larger organisations is the availability of data and consistency across different enterprise resource planning (ERP) platforms. A pragmatic approach should be taken to establish measurable KPIs as soon as possible. Initially, the approach may be manual, but as the process and structures gain maturity the ability to move towards an integrated or automated solution is essential – with provision to the parties involved of a dashboard using near real-time data to help steer the business more effectively.

4.2.2 BENCHMARKING

Benchmarking can provide answers to the following questions:

- How well is the company performing historically or compared with other companies (i.e. peers) operating in the same segment or sector?
- What are the best practices?
- Which improvement opportunities should we try to capture first and what are the key priorities?
- What external financial solutions could a company consider in order to support its working capital performance? Receivables financing, factoring, supply chain finance and procurement card solutions are possible examples of financial solutions companies use.

Working capital benchmarking usually involves popular metrics such as net working capital as a percentage of sales, days working capital (DWC) or cash conversion cycle (CCC), DSO (days sales outstanding), DIO (days inventory outstanding) and DPO (days payables outstanding).

FIGURE 4.1 DAYS WORKING CAPITAL/CASH CONVERSION CYCLE

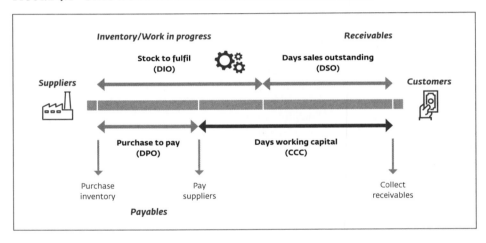

Net working capital as a percentage of sales
It is important for an organisation to minimise the amount of cash tied up in the supply chain as that will help to reduce its financing needs. One of the best ways to determine changes in overall use of cash over time is to use the ratio of net working capital as a percentage of sales. This shows the amount of working capital required to maintain a certain level of sales.

Days sales outstanding (DSO)
DSO is a measure of the length of time it takes a company to collect cash from customers. It is influenced by the position of a company in the supply chain, its power versus the custom-

ers, the industry, the creditworthiness of its customers and last but not least the countries in which the company does business. In addition, DSO is affected by the efficiency and effectiveness of the collection process (billing and collection), product quality and by the pattern of shipments within the quarter or year (seasonality).

Days inventory outstanding (DIO)
A firm's inventory is the necessary investment it needs to make in raw materials, work in progress and finished goods to ensure the normal operation of business and a certain level of customer service. Because of their operating or commercial structure, some firms need to make a large investment in inventory while others can operate with a lower level of inventory. Purchases are driven by expected sales and the so-called long lead times related to certain components. The level of a company's inventory therefore reflects the total value of the goods in inventory as measured by their appropriate costs.

Days payables outstanding (DPO)
Accounts payable increases every time the firm receives a new shipment of goods and decreases every time it makes a corresponding payment. DPO represents a company's average payable behaviour. It refers to the average number of days it takes a company to pay invoices received from suppliers. The DPO level is influenced by the position of a company in the supply chain, the power versus its suppliers, the industry and the countries in which procurement takes place. Purchases are usually driven by expected sales. The determinants of suppliers' trade credit are sales volume, the price of raw materials and days of credit.

Days working capital (DWC)
Changes in accounts receivable, inventory and payable balances affect a firm's overall operating efficiency. Inefficiency in managing working capital can lead to excessive quantities of accounts receivable or inventory in relation to sales or very small amounts of accounts payable. To measure overall efficiency, companies add the current balance of accounts receivable and inventory, and subtract accounts payable divided by one period of sales. Days working capital (DWC) or the cash conversion cycle (CCC) indicates how efficient a company is using cash in its day-to-day operations. The longer the CCC, the less efficiently it operates and the shorter the CCC the more efficiently it operates.

To perform a competitor analysis, it is useful to look at the profit and loss statement and balance sheet statements for relevant data, although that information can only be obtained if a company publically reports its financials. Key information needed includes revenues, cost of goods sold, inventory balance, accounts payable (A/P) balances and accounts receivable (A/R) balances for each competitor. Using a multi-year data overview and performing a sector peer group analysis will help to establish a more robust analysis and identify trends and working capital upside potential.

Setting industry and regional working capital benchmarks
When creating benchmarks, it is important to set reasonable goals based on industry conditions and by region. Industries like retail, telecommunications, utilities and oil & gas are characterised by a relatively low CCC. Retail, for example, has low DSO levels as customers either pay using cash or a credit card.

FIGURE 4.2   WORKING CAPITAL METRICS 2016, WORLDWIDE PER SECTOR

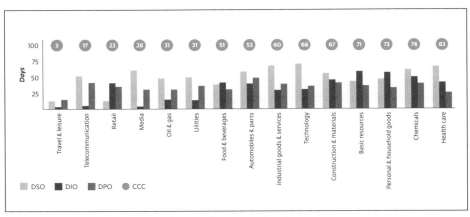

Source: Capital IQ, ING. DSO, DIO and DPO for comparison purposes based on sales.

Industry benchmarks allow the firm to set expectations based on industry best practices. The various differences between countries include cultural differences, banking practices, communications infrastructure, legal and tax issues, time zones and language barriers. For example, Scandinavian countries usually have credit terms of 15 to 30 days. Other countries – such as Italy and Spain – stretch terms from 90 to 120 days and beyond. Having the appropriate regional benchmark figures allows for a firm to adjust working capital more easily and identify opportunities that can enhance the value of working capital throughout the organisation.

FIGURE 4.3   WORKING CAPITAL METRICS 2016, WORLDWIDE PER GEOGRAPHY

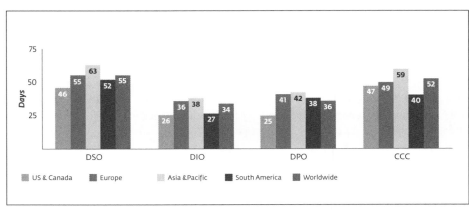

Source: Capital IQ, ING. Median DSO, DIO, DPO and CCC overview, based on sales.

Negative working capital

Some industries have low levels of working capital. Managing working capital to nearly eliminate current assets and liabilities requires that cash not be expended to pay for inventory or other operating costs and that vendors hold title to goods until delivery is required (just-in-time delivery). Under these conditions, a firm is likely to be able to self-finance its operations and to require lower or perhaps no external working capital financing.

4.2.3   SECTORS SHOWING IMPROVEMENTS

Working capital was traditionally viewed as a positive component in managing a business. However, the modern view is that it may constitute a burden on financial performance. A firm's working capital development tends to change over time and the strength of the economy is also likely to be an important determinant.

Free cash flow is important because it allows a company to pursue opportunities that enhance shareholder value. Without sufficient available cash, it is a challenge to develop new products, make acquisitions, pay dividends and reduce debt.

FIGURE 4.4   HOW WORKING CAPITAL IMPACTS SHAREHOLDER VALUE

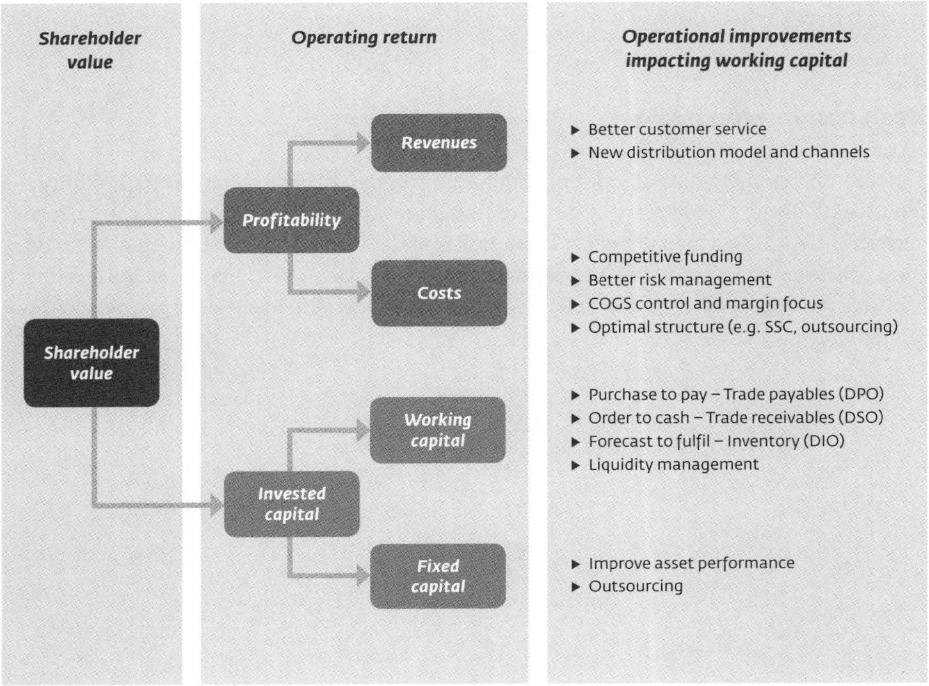

Proper working capital management helps to maintain or increase shareholder value through the creation of free cash flow – the measure of financial performance calculated as operating cash flow minus capital expenditures. Free cash flow (FCF) represents the cash that a company is able to generate after laying out the money required to maintain or expand its asset base. When net working capital increases, FCF has the tendency to decrease as more cash is used to fund day-to-day operations.

Smart investors are attracted to companies that generate an increasing amount of FCF. This signals a company's ability to repay debt, pay dividends, buy back shares and facilitate the growth of business. Those are all important undertakings from an investor's perspective. Growing FCF is frequently a prelude to higher earnings. Companies that experience surging FCF – due revenue growth, efficiency improvements, cost reductions and working capital reductions – are able to provide an attractive shareholder remuneration, reduce debt and therefore reward investors and maintain solid credit ratings. That is why many in the investment community cherish FCF as a measure of value. When a company's share price is relatively low and FCF is on the rise, it is likely that earnings and shareholder value will also increase.

By contrast, shrinking FCF can indicate trouble ahead. In the absence of sustainable FCF, companies may be unable to sustain earnings growth. If a company has insufficient FCF for earnings growth, it may be forced to boost its debt levels. Even worse, a company with insufficient FCF may not have the liquidity to stay in business. In general, many smaller and growing businesses do not have positive FCF as they are investing heavily to expand their operations.

4.3
Cash conversion cycle

The size and composition of working capital largely determines a company's liquidity. As mentioned above, a good starting point to link liquidity to working capital is the cash conversion cycle (CCC), which describes the number of days it takes a company to move money from procurement, production and sales into cash collection from customers. As a result, it captures the time it takes to sell inventory and collect receivables as well as pay bills without incurring penalties.

FIGURE 4.5   WORKING CAPITAL MANAGEMENT CYCLE

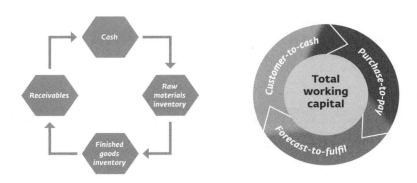

DWC = DSO + DIO - DPO

As a ratio, the cash conversion cycle (CCC) is defined as days working capital (DWC), which equals days sales outstanding (DSO) plus days inventory outstanding (DIO) minus days payable outstanding (DPO). The optimal situation is to minimise DSO and DIO while maximising DPO (subject to company and sector-specific constraints). It is important to note that the efficiency by which the CCC is executed is not the only determinant of net working capital performance. A company's business model is equally as important, as are features such as terms and conditions with suppliers/customers and mergers and acquisitions activity that may drain cash flow. Longer cash conversion cycles are one of the first signs that a company is mismanaging cash and requires an additional working capital improvement effort. However, securing working capital improvements in the business cycle is far from simple. The problem is that the employees managing different processes have traditionally been driven by different metrics, often with little integration.

Basic level of working capital

Although working capital needs vary among sectors, there is a basic level of working capital in every sector that should be treated as permanent and unavoidable. In most growing businesses, the basic level of working capital required will steadily increase. If the investment in an efficient working capital process does not rise in sync with sales, the cash position of the business is likely to deteriorate.

Businesses that grow too rapidly may risk failure by over-trading without an adequate capital base. It is clear that business-to-business and business-to-consumer models inherently call for different demands on liquidity and working capital planning. Retail companies embrace trend analysis (regression analysis) to do cash flow forecasting while utility companies in the oil and gas sector have more predictable cash flows that allow for greater forecast accuracy.

Businesses in fixed capital-intensive sectors often focus more on funding their capital base whereas retail trade and the more working capital-inclined sectors tend to be less capital focused in the short term. In essence, firms need enough working capital to provide a safety margin over and above a basic level in case sales dip, customers fail to pay or unexpected costs arise. Adequate planning can prevent unexpected cash shortfalls.

Cash flow forecasting
Cash flow forecasting is one such activity. It involves an analysis of the cash flow statement's key sections – cash flow from operating, investing and financing activities. Within the statement, some components to consider are highlighted in the table below.

Cash-flow forecasting – components to consider	
Incoming cash flow	**Outgoing cash flow**
– Payments of customer invoices recorded in accounts receivable	– Payments of supplier invoices recorded in accounts payable
– Cash payments by customers	– Salaries, wages and social security
– Profit transfer from associated companies	– Dividends
	– Interest paid
– Loan payouts	– Repayment of borrowings
– Investment / loan payback	– Investments
– Interest received	– Tax payments
– Tax return	– Acquisitions
– Payment from divestment	

Cash flows generated through accounts receivable/payable are part of the operational working capital management scope, while the cash component in the cash flow statement falls under investing or financing flows. Because working capital is a component of operating cash flow, the forecasting of cash requirements requires an understanding of working capital.

Effective cash flow management involves matching inflows and outflows to minimise the need for funding. As a result, a treasurer needs a solid grasp of working capital theory in order to leverage all available liquidity sources and supply chain finance while retaining an overview of the overall organisational mandate.

4.3.1   STRATEGIES TO MAKE WORKING CAPITAL A PRIORITY

Working capital decisions affect cash flow. The cash a company generates on its cash flow statement and profitability on its income statement are two related but separate concepts. A business can be profitable while at the same time unable to pay creditors because of negative cash flow.

The cash flow statement considers actual flows while income statement items are recorded at the time of the sale or purchase. Financial markets therefore correctly place greater emphasis on the cash flow statement to interpret working capital-related issues. This is because flows in working capital items also show up on the cash flow statement – whether in the operating, financing or investing section.

Operating working capital management breaks down into:

- – Accounts payable management
- – Accounts receivable management
- – Inventory management

In the following sections of this chapter, we will discuss the components of working capital management.

4.4
Accounts payable management

In this section, we will highlight the element of working capital that is often defined as accounts payables. We will also focus on the balance sheet liabilities that result in trade creditor balances, i.e. the money owed to the suppliers of component parts or raw materials.

Highly effective procurement and accounts payable processes provide businesses with a means to increase cash flow and service performance while also reducing costs and risks. However, releasing cash from procurement and accounts payable requires more than managing sourcing strategies. It requires a complete review of the sourcing-to-settle process in order to fully optimise working capital while ensuring that cost, service and risk are successfully balanced.

4.4.1   SOURCING-TO-SETTLE

Sourcing-to-settle (S2S) – often referred to as purchase-to-pay (P2P) – covers all processes and activities from planning the budget to the payment of the final invoice to the supplier of a good or service (see figure 4.6). Many multinational corporations employ a considerable number of people who are authorised to make purchases. Keeping track of which suppliers should be paid when and managing them effectively can be a complex job. If the payment process becomes muddled, the company may lock significant amounts of capital in profitless activities. This can place a company at a disadvantage to competitors who have put their resources to more efficient use.

In many organisations, there are functional responsibilities assigned to each process step. However, the added value that is often not deployed involves to utilise a cross-functional approach and leverage the results across the entire S2S process.

4.4.2   THE SOURCING-TO-SETTLE (S2S) PROCESS

An overview of the activities and typical best practices for each step – as related to effective accounts payable management and the optimisation of working capital – are described by section below.

FIGURE 4.6 S2S PROCESS

1 Planning and strategy

Planning and strategy is a key step in the S2S cycle as it defines the strategic vision for overall ownership and governance of the process. This vision should align with that of the business owners, i.e. to optimise efficiency and value of the supply base, and provide consistent management of purchasing behaviour to enable maximum leverage of purchasing power and financial controls.

The best practice in this field is a clear, mandated and effectively communicated corporate policy that considers cost, cash and service goals that align with procurement, finance and operations targets. Compliance with policy should be closely monitored by a cross-functional team and corrective actions taken to ensure it remains fit for purpose for all parties concerned.

2 Selecting and contracting

Defining the selecting and contracting requirements is an important second step in the S2S cycle. It should provide a further definition of the tools, process and strategy used for appraisal, negotiation, selection and contracting with the supplier base. The objective is a selection and contracting approach to optimise the purchasing operations, tools and processes to effectively manage supplier cost, cash and service performance.

In this area, it is essential to develop and communicate a clear and simple general corporate policy governing sourcing and procurement while closely monitoring performance and compliance. World-class companies review and update their sourcing strategy annually and develop purchasing strategies based on supplier segmentation.

The procurement framework uses standardised tools and processes to analyse current spend, research the market, negotiate with current and prospective suppliers and provide overall visibility and accessibility to contracting obligations. Vendors and internal stakeholders are given real-time feedback on their performance. A key enabler is the linkage to the company business plan. Meanwhile, emphasis is placed on enhancing supplier relationships and aligning the supply base with overall sourcing and procurement strategies.

3 Requisition and ordering

Developing and communicating purchase order guidelines is the third step in the S2S cycle and a core component of the corporate policy. The objective is to actively support the corporate policy by ensuring that an appropriate mix of purchasing channels is used. This enables the minimisation of purchase effort while maximising financial controls, particularly in high volume areas, to ensure the best return on investment for procurement, finance and operations stakeholders. It should also drive demand reduction through demand management while delivering optimised order execution for the internal and external customers to encourage compliance.

Many global companies are now focused on the development of an appropriate mix of purchasing and establishing optimal buying tools and appropriate transactional controls, by spend category, based on control level and risk factor.

4 Receipting and evaluating

This stage in the S2S cycle concerns the development and communication of detailed receiving policies and procedures. These should support the corporate strategy, provide feedback into supplier relationship management and purchase channels, as well as providing a foundation for accounts payable automation.

The objective of this step is to support the corporate policy by ensuring that the purchase order and goods or service receipt note are accurate and timely. This will enable purchase order commitment reporting, cash flow reporting and stock availability, while supporting timely supplier payments.

Best practice

Some of the best practices in this field include the measurement of on-time delivery and the availability of goods and services. Many successful multinational corporates use formal goods receipt and direct entry into system, integrate receiving systems with fixed asset systems (such as bar codes to record serial numbers), measure goods/services received but not invoiced as well as put processes in place to match accruals to incoming invoices. They also provide real-time information on supplier performance, business compliance and quality issues. A key enabler is the ability to integrate receiving systems with purchasing, inventory and payables systems.

---

5 Invoice processing

An essential part of the S2S cycle is the development and implementation of a robust invoice process to support accurate and timely capture of liabilities. This can provide an ability to forecast cash, measure performance and drive continuous improvements while supporting on-time supplier payment and corporate policy governance of both finance and procurement.

6 Discrepancy management

An invoice that a customer perceives to be issued in error or that contains erroneous information may lead to the delay or non-payment of the invoice. In such cases, it may be classified as a dispute or discrepancy. Disputed invoices are one of the leading causes of past-due accounts payable and can affect days payable outstanding (DPO) and cash forecast positions as well as create higher administrative costs. The process of identifying, resolving and clearing disputes is referred to as dispute management.

Among the best practices is the operation of accurate, timely and efficient invoice-matching processes linked to finance, inventory and purchasing systems. Such processes can allow the central maintenance of a single enterprise-wide supplier master file that has full integration with other key systems.

In addition, best practice includes the monitoring and review of invoice discrepancy tolerances. It is useful to maximise the usage of technology for document storage and maintain delegation of authority rules for (electronic) workflow validation and approval of electronic and imaged invoices. This ensures good financial controls for tax and supporting procurement policy controls. A key support for this is cross-functional communication.

The goal of this step is to develop a robust process to support accurate and timely capture of liability discrepancies with the ability to measure performance, impact cash flow forecasting and drive continuous improvements. The key elements of an effective dispute management process include the early identification of disputes, timely resolution of disputes and the root cause analysis and eradication of recurring preventable disputes through the collection of volume, value and cycle time data.

Many successful companies manage disputes that affect supplier liabilities and performance and then link that information back to suppliers. They often also ensure – through rigorous cash recovery, discount and credit note processes – that only true liabilities are settled and creditors reflect true liability position. Supportive actions include the development of regular reporting and collaborative reviews with continuous improvement actions jointly defined and linked into the cash forecasting model. A key enabler is a well-defined, robust and automated set of processes.

7   Settlement

The final step is often seen as the ability to process outgoing payments in line with corporate policy and the delegation of authority. In fact, there are additional opportunities for improvement. These include checking whether actual payments are made in accordance with forecasts so that the information can be used to understand variances and improve future processes. In addition, this can assist in the maintenance of a sustainable positive cash position based on cash flow forecasts.

4.4.3   TYPICAL ISSUES AND CHALLENGES

Although there are some specific issues that affect each stage, there are also some generic challenges that can affect S2S effectiveness. These include:

KEY ISSUES AND OPTIMISATION ACTIVITIES – SOURCING-TO-SETTLE (S2S) PROCESS

Process area	Potential issues	Mitigating actions
Planning and strategy	– Purchasing authority is not well defined – Lack of accountability for spend (indirect spend often neglected) – Limited control of/insight into departmental spend outside budgets – No influence over purchasing policies (compliance measures, enforcement) – Inexistent spend consolidation – Compliance to purchasing policies is not measured and enforced	– Develop a sourcing and supply base strategy plan that aligns with business owners to optimise efficiency and value of supply base – Provide consistent management of purchasing behaviour, as well as visibility to spend amounts, future demand and maverick spend – Leverage purchasing power – Define responsibilities, policies and controls
Selection and contracting	– Limited compliance to corporate purchasing policy – no measurement of compliance – Fragmented purchasing processes, systems and organisation – Supplier master file is outdated and/or not integrated into the ERP system – Lack of a rigorous process for the approval of new suppliers – Price is negotiated with limited consideration of payment terms	– Use strategic procurement framework to manage supply base and monitor supplier performance against set of agreed measures – Develop a selection and contracting approach to optimise purchasing operation – Create standardised tools and processes to understand current spend, research the market and determine the best strategy to maximise sourcing value – Provide visibility to supplier performance – Reduce or eliminate maverick spend, aggregate supply base and increase purchasing power – Manage contracts centrally with one operating system
Requisitioning and ordering	– Large amount of supplier commitments made with no P.O. – P.O. issued without validating contractual and commercial aspects – Unclear or undefined purchasing authorisation limits – Limited use of alternate purchasing channels (i.e. P-cards, e-procurement, etc.)	– Develop and communicate purchase order guidelines. – Actively support appropriate mix of purchasing channels used – Minimise purchase effort particularly in high-volume areas – Drive demand reduction through demand management; optimised order execution

▶

▶ *Requisitioning and ordering (continued)*	– Purchasing only invited to formalise an agreement already reached with a supplier – Purchase requisitions are done manually – Contract database doesn't exist or not clearly identified – Purchase orders do not refer to terms and conditions – Discount are agreed against early payment with suppliers randomly	
Receipting and evaluating	– There is no formal goods or services receipt process (GRN/SRN) – Quality issues with suppliers not being identified and tracked properly – Poor visibility of goods/services received but not invoiced – Invoices are sent to individual budget holders for authorisation	– Develop detailed receiving policies and procedures to currently reflect receipting activity and provide feedback into SRM and purchase channels including quantity and quality reporting – Integrate receiving and evaluating systems with purchasing, inventory and payables systems – Ensure receipting process captures relevant information to support cash forecasting and stock management policies – Track and report quality issues to procurement and demand planning for root cause evaluation and performance monitoring
Invoice processing	– Invoices are matched manually – Physical invoices are moved around the organisation – Invoices cannot be matched to a purchase order – First match pass rate is very low – High volume of low-value invoices – Invoices are not booked by accounts payable on the day of receipt – Budget holders go on holiday/ business trips and the invoices/ credits stack up in their in-trays – Copies of invoices are required to replace lost invoices	– Implement robust invoice process to support accurate and timely capture of liabilities with the ability to measure performance and drive continuous improvements – Implement accurate, timely and efficient invoice-matching processes linked to finance, inventory and purchasing systems – Develop central maintenance of a single enterprise-wide supplier master file that has full integration with other key systems – Monitor and review invoice discrepancy tolerances

Invoice processing (continued)		– Maximise usage of technology for document storage – Maintain Delegation of authority rules for (electronic) workflow validation and approval of electronic and imaged invoices
Discrepancy management	– Disputed invoices are not blocked for payment – AP is not informed of discrepancies – No formal responsibility for managing disputes with suppliers – Lack of queries classification – Credit notes are not always requested from suppliers – Information about discounts is not shared with AP – Invoices are not recorded at all until fully approved – Discrepancy not logged or classified by cause into the system – Discrepancy resolution roles and responsibilities not clearly identified – No defined timeframe to resolve queries, no follow-up of the credit note query – No clear threshold identified to facilitate discrepancy resolution	– Develop robust process to support accurate and timely capture of liability discrepancies with the ability to measure performance, impact on cash-flow forecasting and drive continuous improvements – Develop effective dispute management process that includes the early identification of disputes, timely resolution of disputes and the root cause analysis and eradication of recurring preventable disputes through the collection of volume, value and cycle time data – Manage disputes that affect supplier liabilities and performance with feedback loop to supplier – Ensure that only true liabilities are settled through rigorous cash recovery, discount and credit note processes – Develop regular reporting and collaborative reviews with continuous improvement actions jointly defined and linked into the cash forecasting model
Settlement	– No controls to ensure payments made to terms – Payment runs made in advance – Daily payment runs at local level – No formal review of opportunities for taking discount for early payment – Payments are usually delayed because of internal purchaser errors – Limited use of electronic payment methods (manual payment proposal process) – Direct debit payment process	– Process outgoing payments in line with corporate policy and delegation of authority – Ensure payments are made in accordance with forecast and variances to forecast are measured, managed and improved – Establish cash flow forecasting based on predictive model driven by transactional data to define future cash requirements and based on multi-functional approach drawing from demand planning, AR, AP, and treasury

▶

Settlement *(continued)*	– Large volume of returned payments – No cash forecasting	– Define emergency/early payment procedures with authorisation levels and routings in conjunction with treasury – Optimise payment frequency to match supplier payment terms – Precede payment process by duplicate payment audit

4.5
Accounts receivable process

Accounts receivable is another primary component of working capital. Its effective management directly contributes to the optimisation (i.e. reduction) of working capital and the availability of cash. A receivable is created when an invoice for a good or service has been issued. It is resolved – or cleared – upon the receipt of payment against the invoice. This is a company's primary source of incoming cash flows.

At a high level, accounts receivable can be measured by the metric days sales outstanding (DSO). Very simply, DSO represents the number of days it takes an organisation to convert earned revenue to cash (i.e. payment against an invoice). Faster collection of payments will lead to a reduction of the receivables position and therefore a reduction in capital employed. A one-day reduction of DSO is equivalent to a one-day reduction of working capital. In turn, that is quantified as the equivalent of an average day of sales revenue in cash flow improvement.

In this section, we will discuss the issues leading to ineffective receivables management and the practices that can address these challenges, reduce DSO and ultimately improve cash flow.

4.5.1   CUSTOMER-TO-CASH (C2C)

Customer-to-cash (C2C) – Definition
Customer-to-cash – alternatively called order to cash (O2C) – is the overall end-to-end process that includes: – Bad debt mitigation through sales to customers whose financial and commercial state has been evaluated and receivables are reasonably assured for payment   – Terms and conditions for delivering goods and services to customers   – Order fulfilment converting orders to invoices and submitting to the customer for payment at the earliest time allowed by contractual agreements governing this process   – Minimisation of past-due receivables through strategic collections efforts and an efficient cash application process.

Accounts receivable management

The management of accounts receivable and its contribution to the cash conversion cycle is often seen as residing within the direct control and responsibility of the finance department. However, true accounts receivable management is multi-functional and should commence even before a new customer is identified. It should then continue seamlessly throughout multiple activities – such as assigning terms and conditions, taking orders for goods or services, creating and issuing invoices, resolving customer issues and collecting, receiving and applying payments.

No single function holds sole ownership for the performance of working capital, nor can any individual be held responsible for the mismanagement of working capital represented by accounts receivable. It is the collective cooperation and participation of several departments in accounts receivable management strategy that is often referred to as customer-to-cash (C2C). The accounts receivable management strategy is depicted by the C2C seven-step diagram.

FIGURE 4.7   SEVEN STEPS OF CUSTOMER-TO-CASH (C2C)

1   Sales and quote management

Sales and quote management is the first process within the C2C cycle and begins with the identification of a sales lead or potential new customer. This is often followed by a creation of a quote that dictates the proposed pricing for a good or service.

If some form of the quote is accepted by both parties, it results in the conversion of the lead to a customer and finally the negotiation of terms and conditions of the relationship with the customer. The objective of the sales and quote management function is to align marketing and sales activity with company financial goals to secure revenue through active sales.

It is also to support cash flow generation as part of the C2C cycle by helping convert sales into payments. However, revenue does not become cash flow until payment is received. Therefore, the sales process is only the beginning of the cash cycle. In order to achieve the stated objective, it is critical to ensure thorough integration with the next function – credit and risk management – particularly with regards to the negotiation of terms.

In order to actively engage the sales function in the management of working capital, an element of cash flow may be incorporated in the existing sales incentive or bonus schemes. Typically, incentive programs for this function are linked to revenue. This is often recognised at the time of booking an order, not at the time payment is received, and provides little motivation to see the sale through to collection of payment.

In order to determine whether profitable sales are being made while working capital objectives are simultaneously being achieved, the credit and risk management function should be engaged during the contract negotiation process. Financing or credit terms offered to the customer should seek to minimise risk and optimise cash by ensuring payment is required within a reasonable time. Terms discipline – i.e. the use of a limited list of standard agreed terms – can simplify the process, reduce the opportunity for unprofitable agreements and minimise delays between revenue recognition, billing and the collection of cash.

Once terms are agreed and in place, it is important that the sales function continues to maintain effective contact with customers to identify and manage non-compliance. In addition, customer administration processes should be standardised. The use of standard invoice formats and procedures is a good example. For new customers, details should be captured in a standard form with mandatory fields and terms in the system matching the terms agreed with the customer. Access to the customer master file should be restricted to authorised personnel only, to retain the integrity of the data and avoid duplication.

2   Credit and risk management

Credit and risk management refers to the process of minimising financial risk exposure to a business by assessing potential customers to determine if trade should be conducted against credit terms. Credit terms relate to the process of allowing customers to purchase goods or services and pay a period of time afterwards (rather than at the point of sale). If the candidate is deemed too risky, then a decision must be made to reject the prospect or establish an agreement which dictates that all transactions must be paid in advance or at the point of sale.

From a financial risk perspective, it is the responsibility of the credit department to assess a customer throughout the course of the business relationship to ensure credit terms are being adhered to as contractually agreed. The financial stability of a customer may fluctuate and any perceived increase in risk should be mitigated accordingly.

Ultimately, the objective of the credit and risk management function is to reduce bad debt while enabling profitable sales and collection of invoices. Poor credit decisions may lead to late or non-payment of invoices and contribute to a high past-due accounts receivable balance and extend DSO (as well as costly administrative functions related to the collections of unpaid balances).

Credit risk is most effectively mitigated when managed dynamically – through a multi-faceted process that includes the standardisation and automation of the credit assessment process for new and existing customers. That can ensure consistency and accuracy of credit decisions while increasing the confidence of the sales department in the process. It can also allow for a rapid evaluation of credit information and a timely credit decision as well as a reduction in the time until a customer places the first order.

In addition, a continuous systematic assessment of risk for all customers should occur monthly by defining evaluation criteria within the credit management system. Manual reviews of accounts will occur by exception, based on the results of the systematic review rather than at static periodic intervals.

If the pre-defined customer criteria are collected and reviewed systematically on a monthly basis against established acceptable thresholds, it can allow for the timely identification of increases in risk which a static review process may not have picked up on until much later.

Any increases in risk should result in a manual account review with mitigating actions taken. This assessment can also determine where increases, decreases or the with-drawal of credit limits should take place – based on changes in payment behaviour and purchasing patterns.

3   Order processing

Once a trade agreement has been forged with a new customer, orders for goods and services can be placed. Order management includes all processes associated with obtaining, entering and fulfilling an order (including the administration of customer information such as shipping and billing address information).

As the order will ultimately become an invoice, accuracy is critical. It is important that all orders are confirmed immediately after being received and controls are in place to capture entry errors prior to shipment. Finally, the order should be fulfilled as soon as possible so as to quickly convert the order into a receivable (invoice) and start the clock for payment.

4   Invoicing

Typically, the process of invoicing means converting the details of an order to a form that contains the details of the price as well as the terms and conditions (such as the date the payment is due). The customer contract will usually define the point at which an invoice can be created following an order. For example, this may be once the goods have been delivered or service has been completed, or even as early as when the order is placed.

An ideal situation occurs where an invoice is created and issued as early as contractually possible. The reason for this is that the revenue represented by the goods or service may be legally earned but will not be paid until the invoice has been created and the terms have been initiated. For example, a payment term of 30 days may not start until the invoice has been issued – regardless of whether the contract states payment is due from the date of delivery plus terms. As a result, timing is of the essence.

As with order processing, the accuracy of an invoice is equally important. Any error identified by the customer (whether perceived or real) becomes a disputed item and may prevent payment until the error has been rectified. As a result, quality control is essential. In addition, the information available on the invoice document contains clearly stated data on the amount due for payment, the payment due date, the remittance (payment) instructions for both cheque and electronic payment methods, and any other terms and conditions which should be included to protect the interests of the company.

5   Collections management

This describes the activities undertaken to obtain payment from a customer for an outstanding invoice. It is the area in which most organisations identify with accounts receivable management. Collection activity most often takes the form of payment requests through contact with a customer.

The most effective method to ensure collections efforts have a significant impact on accounts receivable is to segment the customer base and create a series of collection strategies (i.e. based on frequency, timing, type or order of activities) in order to achieve the desired behaviour from each group.

An escalation process whereby problem past-due balances are communicated to other functions (such as sales) will complement collection efforts. Indeed, it is often the sales representative who has the closest relationship with the customer and can play an important role in ensuring the money is paid.

It is critical that the performance of collectors is monitored across key metrics such as percentage past due for the customer base, percentage of past due debt older than 90 days (a period of time after which the risk of non-payment becomes much higher), percentage of bad debt (i.e. receivables that were never paid or recovered) and collections effectiveness (value of receivables collected compared with the amount of collectible receivables within a period).

6   Dispute management

An invoice the customer perceives to be issued incorrectly may lead to the delayed or non-payment of part or all of the value of the invoice. The invoice or erroneous item is then classified as a dispute. Until a dispute is satisfactorily resolved or dismissed, the invoice is likely to remain unpaid. If the dispute is never resolved, the invoice may become a bad debt. Disputed invoices are a leading cause of past due AR and high DSO, as well as a driver of administrative costs due to the effort required to investigate and resolve a dispute.

The process of identifying, resolving and clearing disputes is referred to as dispute management. A business may have a discreet function solely focused on the management of dispute
resolution, although most corporates relay the responsibility for this back to the originating
functions in order to disperse accountability across the business. Put simply, the sooner a
dispute is identified and resolved, the sooner the invoice or remaining invoice balance will
be paid and cleared from AR. In addition, by reducing the occurrence of disputes, customers
will have fewer justifiable reasons not to fulfil their financial obligations.

Best practice

One of the most effective mechanisms to guarantee the timely resolution of disputes
is to implement targets. These may vary according to the complexity of the issue. To be
successful, the targets need to be tracked, monitored and reported to senior management. Organisations can also look to eradicate preventable disputes. In order to understand which efforts require focus, data must be gathered and a root cause analysis
program implemented to understand the origin of the dispute. The process can then be
engineered with the aim of preventing the same issue from arising again.

---

7   Cash application

Cash application is the process that occurs once payment for an invoice has been received.
The goal of the function is to match the payment to the correct invoice and clear the invoice
from the accounts receivable ledger. Paid invoices should be cleared from the ledger as
quickly as possible so as to not complicate the collection process and to ensure collection
activities are focused only on unpaid items. In addition, the timely allocation of payments is
important to provide real-time visibility of the customer's use of credit limits.

The types of payments applied are typically cheque, direct debit, credit card, bank transfer,
wire as well as other electronic forms. The process for applying cash varies according to the
payment method. While the majority of payments made in Europe are electronic, manual
cheque payments remain highly common in some countries. As a result, lockboxes – located
at the banking institution used by the business – are often used to receive cheques.

If possible, it is highly desirable that the process of matching payments and the associated remittance advices to invoices can be automated. This frees up manual resources to focus on the investigation and clearance of unmatched items or unapplied cash so that the collection function has a good overview of what is a collectable.

Prior to the automation of the cash application process – and as an argument to justify the cost of automation – there must be a high first-pass match rate. If the current first-pass match rate is low, the process needs improvement. This may include the provision of enhanced information to customers on the remittance advice or internal improvements (such as enhancing the remittance instructions available on the invoice document).

Banks are now offering virtual account structures to further optimise the cash application process by assigning an individual 'virtual' bank account to customers where all collections will be made. This vastly improves the process.

4.5.2   BEST PRACTICE MANAGEMENT

The table below describes some of the issues encountered and mitigating activities that may be undertaken to improve the performance of the function.

KEY ISSUES AND OPTIMISATION ACTIVITIES – CUSTOMER-TO-CASH (C2C) PROCESS

Process Area	Potential issues	Mitigating actions
Sales & quote management	– Sales has limited awareness of and involvement in working capital – No standard payment terms exist, terms and conditions dependent on sales person – Lack of clarity over whether profitable sales are being made – Complex and inconsistent processes – Delays between revenue recognition, billing and the collection of cash	– Regular training on working capital and cash flow management principles and goals – Clear policies on customer contract information requirements, billing guidelines, revenue recognition policies and terms and conditions – Credit and risk management function should be engaged during the contract negotiation process – Financing or credit terms offered to the customers should minimise risk and optimise cash by ensuring payment is required within a reasonable time – Use of standard invoice formats and procedures – Access to the customer master file restricted to authorised personnel
Credit & risk management	– Assessment process is not standardised – Credit decisions are subjective and inconsistent – Irregular scheduling – Credit limits are regularly exceeded without consequence	– Subjectivity of credit evaluation removed by defining the information being assessed and the weighting of importance – Exceeding of credit limits results in automatic order hold through the ERP system, triggering an associated action such as an account review – Credit risk managed dynamically through standardised and automated assessment process – Automation promotes consistency and accuracy of credit decisions while increasing the confidence of the sales department in the process

▶

▶ Credit & risk management (continued)		– Regular assessment of risk for all customers should occur by defining evaluation criteria within the credit management system – Timely identification of increases in risk – Manual account review where necessary to determine where increases, decreases or the withdrawing of credit limits should occur
Order processing	– High level of order errors, with errors not systematically identified or tracked – Side agreements not reflected in terms of contract exist and are not communicated.	– Order entry personnel have targets in terms of order accuracy and cycle time, supported by the appropriate level of reporting – Systematic checks are performed at the time of order entry and fulfilment to ensure terms of contract are being met
Invoicing	– Lengthy delay exists between order fulfilment and invoice creation – Invoices are only created at week's end or month's end instead of daily	– Trigger between order fulfilment and invoice created is systematic – Invoice processing is a daily activity and measured as such – Invoices created and issued as early as contractually possible
Collections management	– First collection contact occurs after the invoice has already become past due – Collection strategy is not defined and varies from collector to collector	– Collection activities and/or reminders are automated by invoice based on pre-defined timing – Manual activities – such as telephone contact – are focused on larger corporate customers – Different collection strategies for each customer segment
Dispute management	– Disputes are identified after the invoice becomes past due – No targets exist to ensure dispute resolution occurs in a timely manner	– Proactive collection contacts bring disputes to the surface in advance of the invoice due date to ensure early resolution – Resolvers have realistic resolution cycle time targets relating actual performance to targets reported

Cash application	– First pass match rate of applied payments is very low	– Root cause eradication activities are conducted to eliminate issues leading to failed matches
		– Matching payments and remittance advice to invoices should be as automated as possible
		– A high first pass match rate is essential

4.6
Inventory management

This section will focus on the inventory element of working capital. All companies hold inventories of materials and/or products that have been processed or transformed to various degrees. Assets in the form of inventories therefore make up a major balance sheet item for most companies. By reducing inventory levels, substantial amounts of cash can be released.

4.6.1   FORECAST-TO-FULFIL (F2F) – DEFINITION

From the moment that customer demand occurs, there are a number of decisions and events that will have an impact on inventories, and consequently on the amount of cash that is being tied up in a company's supply chain. The term forecast-to-fulfil (F2F) captures this process and all the decisions and events that take place throughout the process.

4.6.2   THE SEVEN STEPS OF F2F

The F2F process is made up of a series of steps as can be seen below. Each step represents an activity that affects several different functions in a business. There is a concern in trying to focus too much on the optimisation of a specific step in isolation because it may conflict with the optimisation of another. The companies with the best performing F2F process are the ones that understand these conflicts and take an end-to-end approach to the management of the process.

FIGURE 4.8   F2F PROCESS

1   Product range management

Product range management is the first step in the F2F process. Here, customers' demands are translated into product requirements. It is of utmost importance that the product range and the introduction of new products are well-managed. Uncontrolled product proliferation can lead to increased stock holding and the creation of SLOBS (slow moving and obsolete stock). It requires management time and effort to ensure that efficient processes are in place for product category maintenance, product life cycle management, product classification and product data maintenance.

2   Inventory management

Finding the right balance between stock holding and service provision is the eternal challenge in inventory management. Nobody would dispute that excessive levels of inventory tie up unnecessary amounts of cash and create costs, whereas insufficient levels carry the risk of reducing customer service levels and jeopardising revenues.

The ultimate goal is to have the right amount of inventory in the right place at the right time, and at the right cost to meet customer service and revenue goals but no more than that. The aim is to define the optimal level of inventory. Throughout the supply chain, there are various types of inventory.

> *Best practice*
>
> Best practice in inventory management starts with a well-defined and communicated stock-keeping strategy that classifies products. Business rules to enforce this strategy need to be implemented and clearly understood. In addition, the service strategy needs to be defined that will determine which service levels the company will provide to its customers.

3   Forecasting and supply chain planning

Efficient forecasting and supply chain planning are a prerequisite for the long-term success of a business. These involve the creation of an accurate sales forecast, communicating that to operations, agreeing on what is achievable (based on supply chain and operational constraints) and putting a plan in place.

Poor execution of these steps can lead to a shortage of products or excess inventories (or both). That can have an adverse impact on cash and revenue. Objective, realistic, and data-driven decisions must be made in the areas of forecasting, definition of constraints, alignment and planning.

4   Sales order processing

A very common reason behind building unnecessary inventories is making stock reservations. In some circumstances, administrators and clerks may feel a need to protect their customers and ensure they are able to receive products when they need them. This can be done by reserving stock for these customers, but it means the reserved stock cannot be delivered to any other customers. As other customers cannot be served from this blocked stock, such a situation may lead to the launch of new production even though there is plenty of physical stock on hand. Companies with an extensive use of reservations almost always carry surplus inventories.

Another common reason for excess inventories is the use of call-off orders. These orders are used when the customer only commits to a yearly quantity. The exact quantities are called off with a certain lead time when needed by the customer. The lead times are very often shorter than the production lead time. To ensure that the product can always be delivered, stock may be produced unnecessarily far in advance. The building of such stock is often magnified by a lack of maintenance of such call-off orders.

Best practice

To ensure that there is complete order visibility from entry to receipt, many corporations use web-based applications. Their order processing systems may be integrated or may interface with their customers' systems. Confirmation of the delivery date and the order verification are likely to be fully automated in order to reduce manual checks (which can be time consuming and can lead to human error).

Order entry, order allocation/reservation rules and priorities should be well-documented and followed, and customer orders should be processed according to target service levels. These service targets – as well as the definition of the service measurements – need to be fully understood by the order entry clerks so that any discrepancies can be quickly addressed.

5   Material scheduling

An effective material scheduling process will ensure that raw material inventory needs are reflected in accurate information flows so that there is enough of the right material at the right time. There are many conflicting objectives involved in the acquisition of raw materials. For example, the purchasing department is often assessed on its ability to obtain low pricing. On some occasions, low price is achieved by accepting bigger purchasing quantities (i.e. lot sizes) and longer lead times.

Both long lead times and big lot sizes can have an adverse impact on inventory levels. The production department always wants to be sure that raw material is available for production and that production can be changed at short notice. However, logistics would like to see big lot sizes and delivery by full truck loads (as this will help achieve better transport economy). It is therefore important to ensure that the scheduling process is trans-functional, i.e. with cooperation between purchasing, manufacturing, planning and logistics. When all departments work together, this can help create a balance between the costs of supply and stocking.

The main purpose of the material scheduling function is to make sure that materials are supplied at the right quantity at the right time and at the right costs. The companies that achieve the best results in this area are the ones that closely cooperate with their suppliers. These companies regularly share information with their suppliers, and the suppliers have maximum insight into the true consumption of their customer. One way of accomplishing this is through vendor-managed inventory (VMI) where the supplier takes over the responsibility to plan and replenish the customer's raw material stock.

6   Manufacturing execution

In order to gain production efficiency, reduce costs and achieve high levels of adherence to schedule, companies need to optimise planning and schedules around capacity constraints, and evaluate planning techniques to minimise stock levels.

Best practice

Best practice manufacturing execution incorporates a good understanding of all capacities, capabilities and constraints, including process and packaging line capacities, change-over times, downtime, resource requirements and storage. It is conducive to good business if these are quantified and documented. Key manufacturing processes should also be documented and the method of operation defined (including factors such as responsibilities or timing). Cross-functional collaboration should be in place to identify and eliminate any manufacturing process waste.

It is important for machines and equipment to be flexible and reliable as this will allow for quick and frequent changeovers (which is a must for small production batch sizes and low cycle stock).

7   Warehousing and distribution

Warehousing processes and design can have a significant effect on inventory levels and costs. The network design – i.e. the number and location of distribution centres – requires decisions based on trade-offs between cost, service and cash. The fewer the number of distribution centres, the less inventory is required. Nevertheless, transportation costs are likely to increase and service may suffer.

The choice of a transport solution will also have an impact on transport lead times and consequently on inventory and service. A speedy transport solution may be preferred from a service and inventory perspective but may not be justifiable from a transport cost point of view, particularly if the value of the goods in relation to weight is low (e.g. certain commodities).

The use of cross-docks, where shipments are unloaded and reloaded without passing through the shelves of the warehouse, is a way of speeding up the delivery process and reducing lead times and inventory. Some companies require their suppliers to keep products in consignment stock. A consignment stock refers to inventory that is being held in the customer's warehouse but is still owned by the supplier. Ownership is only transferred to the customer at the moment of the consumption. Although there are some strategic advantages to accepting a consignment stock, it almost always leads to increased inventories for the supplying company.

The design of the supply chain must take the impact on inventory into account. A solution that is optimal from a service and transport cost point of view may require more distribution centres. That may increase costs and inventory. Likewise, sourcing from distant countries will probably increase lead times and drive up stock in transit. These factors need to be considered.

Transportation routes must be planned in an optimal way, and orders to the same destination must be consolidated to reduce transport costs. It is important to have online visibility of the entire supply chain so that, at any given moment, employees can locate a shipment as well as check availability of specific products in all stocking locations. In a smoothly operating supply chain, there should be very few customer returns. On the few occasions where they occur, there should be a well-documented and understood process in place for quick handling these returns so they can be made available from stock without delay.

4.6.3 ISSUES AND CHALLENGES

As we have discussed, there are many factors that can lead to a business holding unnecessarily high levels of inventory. Below are a number of such issues and challenges.

KEY ISSUES AND OPTIMISATION ACTIVITIES: FORECAST-TO-FULFIL (F2F) PROCESS

Process Area	Potential issues	Mitigating actions
Product range management	– Poorly managed introduction of new products leading to obsolete stock of replaced products – Lack of product differentiation – Uncontrolled product proliferation	– Efficient processes implemented to control product life cycle management, classification and data – Cross-functional approach to product range and life cycle management – Products classified in a way that takes value and risk into consideration
Inventory management	– No correlation between stock levels and customer service, causing unnecessary high stock levels for some products and insufficient stock levels for other products – Insufficient inventory leading to risk of losing revenue – Excessive stock levels leading to risk of SLOBs	– Controls and methods in place to ensure that the business has the right amount of inventory in the right place, at the right time and at the right cost – Ensure that products and customers are given a service level that reflects their importance to the business – Proactive process in place to identify SLOBs and prevent their recurrence – A clear and well defined stock-keeping strategy
Forecasting and supply chain planning	– Poor forecasting accuracy can lead to a shortage of products or excess inventories – Misalignment of demand and supply causing shortage or excess of inventories	– A demand forecasting process that supports the establishment of a consensus-based forecast – Forecast accuracy measurement in place with regular follow-up and root cause analysis – Critical that there is a cross-functional and formalised sales and operations planning process in place to reconcile demand forecast with production capacity
Sales order processing	– Stock reservations building unnecessary inventory for customers that don't need the stock right away and may, at the same time, prevent customers who urgently need the stock from getting it – Unrealistic delivery parameters that increase inventory and/or delivery costs	– Clear and well-defined business rules that govern the order entry and order handling process, and enforced discipline to ensure these rules are being adhered to – Implementation of differentiated service levels that reflect the importance of the customer to the business

Sales order processing (continued)	– Lack of consistent or targeted service levels can cause poor business performance	– IT systems that with parameters set and controls in place to avoid promising unrealistic delivery times to the customers
Materials scheduling	– Poor data integrity causing incorrect replenishment decisions leading to shortage or surplus stock of raw materials – Low materials price is achieved by accepting larger purchasing quantities and longer lead times – this can have a detrimental effect on inventory levels – Poor supplier peformance and/or management is causing increase of safety stocks of raw material	– Enforce high data integrity in master files and MRP system – Close cooperation with suppliers helps to ensure that the right materials are supplied at the right time – Regular sharing of information between a business and its suppliers through web based applications for instance – VMI (Vendor Managed Inventory) where the supplier takes over the responsibility to plan and replenish the raw material stock may prove useful
Manufacturing execution	– Inaccurate planning parameters and unnecessary time buffers may increase waiting times between machine operations and increase lead times and WIP (Work in Progress) – Inflexible machines and equipment cause long changeover times and increased batch sizes, and consequently higher stock levels – Poor management of bottlenecks causing queuing and increased WIP	– In order to gain production efficiency, reduce costs and achieve high levels of adherence to schedule, companies need to optimise planning and schedules around capacity constraints, and evaluate planning techniques to minimise stock levels – Implementation of lean principles such as JIT, Kanbans, standardised processes, zero defects etc. will eliminate or reduce non-value adding waste, including inventories – Machines need to be flexible, allowing for quick changeovers and able to run when needed (as well as allow for high schedule adherence maintenance needs to be based on total productive maintenance – TPM)
Warehousing and distribution	– Sub-optimal supply chain design increasing costs and/or inventory levels – Ineffecient processing of return shipments causing pile of returned goods	– Supply chain needs to be designed taking into account the impact on inventory in addition to cost and service – To minimise customer returns, there should be a well-documented and understood process in place for quickly handling returns so that they can be made available from stock

4.7
Combining working capital management and financial solutions

The overview below combines internal optimisations, which a company can implement in order to strengthen working capital performance, and external financial solutions, which are offered by financial institutions to support the (financial) supply chain of a company.

FIGURE 4.9   INTERNAL OPTIMISATIONS AND EXTERNAL SOLUTIONS LEAD TO WORKING CAPITAL IMPROVEMENT OPPORTUNITIES

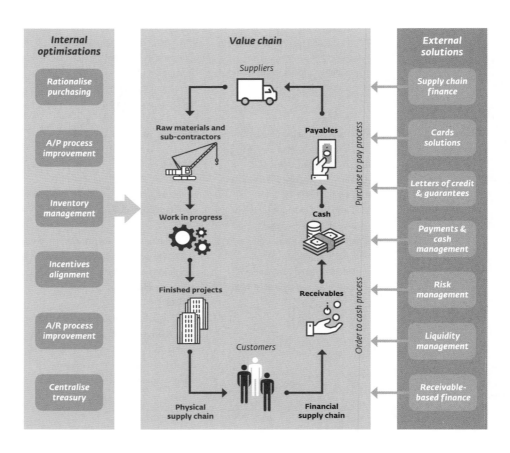

In order for a company to achieve its working capital improvement targets, any management of receivables, inventory and payables needs to be supported by a targeted KPI and incentive structure, and a centralised approach to treasury management. Besides these internal measures, financial solutions like receivables, purchase financing (including factoring), supply chain finance (reverse factoring), purchase card solutions, letters of credit and certain payment and cash management techniques can be used to manage and reduce working capital.

Chapter 5

Supplier and Receivables Finance to Support Trade and Working Capital

5   Supplier and Receivables Finance to Support Trade and Working Capital

5.1
Introduction

The chapter on working capital management (chapter 4) focused on working capital metrics like days sales outstanding (DSO), days inventory outstanding (DIO), days payables outstanding (DPO) and on internal optimisation measures a company can take to strengthen working capital. This chapter introduces several solutions offered by financial institutions and technology providers that companies can use to further accelerate existing working capital initiatives and capture additional working capital upside with respect to receivables and payables. Both supplier finance and receivables purchase finance will be covered, in combination with the organisational requirements for implementing a successful programme. As with regular working capital management, implementing supplier finance and receivables finance assumes that organisational key performance indicators (KPIs) are aligned and senior management is supportive.

5.2
What is supply chain finance (SCF)?

Since 2000, supply chain finance (SCF) has increasingly propagated and is now better understood and utilised as an important tool to help treasurers increase economic efficiencies in relation to how corporates either receive cash from customers or pay out cash to suppliers. Major banks, specialist technology firms and physical supply chain logistics providers have all recognised that considerable inefficiencies exist in complex, modern, international (and domestic) supply chains. These inefficiencies require an analysis of how traditional trade relationships are conducted in order to find new ways of making them more streamlined and efficient.

The broad definition of SCF describes it as a form of receivables-based financing designed to benefit both suppliers and buyers of goods and services by introducing a new source of competitive funding into (and based on the strength of) the trading relationship. It hinges on the purchase of receivables generated during the course of sales from a supplier to a buyer. Since most corporates are both buyers and suppliers in their own right, it can help improve metrics on both the payables and receivables side of the business.

SCF is short-term in nature, typically uncommitted, priced keenly and can be a key component of the working capital strategy of both the supplier and the buyer. It is not designed to replicate or replace other forms of established short, medium or long-term financing but to complement them. In effect, well-structured programmes can provide both entities with an alternative source of funding, allow funding priced on the specific qualities of a trading relationship and help improve the working capital position of both supplying and buying entities. When extended internationally, this may also include the opportunity to provide financing at considerably improved margins compared to those readily available in a local market.

There are two main receivables-based SCF solutions. The first is often known as either:

–   Supplier finance
–   Buyer-centric receivables purchase

In this first solution, the corporate is the buyer of goods or services and it focuses on the corporate's payables. The second is commonly known as:

–   Receivables finance
–   Receivables purchase finance
–   Seller-centric receivables purchase

Here, the corporate is the supplier of goods or services and the financing is related to the corporate's receivables. The diagram below illustrates the two solutions in relation to the corporate.

FIGURE 5.1   SUPPLIER FINANCE AND RECEIVABLES FINANCE MODELS

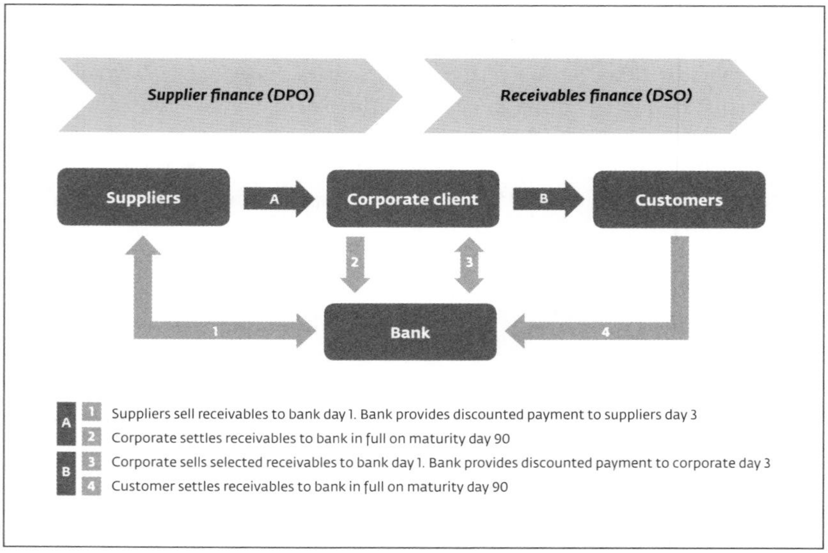

Supplier finance (DPO)   Receivables finance (DSO)

Suppliers   A   Corporate client   B   Customers

2   3

Bank

1   4

A
1   Suppliers sell receivables to bank day 1. Bank provides discounted payment to suppliers day 3
2   Corporate settles receivables to bank in full on maturity day 90
B
3   Corporate sells selected receivables to bank day 1. Bank provides discounted payment to corporate day 3
4   Customer settles receivables to bank in full on maturity day 90

SCF should not be confused with the financial supply chain (FSC). The former is a working capital financing solution whereas the latter is the existing (or proposed) design and business process involving payments between *all* the different entities (both internal and external) of a corporate.

5.3
Supplier finance

Supplier finance is a way of providing key suppliers with a new stream of funding based on the buyer's credit rating (which tends to be stronger). The buyer is usually in the lead in these programmes and recognises that it is in the interest of the buyer to help ensure that strategic suppliers remain eager to supply. It can be that the buyer has decided to extend payment terms with suppliers (i.e. days payable outstanding (DPO) or how long the company takes to pay its trade creditors) as a way of freeing up working capital.

By implementing a supplier finance solution, suppliers can choose to join and then take advantage of discounted early payments or receive payment from the buyer at maturity, depending on their business needs. This is achieved because the enrolled suppliers offer to sell their eligible receivables that the buyer owes to the bank. In addition to access to competitively-priced financing, it can provide the supplier with a way to free up its own credit lines so they can be used appropriately.

These programmes are typically offered at no cost to buyers since they only consume part of their banks' credit lines, up to an agreed limit. The suppliers pay to join the programme via the discount applied by opting to receive their cash more quickly from the bank (rather than at normal maturity date from the buyer).

The diagram below (figure 5.2) explains the mechanics of a supplier finance solution in more detail.

FIGURE 5.2   THE MECHANICS OF SUPPLIER FINANCE

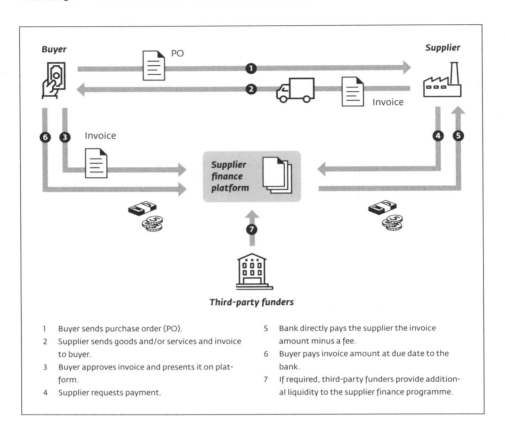

1   Buyer sends purchase order (PO).
2   Supplier sends goods and/or services and invoice to buyer.
3   Buyer approves invoice and presents it on platform.
4   Supplier requests payment.
5   Bank directly pays the supplier the invoice amount minus a fee.
6   Buyer pays invoice amount at due date to the bank.
7   If required, third-party funders provide additional liquidity to the supplier finance programme.

Benefits
Supplier finance benefits both buyers and suppliers.

Buyers	Suppliers
Working capital reduction by lengthening DPO, resulting in higher free cash flow	Working capital reduction by shortening DSO, resulting in higher free cash flow
Strengthening supplier relationships in combination with optimised trade terms and conditions	Potential attractive source of working capital funding based on buyers' credit quality
Streamlined payment processing	Possible saving on credit insurance
Reconciliation and process improvement	Transparency regarding the status of invoices and payment timing

Implementing a successful supplier finance programme requires close co-operation and alignment between procurement, corporate treasury, legal, finance and accounting (including the accounts payables department), operations and IT. One of the key objectives should be to establish straight-through processing (STP) between the buyer's ERP system, the supplier finance platform and the suppliers.

Procurement

The first step in evaluating supplier finance is to analyse and involve procurement, which is the crucial department for any successful supplier finance programme. This analysis usually involves the provision of supplier names, locations, agreed payment terms, actual payment terms and intended payment terms. It is sensible to split suppliers into domestic and international categories. Typically, it makes sense to include suppliers selling more than EUR 1 million in goods or services to the buyer each year.

Suppliers with lower volumes may well be more suited to a procurement card rather than a supplier finance solution. Procurement card solutions (often not delivered with actual cards but instead in the form of software connected to the buyer's procurement and finance systems) provide faster payment options to high volumes of lower value suppliers enrolled in such a programme.

Procurement information can then be shared with the buyer's key banks that offer SCF solutions. They will help to analyse and evaluate an appropriately-sized programme. Since it will be required to mark a credit limit against the buyer, capacity must be available (or made available) to accommodate a supplier finance facility. Given sensible analysis of the suppliers, certain categories may be more likely to join a programme than others. Again, the bank should advise the buyer on this detail.

The facility amount will be determined at this stage. It may be capped at a smaller level than is actually required should credit lines with the bank be full. Otherwise, the facility amount should reflect as conservative a requirement as the programme warrants. More experienced banks may advise the buyer to start with a smaller facility that can be expanded later as more suppliers join and facility utilisation is higher. It is worth remembering that very large over-ambitious facilities can consume credit lines and may be subject to withdrawal by the bank if utilisation is low.

Dynamic Discounting

Dynamic discounting is a solution that can be used by corporates that have excess cash and liquidity. Whereas corporates are seeking to extend their payment terms in traditional supplier financing, with dynamic discounting corporates pay their suppliers early by using available excess cash and liquidity in order to collect an early payment discount. This early payment discount is calculated automatically based on a pre-agreed financing rate and the original payment term, and the corporate can increase the competitive tension among suppliers by putting regular auctions in place and attracting the best possible discount rates.

5.4
Receivables purchase finance

Receivables purchase finance is the purchase of selected receivables by the bank from sales generated by the corporate (client) from their customers (debtors) selected and approved to join the programme. It focuses on the improvement of days sales outstanding (DSOs).

Depending on the structure designed for the corporate, receivables purchase finance often has the following characteristics:

– Improves liquidity, reduces DSOs and frees up capital
– Acts as an alternative source of financing
– Has straightforward documentation
– Non-recourse to the corporate, with efficient payment risk management
– Off-balance sheet to the corporate because of the true sale of receivables to the bank

FIGURE 5.3   THE MECHANICS OF RECEIVABLES PURCHASE FINANCE

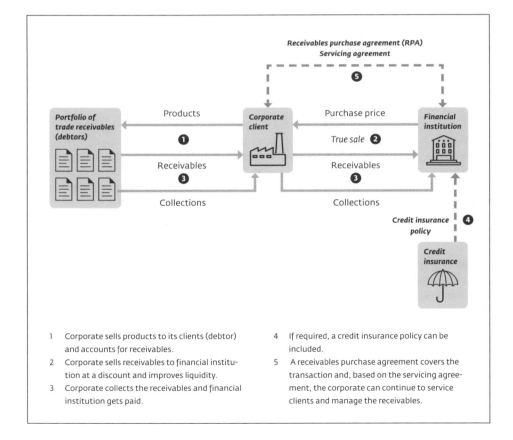

1   Corporate sells products to its clients (debtor) and accounts for receivables.
2   Corporate sells receivables to financial institution at a discount and improves liquidity.
3   Corporate collects the receivables and financial institution gets paid.
4   If required, a credit insurance policy can be included.
5   A receivables purchase agreement covers the transaction and, based on the servicing agreement, the corporate can continue to service clients and manage the receivables.

While this solution will not be appropriate for all the corporate's customers, it may be suitable for selected customers with whom the bank typically has both credit relationships and credit capacity available to support the corporate. The bank will indicate which criteria it uses to help the corporate identify which customers to include in the programme. The corporate pays the bank for this form of financing via fees and the discount rate applied to the receivable based on the credit quality of the debtor entity and the time of financing (i.e. the maturity date).

In practice, receivables purchase financing comes in different forms, where smaller firms often use factoring to accelerate the collection of receivables and improve DSO while larger companies use a more flexible approach to receivables financing. The latter may include the securitization of large granular portfolios of trade receivables and the financing of a selective subset of receivables from a single debtor or multiple debtors. Depending on the number of debtors, the size of the receivables and the granularity of a portfolio, these types of receivables financing solutions are offered to corporates.

In a factoring transaction, a smaller corporate usually sells accounts receivables to a financial institution, which subsequently collects these receivables from the corporate's customer once they become due. This is shown in figure 5.3. An important element in a factoring transaction is the fact that the customer needs to be notified (disclosure) and will be required to make payments to the factor instead of paying the corporate that has sold the receivable. In general, the factor will not have any recourse to the corporate if the customer fails to pay.

The disclosure element in a factoring transaction and the fact that collection of receivables is transferred to the factor is unattractive for larger corporates who prefer to retain control with respect to the collection of their receivables. For larger companies, alternative and more flexible receivables purchase solutions are available whereby they continue to be responsible for the collection and servicing of receivables and maintain the full relationship with customers. These transactions can be structured in a way that they remain undisclosed to the customer, obtain off-balance sheet treatment (true sale of the receivable), cover multiple jurisdictions, multiple currencies and different subsidiaries, and include or exclude credit insurance.

Implementing a receivables purchase finance transaction requires thorough preparation and, depending on the specific characteristics of a transaction, the corporate may be required to provide the following information:

- Receivables balances (month-end)
- Monthly sales figures
- Monthly receivables collection, bad debt, ageing and delinquency statistics
- Overview of payment terms offered
- Receivables dilution statistics resulting in receivables becoming uncollectable (e.g. from credit notes, trade discounts, disputes etc.)
- Concentration exposure to certain customers
- Collection procedures

Over the years, receivables purchase financing has continued to grow and this trend is expected to continue. This form of working capital management has attracted a broad range of companies, from small to large and from investment grade to below investment grade.

5.5
Successful supply chain finance programmes

As with any significant business improvement programme, it is important that the many internal and external stakeholders are all engaged and understand the business rationale from the outset. Managing these stakeholders – as well as breaking the programme into manageable parts – will help to define, develop and implement a solution that works well for all parties involved.

5.5.1   INTERNAL EVALUATION WITHIN THE CORPORATE

Strategic drivers
Usually, a corporate's readiness to embark on an SCF programme is preceded by a thorough analysis of working capital needs, the awareness that solutions such as SCF exist and the development of a pragmatic working capital strategy that recognises SCF as a key pillar of support.

All businesses are complex in nature and are frequently not only at the mercy of ever-changing market dynamics but also under the increasing scrutiny of financial analysts and commentators regarding how the corporate is performing against its peers. Therefore, in addition to active market interest in new products or services that are in development or being launched, the financial markets are keen to know how efficiently the corporate is run as a business.

Finance-led but procurement buy-in and executive support essential
While implementing SCF will ultimately be driven by finance, the motivation will initially be strategic. As a result, executive support and sponsorship is required. For supplier finance, the focus is on procurement so early buy-in here is also essential.

The procurement function will go beyond the statistical data available from finance that is related to the relationship, terms and strategic importance of each supplier (or group of suppliers). Procurement will also need to work with finance and support the strategy as they are primarily responsible for supplier relationships.

Examine your business
Most medium-to-large corporates have a sizeable number of suppliers – typically as many as 5,000 or more – but the bulk of their procurement spend is often with a smaller number of large suppliers. The most optimal programmes tend to focus on the top 200 suppliers as this is where greater benefits may occur. Smaller suppliers below a certain value of spend may find a procurement card solution is more appropriate.

On the receivables purchase finance side, it is important to select clients that are both large and interesting to banks from a credit perspective. Banks will not take over commercial risk from a corporate with such programmes and so the type of customer, their rating, the size of the transaction and the jurisdiction are all important.

Adopting a phased approach

Launching any solution of relative complexity needs to be broken into manageable parts or phases. Breaking up the work will enable corporates and banks to keep the project run tightly and will continually match the parties' mutual requirements in order to set realistic expectations. It is important that both parties have adequate project management skills to keep the programmes on track.

5.5.2 SELECTING BANKING PARTNERS

Most of the major international banks currently have SCF capabilities in place. These include the expertise to evaluate, structure and deliver programmes – as well as technology platforms with which to operate them efficiently. The selection of an appropriate bank is essential.

Criteria for selecting banking partners
Criteria should include:
– Relationship to the corporate
– Expertise and experience in supply chain finance
– Geographical strength and supplier on-boarding capabilities
– Technology solutions
– Access to credit capacity

In most cases, the facility requirement may also exceed the bank's own threshold for a facility for that particular corporate. Here, the chosen bank's capability to lead other banks is invaluable. The banking partner should be able to manage and bring other banks into the transaction and to sell it down (risk distribution) accordingly – either via their own market access or with other relationship banks proposed by the corporate.

Selecting a region

The business of the corporate will have a direct bearing on the bank(s) that would be most suitable for a specific programme. For large global corporates with operations worldwide, it may be prudent to split the business on a regional or country level, and then select banks that are strong in each region.

Other corporates may have a disproportionally large domestic business, in which case strong national banks may be more suitable. Nevertheless, it is sensible to spread the risk of having a single bank provider and consider different regions with different banks. This also provides scope to actively benchmark the service received from the selected banks.

- Channel solutions – need to be flexible, scalable and easy-to-use
- Proprietary bank channels – can often receive data from corporates automatically
- Third-party channels – where technology specialists develop their own channel solutions
- Corporate (in-house) channels – where a corporate develops its own platform.

5.6
Managing/extending a programme – evaluating performance

SCF programmes can and do take some time to establish and bring up to full speed. As with any relatively complex solution with multiple stakeholders, it is important that this process is managed well and that all stakeholders are functioning effectively. It should be possible to quickly take corrective action to ensure the implemented programmes are run in the best manner and that issues that may arise are addressed swiftly.

Expanding a programme

Once a programme is running, it is then possible to take time to consider how it could be extended – for example to other regions or with other service providers. Because most banks will have credit restrictions on corporates, looking at programmes where multiple banks can be brought in to share the exposure to a corporate are becoming increasingly important. Flexible channels that can support growth and choosing providers that have strong experience (whether technological, geographic or in a specific sector) are important. It is in everyone's interest to start a programme and ensure it will grow successfully for all parties.

5.7
Future developments and outlook

SCF is still relatively new in the marketplace but it is clear that it is a solution that will continue to grow in importance. Banks and technology providers continue to invest in both their hard (e.g. finance or technology) and soft offerings (such as advisory or consulting). Indeed, these solutions are seen as very much core in the delivery of working capital gains for each entity in a modern supply chain.

However, SCF does not offer the same potential scope to transact across multiple trading chains as the Bank Payment Obligation (BPO). It is clear that the BPO can provide new opportunities through which a corporate entity can generate competitive advantage. Classical trade finance is based around traditional trade instruments such as letters of credit. The nature of supply chain finance solutions is that they are based on receivables purchase – known commonly as open account solutions. Given that open account trading now covers more than 80% of the major global trade patterns, this growth trend will certainly continue.

The importance of understanding how a corporate trades and then designing a realistic solution that is built around that will ensure that the implementation of SCF solutions can bring real value and efficiency to complex international (and domestic) supply chains.

As with the physical supply chain, collaboration between banks, technology providers, corporates and their trading partners must continue so that each partner achieves realisable benefits and cost efficiencies that are for the overall benefit of the end consumer in the final marketplace. The kinds of solutions we have discussed in this Chapter look set to continue to evolve as the benefits of e-trade and increased interoperability become significantly more pronounced.

Chapter 6

Trade Finance

6   Trade Finance

6.1
Introduction

Historically, trade finance has been a highly effective tool used by exporters to finance and support sales in international markets. In addition, it has been used by importers to finance the purchase of goods.

Trade finance itself is a generic term that has a number of definitions. However, most treasurers agree that it describes a series of corporate activities which are primarily concerned with the management of the capital used in international trade flows.

Although trade finance was originally focused on risk management, over the last few decades (until relatively recently, at least) it had started to become less important as a result of a lengthy period of more stable market conditions and the advent of supply chain finance (SCF) solutions.

Due to a prolonged period of market instability, there has been a renewed focus on risk management through the use of traditional instruments combined with more powerful technology. The discounting of letters of credit has also become popular since the last revision of UCP600 combined with the historically low interest levels. Provided the transactions are structured correctly, financing can be provided without the use of borrower's credit limits.

In this chapter, we will describe trade finance as well as the common challenges associated with international trade. In addition to discussing the trading relationships that occur between a buyer and seller, and the risks and requirements that can arise from such activity, we will also be highlighting how delivery channels have developed to make traditional products and services more accessible to users.

In addition, we will look at some of the recent developments in the trade world and at the growing impact of digitalisation on the world in general and on trade in particular.

6.2
What is trade finance?

Trade finance is directly linked to an underlying trade transaction. Companies buy and sell goods and services, and the process of fulfilling the underlying sales contract can be broken down into stages such as order, dispatch, billing, delivery and payment. These represent simple financial and logistical steps.

There are various documents that help facilitate each step in the process and the evidence provided by a confirmed purchase order, an invoice or an acceptance certificate can be used to manage risks associated with trade. For example, a buyer may delay payment until there is clear evidence of dispatch or delivery.

Trade finance can also be structured to mirror the underlying stages of the transaction. This can make it easier to raise higher levels of finance as there is more opportunity for the finance provider to monitor and control the way the finance is used. As a result, associated risks can be more readily managed.

It is also a characteristic of trade finance structures that they are closely aligned to the ultimate source of payment. For example, there will often be a clear line of sight through to an end buyer and the means by which they will pay.

As trade finance is directly linked to an underlying trade transaction, it can be used to manage risk as well as an additional source of finance for one or more of the trading companies. There can also be a close linkage with a payment or payment process.

Traditionally, banks have provided services that help buyers and sellers in different markets to conduct trade by undertaking defined roles in the settlement terms agreed. These can include important aspects such as authentication, validation, guarantees, funding and effecting payment. This activity is illustrated well by services such as letters of credit, documentary collections, bonds, guarantees and forfaiting. A set of international standards has been developed to facilitate this process (and will be covered in greater detail later in this chapter).

Governments, authorities and organisations such as the World Bank have a role in the provision or facilitation of trade finance. Governments can do this through export credit agencies, who may insure or provide guarantees that enable trade finance proposals which might not otherwise be attractive in the private market. Typically, these will operate under a set of rules such as those developed by the Berne Union (a leading association of export credit agencies and insurers that develops guiding principles for such activity). In recent decades, there has been considerable activity dedicated to the modernisation of trade and trade finance.

- Trade finance is directly linked to an underlying trade transaction
- It facilitates the buying and selling of goods and services
- Finance can be structured to mirror the stages of the transaction
- Documents used include documents evidencing shipment of goods
- Governments and organisations can help to facilitate trade finance

6.3
Common challenges associated with international trade

As a result of the separate regulations and various differences between markets, trading on an international basis can be much more challenging than doing so in a single market.

6.3.1   DISTANCE

If there are great distances involved in trading, associated challenges can arise such as delay or a lack of knowledge about how to resolve issues in more remote locations. This factor can affect both goods and services (especially where certainties are needed to assure delivery of services, often over a longer period of time).

6.3.2   CUSTOMS AND LOCAL PRACTICE

Language differences can create barriers between potential buyers and sellers. Specific markets can have quite distinct preferences in branding, packaging or even preferred trading terms. Seasoned international traders are accustomed to scenarios where the branding used in one market is not suitable for another. The basis of competition and local market dynamics can vary considerably. For this reason, multinational corporations will often use distinctive market penetration strategies in specific geographies. An understanding of the local context is therefore important.

6.3.3   REGULATION

Regulation can vary from market to market in a number of respects. Despite international harmonisation, factors such as accountancy standards, trade regulations and customs clearance, the basis of taxation and collection can vary considerably. Such factors can have a significant impact on how business is conducted. In chapter 5 we already discussed supply chain finance (SCF). It is worth noting that any finance provider delivering a programme in multiple jurisdictions may have to take specific steps in each location in order to perfect individual agreements.

6.3.4 COMMERCIAL RISKS

When buying and selling, a number of commercial risks arise. These can be broken down into risks such as contract frustration, failure to perform across a range of obligations, litigation risk, failure to effect payment and failure to deliver. Many apply to domestic trade as well. However, the factors involved can become more complicated when trading in a series of different jurisdictions. For example, customs clearance can certainly become less clear. Such factors can affect how these risks are assessed.

6.4
Risks for buyers – getting the right goods

Fundamentally, a buyer seeks assurance that the goods or services will arrive on time and to the correct specification. This can be harder to manage where there is greater distance in either physical or cultural terms. There is comfort in dealing with locally sourced goods or services, or even with a well-embedded trading relationship where a good understanding has been developed.

Another consideration is the level of risk the buyer is willing or able to tolerate. For example, let us consider the buyer's dependence on the supplier. If a supplier fails to perform, a key question is how quickly – and materially – it will affect the buyer's own offering. It is also worth considering a supplier's ability to finance the contract and any potential reliance on the buyer as a source of funding. Such factors can determine the nature of the relation- ship and, more narrowly, the terms of trade and approach to trade finance.

6.5
Risks for sellers – being paid

Being paid on time is a fundamental consideration. However, it can be complicated by distance and unfamiliarity and, in turn, this can impair the ability to assess buyers and reach a common understanding of terms. This is known as payment risk. Concerns will often be higher if the seller is delivering to a country with a relatively weaker risk profile.

When selling to less developed markets, the ability to mitigate the risk by using credit insurance or bank trade instruments (described later in this chapter) has become more difficult. In addition, the appetite of the service providers in question may be limited.

Political disruption or imposition of sanctions can also frustrate a contract. These are just two elements of what is referred to as political risk. Even if there is risk cover via insurance, it may not include all eventualities. As a result, this aspect needs to be carefully considered.

6.5.1   FUNDING IMPACT

Despite globalisation and improvements in transport, longer transit times and potentially longer credit terms can affect international trade transactions. It can take longer to recoup costs unless the problem can be transferred to another party. An extended funding requirement may affect the seller's ability to access finance or the cost at which that finance is available. The challenge becomes even more difficult where the perceived risk of ultimate payment is higher.

6.6
The risk ladder

The opposing interests between buyer and seller can be graphically illustrated in the risk ladder. The core principle underpinning the risk ladder is that there is a trade-off between what is best for the buyer and the seller in terms of risk mitigation. The trading terms that afford buyers the greatest assurance of getting what they have paid for leave sellers most exposed to not being paid. Conversely, the trading terms that provide sellers with the greatest assurance of being paid leave buyers most exposed to non-receipt of delivery.

FIGURE 6.1   RISK LADDER FOR BUYERS AND SELLERS

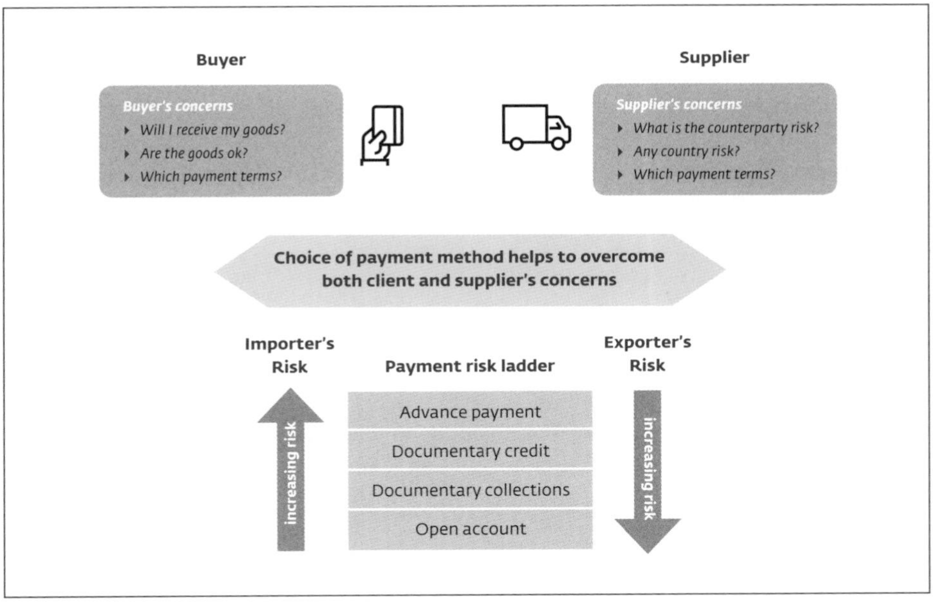

Figure 6.1 portrays the relative level of risk (or conversely assurance) associated with common trade products. However, the key principle (at least from a seller's perspective) is that where there is higher risk, more secure terms should be considered. For example, Dun &

Bradstreet Country Risk Reports include a number of indicators of risk and recommend a range of suitable payment terms to reflect this as well as local practice.

6.7
The trade cycle

A timeline can be constructed that maps the stages from initial order through to ultimate payment. This can be overlaid with a further timeline indicating when money must be paid or will be received. In turn, this defines the element within the overall arrangement that is not self-financing and determines the 'funding gap'.

FIGURE 6.2 THE TRADE CYCLE

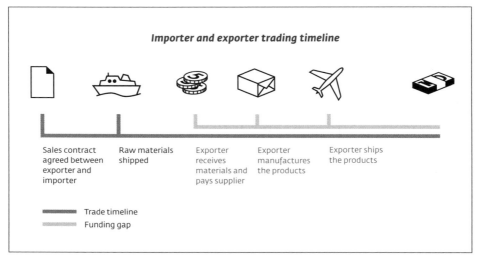

*Payment format will be agreed at the sales contract stage

Figure 6.2 illustrates how the trade cycle is put together. These building blocks can be used to determine the overall funding requirement. Different terms of trade can be used within this model to assess the relative impact of each on the funding requirement. For example, payment in advance to suppliers requires more funding than an extended credit period.

6.8
Terms of trade

In this section, we describe in more detail the trading terms that are used in the risk ladder. To place this in context, we also highlight the process of drawing up a contract and focus on elements that are particularly relevant to trade and terms of trade.

6.8.1 DRAWING UP A CONTRACT

The contract is the legal document (or set of documents) that defines the rights, responsibilities and obligations of the trading parties. This is a familiar process to all businesses. It often involves an enquiry, a quotation, an order and an order acknowledgement. This process can be very easily standardised in domestic markets with regular trading parties. However, it can become more complicated when trading across markets. For example, one common issue involves determining which law governs the contract and which jurisdiction will be used to resolve any disputes.

The International Chamber of Commerce (ICC) is the primary body involved in drawing up rules that are chosen frequently by parties to govern these arrangements. Its guidance ranges from areas such as model contracts, to form the basis of the commitment, to services such as the International Court of Arbitration (a body whose purpose is to help resolve disputes).

The ICC developed International Commercial Terms (Incoterms), which are a set of relevant rules that define the responsibilities of buyers and sellers for the delivery of goods under sales contracts. They are used to make sure buyer and seller understand:

- Who is responsible for the cost of transporting the goods, including insurance, taxes and duties
- Where the goods should be collected and transported
- Who is responsible for the goods at each step during transportation

These rules are often referenced in traditional trade instruments such as letters of credit and documentary collections.

Drawing up a contract

- A contract defines the rights, responsibilities and obligations of parties
- It normally entails an enquiry, a quotation, an order and an acknowledgement
- The ICC draws up rules that govern these arrangements
- Incoterms help to define responsibilities and determine costs and risks

---

6.8.2 COMMON PRINCIPLES

From the seller's perspective, terms of trade can be split between 'unsecured' and 'secured' terms.

Unsecured terms
The most commonly used term for this is 'open account'. It is, in many ways, the most convenient. However, it is associated with a higher risk of not being paid on time or not being paid at all. However, the associated risk can be mitigated, particularly in circumstances

where there is a high level of repeat purchase or buyer dependency on the seller. Often, corporates have internal limits on their buyers in cases of open accounts. Should the buyer pay late, and these credit limits are exceeded, delivery of goods will be stopped until the debt is back within the pre-defined limit.

A range of working capital solutions (such as supply chain finance – see chapter 5) fit within this category. Similarly, credit insurance is frequently used to mitigate the risk of delays in payment and default. Factoring is a form of invoice finance that can fulfil a similar role for the seller.

Many forms of invoice finance provide an advance, or discount a future receivable, but reserve a right of recourse if that payment is not received, while factoring can provide fuller risk transfer. This is achieved when the provider formally purchases the debt from the seller without recourse.

Secured terms

These terms build on the traditional role of banks as intermediaries in trade. For example, under a documentary collection or a (documentary) letter of credit, companies will present documents through a bank or chain of banks. The net effect is to provide the buyer with assurance that they will receive what they have paid for. The seller is also potentially better placed to receive payment for what has been delivered.

6.8.3 PAYMENT/CASH IN ADVANCE

This term means exactly what it says. Goods or services are not delivered until they are paid for. There is a direct parallel with a consumer transaction in a retail outlet – payment for the goods occurs before they can be taken away. In a business context, such terms can be difficult to obtain unless the seller is in a powerful position.

One variant is where there is a contract that involves stage payments. This may occur where the seller is building an expensive machine. For example, a deposit may be required but subsequent payments will be made against delivery.

A risk of asking for cash in advance is that it may trigger a request from a buyer for an advance payment guarantee (see below) because the buyer may want recourse if what has been paid for is not delivered.

Unsecured terms
- Open account is common and SCF can fit within this category
- Factoring is a form of invoice finance that can fulfil a similar role for the seller

Secured terms
- Builds on role of banks as intermediaries
- Can assure buyers they will receive the goods and services
- Can help to ensure seller receives payment for what has been delivered

Cash in advance
- Goods/services not delivered until payment has been made
- Similar to consumer retail transactions
- Unless the seller is in a powerful position, such terms can be a challenge
- Can include stage payments
- May result in a buyer request for an advance payment guarantee

Letters of credit (also documentary letters of credit)
- An issuing bank undertakes to pay a sum within a specified period
- Typically requested by a customer that is an importer
- The beneficiary (typically an exporter) will often be counselled by its advising bank to use a letter of credit
- Where further assurance is needed, the letter of credit can be 'confirmed' by another bank
- The beneficiary needs to present compliant documents to meet the terms
- Letters of credit are irrevocable instruments

6.9
Letters of credit (also known as documentary letters of credit)

This section describes letters of credit (one of the secured terms described in section 6.8.2) in more detail. The ICC plays a role in ensuring a common understanding between parties who use letters of credit. These letters of credit are governed by an obligatory set of ICC rules – Uniform Customs and Practice for Documentary Credits (UCP). The latest version is UCP 600.

6.9.1 DEFINITION

A letter of credit (LC) is a method of settlement under which the issuing bank undertakes to pay a specified sum upon presentation of compliant documents within a specified period. The issuing bank does this at the request of its customer (the applicant) who is typically an importer.

The beneficiary (typically an exporter) is often advised to use a letter of credit by a separate bank (known as the advising bank). The advising bank is often a bank that is familiar to the exporter whereas the issuing bank may be less so. This process serves the purpose of authenticating the letter of credit and advising the exporter of conditions they need to meet in order to get paid.

If the exporter wants a stronger assurance of payment, the letter of credit can be 'confirmed' by another bank. There is still an onus on the beneficiary to present compliant documents to meet the terms of the letter of credit. However, this may appeal where the confirming bank has a stronger credit rating than an issuing bank, thus improving the prospect of payment. An exporter may be more comfortable with a commitment from a familiar bank, particularly if it is one with whom they have a relationship.

Letters of credit are irrevocable. This means that once they have been advised they can only be changed or cancelled by agreement between the parties.

Once a letter of credit has been advised, the exporter is obligated to present documents in accordance with the terms of the letter of credit. These terms may mirror key elements of the contract. For example, this may include providing evidence of the latest shipment dates, certifying origin or evidence that the shipment has been inspected and conforms to a defined standard. In this context it is vital that parties are familiar with the generally accepted industry standard (but still voluntary) Incoterms – published by the International Chamber of Commerce (ICC) relating to the various risks, tasks or costs concerning the delivery of goods in international commercial transactions.

6.9.2   RISK MITIGATION FOR THE EXPORTER

The primary benefit of this form of settlement to the exporter is that it provides greater assurance of being paid as long as the documents are presented correctly. The fact the letter of credit is issued illustrates that the issuing bank is prepared to support the applicant (by demonstrating a certain credit standing with them). The exporter is reassured by one or more banks that payment will be made if the terms of the letter of credit are met. A further advantage is that finance can be linked to the letter of credit. The finance provider may also have more appetite to lend because a more secure source of repayment is in place (see section 6.9.4 below).

6.9.3   RISK MITIGATION FOR THE IMPORTER

The primary benefit for the importer is greater assurance that the exporter has to meet its obligations in order to be paid. The documents and timing will often reflect elements of the underlying trade transaction. A range of documents can be called for under a letter of credit. For example, evidence of shipment or an inspection certificate can provide greater assurance of ultimate physical delivery or of the quality of the goods.

6.9.4 FINANCE OPTIONS

Finance can be structured in a number of ways using letters of credit. From an importer's perspective, it is a way of achieving a period of credit from the exporter that would not otherwise be available. The presence of a bank risk-undertaking provides an exporter with more confidence to extend credit because there is greater assurance of payment. A disadvantage for an importer may be that the bank is likely to mark a commitment against the importer's credit lines – potentially restricting access to other facilities.

Often, the exporter/producer is able to use the LC it receives as beneficiary as a collateral to obtain pre-export finance to help with the cost of meeting the order. Finance providers may be willing to do this because there is a clear contract and a secure source of repayment in due course. This is one of the main reasons for the existence of LCs issued in Europe for Asia.

More typically, letters of credit enable post-export finance. So for example, if the letter of credit allows for a period of credit to the importer, the exporter may be able to get payment advanced or accelerated (effectively a pre-payment) upon presentation of compliant documents. The term discounting is used to describe this option.

6.9.5 VARIATIONS

There are many variations and derivatives of letters of credit. They build on common principles for the trading parties such as the use of the bank's conditional guarantee to provide a level of assurance that facilitates trade, using an underlying bank commitment to reduce or transfer risk, or building on the presence of that commitment to raise finance.

In markets such as the US and Canada, standby letters of credit are used for the same purpose as a demand guarantee. They are normally in letter of credit form and subject to similar rules. For example, ISP98 (ICC590), which is more appropriate for standby LCs than UCP600. One way in which they are used is to underpin a series of transactions without the need to call for presentation of documents each time. This allows regular trading to take place with similar freedom to open an account with the support of a clear fall-back position for the seller should the buyer fail to pay.

Transferable letters of credit have a specific clause that authorises the advising or confirming bank to pass on benefits under the letter of credit to someone other than the named beneficiary. An exporter may seek to enter into this arrangement to meet obligations to suppliers by offering the comfort of ultimate payment from a 'secure' source. This can eliminate the need for the exporter to use its own cash or credit lines with its bank. This form of LC can be used to help traders or smaller intermediaries. However, LCs transfers often fail to achieve their intended purpose. The system attracts inexperienced parties or parties with a low credit standard. Operational risks can be quite substantial for all parties.

6.10
Documentary collections

In this section, we discuss documentary collections which are another of the secured terms described in 6.8.2. As is the case for letters of credit, the ICC has developed Uniform Rules for Collections (URC). The latest version is URC 522.

Documentary collections are a method of settlement where a bank conducts the transaction in such a way that documents are released either when goods are paid for or against a signed document (like a bill of exchange) that commits to the payment of a specified sum at a defined future date. There are a number of terms for these options, including the commonly used 'cash against documents' and 'documents against acceptance'. The key distinction compared to a letter of credit is that there is normally no bank undertaking to make payment. That obligation is solely with the buyer. As a result, from an exporter's perspective this is a less secure form of settlement in the risk ladder.

A bill of exchange (often referred to as a draft) is a written acceptance of a debt that is signed by the person extending it. The amount and date due are specified. Because these can often be future-dated, they have traditionally been a common way of creating and evidencing a debt in a form that can be sold or discounted. A very similar instrument is a promissory note. This has a similar legal effect but is drawn up by the debtors themselves rather than being merely signed.

While cheques share some common characteristics with bills of exchange and promissory notes, they are not normally seen as an integral part of trade finance. Bills of exchange and promissory notes have stronger underpinnings in terms of established practice, international standards and legal recognition for this form of activity.

6.10.1   RISK MITIGATION FOR THE EXPORTER

If the documents being released under a collection are documents of title (such as bills of lading), this impairs the importer's ability to collect goods if they have not paid or accepted such goods as the collection requires. Failure to pay – particularly when a bill has been accepted – provides clearer evidence of non-payment than non-settlement of an invoice (which may, in certain circumstances and jurisdictions, make it easier to pursue the debt).

6.10.2   RISK MITIGATION FOR THE IMPORTER

Risk can be somewhat reduced on behalf of the importer if it has more evidence that the exporter has taken steps to deliver before the importer has to pay or sign an acceptance that commits to payment.

6.10.3   FINANCE OPTIONS

There are financing opportunities available with documentary trade. Often, an exporter may be able to obtain an advance or discount a future payment by using trade products – particularly where a bill has been accepted by a company or bank with a good credit rating. Sometimes, banks will also avalise bills to aid the process of raising finance in this way.

6.10.4   VARIATIONS

One important variation is forfaiting. In its traditional form, this involves the purchase of negotiable financial instruments – mostly avalised bills of exchange without recourse to the seller. Negotiation in this case can be defined as the passing on of the rights under the bill. An aval is essentially a simple acceptance – often by a bank. It is a mechanism that can be used to raise finance in the first place, whereby the risk is distributed among 'investors' who have an appetite for it.

6.11
Bonds and guarantees

The terms bond and guarantee represent the same commitment for most trading purposes and are often used interchangeably. Essentially, a bank or a specialist surety company stands behind a commitment on behalf of a client. If there is a claim and banks or sureties have to pay up, they will ask for repayment from the client under a separate counter-indemnity that will have been signed when the client engagement was made.

6.11.1   CLASSIFICATION

One key distinction that should be made is between contract bonds (that directly support performance of a contract) and financial guarantees (that stand behind a debt or financial commitment). Typically, contract bonds will be used at the buyer's insistence. Financial guarantees are often driven by the needs of a provider of finance or credit.

A further distinction is between conditional bonds and unconditional on-demand bonds. As the name implies, conditional bonds require a higher threshold to be met before payment is made. Unconditional on-demand bonds afford less protection against capricious or unfair claims. The ICC has developed guidelines (which are not obligatory) for the demand bonds: Uniform Rules for Demand Guarantees (URDG).

6.11.2   CHALLENGES

Bonds and guarantees can be affected by local law, customs and practice. In some markets, it is a common requirement that bonds are issued by a local bank (albeit indemnified by the exporter's bank).

Even where a bond has a defined expiry date, there may be no assurance that the commitment is released at that date in certain jurisdictions. Bond wordings can also be onerous and have limited scope for negotiation. In summary, this is not an area for the unwary. It is one that requires both legal advice and specialist input from banks before commitments are undertaken. Companies that issue a large number of bonds can find that they use up an unwelcome proportion of available credit lines with finance providers. This problem can be exacerbated if the company for whom the bonds are issued encounters delays in getting them cancelled.

6.11.3 TYPES OF CONTRACT BONDS

There are many types of bonds issued in support of trade contracts. Common varieties follow the structure of a contract, including performance, tender, advance payment, or warranty bonds.

Performance bonds
A performance bond is a guarantee written by a third-party guarantor, such as a bank, to a contractor's customer. It is usually issued to cover the price of a contract and it ensures that cash will still be paid if the contractor does not succeed in undertaking the specified terms or requirements of the contract.

Tender bonds
Tender bonds are sometimes known as a tender guarantee or a bid bond. In this case, the bond issuer, such as a bank, undertakes to pay a specific sum to a beneficiary on behalf of a contractor that wins a tender but does not enter into a contract. The sum is normally a stated proportion of the contract's full value.

Advance payment bonds
These bonds are designed to help facilitate an advance payment from the buyer for a contractor. Sometimes they are known as advance payment bonds. Normally, they are used by a bond issuer to pay the beneficiary a sum of money in circumstances where a payment has been made on a contract but the contractor does not undertake the work required.

Warranty bond
Warranty bonds are sometimes known as retention or maintenance bonds. They are used by contractors to pay their buyers if the former is unable to meet warranty obligations for the products (or services) listed in the contract. Warranty bonds are often required before a buyer is prepared to make the final payment of a contract.

6.12
Other common forms and features of trade finance

In addition to the above-described forms of trade, there are a number of common trade features in the market, including:

6.12.1   DISCOUNTING

The term discounting is used to describe the process of advancing future receivables linked to a trade instrument. This process has the same effect as providing a loan for the term in question. However, the structure usually involves calculating the interest obligation for the period until payment is due and advancing to the borrower the amount ultimately due less this interest.

It is possible to provide finance in this way without a trade instrument. This can be referred to as invoice finance and invoice discounting. It is a technique used by a wide variety of trade finance providers. The terms of finance will typically be governed by a lending agreement and may cover a range of invoices (defined as eligible for finance) or single invoices.

6.12.2   RECOURSE

A lot of trade finance is said to be 'with recourse'. This means that if the source of repayment in question is in default, the finance provider will require repayment from the borrower. As a result, there is no transfer of risk from a seller of goods or services who obtains non-recourse finance. With recourse finance, the finance provider will have purchased the debt from the borrower and in the event of default, will normally pursue recovery from the debtor.

6.12.3   EXPORT CREDIT AGENCY SUPPORT

Export Credit Agencies (ECAs) are government agencies that provide support in various guises to facilitate exports. There are a range of agreements that govern the practice of ECAs. For example, the OECD has provided guidelines for credit support of more than two years (known as the Consensus) to discourage unfair competition between states in the provision of subsidies. Similar rules are agreed via the Berne Union about the appropriate term and structure of such support.

In most cases, the ECA steps in to provide a guarantee or insure a debt and take on a percentage of the risk under defined circumstances that can include buyer default and political risks. The aim is usually to make it more attractive for finance providers to lend by participating in the risk. In some cases, ECAs will provide direct finance.

6.13
Channel delivery – historic context

Traditionally, trade finance has been associated with a heavy use of paper. And when documents move around between various organisations and locations, there is a greater risk of delays. For example, one factor in the relative decline of documentary collections in short-haul trade has been that the movement of documents can struggle to keep pace with the movement of goods.

Other objections relate to the burden of monitoring less automated processes and the perceived complexity of some of these trade instruments and processes.

6.13.1   PROPRIETARY E-CHANNEL DELIVERY

A partial response by banks has been the development of proprietary e-channels. This has the benefit of speeding up secure communication but it has not eliminated the requirement for paper documents. Other services have been offered to limit this inconvenience (such as when banks pre-check or prepare documents on behalf of customers). Even so, a common objection among companies using multiple banks has been the need to maintain multiple delivery systems.

6.13.2   MULTI-BANK AND THIRD-PARTY SYSTEMS

In response to the objections associated with proprietary e-channels, ways of communicating with banks have been developed using common formats. One example of this is the MT798 SWIFT format used for guarantees and letters of credit.

In addition to efforts by banks and corporates to devise such solutions, a number of independent third-party providers have also developed operating systems to enable such formats. Examples include internet applications which offer multi-bank applications for letters of credit, guarantees and collections and/or allowing for the electronic exchange of trade documents between parties. Meanwhile, some third-party providers offer multi-bank trade finance solutions for corporations and financial institutions, and have a platform with functionality designed to save users money and time while reducing risk and improving monitoring and control. Other third-party systems provide a multi-bank portal that enable corporates to undertake the secure and authenticated electronic transmission of approved trade-related instructions.

There are several overall advantages to these platforms. They offer functionality that allows corporations and financial institutions to save users money and time while reducing risk and improving monitoring and control of the various head office departments as well as managing their often remote subsidiaries and trading units.

Such solutions depend on investment by the companies involved (and therefore appeal more to large users of trade services) and cooperation from participating banks. The ICC has tried to facilitate this process by developing standards that support the practice. For example, eUCP was developed to support the electronic presentation of records under letters of credit.

6.13.3 OPEN ACCOUNT TRADING

Open account trading has become increasingly popular in international terms of trade and this affects the choice of trade finance solution. Open account trading refers to a situation where goods are dispatched or delivered but payment is invoiced at a later date – for example 30 or 90 days after delivery. As businesses have become increasingly comfortable trading across markets, they have continued to retain a demand for simple solutions that can integrate with their processes in a similar way to that of domestic transactions. This is often more readily achieved in markets with a strong credit rating and a legal and commercial infrastructure that is supportive of the recovery of debts created on such terms.

The financial crisis of 2008/2009 highlighted that open account settlement can potentially expose exporters to risks that were often previously mitigated by letters of credit (LCs). One of the main challenges involves minimising such risks from open account trading while reducing the labour-intensive aspects of LCs. In response to these needs, SWIFT launched the trade services utility matching tool, which was later developed by ICC into the bank payment obligation (BPO) product. To date, however, the BPO product has not seen much traction in the market as a potential replacement of the LC.

6.14
Anticipated future developments

As mentioned earlier, trade is still very dependent on paper-based documents to evidence shipment and title. Transporting these title documents (e.g. bills of lading) and the various accompanying documents and certificates (including packing lists, certificates of origin, certificates of inspection, etc.) is cumbersome, time-consuming and prone to loss. A number of parties in the industry are investigating initiatives to remove the paper flows underlying the transactions and move to electronic-based documentation. These initiatives include removing paper from trade processing by using electronic documentation. One challenge will be on-boarding the many parties involved in trade transactions (buyers, sellers, agents, shipping companies, port authorities, etc.) onto these various platforms, especially given the often remote locations of many of these parties.

One of the more exciting but untried challenges at the moment involves leveraging the blockchain or distributed ledger technology for trade transactions. The underlying paper-based aspects, combined with the remoteness of the parties, would appear to make this an ideal platform for managing trade transactions.

A blockchain is a distributed database that is used to maintain a continuously growing list of records, called blocks. Each block contains a timestamp and a link to a previous block. A blockchain is typically managed by a peer-to-peer network collectively adhering to a protocol for validating new blocks. By design, blockchains are very difficult to change. Once recorded, the data in any given block cannot be altered retroactively without the alteration of all subsequent blocks and the cooperation of the network. Functionally, a blockchain can serve as an open, distributed ledger that can record transactions between two parties efficiently and in a verifiable and permanent way.

Blockchain lends itself easily to the trade finance industry, which heavily relies on the settlement of sensitive information. This technology could be used to digitise sales and other legal contracts (smart contracts), allow the location of goods to be monitored and facilitate payments in close to real time. Potentially, business transactions can be executed directly on the platform itself through the use of 'smart contracts' embedded in the platform and the platform could be further connected to payment systems and distribution networks for a smoother flow of payments, goods and services.

The expectations are that the industry will embark on a period of increased automation and reduced use of paper. Still, this will be a challenge given the many parties and often remote locations involved.

Payments and Receivables

Chapter 7

Cash Flow Management

7 Cash Flow Management

7.1
Introduction

As we have seen in chapter 2, one of the core cash management responsibilities is to manage the funds that flow in and out of a company. These include, for example, ensuring there is an efficient account structure for collections and cash concentration, and that there is enough liquidity to make payments in the right currency, at the right location and at the right time when they fall due. Receivables and payables management also falls into this category, which involves selecting the most efficient payment instruments for the collections and payables.

In order to do that, many transaction instruments are required, as well as electronic interfaces with the banking industry. We will discuss these transaction tools in this section of the book. First, however, we will discuss the policy aspects of cash flow management and identify the essential aims and objectives that companies wish to achieve through first-class cash flow management. In particular, we will focus on strategies to reduce transaction costs and help ensure cash flows are tightly controlled.

We will explain the basics of cash flow management as well as provide our view on its definition, objectives and relevance. We will also discuss the options available to reduce the costs of the payments process. In addition to pushing down transaction fees and handling costs, operational costs can also be reduced by reviewing and optimising the overall structure of cash flows. This may involve the re-routing of international payments through offshore accounts or the netting of inter-company payables and receivables. Alternatively, the company may improve efficiency by centralising the internal transaction processes in an in-house transaction centre.

7.2
What is cash flow management?

Cash flows can originate from many sources including trade transactions, social security and tax obligations, and financial contracts. These settlements create cash movements between the company and its third parties as well as between the company's own operating entities. As we know, corporate cash flows can occur at any moment in different currencies, via multiple bank accounts and in various countries. As a result, managing these flows can be challenging but important, as each cash flow can have a direct impact on the company's liquidity position and will generate operating costs.

The majority of the cash flows are likely to originate from commercial transactions such as those with customers or vendors. These counterparties can be external customers and suppliers or internal entities that buy and sell goods and services within the group. In addition, non-commercial cash flows need to be included, such as social security and tax payments, treasury transactions and capital transactions.

Cash flow types	
Outgoing transactions	**Incoming transactions**
– Vendor payments	– Customer receivables
– Inter-company payments	– Inter-company receivables
– Tax payments	– Recovered tax such as VAT refunds
– Social security payments	– Subsidies
– Payroll payments	– Treasury receipts
– Treasury payments	– Corporate divestments
– Corporate investments	
– Dividend payments	
– Interest payments	
– Loan repayments	

Other receivables:

- Proceeds from the sale of assets
- Royalties
- Rent received

Other outgoing:

- Cash purchases
- Marketing costs
- Lease payments

In order to evaluate a company's cash flow management, it can be clearer to use a diagram to highlight the most important external and internal cash flows. A simple cash flow structure is shown in figure 7.1. When the company operates in a number of countries, with different operating companies and varied currencies, it is useful to identify the cross-border flows in each currency.

FIGURE 7.1   A TYPICAL CASH FLOW STRUCTURE

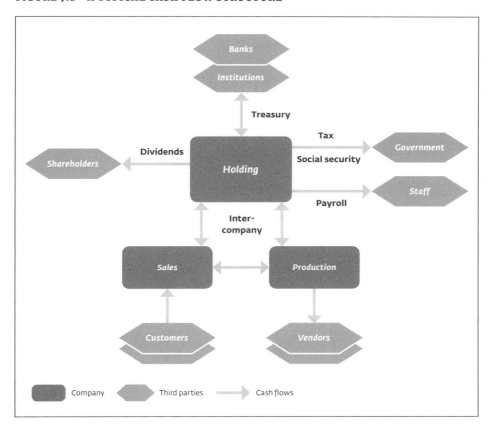

7.2.1   CASH FLOW MANAGEMENT – DEFINITION AND OBJECTIVES

Cash flow management focuses on the management of the company's transaction flow with third parties and between its entities. This includes the settlement of transactions on bank accounts as well as through internal accounts.

Cash flow management – definition and objectives
The management of internal and external transaction flows settled on bank accounts and internal accounts in order to:
– Minimise internal and external transaction costs
– Influence the timing of the transactions to optimise a company's liquidity position

Very often, corporate treasury is not responsible for the daily execution of transactions. However, we believe that the treasurer has a key role in ensuring that the operational transaction process is organised in such a way that transactions happen at the right time, in the right place, in the right currency, with the right information and in the most efficient way. Operational transactions have a direct impact on the liquidity position of the company so it is in the treasurer's interest to influence the timing of such transactions.

Good examples of positive influence could include the spreading of transactions over a certain period so as not to create a peak in outflows, or to accelerate inflows and delay outflows so as to avoid expensive overdrafts on foreign currency accounts. Nevertheless, in practice it is often difficult to change the timing of transactions. Incoming payments are particularly problematic because they are determined by factors beyond the control of the treasurer or even the company itself.

7.2.2   STRATEGIES TO IMPROVE CASH FLOW MANAGEMENT

Sometimes, the scale of the transactions carried out in a large international company grows significantly when a consistent strategy is not applied. It is therefore useful to review cash flow practices within the company and identify options to reduce operating costs and improve control over daily cash flows. Standardisation and automation are critical instruments to improve efficiencies and they also enable the straight-through processing of transactions. Standardisation of message formats and security protocols is required for companies to communicate efficiently with their transaction banks and achieve full data processing integration.

There are various options open to those who wish to improve cash flow management. As a first step, companies can begin by reviewing cost-saving opportunities within the existing cash flow structure. Are the conditions agreed with the transaction banks competitive? Are the most efficient transaction instruments being used, is the account structure optimised for the receivables and disbursements it has to support? As a second – more fundamental – step, companies need to review the overall cash flow structure. Can the company benefit from the re-routing of transaction flows through different banks, countries and accounts? Finally, internal transaction processes may be reviewed and streamlined by centralising processing into a central unit with a single interface to the banking industry.

Strategies to optimise cash flow management
– Cost-saving measures within the existing cash flow structure
– Changing the cash flow structure
– Changing the internal organisation

7.3
Realising financial benefits by optimising the existing cash flow structure

A company can reduce payment costs in various ways without adjusting its existing cash flow structure. These measures include:

- Payment charges
- Bank float and value dating
- Use of payment instruments
- Internal handling costs
- Timing of collections and payments
- Bank account structure

7.3.1   NEGOTIATING LOWER PAYMENT CHARGES

The costs that banks charge for payment services are often negotiable, especially where high transaction volumes are involved and/or in combination with cross-buy of other bank services. This can be supported by the consolidation of the numbers of transaction banks a company is dealing with. In the US and Europe in particular, payment products have become commoditised. Prices have been driven down by fierce competition (although this does not necessarily apply to small or medium-sized companies or to transaction services in emerging markets). As a result, a treasurer is well advised to regularly check whether the company is still paying the going market rate. Another important factor is the manner in which payment services are purchased, whether at a decentralised level by the operating companies or at a centralised level by the corporate treasurer. Companies that opt for centralised purchasing can often benefit from lower rates.

7.3.2   REDUCING BANK FLOAT AND VALUE DATING

Bank float is the time that a transfer is 'in transit' – the time lapse between the moment that the payer's account is debited (book date) and the moment that the beneficiary's account is credited (book date). Bank float particularly affects international payments involving two or more banks. When several banks take part in a transfer, it is often very difficult to ascertain which bank is still 'sitting on the money' i.e. enjoying the liquidity benefit of the transaction. However, the interest rate environment and funding cost for specific currencies may influence this as well.

To reduce or prevent excessive bank float, companies can try to avoid cross-border transfers by using offshore accounts to disburse and collect funds in a foreign country. Bank float can also occur in domestic payments processes, although this depends on the countries in which the payments are made. Inter-company payments are sometimes concentrated in a single bank so that zero float conditions for inter-company payments can be negotiated.

Banks may also apply value dating. That means the amount transferred only starts earning interest one or more days after it has been posted to the account. Value dating is traditionally used by banks as compensation for transaction services as it enables them to apply lower transaction fees.

Value dating can often be influenced by the customer. In many countries, banks can reduce or switch off value dating should the company prefer to pay transaction fees. Since 2008, under the rules of the Single Euro Payments Area (SEPA) and the Payment Services Directive (PSD) value dating can no longer be applied by banks transferring euro payments across the euro area. In some non-EU countries however, value dating practices may not always be clear and transparent. It is worth investigating how banks handle value dating in order to select those that offering transparent pricing.

7.3.3 SUBSTITUTING EXPENSIVE PAYMENT PRODUCTS WITH COST-EFFECTIVE INSTRUMENTS

In many markets, companies can choose between instruments such as urgent payments, single credit transfers, batch payments, cheque payments and cheque collections, direct debits, credit and debit card transactions, and cash payments. The company needs to select the correct payment instrument for each outgoing and incoming transaction according to the requirements of the underlying transaction in terms of execution time, cut-off time, value dating, remittance details, payment finality, local practices, specific requirements of the customer or vendor and – most importantly – the related costs. For example, treasury transactions such as investment and foreign exchange transactions are often executed through an 'urgent' or 'high-value payment' with fast and unconditional settlement, a late cut-off time, no value dating, limited remittance data and relatively high costs. Typically, a regular vendor payment is executed by a single low-value or batch payment where immediate execution is often not required but sufficient room for remittance details is important and low transaction costs are critical.

Requirements for selecting the optimal transaction instrument
– Execution time
– Cut-off time
– Value dating
– Remittance details
– Payment finality
– Costs
– Availability (not all banks offer all products in all regions of the world)

In general, it makes sense for a company to seek the lowest possible costs with the lowest associated risk. This means that relatively expensive and inefficient instruments such as cheque collections, cash payments and manually initiated transfers should be avoided. More efficient instruments include direct debits, where the payer signs a direct debit mandate allowing the company to automatically debit the debtor's account. This gives the company better control of the date of the collection.

In summary, it is firstly important to establish which instrument is used for each type of payment. Secondly, it is essential to find out whether an alternative payment instrument is cheaper or provides tighter control in terms of execution time.

7.3.4   REDUCING INTERNAL HANDLING COSTS

The internal costs of preparing and delivering payment instructions – as well as processing collections – are often significantly higher than the external costs. Companies regularly use electronic banking connections to deliver payment instructions and to receive information about receivables. In order to minimise processing costs, these electronic banking systems must be connected to the accounts payable and the accounts receivable systems. In addition, it is critical that the information between the company's applications and its bank can be exchanged fully automatically without manual intervention. This is known as straight-through processing. The higher the degree of automation, the lower the costs.

Electronic banking technology and industry standardisation have been developed extensively in the last couple of years and this has enabled companies to establish automatic interfaces with virtually every accounting or enterprise resource planning system. The biggest challenge now is to achieve a high degree of standardisation of remittance information. This is the data in the payment instruction needed for the receiver to automatically identify which client has paid which invoice. Software companies and banks have developed systems that enable companies to reconcile outstanding receivables and incoming receipts almost automatically, and this can result in significant savings.

7.3.5   COLLECTING FAST AND PAYING LATE TO OPTIMISE WORKING CAPITAL

Additional savings can be achieved by optimising working capital through speeding up the collection of receivables and delaying payment of outstanding payables until it is economically and commercially needed. Outgoing payments need not be made before the payments are due according to the agreed terms of payments, or before the day deemed acceptable by the company doing business with the supplier. Yet, they should also not be made late, as this may trigger penalties or worsen the relationship with strategic suppliers which, in turn, could cause issues and additional costs. It is critical to organise the payments process in such a way that it facilitates these 'just-in-time' payments.

As can be seen in chapter 4, there are various ways to accelerate the collection of receivables. These can help companies to substantially reduce their borrowing requirements or increase their excess liquidity positions. In turn, this can help to minimise a company's interest charges or maximise its interest income.

7.3.6   OPTIMISE ACCOUNT STRUCTURE

There is no one-size-fits-all account structure. Indeed, there are nearly unlimited variations when it comes to designing such a structure.

Typically, choices are made based on the needs of the organisation, its business character, and treasury needs. In addition, there are many different drivers/influences affecting account structure decisions. These may include regional or country regulatory requirements, availability of payment instruments, systems on the corporate and the banking side and the need to have responsibilities and operations focused locally or centrally.

In general, the aim is to reduce risk through optimisation of visibility and availability of cash while enabling the company to receive and pay cash and manage currency exposures as efficiently as possible.

Tax implications of proposed structures are reviewed by the tax advisor/department before being implemented.

Where to start:

1. Decide if and where to keep accounts denominated in non-functional currencies (i.e. only functional/local currency accounts with one local bank and the use of spot foreign exchange (FX) conversion for all foreign currency (FCY) transactions, or keep FCY accounts in one location – such as a shared service centre (SSC) or a treasury centre – or to keep FCY accounts in the currency centres). Part of this exercise will be determined by the company's appetite for exposures in non-functional currencies.

2. Decide on the level of centralisation. Particularly in larger international companies, the level of centralisation will have a great impact on the number of current accounts because part of the structure will have to be replicated for each entity or business unit (BU). Such a replicated structure can be expensive as each additional account will not only add to the annual cost for maintenance (both banking fees as well as internal costs related to maintaining/monitoring/reporting/auditing the account) but increase risk (i.e. fraud risk). Decentrally organised companies benefit less from economies of scale to coordinate and leverage across banks and have fewer FX matching efficiencies.

International account structures to enable collections and disbursements may be integrated in pooling structures (either notional, cash concentration or virtual cash management).

- Negotiating competitive transaction fees
- Reducing bank float to a minimum
- Avoiding value dating costs
- Using cost effective transaction instruments
- Reducing handling costs through automation and standardisation
- Collecting fast and paying late
- Optimising account structure

7.4
Changing a company's cash flow structure

Another way of realising cost savings is to make changes in the company's cash flow structure. To assess the possibilities for cost reduction, it is essential to create an overall view of its most important cash flows. The following cash flows must be made visible:

- Inflows and outflows of each operating company
- Inter-company flows – domestic and cross-border
- Cross-border flows with third parties
- Separate flows in the most important currencies

Once a company has an accurate understanding of the cash flow structure, it can explore the various opportunities for changing the routing of payment flows to achieve additional cost savings. We will focus on two opportunities:

- Changing the routing of cross-border cash flows
- Changing the routing of inter-company cash flows

7.4.1 CHANGING THE ROUTING OF CROSS-BORDER CASH FLOWS

The Single Euro Payments Area (SEPA) was implemented in Western Europe, creating a Europe-wide clearing infrastructure and allowing cross-border payments in euros to be processed as domestic payments at domestic rates with zero float. However, cross-border payments outside Western Europe and payments in non-euro currencies within the EU are still processed through the correspondent banking system, which involves multiple banks. As a result, these payments can attract relatively high fees and float costs. To reduce transfer costs, a company may wish to consider replacing cross-border payments with local transfers. We will look at incoming and outgoing cross-border payments successively.

Incoming cross-border payments
A company receiving export orders from many different customers in a given country will be faced with a large volume of incoming cross-border payments from that country. It will not always be possible or desirable for it to pass the costs of the cross-border transfers on to

its customers. One solution is to open a 'non-resident' or 'offshore' account in the country in question. If such an account is mainly used to receive incoming payments, it is called a collection account. In that case, the cash manager will open the offshore account with a local bank or a foreign branch of an international network bank.

Customers in that country can then transfer money via the local clearing system – at the lower local rates – to the exporter's local account. The incoming amounts collected in this manner can then be transferred periodically (automatically or manually) to the central account the company maintains with its cash concentration bank in its home country. As a result, the company will only be charged the higher costs of a foreign transfer when the funds are transferred periodically to the home country.

Outgoing cross-border payments

Some companies need to make many payments to suppliers abroad. If these payments are made from a bank account in the company's home country, the resulting cross-border payments will often be processed through correspondent banks. To avoid the high costs of such cross-border payments, companies may open a non-resident account abroad in the country of the beneficiary. The payments to the beneficiaries in that country can then be made out of this account. The payment instructions are delivered to the foreign bank using an electronic banking system. These 'remote local payments' will be processed through the local clearing system in the country of the beneficiary.

Examples of re-routing cross-border cash flows

Below are two examples where a decision is made to change the routing of cross-border cash flows. The first example concerns a company based in France with suppliers and customers in the UK. Initially, the company did not have a non-resident account in the UK. Both the company and its suppliers invoice in GBP. In the company's cash flow structure, we see parallel cross-border payment flows in GBP going in opposite directions. This is shown in the figure below.

FIGURE 7.2   OLD CASH FLOW STRUCTURE OF FRANCE-BASED COMPANY

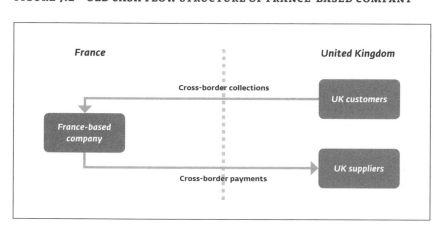

To save costs, the France-based company can decide to open a non-resident account in the UK. This account can be used to receive local payments from customers and to make local payments to suppliers. From time to time, the central treasury will have to fund the offshore account or transfer excess cash to the company's bank in France. A diagram of the company's cash flow structure now looks like this:

FIGURE 7.3   NEW CASH FLOW STRUCTURE OF FRANCE-BASED COMPANY

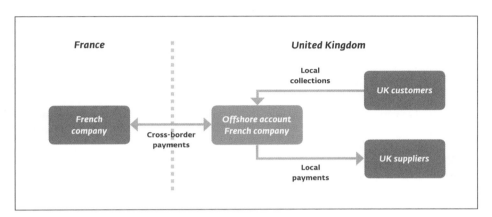

By re-routing the cross-border payment flows, the France-based company will benefit from the following advantages:

- Local rates – the company pays local rates in the UK for its outgoing and incoming transactions
- Reduced bank float – incoming payments are received earlier and outgoing payments can leave later, resulting in improved liquidity and enhanced interest results
- Better service to local customers – they can pay to a local account more easily and cheaply
- Better commercial position – the company improves its position by showing a local presence in the UK market

These benefits should be weighed against the costs of running the offshore account. Alternatively, the company could consider alternative arrangements such as the global cross-currency payment instruments offered by banks and other service providers. These tend to be suitable and cost effective for low-value cross-border payments from one account in the company's base currency. Another option used by large international companies is to replace cross-border payments with domestic transfers initiated by local subsidiaries who make payments on behalf of another sister company with internal settlement through in-house systems.

In our second example, a company based in Japan sells its computer hardware through operating companies in various countries around the world, including Germany, Italy and the United Arab Emirates (U.A.E.). Invoicing takes place in USD. All operating companies have a USD account with a local bank in the country where they operate. Local customers in these countries send payment instructions to their local bank, which instructs their correspondent bank in the US to move dollars to the correspondent bank of the beneficiary bank. The correspondent bank of the beneficiary bank receives the funds through the US clearing system, and sends a SWIFT message to the beneficiary bank stating that the funds have been received. The payer's local bank sends a SWIFT message to the local bank of the company in Japan asking to credit the funds to the receiver's account. While this method of collecting USD payments through the correspondent banking system is quite common, it has two disadvantages:

- Complicated routing makes payments error-prone and expensive – every transfer goes through correspondent banks and must cross borders twice each time
- USD balances are spread over the USD accounts maintained by the selling company in different countries with local banks, which makes it more difficult for the company to manage its USD liquidity

The Japan-based company now decides that all operating companies must maintain an account with one and the same bank in the US. The operating companies open an offshore account in their name with a bank in New York. The optimised cash flow structure is as follows:

FIGURE 7.4   OPTIMISED COLLECTION STRUCTURE

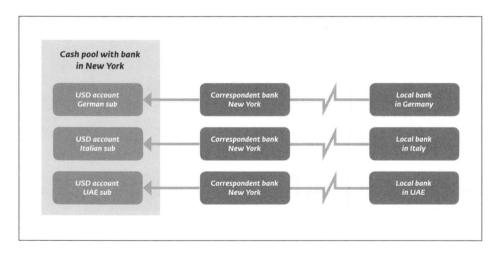

Once the transfer instructions are delivered by the customers and their local banks, the routing of the payments is now much shorter. The transfers can take place in just two steps. The first is from the customer's local bank to the correspondent bank in New York. The second, from the correspondent bank with a local transfer to the beneficiary bank in New York. The transfer only crosses the border once. This means the company in Japan no longer needs to involve correspondent banks and thus avoids the related costs. This solution is also beneficial to cash-balance management. All USD cash balances are concentrated in New York and the accounts are included in the same cash pool. The overall balance can be managed easily by the company from its headquarters in Tokyo.

The customers of the Japan-based company do not realise any cost savings as they still need to use their own correspondent banks and pay the costs of these services. These costs can only be reduced if they also open non-resident accounts in New York. Alternatively, the company may decide to invoice its deliveries in the local currency of the buyer and collect its receivables through local collection accounts.

Improving the cross-border account structure
From the above examples, it is clear that efficiencies can be achieved by routing transactions through bank accounts in the country where the respective currency is cleared. For instance, payments and collections in USD can most efficiently be managed via an account in the US connected to the local clearing.

The reason not all companies are doing this is that they consider access to a local bank in their home country important for service and local language considerations. Another factor is that the company may wish to concentrate all bank accounts in different currencies in one place, such as London or Amsterdam. However, when companies have very large volumes of transactions in a certain currency, it is beneficial to use accounts in the country of that currency (for example USD in the US) because the costs on a per-transaction basis are much lower. If the number of transactions are high, cost savings will outweigh the disadvantages of maintaining an additional account.

WHERE TO MAINTAIN ACCOUNTS IN FOREIGN CURRENCY

	Clearing country	Home country
Local access to clearing	✓	–
Low transaction costs	✓	–
Late cut-off times	✓	–
Local service	–	✓
Integrate with corporate liquidity	–	✓

7.4.2 CHANGING INTER-COMPANY CASH FLOWS

Inter-company payments are payments between the business units of one company. The volume and values involved can be substantial (particularly within large multinational companies). Typically, the business units deliver services and products to each other and that gives rise to mutual payables and receivables that must be settled by means of inter-company payments. Very often, these inter-company transfers are cross-border payments. When they are executed through the correspondent banking system, the company will be confronted with significant transaction costs. There are a number of ways to reduce these costs using:

- Internal accounts within the company
- Multi-currency accounts with one bank
- Virtual cash management
- Inter-company netting

The first three options are discussed below (inter-company netting is discussed in section 7.4).

Settlement through internal accounts

A company can set up an internal system of current accounts to effect inter-company payments. Many enterprise resource planning (ERP) systems have this capability. The internal transactions are settled through these internal accounts without any money actually being transferred via the bank. A disadvantage of this solution is the significant effort required to set up and maintain the system. However, the savings on transfer charges may outweigh the administrative workload and costs, particularly if the company has large volumes of cross-border payments.

Settling through a multi-currency centre

Alternatively, a company can channel all of its inter-company transactions through external bank accounts. Typically, these transaction accounts are held with one bank in one country. Many large international companies operate multi-currency accounts in cities such as London or Amsterdam. They have accounts set up in the name of their subsidiaries and these accounts are combined in a multi-currency cash pool (this solution is explained in chapter 14).

Because the transaction costs for the bank are quite low in this instance (as funds are only moved within one bank branch), companies can often negotiate very attractive rates and zero float transfers. Funds can be moved quite easily and cheaply between subsidiary accounts. When the operating companies have decentralised administrations and decentralised payments initiation, they will use an electronic banking system to initiate inter-company transactions and to monitor their balances in the multi-currency centre. For transactions between two accounts with different currencies – such as from a GBP account to a EUR account – special exchange rates may be negotiated with the bank.

Virtual cash management

This option is somewhat comparable to settlement through internal accounts. With virtual cash management it is possible for each entity to have their own virtual account on which they can monitor their balance, initiate and collect payments to and from other entities as well as third parties. If an intracompany payment is made by entity A to entity B, it will be debited from the virtual account of entity A and credited to the virtual account of entity B. There will be no real transfer of funds over a traditional current account and hence there will be no transaction fee, reducing the costs associated with such transfers.

Although the virtual cash management offering can vary widely between various service providers and banks, it is often the case that netting functionality is also supported with virtual cash management propositions (see chapter 13 for more details on virtual cash management).

FIGURE 7.5   INTER-COMPANY TRANSACTIONS THROUGH A MULTI-CURRENCY CENTRE

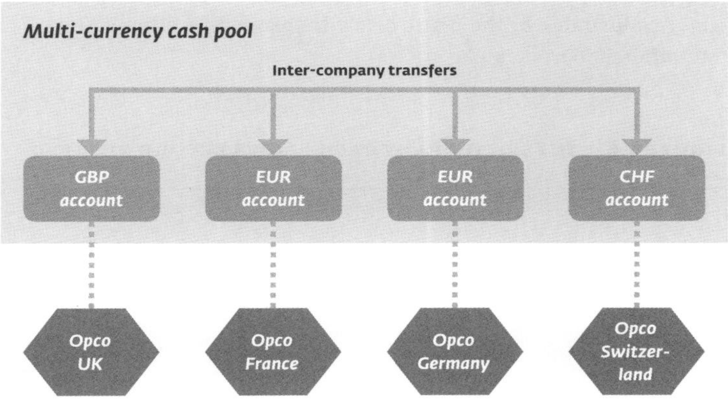

7.4
Inter-company netting

Netting is an important method to optimise a company's cash flow and working capital management. It focuses on the administrative off-setting of reciprocal cash flows. There are two forms of netting. Bilateral netting occurs between two parties where one of the two parties keeps the administrative records. Multilateral netting occurs between more than two parties and usually requires the company to set up a separate unit called a netting centre. This unit collects, orders and nets all inter-company obligations (insofar as possible). Sometimes, the netting function is outsourced to a bank or other service provider.

Apart from the settlement of inter-company commerce, various other internal transactions can also be effected through the netting system, including:

-   Intra-group loans
-   Interest payments
-   Dividends
-   Investments
-   Commission payments

In addition, external transactions can be streamlined through a netting system when large numbers of reciprocal transactions occur with external parties. In agreement with those parties, invoices can be logged into the netting system and settlement of the net amounts carried out on the same day as the internal settlements.

7.4.1   EXAMPLE OF NETTING

The following example shows the impact netting can have on the cash flows of a multinational company. The company has various business units delivering goods to each other with each company unit issuing an invoice in its own local currency. The first overview is of the inter-company payments that can be expected before the company changes to a netting system. As illustrated by the figure below, there are nine different inter-company cash flows in four different currencies.

FIGURE 7.6   INTER-COMPANY CASH FLOWS BEFORE NETTING

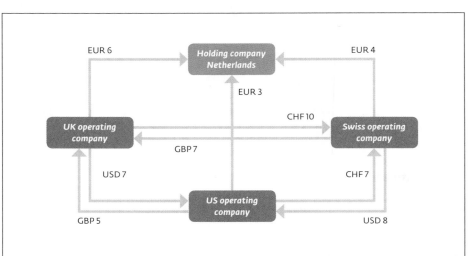

We will now see how a netting system can reduce the volume and the value of these payments. The netting centre processes all inter-company payments and compresses them into a single payment for each participant. Net payers make a single settlement payment to the netting centre in their own local currency, while net recipients are paid out in their own local currency by the netting centre.

The table below shows the cash flow values before netting (gross payments and receipts) and after netting (net payments and receipts) with all transactions converted into euros.

FIGURE 7.7   CASH FLOW VALUES BEFORE AND AFTER NETTING

	All amounts in EUR				Gross payment	Net payment
	NL receives	UK receives	US receives	SW receives		
NL pays	–	–	–	–	–	–
UK pays	6	–	5.2	8	19.2	5.8
US pays	3	5.6	–	5.6	14.2	3.1
SW pays	4	7.8	5.9	–	17.7	4.1
Gross receipt	13	13.4	11.1	13.6	51.1	
Net receipt	13	–	–	–		13

The above netting of inter-company payments leads to four settlement transactions in the respective foreign currencies (as can be seen in figure 7.8).

FIGURE 7.8   INTER-COMPANY CASH FLOWS AFTER MULTILATERAL NETTING

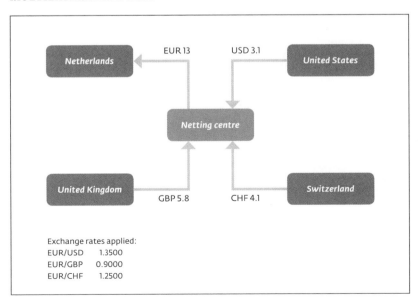

7.4.2 THE NETTING CYCLE

We will now describe how netting works in practice. The company is likely to organise a periodic netting cycle. This might be once a week or once a month. A netting cycle typically spans five to seven days. Below, we have listed the various actions that can be identified from the beginning of such a cycle – six days before the actual netting on day x – until the reconciliation just after the netting.

EXAMPLE OF A NETTING CYCLE

1. **Day x-6**
   The participants (i.e. operating companies) deliver the invoices to the netting centre.

2. **Day x-5**
   The netting centre sorts the invoice data according to participant, currency type and nature of the payment, and enters it into the netting system.

3. **Day x-4**
   Provisional pre-calculation of netting and reporting of this pre-calculation to the participants. Opportunity for participants to make adjustments.

4. **Day x-3**
   Second pre-calculation to determine the foreign currency to be bought / sold in the market on x-2.

5. **Day x-2**
   The netting centre carries out the foreign exchange transactions and makes a definitive netting calculation on the basis of the effective buying and selling rates of those transactions. It then sends a report to the participants.

6. **Day x-1**
   Net paying participants pay the amount they owe via the local bank. The netting centre pays the resulting net amounts to the receiving participants. All transfers take place on value date x.

7. **Day x**
   Actual netting. Banks execute the payment instructions on value date x.

8. **Day x+n**
   Reconciliation is checked and any execution problems are resolved.

7.4.3 THE COSTS AND BENEFITS OF NETTING

Setting up a netting system can yield significant benefits for the company. However, these must be weighed against the costs of operating such a system.

Benefits of netting
– Reduction in transaction costs
– Alleviation of administrative workload
– Reduction in foreign exchange costs, larger tickets, centrally traded
– Intangible benefits

Reduction in transaction costs

Netting will substantially reduce the number of payments that the participants must initiate to one transaction in each netting period. In our example, the number of transactions decreases from nine to only four transactions – a reduction of more than 50%. The total value of the transactions decreases from EUR 51.1 to EUR 26.0, representing a reduction of almost 50%. The lower value of the payment flows will reduce the loss of interest from bank float and value dating.

Alleviation of administrative workload

Netting will reduce the costs of managing inter-company payables and receivables. Instead of creating a payment for each individual invoice, subsidiaries can now view their outstanding payables and receivables in the netting system. When they have given their approval, only one physical transaction will have to be processed at the end of the netting period. This means less work to send payment reminders and reconcile incoming payments with outstanding receivables.

Back office activities related to foreign exchange transactions will also be eliminated at operating company level. In addition, all inter-company payments take place at fixed times, which provides more certainty as to when transactions occur. Though delays in inter-company payments have no impact on group liquidity, they can still lead to unbalanced positions at a subsidiary level.

Reduction in foreign exchange costs

In our example, we saw that the operating companies had to buy foreign currencies and that a total of nine transactions were executed. Netting centralises all foreign currency transactions at the netting centre and substantially reduces the number of transactions. In addition, opposite FX flows can be matched. For instance, when one entity wants to sell USD for EUR and another wants to buy USD for EUR, netting can prevent both entities from paying an FX conversion margin on each side.

The use of theses technique allows companies to reduce their foreign exchange costs, as only the net positions are traded externally. This will reduce operating costs at subsidiary level and concentrate foreign exchange activity in the centre. The centre itself will be more specialised and capable of negotiating competitive rates with the banks.

Leading and lagging

The netting centre can optimise inter-company liquidity by speeding up or slowing down payment transactions.

Leading: speeding up payment transactions to fund cash-poor beneficiary subsidiaries. The beneficiary's days sales outstanding are reduced through a decrease in the days payable outstanding of the paying entity.

Lagging: slowing down payment transactions to fund cash-poor initiating entities. The initiating entity's days payable outstanding are increased through an extension of the days sales outstanding of the beneficiary

Intangible benefits

Netting also creates some less obvious benefits. Although these are not always clearly visible, they are often just as important for the company as the tangible benefits. The most important additional benefits are:

- – Stronger payment discipline among participants / guaranteed payment dates
- – Improved liquidity forecasting
- – Better internal communication between subsidiaries
- – Centralisation of foreign currency liquidity
- – Better and more timely information
- – Reduced administration burden at group level
- – Standardisation of procedures

Operating costs of netting

The most significant costs involved in operating a netting system are management costs and system costs. There are different ways to manage a netting process. Companies can choose to operate the netting system in-house through the central treasury team or the central accounting department. This will require resources and create operational risk through exposure to specialised manpower. Alternatively, a company can outsource the netting operations to a bank or other service provider. The fees paid to the external service provider are usually lower than the costs of internal handling and the operational risks will be much smaller.

System costs can differ significantly according to the type of netting system used. Many companies still use spreadsheets to keep system costs very low (although operational risk remains very high). However, management costs will be substantially higher because no automated interfaces exist with the company's back-office systems. Alternatively, companies may use enterprise resource planning systems to operate netting. While this can resolve the interfacing issue, relatively high management costs can remain. Banks and third-party service providers are increasingly offering web-based netting systems. These are easily accessible for all subsidiaries and relatively low in cost to operate. They can also be linked to general ledger systems, which can help to decrease internal management costs.

Weighing up the advantages and disadvantages
It is useful to carry out a feasibility study to establish whether the potential benefits outweigh the operating costs. The outcome of such a study is likely to vary according to the following factors:

- Number of foreign operating companies with cross-border payments
- Number of inter-company payments
- Countries where the participants are located
- Current invoicing method
- Number of currencies used
- Extent to which the company has already streamlined its inter-company payments

7.5
Benefits of optimising a company's cash flow structure

In many multinational companies, payments and collections are carried out by the local operating companies. They send their payment instructions to their local banks for execution. However, an increasing number of companies have integrated payment processing into a centralised service unit known as a shared service centre (SSC), a payment factory or a collection factory.

An SSC is a specialised unit which carries out certain business support activities for a corporation and enables operating companies to focus entirely on their core business activities. Examples of such non-core business activities include finance and accounting, accounts payable administration, accounts receivable administration, processing of payments and collections, treasury operations, centralised purchasing, human resources administration and support, IT functions and real estate management. By centralising these activities into one dedicated service unit, companies seek to reduce operating costs and increase quality.

While SSCs usually handle many different functions, a payment and collection factory focuses exclusively on the execution of transactions. This is one way in which large companies try to improve the management of their cash flows. When we discuss payment and collection factories, please bear in mind that the same functions can be fulfilled by an SSC.

7.5.1   THE PAYMENT FACTORY

A payment factory is a central unit which executes payments on behalf of several or all operating companies within an organisation. When payments need to be executed, the local operating companies send relevant payment data via an internal network to the payment factory. The payment instructions are collected in a central system that prepares a batch of payment instructions and sends this batch to the bank.

As all of the corporation's payment instructions are sent via a single channel to the bank, the company only needs one electronic interface with the bank. This is called a 'single pipeline'. The operating companies are often based in different countries and increasingly connected to the central system via a company-wide enterprise resource planning (ERP) system. In addition to creating the single batch of payments, the payment factory may provide other services, such as settling inter-company payments on internal accounts, buying foreign currencies or handling central bank reporting of international transfers.

As we can see in figure 7.9, the bank receiving the payment instructions will send these to its local branches in the country of the beneficiary for execution in the local clearing system.

FIGURE 7.9   ROUTING OF PAYABLES THROUGH THE PAYMENT FACTORY

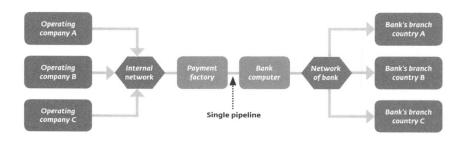

	Benefits of a payment factory

- Reduced workload for the operating companies
- Reduction of transaction costs
- Single interface to the bank
- Concentration of foreign exchange transactions

Reduced workload
The operating companies do not have to make a distinction between inter-company and external payments. They can send both types of payments to the payment factory. In addition, the payment factory will handle the purchase of foreign currencies needed for international transfers so that the operating companies will only pay in their own local currency. The payment factory also alleviates the administrative workload of the subsidiaries by preparing the international transaction reports for the central bank in countries where the reports are still required.

Reduction of transaction costs

The payment factory is able to route the payments through the most appropriate channel. For instance, cross-border payments will be executed through in-country clearing systems to reduce transaction fees. Urgent payments will be processed via a gross settlement clearing system to ensure immediate execution while non-urgent payments are channelled through the lowest cost clearing system. Given the large volume of transactions, the payment factory will be in a position to organise the optimal routing of the payments and negotiate competitive transaction fees with the bank.

Single interface to the bank

The operating companies no longer need to maintain electronic interfaces with local banks. This can lead to significant savings because the operating companies do not have to adapt their systems to changes in electronic banking systems to ensure straight-through processing, and they avoid electronic banking and service fees. The payment factory is the intermediary between the entire company and the bank. This will help to make sure the external and internal systems are compatible.

Concentration of foreign exchange transactions

As we mentioned previously, the payment factory may be tasked with the handling of all foreign exchange transactions. That will simplify operations for the operating companies and enable the whole group to achieve more control of foreign exchange exposures, while minimising the external costs of the currency conversions.

7.5.2 THE COLLECTION FACTORY

The processing of incoming payments can be centralised in a collection factory. This entity is similar to a payment factory and will usually select one international network bank to streamline its collections. Local collection accounts will be used with the network bank in the countries where the customers are located. The network bank collects all information on the incoming receipts and sends a single file containing all transaction information to the collection factory. In turn, the collection factory splits this file into various sub-files for the operating companies and sends the relevant information on incoming payments to each one. The operating companies will use this information for reconciliation in their accounts receivable administration. If the company is operating an SSC, that centre will handle the collections as well as the centralised accounts receivable administration (including the reconciliation of incoming payments).

The major advantage for the operating companies is that all information on incoming payments is delivered to them in a single standard format. And the company as a whole will benefit because it will achieve greater control of the receivables, which will enable the company to reduce operating costs and optimise its liquidity position.

7.6
Evaluation of cash flow management

Many companies find it useful to evaluate cash flow management at regular intervals. This may occur approximately once every two or three years. The starting point of this evaluation is the company's actual cash flow structure – an overview of all major cash flows by operating company, by country and by currency. The individual cash flows need to be reviewed. In addition, transaction instruments must be assessed, as do operating costs and straight-through processing possibilities. Are the most efficient transaction instruments being used? Are there ways to reduce the transaction costs? As the payments market is continuously changing, it is recommended that advice be sought from the banks or specialised consulting firms when carrying out this exercise.

Review of cash flow management performance
1   Map out current cash flow structure
–   By cash flow type
–   By country
–   By currency
2   Investigate operational issues
–   Bank charges
–   Bank float and value dating
–   Use of transaction instruments
–   Internal handling costs
–   Timing of transactions
3   Review cash flow structure
–   Routing of cross-border transactions
–   Routing of inter-company transactions
4   Consider internal organisation opportunities
–   Payment factory
–   Collection factory
–   Shared service centre

Chapter 8

Transaction Types

8   Transaction Types

8.1
Introduction

Companies have a variety of instruments available for both incoming and outgoing payments. These instruments and their specific advantages and disadvantages are described in this chapter. Banks and other payment service providers (PSPs) continue to offer multiple channels through which companies can submit and process such instructions. Banks have developed a wide range of instruments for the purpose of transferring funds. Most of these instruments are national, regional or global industry standards – a payment from one bank is a collection from another. Some banks have developed specific features on top of these standards. As will be shown, each instrument has specific advantages and disadvantages for both the payer and beneficiary.

There are a number of different ways to send funds and there are an equal number of ways to receive them. Some are automated while others require manual intervention by the company or their banks. When two parties enter into a business transaction, it is often the case that one party – the buyer – purchases goods or services from the second party – the supplier. This process can simply consist of the following three activities:

1. The buyer places an order with the seller or supplier
2. The supplier delivers the goods or services and invoices the buyer for payment
3. The buyer settles the account by paying the supplier for the goods or services

The third activity can be further broken down into the following:

1. The buyer (payer) instructs its bank to make a payment to the bank account of the seller (beneficiary)
2. The payer's bank transfers the funds (in some cases to an agent or intermediary bank to forward on)
3. The funds are received by the beneficiary's bank and made available to the account of the beneficiary

Typically, a distinction can be made between payment products and collection products. This will be covered in more detail in this chapter.

Payment products

Paying in cash for goods or services has been common for thousands of years. Even today, cash remains important, for example for purchasing low-value goods and services. However, in many countries paying in cash is in clear decline due to the wide availability, ease and efficiency of electronic means of payment such as mobile payments and (contactless) debit and credit cards as well as due to the increase of e- and m-commerce, i.e. purchases made via webshops and mobile phones.

For companies that trade with each other, the high value of the transaction, the geographic location of the parties and the desire to maximise cash flow means that cash is rarely used. Instead, such businesses use the payment instruments available from their bank. The buyer's bank can offer a choice of how the instruction can be given as well as the option of a number of different payment products or services. Regardless of the chosen method, the process will be as defined as above.

The instruments the buyer can choose from include:

- Credit transfers
- Documentary credits
- Cheque/draft payments
- Card payments

Collection products

The supplier may want to have control over the receipt of the payment under a direct debit authority by claiming them from the bank account of a (wholesale or retail) buyer. For instance, within the Single Euro Payments Area (SEPA), SEPA Direct Debit (SDD) claims can be initiated in euros across national boundaries.

For collections, the supplier can choose from the following instruments, among others:

- Incoming credit transfers
- Documentary collections
- Cheque collections and negotiations
- Card collections
- Direct debits
- Online banking-enabled payments
- Cash receipts

8.2
The credit transfer

Making a payment and collecting receivables from companies require funds to be transferred from one current account to another. These accounts can be denominated in different currencies and held in different countries but in order to initiate an outgoing payment, a company must raise a payment instruction.

8.2.1 THE CREDIT TRANSFER PROCESS

Credit transfers involve funds moving from one account to another without meeting any specific conditions agreed between the trading partners. These unconditional transfers are sometimes referred to as clean payments as opposed to documentary payments, where documents need to be presented and validated before the transaction can be executed. A credit transfer is regarded as an outgoing transfer because the paying party takes the initiative and funds are 'leaving' the account/bank of the originator (payer).

Credit transfers can be used for both low-value payments and high-value payments. Payments processing and cut-off times, allowed currency and reach can differ per type.

High-value payments often need to be executed and settled urgently. They are used for all kinds of time-critical transactions, such as treasury payments (i.e., money market and foreign exchange transactions), real estate transactions and tax payments. High-value payments are also commonly used in the transport sector to secure the rapid release of goods at seaports.

Low-value payments are relatively small amounts used, for instance, for normal vendor payments as well as for payroll payments. These payments, where time is not very critical, are also referred to as retail or bulk payments.

An increasing number of countries have recently started offering (or planning) a new and faster type of credit transfer that allows (near) real-time payments (and access to the transferred funds), 24 hours per day, seven days per week.

In the case of a credit transfer, the payer delivers a payment instruction to the bank specifying details such as: amount and currency, beneficiary details such as account number or IBAN (International Bank Account Number), name and address, execution date, beneficiary bank details, charges, routing instructions, etc. The required information and options can depend on the specific credit transfer instrument used.

Most banks distinguish between domestic, SEPA and cross-border or international transfers. Domestic transfers are typically characterised by a transfer between banks in local currency within a country. The SEPA Credit Transfer (SCT) is special in the sense that it can be considered a domestic (euro) payment within the multi-country SEPA zone (for further details, please also refer to the section on SEPA below). International payments are typically between accounts held in different countries and/or in a different currency than the payer's or the beneficiary's local currency. Cross-border payments tend to be more complex, with requirements for currency conversion and additional intermediary parties.

SEPA

Through the Single Euro Payments Area (SEPA), a new and regional (i.e. European) set of payments instruments were introduced. The objective was to contribute to the EU single market by removing the difference between cross-border and domestic payments in euros. Initially, three SEPA schemes were created: one for the SEPA Credit Transfer (SCT) and two for Direct Debit (SDD) (including C2B and B2B). As a result, national euro credit transfers and direct debit schemes have been replaced by the SEPA instruments. SEPA now consists of the 28 European Union (EU) members and Guernsey, Iceland, Isle of Man, Jersey, Liechtenstein, Monaco, Norway, San Marino, Saint-Pierre-et-Miquelon and Switzerland.

A new scheme for SEPA instant payment credit transfers was launched in November 2017. This scheme is optional for banks and will allow payments execution and funds availability to the beneficiary in seconds, 24 hours per day, seven days per week. Some banks and banking communities will be offering SEPA instant payments from the start, others in the course of the next year or two, and some are still considering the best course of action.Expectation is that instant payments will become the new normal for single credit transfers in the SEPA area and will replace the current SEPA Credit Transfer in the near future.

SEPA is underpinned by the Payment Services Directive (PSD). The PSD is an EU directive that establishes common rules for payments within the European Economic Area.

Global payments initiative
To further improve international payments processing, SWIFT has recently launched in collaboration with a growing number of banks, the global payments initiative (GPI) to make international credit transfers an improved payment experience, with same day use of funds, transparency of fees, end-to-end tracking, and transfer of rich payment information.

8.2.2 COSTS OF OUTGOING CREDIT TRANSFERS

Typically, banks will charge a fee when making a payment. The charge(s) may be in the form of an overt, published transaction charge for the payment, a value date that is different from the booking date (however, this is not allowed by the PSD), an agent or intermediary charge for routing an international transfer, or as a margin factored into any currency exchange rate used when sending the payment. These charges are not mutually exclusive and companies can often expect to incur all four. The value of the charge can be affected by a number of factors, which are clearly visible to the user:

- *Competitive differences between payment providers*
  These may involve discounted charges to specific market segments or volume-based discounts
- *Country or regional 'norms'*
  This may mean a global bank has to adjust its charges to remain competitive in certain countries or regions
- *Method used to provide the bank with the payment instruction*
  Most banks offer a technology-based solution that automates the receipt of the instruction and incurs a reduced charge compared with payment instructions delivered by letter or fax
- *Speed of transfer*
  Most banks implement a strategy where the quicker methods of transfer attract higher charges (so less urgent transfers incur lower charges)

Once such factors have been considered, the payer will generally then be responsible for covering the payment charges. However, there are other options and it is therefore important that prior to completing the transaction, the companies involved confirm who has responsibility for paying the payment charges. Some products mandate a certain charging principle – for example, for the SEPA Credit Transfer (SCT), only the SHA option is possible – and under certain regulations, such as the PSD, value dating is not allowed for certain transactions.

Three charging options a bank can apply

OUR
The payment charge is paid by the payer that initiates the transfer.

BEN (beneficiary)
Where the payer's bank charges are paid by the beneficiary, whereby the charge is deducted from the value of the funds sent.

SHA (shared)
The charges of the payer's bank are paid by the payer. All other costs are paid by the beneficiary.

8.2.3 ADVANTAGES AND DISADVANTAGES OF OUTGOING CREDIT TRANSFERS

The advantage for payers is that they can control when the funds leave their account, as well as which charging structure is applied to the payment and the speed of the transfer.

Both the payer and receiver benefit from the knowledge that banks have invested in the technology to quickly, efficiently and securely transfer funds around the globe. The systems used are robust and offer the banks a high level of automation (which ensures costs are relatively cheap).

Based on the requirement for speed of delivery and the consideration of the associated costs, the bank will make a decision about how to route the payment. Increasingly, treasury departments are adopting cash-management techniques and are making such selections themselves to maximise their returns and reduce costs.

Historically, the most common means of making a transfer has been a cross-border (wire) transfer. This generally involves the sending bank passing the funds on to one of its pre-approved partner banks or intermediaries in the end-beneficiary bank's country or region. The partner/intermediary bank will assess an additional charge before sending the funds to the intended beneficiary's bank for the benefit of the payee.

For non-urgent low-value payments, banks will use an (in-country) automated clearing house (ACH) to deliver the funds to the beneficiary's bank account. Although the process takes longer, the charges are lower. As both banks and clients seek to reduce the charges they pay, in some cases banks are using their global branch and back-office network to 'send' funds internally and then disburse them in-country.

The main disadvantage of this type of payment is the potential risk that both parties face. The beneficiary has no insight into when the funds were sent or when they will be received, so the risk is that goods or services may have been provided before the payment arrives. Conversely, the beneficiary may ask for funds to be received prior to the release of goods or services. In that case, the risk is with the payer – effectively, they have paid for goods and services on the promise that they will be delivered. In that case the bank of the payer could also provide a 'proof of payment', declaring that the payment of the originator was successfully processed and sent to the bank of the beneficiary.

8.3
Documentary credits

One risk faced by exporters is that the payer – or the payer's bank – is unable to meet its obligations. This is called 'credit risk'. Such risk exists with domestic payments but is increased in the case of cross-border transactions as a result of a lack of detailed knowledge or insight into the creditworthiness of the other parties involved in the transaction. This effect can be compounded when trading with companies in less developed economies while trying to understand the local legal framework in those regions.

Exporters are keen to mitigate such risks. One way they can do so is by getting the importer to issue a documentary credit. A documentary credit is applied for by the importer, i.e. the payer. It is therefore an outgoing payment product. In the case of a documentary credit, the bank enters into an obligation to pay the exporter (or 'beneficiary') during a certain period of time (the period of validity) when certain documents have been submitted.

8.3.1   THE DOCUMENTS WITH A DOCUMENTARY CREDIT

In order to be eligible for the payment, the exporter must meet certain credit conditions and will be required to present a number of documents to the bank. The documents that the importer wants to receive before the bank is permitted to make the payment are specified in a letter of credit (LC). The LC is drawn up by the importer's bank in cooperation with the importer. The importer stipulates which documents must be handed over before the bank pays the exporter. This process involves the following documents:

1. Proof of ownership
2. Transport document proving that the goods have been dispatched
3. Certificate of insurance
4. Quality certificate

The payment of the documentary credit is contingent on the exporter supplying the required documents. However, the delivery of the correct documents does not in itself prove that the actual goods will be delivered. The documents simply provide an assurance that the goods have been dispatched, are insured and were in a good condition at the time of inspection.

They do not guarantee the accepted quality of the goods upon arrival at the importer's premises, nor even whether they will arrive at all. In addition, the documents could be perfect but the goods worthless. Disputes over the quality of the goods must be settled on the basis of the contract of sale between buyer and seller and not on the basis of the documentary credit.

8.3.2   THE PARTIES INVOLVED IN A DOCUMENTARY CREDIT

Parties involved in a documentary credit
1.   The payer / issuer (i.e. the importer)
2.   The payer's bank or issuing bank
3.   The beneficiary (i.e. the exporter)
4.   The beneficiary's bank or nominated bank

The payer's bank
This is the importer's bank and is also referred to as the 'issuing bank'. The issuing bank makes the credit available and draws up the letter of credit together with the importer.

The beneficiary's bank
The issuing bank sends the letter of credit to the beneficiary's bank – also called the 'nominated bank'. The nominated bank passes the letter of credit on to the exporter and pays the outstanding amount if the exporter presents the specified documents.

If the nominated bank does not undertake to pay the outstanding amount, it is referred to as the 'advising bank'. In that case, the nominated bank sends the documents to the issuing bank and waits for it to pay. Once the advising bank has received payment, it will pay the amount in question to the exporter. In this case, the documentary credit is called 'advised'.

Sometimes, the exporter will negotiate additional assurances because he does not know the issuing bank. In that case, the exporter can ask the nominated bank to 'confirm' the documentary credit. This means that the nominated bank enters into an obligation to pay immediately upon receipt of the specified documents. It is then referred to as the 'confirming bank'. The documentary credit is described as 'confirmed'.

8.3.3   THE ROUTING OF A DOCUMENTARY CREDIT

In this section we will describe the end-to-end process that a documentary credit follows from application to final payment. In the example below, we assume that a consignment of agricultural products is to be delivered from Germany to Nigeria under a confirmed documentary credit.

The Berlin-based company Agri4 GmbH (the exporter) concludes a contract in January 2017 with Wholesale Ltd. based in Lagos, Nigeria (the importer) for the delivery of agricultural tools valued at EUR 50,000.

The delivery will be in Lagos and the shipment will be carried out by African Lines with the latest date of shipment being 30 May 2019. Payment under an LC is to be issued by bank A in Lagos (the bank of Wholesale Ltd) and confirmed by Bank B in Berlin (the bank of Garden GmbH). Both parties pay the costs charged by their own banks. In figure 8.1, we show the different steps in the routing process of this documentary credit.

FIGURE 8.1   ROUTING OF A DOCUMENTARY CREDIT

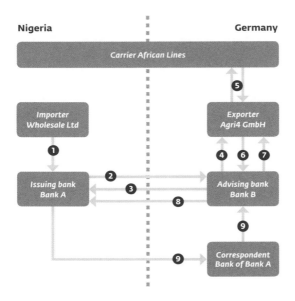

1. Wholesale Ltd requests its Nigerian Bank A to issue a documentary credit to be confirmed by German Bank B
2. Nigerian bank A assesses the application from Wholesale Ltd, issues the letter of credit and requests German Bank B to confirm this letter of credit
3. German Bank B responds positively to the request for confirmation
4. After adding its confirmation, German Bank B sends an advice note, together with the letter of credit to Agri4 GmbH
5. Agri4 GmbH ships the goods via African Lines, from which it received the bill of loading, and creates/receives other required documents
6. Agri4 GmbH presents the documents to German Bank B
7. German Bank B examines them and, upon approval, pays Agri4 GmbH Euro 50,000, less costs
8. German Bank B sends the documents to Nigerian bank A, which also examines them
9. Upon approval, Nigerian Bank A transfers the funds to German Bank B via its correspondent bank in Germany

When the issuing bank receives the correct documents, it will charge the importer's account. Their next step is to transfer the money to the exporter's bank. The payment made under the documentary credit is a straightforward cross-border transfer.

If the credit has not been confirmed, the advising bank will credit the beneficiary's account on receipt of payment, applying the usual value dating rules. With a confirmed credit, the confirming bank credits the beneficiary's account when the beneficiary presents the required documents. In determining the value date of this credit entry, the confirming bank will take into account that it, too, will only receive the amount after a certain delay. After all, this bank must first send the documents to the issuing bank, which will then examine the documents. It is only after examining and approving the documents that the issuing bank will transfer the credit amount to the confirming bank.

8.3.4   ADVANTAGES AND DISADVANTAGES OF A DOCUMENTARY CREDIT

For the importer, the most important advantage of a documentary credit is that it receives:

1. The proof of title to the goods
2. The documents proving that the goods have been dispatched, insured (optional) and inspected

However, the proof of title and the document do not provide a guarantee that the goods will actually arrive in good condition. The documentary credit gives the exporter a high level of payment security. This is particularly true with a confirmed credit. In this case, the exporter's own bank guarantees the payment. If the credit has not been confirmed, the exporter still has a claim on the importer's bank. Of course, a claim on the bank provides better payment security than a claim on the importer company.

One disadvantage of the documentary credit is cost. The processing of a documentary credit is largely a manual process with the need to read and review the associated documents. The banks involved will seek to pass these costs on to their customers.

1. The issuing bank must issue the documentary credit and draft the letter of credit
2. The issuing bank must inform the advising bank
3. The advising bank must take receipt of the documents and forward them to the issuing bank
4. The issuing bank must examine the documents

8.4
Outgoing cheque payments

The issuing of cheques for domestic and cross-border fund transfers is in decline. Nevertheless, in some countries (like the US, France, India, etc.), the convenience and habit of having immediate access to a (paper-based) payment instrument is a convenience that is still preferred by some payers over the security and automation of a credit transfer.

8.4.1   THE PARTIES INVOLVED IN CHEQUE PAYMENTS

The following parties are involved in the process of issuing and collecting a payment by cheque:

1. The payer
2. The payer's bank
3. The beneficiary
4. The beneficiary's bank

The payer
The payer writes the cheque or arranges for a bank cheque to be issued on its behalf. The payer, who is also referred to as the drawee, is the party that needs to pay for the services or goods. Other names used for the payer are the 'issuer', 'remitter' or 'drawer'.

The payer's bank
This is the bank upon which the cheque is drawn. In the case of a bank cheque, it is the party who has already taken the client funds on to its books before issuing the bank cheque/draft. The payer's bank is also referred to as the 'issuing bank' or 'drawee bank'.

The beneficiary
The beneficiary or 'payee' is the supplier of the services or goods delivered and will be named on the cheque.

The beneficiary's bank
In most cases, the beneficiary's bank receives the cheque from the beneficiary and sends it to the payer's bank for collection or negotiation. At a later point in time, the beneficiary's bank will receive the value from the payer's bank and will, in turn, apply the funds to the account of the beneficiary.

Two types of cheques are used in the world of international commerce and payments – company cheques and bank cheques (drafts).

8.4.2 COMPANY CHEQUES

A company or personal cheque is an 'ordinary' cheque issued on a current account. This can be an account in the currency of the account holder's domestic currency or an account designated in another currency. It is a cheque that a payer/issuer draws on their bank (i.e. the issuer's bank) and subsequently delivers or sends to the beneficiary and supplier of the goods.

A company or personal cheque does not provide the beneficiary with a guarantee that it will be cleared and the funds credited to their account. This is because it is only once the cheque has gone through due process and is presented to the drawee bank that its fate is determined.

In figure 8.2, we can see how a company cheque is routed through the banking industry.

FIGURE 8.2   CHEQUE PROCESSING

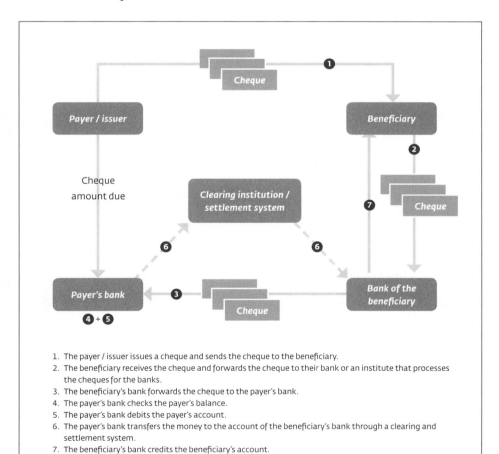

1. The payer / issuer issues a cheque and sends the cheque to the beneficiary.
2. The beneficiary receives the cheque and forwards the cheque to their bank or an institute that processes the cheques for the banks.
3. The beneficiary's bank forwards the cheque to the payer's bank.
4. The payer's bank checks the payer's balance.
5. The payer's bank debits the payer's account.
6. The payer's bank transfers the money to the account of the beneficiary's bank through a clearing and settlement system.
7. The beneficiary's bank credits the beneficiary's account.

8.4.3 BANK CHEQUES (DRAFTS)

A bank cheque is drawn directly on the books of the issuing bank. When the company requests a bank cheque, the funds are taken from their own account and placed on the books of the bank. The bank provides the company with a cheque drawn on its own account. The company can then send this to the supplier. This could be on the bank's own account in-country or – in the case of a currency draft – on an account in the bank's name held in a different country and potentially in a different currency.

The key difference between a bank cheque and a company cheque is that the former is drawn on a bank and hence provides a stronger guarantee than the latter. Payments by cheque normally depend on the commercial relationship between the payer and the beneficiary. It is the beneficiary that decides if payment by a company or bank cheque is acceptable.

8.4.4 ADVANTAGES AND DISADVANTAGES OF CHEQUE PAYMENT

For the payer, the benefit of a company cheque is the time it takes for the funds to be taken from their account. This allows the float of funds to generate a financial return.

A disadvantage for the beneficiary is the time it can take for the cheque to be cleared and for the beneficiary to receive the value.

Therefore, most banks will offer the beneficiary two choices:

1. Credit under usual reserve (uur)
2. Payment after final collection

Credit under usual reserve (uur)
This is a cheque collection where the beneficiary's bank pays the funds in advance (with a future value date). The beneficiary bank maintains the right to reverse the credit if, for a specific reason, the funds are not received from the issuer (bank). This service is offered if the beneficiary has an approval for the so-called uur from the beneficiary bank and that bank has a cash letter service with another bank.

Payment after final collection
This option is a cheque for collection where the beneficiary's bank presents the cheque to the issuer (bank) and waits for final payment. This service is offered if final payment needs to be assured or when there is no cash letter service between banks in place.

A bank cheque provides some reassurance to the supplier as they know the bank itself is holding the funds. For a known client, this may be enough to release goods before the funds clear. However, the potential for stolen and altered bank cheques means that payment can never be fully guaranteed before it has gone through due process and is in the hands of the drawee bank.

As much of these processes are manual, the associated bank charges are often higher than the automated receipt of a payment.

8.5
Card payments

The proposition for paying with a card is one of convenience and security. Convenience is a key factor since most retailers accept card payments. Card payments can be used at the physical point of sale (POS) or remotely: mail order, telephone order and internet payments (e- and m-commerce). Furthermore, cards can be used to withdraw money at an ATM.

At the POS, card payments can be initiated in different ways, including:

1. *Electronically*
    –   By inserting or swiping the card in a POS terminal, often followed by entering a PIN code.
    –   Contactless, by holding the card against the contactless reader of the POS terminal; contactless payments can be made with or without a PIN, depending on the amount of the payment (e.g. > 25 euro) or the cumulative amount of the payment (if this amount reaches a certain value, a PIN is required to complete the transaction).
    –   Using a smartphone with card data electronically stored in the phone, whereby the contactless reader of the POS is used to execute the payment.

2. *Manually*
    –   This is done by taking an imprint of a customer's card, or by taking down the customer's card information, obtaining the customer's signature and processing the credit card later by phone or internet; this method is used relatively rarely and often only as backup as it is less efficient and safe.

Card payments can be initiated remotely in several ways, including:

–   Via phone by providing the card details to a merchant or call centre assistant
–   Via a website by entering card details in a webform
–   Through an electronic wallet that has card details pre-stored (e.g. by an online merchant)

Most emerging types of remote payments involve e-commerce and m-commerce. These are card-based payments initiated on a website using a PC, tablet or mobile phone. Cards are still the most popular instruments for initiating such payments. 'Wallets', where card details are stored on a mobile phone, can be used to make payments in a secure and convenient way.

The various aspects relevant to card transactions will be covered in more detail below.

8.5.1 ACTORS IN A CARD TRANSACTION

In most circumstances, card transactions operate under a so-called four-party model. In this model, apart from the card scheme, four parties can be identified:

1. *Cardholder* – the payer
2. *Merchant* – the beneficiary of the payment
3. *Issuing bank (or Issuer)* – the bank that issues the card to the cardholder
4. *Acquiring bank (or Acquirer)* – the bank of the merchant

The parties involved in a card transaction are depicted in figure 8.3.

FIGURE 8.3   OVERVIEW OF THE DIFFERENT ROLES AND MESSAGE FLOWS RELATED TO A CARD PAYMENT

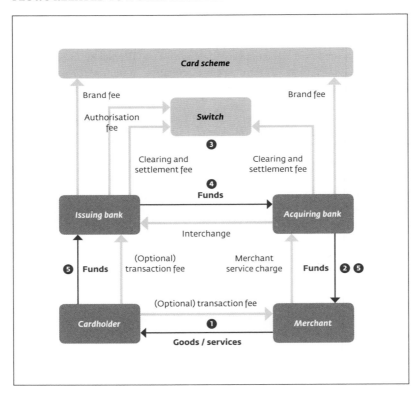

The four-party card scheme consists of a technical and commercial arrangement set up to serve one or more brands of cards. It provides the organisational, legal and operational framework necessary for the functioning of the services marketed by those brands. The issuer and acquirer must have a contractual relationship with a card scheme before they can issue cards or sign up merchants for acquiring services. The actual routing or processing of card transactions is performed by a processor which, in the cards world, is referred to as a switch.

A card transaction in the four-party scheme is performed as follows:

1. The cardholder (i.e. payer) pays the beneficiary using a payment card
2. The beneficiary (e.g. the merchant) performs an authorisation request and, if the transaction is authorised, the goods or services are delivered. The authorised transaction is sent to the acquirer for clearing and settlement
3. The acquirer sends the clearing and settlement request via the switch to the issuer. The switch calculates the net settlement positions of all issuers and acquirers and advises these banks accordingly
4. Net settlement is performed between the banks and the card scheme
5. Banks ensure that cardholders are debited and merchants are credited

Figure 8.3 also provides an overview of the various charges that can be applied during a card transaction. Apart from the four-party card scheme, a three-party card scheme also exists where the card scheme itself acts both as issuer and acquirer.

8.5.2   CARD PRODUCTS – PAYMENT TYPES

Card products differ according to which point in time the actual payment has to be made by the cardholders. This can be before the transaction, at the time of the transaction or after the transaction. A brief summary is given in figure 8.4, followed by more details.

FIGURE 8.4   PAYMENT CARDS – DIFFERENT PRODUCT TYPES

		Now	
Moment of transaction	→ → → → → → → → → → → → → → → → →		
Moment of payment	Pay before	Pay now	Pay later
Card product	Prepaid cart	Debit card	Credit card/charge card
Specifics	No bank account	Connected to bank	Decoupled from bank
	Salary cards	account	account
	Social benefit cards	Access to funds	Higher spending
	Students	Everyday spending	Instalments

Prepaid cards
Prepaid cards are often marketed to offer a solution in a specific sector. As the cardholder and end user, individuals can add funds to the card which they can spend in retail outlets, internet stores or even to withdraw cash from service tills. They provide the reassurance that

users can only spend the funds loaded on the card. Some firms market this as a secure way to take your holiday cash abroad, although ATM and overseas point-of-sale (POS) charges can apply.

Other issuers target the worker's remittance sector where funds are sent home periodically. In that case, the actual cardholder is likely to be in a different country to the person adding funds to the card. When the card is topped up, the cardholder can spend the loaded funds. In other markets, prepaid cards serve the unbanked – people can be supplied with a prepaid card to make salary payments, for example, without the need for the cardholder to have a bank account. In the past, it was possible to obtain anonymous prepaid cards, but tighter regulation nowadays typically requires customer due diligence before prepaid cards can be issued and used to the fullest extent. Prepaid cards can be used for anonymous and fraudulent payments (for instance by terrorists), which is why the issuance of such cards is limited in more and more countries.

Debit cards
A debit card is a bank card that gives cardholders electronic access to their current account. It is a multi-function card that allows the cardholder to use it to withdraw cash from ATMs, to make point-of-sale (POS) purchases (by using the card in a POS terminal or contactless in stores, on public transportation, in vending machines, etc.) or to make payments over the phone or via internet stores where these cards support such transactions. While some domestic schemes still exist, cards are more likely to bear the badge of a global scheme such as MasterCard or Visa. The funds will be debited from the cardholder's current account.

Credit cards
A credit card is a payment card that has a credit facility connected to it. Usually, the issuer will charge interest for the portion of the credit facility used.

Charge cards
Charge cards are cards where full payment is due at the end of the billing cycle.

8.5.3   CARD PRODUCTS – CLIENT SEGMENTATION

Card products can be targeted at specific clients such as consumers or corporate entities. And within these client segments, sub-segmentation can occur as well. Some examples are included in this section.

Consumer cards
Cards targeting the consumer segment are usually of the types mentioned in the previous section. However, in order to attract or target specific customers, these products can be tailored to specific needs. For example, issuers can offer different card products such as classic, gold or platinum, each aiming at a different consumer segment in terms of expected spending or affluence. Other possibilities are co-branding the card with a specific co-brand partner, such as an airline or a sports club, to appeal to customers who have a specific affinity with that particular co-brand.

Commercial cards

Commercial cards are payment cards that are issued to corporate clients and their employees. Corporate cards provide a payment solution that offers high visibility and control of expenditure, and helps customers improve their cash flow and streamline their expense and purchasing processes. Among other options, a corporate card can:

– Allow customers to remain firmly in control of costs while enabling their employees to perform day-to-day business expense and purchasing transactions face-to-face, by phone or online.

– Provide a simple solution to help business cash flow. Suppliers get paid within a few days and customers can gain up to an additional 38/45 days breathing room on top of their standard supplier payment terms.

– Give customers access to comprehensive management information, enabling them to track and analyse their travel, expenses and purchasing spend at merchant, cardholder, department and company level. Plus, it provides the ability to capture additional transaction data and customise transaction data with additional business information, such as cost centres or general ledger codes, and to load that data directly into business accounting systems.

8.5.4   IDENTIFICATION AND AUTHENTICATION

Security is of key importance. Measures to improve security vary per situation, are continuously updated and can consist of PIN codes, using embedded chips (EMV), additional codes and passwords for remote use as well as tokenization.

8.5.5   ADVANTAGES AND DISADVANTAGES OF CARD PAYMENTS

Card payments are an easily accessible payment method that serves as a secure alternative to cash payments. Holding a card is much safer than holding money in cash given that, if the card is lost or stolen, it can be cancelled by the issuer. With Chip & PIN, the chances that the card will be fraudulently used are reduced. Debit cards take the funds almost immediately from the holder's current account which helps budgeting, while a credit card offers an easy way of delaying payment for goods. The cards are widely accepted globally for use in ATMs, at retailers and virtual shops on the internet, and are capable of allowing transactions in multiple currencies. For corporate clients, benefits include increased business liquidity, access to management information and spending control features.

8.6
Incoming credit transfers / collections

The majority of collections relate to the receipt of a credit transfer. After a credit transfer has been received by the beneficiary bank, the bank will advise the beneficiary. This can be an electronic advice or a paper acknowledgement that is posted to the beneficiary. The advice will show all the details of the payment such as who sent it, which bank transferred the funds, gross and net values and the invoice number or goods description. That information will enable the beneficiary's accounts receivable department to process the collection in their records and reconcile invoices issued against funds received.

Payments received by credit transfer do not require the beneficiary to undertake any specific activity, such as examining a documentary credit. The disadvantage is that the beneficiary has no advanced visibility of when the funds will actually be received on their account. The client has to rely on the commercial relationship, trusting that funds will be received on the planned date.

8.7
Documentary collections

Documentary collections provide an opportunity for the beneficiary to act as the initiator of the payment. As with documentary credits, documentary collections are often used for international transactions. With a documentary collection, the beneficiary does not charge the payer's account directly. Instead, the beneficiary hands over the required documentation (including the proof of ownership) to the payer in exchange for either the payment or a promise to pay on a future date. Handing over documents and collecting the payment against them is entrusted to a bank located in the payer's country. The same documents are used for documentary collection as for documentary credits.

8.7.1 THE PARTIES INVOLVED IN DOCUMENTARY COLLECTIONS

The following parties are involved in a documentary collection:

1. *The beneficiary or seller*
   This is the exporter who gives the instruction to their bank
2. *The payer*
   This is the buyer or importer
3. *The 'remitting bank'*
   This is the bank that receives a collection instruction from the beneficiary
4. *The 'presenting bank'*
   The bank that actually presents the documents to the payer

The presenting bank is usually the same as the collecting bank and is assigned by the remitting bank for the collection of the documents. This is normally a correspondent bank of the remitting bank. Or, in the case of a bank with a global network, simply a network branch. However, the payer is able to ask that their bank act as the presenting bank. Regarding documentary collections, banks are merely intermediaries acting on behalf of their customers.

8.7.2 THE ROUTING OF A DOCUMENTARY COLLECTION

The diagram below (figure 8.5) illustrates the process for a documentary collection issued by Global Trading S.A. in France at its bank, French Bank A. The importer is the Taiwanese company F, which holds an account at the Taiwanese Bank B. The Taiwanese Bank B holds an account denominated in euros at the French correspondent Bank of Taiwanese Bank B.

FIGURE 8.5   THE ROUTING OF A DOCUMENTARY COLLECTION

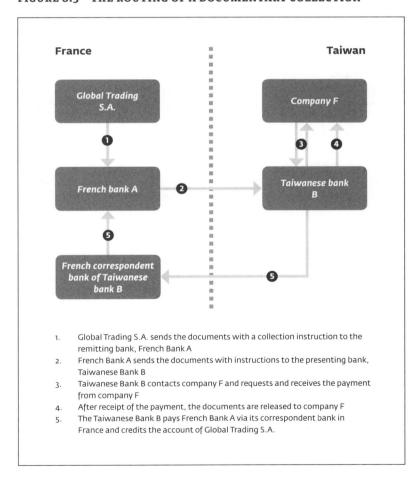

1.   Global Trading S.A. sends the documents with a collection instruction to the remitting bank, French Bank A
2.   French Bank A sends the documents with instructions to the presenting bank, Taiwanese Bank B
3.   Taiwanese Bank B contacts company F and requests and receives the payment from company F
4.   After receipt of the payment, the documents are released to company F
5.   The Taiwanese Bank B pays French Bank A via its correspondent bank in France and credits the account of Global Trading S.A.

8.7.3 ADVANTAGES AND DISADVANTAGES OF DOCUMENTARY COLLECTIONS

For an exporter, a documentary collection has the advantage that payment is guaranteed provided it hands over the correct documents. The importer has slightly less certainty. He will receive the correct documents against payment but still has to wait and see whether the goods are in the right condition. As with documentary credits, the main disadvantage is the fact that, by nature, the process is mostly manual. As a result, it attracts higher bank charges for processing.

8.8
Card collections

As discussed in section 8.5.1, in the four-party card scheme model the acquiring bank (acquirer) is the merchant's bank that performs a role in the collections side of card transactions. The beneficiary needs to consider various aspects before engaging an acquirer. These include the right card schemes to accept, which card products to accept, which channels to support and which transaction types to support.

Card schemes
Acquirers can be licensed by one or more card schemes and card schemes can have a domestic, regional or international footprint. Based on the target customer footprint, the merchant needs to decide which card schemes it wants to accept. If the merchant targets domestic customers only, accepting a domestic scheme might be sufficient. However, those merchants that focus on international clients might need regional or international schemes.

Ideally, one acquirer should fulfil this requirement. However, international retailers that also want to accept cards issued under domestic schemes will, in most cases, have to contract an acquirer in each domestic market they want to serve. The European cards market was an example of such a fragmented market but as a result of SEPA, cardholders are now able to use their cards across the whole euro area, either because the cards are now issued under an international card scheme, or because they are co-badged with an international card scheme.

Card products
Various card schemes can support different card brands and under a card brand different product types can exist. The most general distinction that can be made is that between debit products and credit products. From an acceptance point of view, a difference between the two is the charge-back risk which, in most cases under debit card rules, does not exist. Under credit card rules, consumers have the right to dispute certain transactions. Also, generally speaking, accepting debit cards is less costly than accepting credit cards.

Advantages and disadvantages of card collections
In general, accepting payment cards makes it more convenient for the merchant's customers to pay. By accepting payment cards, merchants avoid having to handle large amounts of cash.

Cards can be used across borders and over the internet. As a result, accepting cards from abroad can increase a merchant's potential customer base.

The costs of accepting cards are clearly visible to merchants on their statements, and such costs can be perceived to be comparatively high. There might also be some risks involved in accepting cards – especially over the internet – but by taking some preventive anti-fraud measures in collaboration with the payment service provider, those risks may be mitigated.

8.9
Incoming cheque payments

Although volumes are in decline, in some regions – such as the US, France, India, etc. – cheques still remain a popular payment instrument. In this section, we will describe the collection, processing, value dating and advantages/disadvantages of incoming cheque payments.

8.9.1 THE COLLECTION OF CHEQUES

The process starts when a company receives a payment by company or bank cheque. In the first instance, it will present the cheque to its own bank in order to receive the value for it. Based on individual bank criteria, the beneficiary's bank may accept the cheque for negotiation or collection.

Acceptance for negotiation
If there are no doubts concerning the beneficiary – he is deemed to be creditworthy and the beneficiary's bank believes that the cheque being presented will be honoured – then the beneficiary's bank may accept the cheque on the basis of negotiation. This means that the beneficiary's bank credits the beneficiary's account with the value of the cheque 'under usual reserve' within days before the funds have been collected from the payer's bank. Banks often charge interest on this amount for the period between the dates when they apply the funds to the beneficiary's account and receive the value from the drawee bank.

Under usual reserve means that the bank has right of recourse. So, in the event that they do not receive value from the drawee bank, they can recover the funds from the beneficiary. Technically, the fate of a negotiated cheque is never known, so the cheque could be deemed fraudulent at a later date and that would result in the funds being reversed from the beneficiary's account.

Once the payer's bank receives the cheque from the beneficiary's bank, there are only two possible outcomes:

- *The payer's bank pays the value of the cheque to the beneficiary's bank*
  In turn, the beneficiary's bank settles it in its own books and this concludes the transaction.

- *The payer's bank does not pay the cheque*
  In this case, the beneficiary's bank will receive an advice from the drawee bank confirming the reason. The beneficiary bank will then reverse the advance provided to the beneficiary's account and confirm that it has done so with the reason provided by the drawee bank.

Acceptance for collection

The beneficiary's bank may accept a cheque presented 'for collection'. Unlike negotiation, the bank does not credit the funds to the beneficiary's account until it receives the funds from the drawee bank. This approach has less risk for the beneficiary bank and is preferred if there is:

1. Doubt about the beneficiary's creditworthiness
2. Risk associated with advancing significant funds
3. Doubt about the payer (issuer) or the issuing bank
4. Potentially an unusual transaction (i.e. first cheque from this drawee or originates from a high-risk country)

The beneficiary's bank sends the cheque to the issuing bank and waits for the issuing bank to pay it the value. Timeframes will vary but it is likely to take weeks rather than days. Again, there are only two possible outcomes:

- *The issuing bank transfers the cheque value to the beneficiary's bank without problem*
  Following receipt of the amount, the beneficiary's bank will credit the beneficiary's account (after deduction of charges).

- *The issuing bank sends the cheque back with the message 'no advice to effect payment'*
  This is a discreet way of saying that the payer does not have sufficient funds in the account or that the issuing bank was unable/unwilling to pay. The beneficiary is responsible for arranging to secure payment or retain the goods.

With a cheque collection, the beneficiary knows that once it has been credited, the entry cannot be reversed due to insufficient funds in the payer's account. However, the funds could still be reclaimed at a later date if the cheque is deemed to be fraudulent.

8.9.2 THE PROCESSING OF CHEQUES VIA A LOCKBOX

When paying for goods or services by cheque, the process often starts with the cheque being posted to the beneficiary. That is the first delay in the process. Then, once the beneficiary has provided the cheque to its bank to process, the receiving bank posts the cheque to the drawee bank. This further delay is often referred to as a 'mail float'. In order to shorten it, banks and other service providers offer a 'lockbox' service.

A lockbox service is essentially a cheque collection and processing service where the beneficiary of the cheque outsources to a third party the physical collection of the cheque and associated documentation. It means that the physical cheque does not have to be sent to the beneficiary. The lockbox service receives the cheques on behalf of the beneficiary, deposits the funds into the local clearing system and sends the information relating to each cheque to the beneficiary for reconciliation. There are three types of lockbox services. Although the basic principle is the same, they cater for the needs of different types of clients:

1. *Retail lockbox services*
    Processing low-value cheque receivables with few accompanying documents – typically, the cheques are similar.

2. *Wholesale lockbox services*
    Processing high-value and more diverse cheque receivables with more accompanying documentation.

3. *Wholetail lockbox services*
    Processing both types of cheque receivables.

FIGURE 8.6   THE LOCKBOX PROCESS

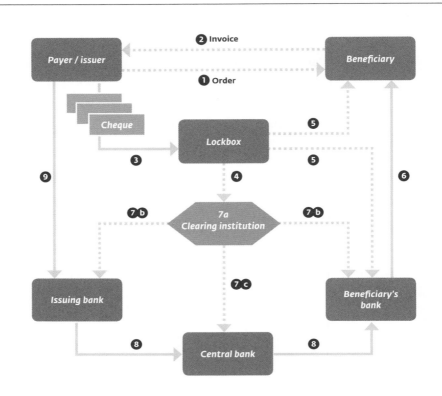

1. The buyer places an order with the seller.
2. The seller sends an invoice to the buyer.
3. The buyer (now called payer) issues a cheque and sends it to the lockbox which is assigned by the beneficiary's bank.
4. The lockbox company will clear the lockbox every day and pass the local cheques into the local cheque clearing system that day.
5. The lockbox company sends the information relating to the cheque electronically to the beneficiary and to the beneficiary's bank.
6. The beneficiary's bank credits the beneficiary's account on the same day that the cheque is received. This goes under usual reserve.
7. Clearing:
    a. Sorting of cheque payment instructions and calculation of settlement claims.
    b. Sending detailed payment information to the issuing bank and to the beneficiary's bank.
    c. Sending settlement instructions to the central bank.
8. Settlement at the central bank.
9. The issuing bank debit's the payer's account.

A lockbox service allows companies to outsource all the activities associated with receiving, handling and processing their cheque receivables. That, in turn, reduces the time companies have to wait for funds to be cleared. This clear confirmation assists with their reconciliation process and reduces the overall costs associated with collecting cheque receivables. In summary, the advantages of a lockbox service are that:

1. It reduces the 'mail float' period by ensuring that the cheques do not enter the postal system in the first instance
2. It increases efficiency by outsourcing the cheque collection activities – allowing the beneficiary to concentrate on its core business
3. Clear advices are sent to the beneficiary to aid with accounts receivable reconciliations

8.9.3 THE VALUE DATING OF INCOMING CHEQUES

When the beneficiary bank advances the value of the cheque to the beneficiary upon undertaking a cheque negotiation, it does so before it receives the funds from the drawee bank.

The beneficiary's bank therefore posts the amount with a later value date than the book date i.e. the expected date of receipt. This difference is based on the number of days the collection procedure normally takes to complete. However, the beneficiary's bank and the payer's bank can make bilateral arrangements so that the date of receipt is usually known beforehand. Depending on the payer's or issuing bank's country of origin, this can mean the dates are not aligned.

8.9.4 ADVANTAGES AND DISADVANTAGES OF INCOMING CHEQUE PAYMENTS

Company cheques benefit an issuer as it can be weeks rather than days before the funds are taken from their account. There is no benefit for the beneficiary in accepting a cheque other than the sale of the goods or service. By accepting a cheque, the beneficiary actually increases its risk as there is no guarantee of payment. In most cases, the processing of cheques is a series of manual activities for the banks and is reflected in the charges that are levied. However, sometimes due to the nature of the business or local habits beneficiaries will need to accept the cheque payment, despite aforementioned drawbacks.

Compared with a company cheque, a bank cheque (draft) is more favourable for the beneficiary. Bank cheques provide greater payment security as the drawer must pay up front in order for the bank to issue the cheque. Nevertheless, payment can still not be guaranteed, as the cheque may have been illegally altered or possibly even stolen from the bank. However, the process for the drawee bank is more streamlined and the drawing bank will settle much more quickly once the cheque is presented for payment. A key benefit of accepting a bank cheque is that the beneficiary's bank will be more inclined to process it as a collection, as the funds are settled quicker and the risk of non-payment is significantly less.

8.10
Direct debits

In cases where a company's debtors elect to pay their bills by credit transfer or cheque, the company has no option but to wait for the funds to be received. To address this and put the company back in control, collection products have been developed where the receiving party takes an active role in securing the payment. These schemes are called 'direct debits' (DDs).

With direct debits, the beneficiary company can claim amounts from the payer's account. The payer will sign an authority that confirms to their bank that they authorise the beneficiary to take the funds. The beneficiary and payer confirm the frequency of the claim. Most commonly, this is monthly, but it could be weekly, annually or a one-off. When the beneficiary requests the funds, in some cases the paying bank will check that an authority (mandate) is in place before it releases the funds. In other cases, the bank will assume that the mandate has been agreed between the beneficiary and payer.

In the event that the payer has insufficient funds or there is no authority in place, the paying bank can stop the beneficiary from taking the money. If the beneficiary takes more money than agreed with the payer, strict rules will ensure a refund is made to the payer as quickly as possible.

8.10.1 CROSS-BORDER DIRECT DEBITS IN THE EUROZONE

Since the introduction of the SEPA direct debit schemes in November 2009, it has been possible to initiate direct debits denominated in euros across SEPA.

These introduce uniform standards, formats, timescales and conditions for direct debits that allow corporates to collect euro payments throughout SEPA as easily, quickly and efficiently across borders as domestic payments. There are two direct debit schemes – the core scheme and the business to business (B2B) scheme. The B2B scheme is specifically aimed at business collections from their business counterparties with no refund right after debit as one of the key differentiators from the core scheme.

8.10.2 ADVANTAGES AND DISADVANTAGES OF DIRECT DEBITS

The direct debit is quick to set up and is a convenient collection method because the processing is fully automated. The advantages for the beneficiary party are that it can decide when the payment will be made, that it will control that the amount due is paid in full and into the desired account, and that there is a degree of reassurance that the payer intends to honour the claims.

However, this does not guarantee that the claim will be met and the funds will be received. For example, the payer may cancel the mandate, block a beneficiary from debiting or might not have enough funds in his account. In addition, in some instances payers have a certain period of time in which they can initiate a reversal of a direct debit that has already been paid.

In a commercial agreement between a beneficiary and a payer, there is likely to be a clause setting out what would happen if claims are not met. Often, this requires the total outstanding value of the agreement to be settled immediately.

8.11
Online bank-enabled payments

Online Banking ePayments (OBeP) is a payment instrument that was developed by the banking industry to address the unique requirements for payments made via the internet. In some countries, these types of payments have been very successful. Examples include iDEAL in the Netherlands, EPS in Austria, giropay and paydirekt in Germany, MyBank, etc.

The typical transaction flow of the OBeP:

- The consumer (i.e. payer) is authenticated in real-time by the payer's financial institution online banking infrastructure
- The availability of funds is validated in real-time by the payer's financial institution
- The payer's financial institution provides guarantee of payment to the merchant (i.e. the beneficiary)
- Payment is made as a credit transfer (push payment) from the payer's financial institution to the merchant, as opposed to a debit transfer (pull payment)
- Payment is made directly from the payer's account rather than through a third-party account

The merchant in the above situation receives a real-time guarantee that it will be payed and can release the goods immediately. The transaction is highly secure as the bank's security infrastructure is used.

8.12
Cash receipts

Though the use of cash is decreasing, some businesses such as shops, bars and cafés still receive many cash payments. These businesses regularly deposit the contents of their tills at the bank. For convenience and security, some may employ the services of a professional money transport firm.

8.12.1 THE COUNTER DEPOSIT

In the case of a direct deposit at the counter of the local branch, the amount of money offered is counted in the presence of the depositor. The number of notes in each denomination is itemised on a special form or keyed into a terminal. If cheques are also presented, these too are checked and totalled. The bank issues a deposit slip and credits the account of the depositor. The depositor is then provided with a receipt for the total cash and cheques deposited.

Some banks offer the ability to deposit cash via a multi-functional ATM. The money is than directly credited to the account of the beneficiary. The benefit for the bank is replenishment of the ATM, which reduces costs.

Some banks also offer a night vault service. Here, the customer deposits the money in a seal bag and the money is counted by the bank or service provider at the next available opportunity.

8.12.2   THE MONEY TRANSPORTER

Where large amounts need to be deposited at the bank, it is often more efficient to use the services of a professional money transporter. This service is commonly carried out by a security firm. In this case, the money transporter delivers the cash and cheques in a locked box directly to one of the bank's cash centres or service provider. The depositor locks the boxes, which can then be opened under dual control at the cash centre. At least two different individuals will count the cash to ensure accuracy and prevent fraud.

8.12.3   ADVANTAGES AND DISADVANTAGES OF CASH RECEIPTS

The main advantage of cash receipts is simply that everyone has access to this type of payment. However, the retailer needs to ensure that the cash they accept is genuine, as there is the potential for both bank notes and high-value coins to be counterfeit. With cash, the risk of theft might also increase. The cost of processing, storing and transporting cash is expensive for the banks and much of this cost is passed back to the retailer in the form of bank charges.

8.13
List of payment and collection instruments

In this final section we will give a summary of the different payment products that are used for both paying and collecting funds, and will highlight the main advantages and disadvantages of each.

PAYMENT METHOD

Product	Suitable for	Advantages for payer	Disadvantages for payer
Cash	– Small value face-to-face purchases	– Universally available and accepted.	– Beneficiaries are increasingly suspicious of high value cash transactions
Credit transfer Non-urgent	– Vendor payables – Salaries	– Cost effective – Payer chooses when the transfer is processed	
Credit transfer Urgent	– Treasury payments – Urgent supplier payments – Tax payments	– Payer chooses when the transfer is processed – Potentially same-day finality	– More expensive than non-urgent transfers
Company cheque	– Vendor payables	– Delayed debiting of account – Ease of issuing	– Potentially higher bank charges
Bank cheque	– Vendor payables	– Provides additional certainty to receiver	– Instant debiting of funds from the account
Documentary credit	– Vendor payables – Import transactions	– Commercially, the exporter is more likely to do business	– Expensive – Time-consuming process
Card products		– International, flexible alternative to cash, grace period	– Not accepted everywhere

COLLECTION METHOD

Product	Suitable for	Advantages for beneficiary	Disadvantages for beneficiary
Credit transfer	– Accounts payable	– Efficient – Cost-effective to process	– No guarantee for collection of funds – Uncertain timing of the collection
Company cheque	– Accounts receivable	– None, other than the sale of goods or service	– No guarantee for collection – Time-consuming procedures leading to delaying the crediting of the funds – Higher bank charges for processing
Bank cheque / Draft	– Accounts receivable	– Confirmation that the bank cheque is drawn on the bank and not the client	– Increased reassurance over a company cheque – Time-consuming procedures leading to delayed crediting of funds – Higher bank charges for processing
Documentary collections	– Export transactions	– Payment is guaranteed when documents are exchanged	– Time-consuming procedures – Expensive bank charges
Debit card / Credit card	– Ideal for retailers and internet-based shops	– Consumer-friendly – Increased trade as buyers can defer paying by using credit card	– Debit card: per transaction charge/Credit card: a fixed percentage of the transaction value
OBeP	– E-/m-commerce transactions	– Secure – Control	– Immediate debiting of funds – Ease of use
Direct debits	– Accounts receivable – Recurring receipts	– Active role in collecting the funds – Control over the timing of the transfer	– The claim of funds may be refused or reversed – Payer controls the mandate
Cash	– Ideal for retailers with low-value transactions e.g. shops, bars and cafés	– Universally available and accepted	– Funds must be held securely before being physically deposited at the bank – High costs associated with holding and processing leading to higher bank charges

Chapter 9

Delivery Channels

9   Delivery Channels

9.1
Introduction

The financial sector has widely adopted digitalisation of banking products and services. Where in the past, banks focussed on electronic payments and reporting on current accounts, most banks now offer all kinds of additional services related to transaction banking. Self-service tracking and tracing of transactions and customer service requests, eBAM (electronic bank account management), online billing, e-signature, predictive data analytics and mobile authorisations are just a few examples of a growing range of internet banking services.

In addition to deeper digital services, the product coverage of internet banking has also been extended from payments only to trade, guarantees, lending, financial markets and securities.

Broadly speaking, delivery channels can be split into online banking systems and direct link systems, also known as host-to-host solutions.

9.1.1   ONLINE BANKING SYSTEMS

The online banking systems (or web-based systems) are primarily used for manual origination of payments and account reporting. Most online banking users work from PCs, but there has been an increase in the use of mobile devices such as smart phones or tablets. This trend started in the retail market and has spread to the corporate sector as banks have begun to provide reporting – i.e. transaction information and alerting – and authorisation functions.

9.1.2   DIRECT LINK SYSTEMS

The direct link systems are used for file transmissions related to automated, straight-through processes between the (ERP) systems of the corporates and their banks. Host-to-host systems come in two guises – bank proprietary direct connections and multi-bank solutions.

Corporates seek multi-bank solutions both for online and bulk systems. The multi-bank aspect meets an increasing desire among corporates for bank-agnostic connectivity. Since the financial crisis in 2008 there has been a spotlight on counterparty risk that has slowed the trend among corporates of concentrating on fewer banking relationships. Instead, corporate treasurers have sought to spread counterparty risk by doing business with many banks. However, implementing multiple proprietary electronic banking systems is inefficient and does not deliver the visibility of nor the control over funds that treasurers are seeking.

The delivery channel(s) that a company selects depends on factors such as transaction volumes, multi-bank needs, accessibility requirements, data integration and security needs. In practice, many corporates implement a combination of host-to-host and online banking.

This chapter elaborates on the benefits and constraints of web-based internet banking and direct link systems. The multi-bank section explains the connectivity options provided by SWIFT, EBICS, bank-independent payment hub providers and the latest developments in open banking via the API technology. We conclude with the importance of properly addressing security. The irreversible digitalisation of banking requires an active and up-to-date corporate cyber security strategy.

9.2
Online banking

The core functionality of web-based systems is that banks provide screens to users, which enable them to manually enter transactions and requests, and to process and read a variety of information. Online banking systems offer a wide range of applications and services including:

- Executing payments
- Authorising transactions
- Account reporting
- Deal initiation
- Trade finance
- Status reports
- Electronic bank account management (eBAM)
- Multi-bank payment and reporting (MT101 and MT940)
- Mobile banking

9.2.1 AN OVERVIEW OF SERVICES AND APPLICATIONS

Executing payments
Online banking systems usually support a number of payment products. In addition to low-value and high-value payments, cheques and direct debits can also be initiated. Some online banking systems can also handle the central bank formalities for payments between residents and non-residents. Payment files can be imported from the online banking systems into the ERP or treasury systems (and vice versa), thus removing a manual operation between the systems.

Authorisation of transactions
Online banking systems also offer the functionality for authorisation of transactions either initiated by the same channel or through direct link channels.

Account reporting

Online banking systems allow cash managers to view end-of-day balances on accounts. Apart from the end-of-day book and value balances of the accounts included in the package, most solutions currently offer intra-day transaction statements.

Balance and transaction reports are usually not the only types of report that online banking systems can generate. Liquidity forecasts can be generated with the aid of most systems while consolidated reports can be prepared in a single currency. Some online banking systems can also prepare various cash pooling reports, such as shadow interest statement reports and notional pooling reports.

FX deal initiation

Some online banking systems include a separate module for short-term investment transactions or foreign exchange transactions with the bank. In the past, these modules were drawn up by systems specifically designed for such transactions but now the deal initiation of these transactions is frequently integrated with cash management applications.

Trade finance

Import and export letters of credit can be initiated via online banking systems. Previously, the process was very paper-intensive. Guarantees and collections are other trade finance instruments which, like supply chain-related products, are generally supported by online banking systems. These products were previously provided to companies in separate systems but are currently also being integrated with the traditional cash management applications.

Status reports

Companies can obtain real-time information about the status of their payments. By accessing the bank's internal tracking system via the internet, a customer can keep track of his own payments. Furthermore, client service inquiries can be initiated and tracked through the same online banking systems. This saves the bank a considerable cost that it may otherwise have incurred handling telephone inquiries.

Electronic bank account management (eBAM)

As part of the ongoing need for self-service, banks are also providing functionality to open, maintain and close bank accounts. This functionality also supports the exchange of documents related to opening an account and a digital signature that replaces an inked signature.

Multi-bank payment and reporting (MT101 and MT940)

Multi-bank payment and reporting initiation is also a common function delivered through online banking channels. Through multi-bank payment initiation, corporates can initiate payments from their accounts from multiple banks using the same online banking channel. This process is based on the MT101 agreements between banks. Through a SWIFT MT101 message (request for transfer), banks support the execution of payment instructions on behalf of a corporate entity. As a result, an account can be debited when this instruction is received from another bank. Multi-bank reporting uses the SWIFT MT940 message to exchange account statements.

Mobile banking

There has been an increase in the use of mobile devices – such as smartphones or tablets – for internet banking. This trend began in the retail market, where many banks enabled their retail services to be conducted through a mobile application. Now banks are providing mobile banking services to corporates.

One key difference with retail is that corporates place less emphasis on initiating transactions and more on reporting functions such as transaction information and payment alerts as well as authorisation functions.

Looking to the near future, it is likely we will see mobile applications becoming more common in the corporate market and there will be further integration with other non-cash functions such as market analysis and real-time FX rate information. It is expected that other functionalities currently already available through banks' portals will become available through mobile applications as well.

9.2.2   TECHNOLOGY

A company that simply wants to make individual payments via the internet, will not need major adjustments to its technical infrastructure. All it needs to arrange is the contract with the banking provider. Communications between the bank and the company take place via the internet, using a web browser. The internet applications are based on TCP/IP (Internet protocol suite) and customers can simply log in through their own internet provider.

The security solution of the online banking channel may require the installation of specific software; this is usually the case when security devices are used that are connected with the computer system running the web browser. For example, a smartcard and smartcard reader connected to a PC via a USB cable. However, most banks offer remote (unconnected) security solutions for authentication and authorisation, such as a hardware token or mobile phone app.

9.2.3   BENEFITS AND CONSTRAINTS OF WEB-BASED ONLINE BANKING SYSTEMS

Alongside the extensive suite of applications described above, web-based systems offer a large number of benefits. At the same time, the characteristics of an online banking system create constraints from a volume perspective and require human interaction.

Access from anywhere

A company can access an internet-based system from anywhere in the world. All it needs is a personal computer, laptop or mobile telephone with an internet connection. The only other condition is that security software has been installed (if applicable).

Personalisation

Web-based systems can offer personalised services. This is an important marketing tool and can be used by banks for cross-selling activities. A bank can tailor a home page to each customer. Basic examples include the storage of personal data supplied by the customer to generate personalised views or product recommendations. A bank can also select certain products for the customer. This means that the customer receives only customised information and does not need to perform his own searches.

Online client support and training
The online banking system often offers the option to communicate with a bank's helpdesk to obtain online support. In addition, a bank can provide an online training module.

Volume limitations
Web-based systems are usually not suitable to handle very large volumes. The interactive nature of an online banking system puts constraints on the size of payment or reporting files that can efficiently be processed and managed by the user via the application interface.

Human interaction required
The most important constraint of online banking is the need for human interaction. Many companies have installed accounts payable/receivable, treasury solutions or ERP systems including payments and reporting functionality and manual input screens. Giving staff access to online banking systems is an extra layer for the administrative organisation and sometimes creates unnecessary duplication of work. Because of the operational risks involved in human access to external internet banking platforms, many companies opt for direct link systems integrated into their internal (ERP) systems.

Online banking

Online banking systems are now mainly internet-based and primarily used by corporates for the execution and / or authorisation of payments, the reporting of account balances and transaction details, and the upload of payment or collection files to banks. These systems are increasingly being used for other applications such as electronic bank account management (eBAM) or client service functions.

Another key development is mobile banking, which is gaining momentum in the corporate market through key cash management functions for reporting, alerting and payment authorisation. Additional services include market analysis data and real-time FX rates, which are becoming available through specific applications.

9.3
Direct link systems

Companies that have implemented ERP and treasury systems with a complete set of manual entry and reporting screens might not be interested in similar and overlapping functionality from banking systems. The key demand will be to link the internal systems to the company's banks in a secure and resilient way. This is typically where direct link systems are introduced, both for transmission of payments and of reporting files.

Direct link systems, also called host-to-host solutions, file transfer, straight-through processing (STP) or bulk processing systems connect the customer's and bank's systems to each other without any manual intervention.

Traditionally, direct link systems were used mainly to submit larger volumes of payments to a bank. Web-based systems are usually unable to handle very large volumes and do not provide an automated end-to-end solution. Driven by corporate security policies, there is now a clear trend to also use host-to-host systems for high value treasury payments and smaller volumes of vendor payments. It is recognised that every manual step in a company's payment flows contains a certain fraud risk. When companies have mitigated these risks within the internal ERP and treasury systems, an unattended direct link will no longer add extra steps and avoids additional user access risk.

9.3.1   TECHNICAL ASPECTS OF DIRECT LINK SYSTEMS

A direct link system has three key technical aspects:

- The file format for submitting the payment orders
- The communication protocol
- The security protocol

With direct link systems, companies can send the payment orders and receive the reporting files in an agreed format directly from their own system. This can be done from an ERP system or a treasury management system. There are also solutions where companies implement a corporate payment hub between different ERP platforms and banks. Some banks also deliver connectivity software to make system integration easier. The format agreed and supported can either be a country-specific standard (such as the BACS Standard in the UK) or an industry global standard (such as ISO XML20022 for payments or MT940's for reporting).

Figure 9.1 shows data communication between a company and a bank, and the interaction between various internal systems in the company's computer network that make use of a direct link system.

FIGURE 9.1   BANK CONNECTIVITY SYSTEMS

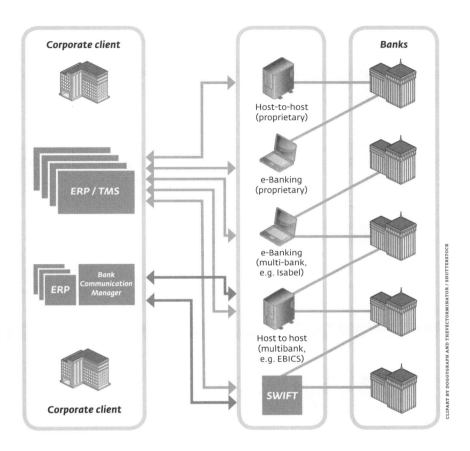

9.3.2   APPLICATIONS OF DIRECT LINK SYSTEMS

The most important applications of these systems are:

–   Automated sending or receiving files with payment orders
–   Receiving balance and transaction information
–   Multi-bank and third-party solutions

With direct link systems, there is no limit to the number of outgoing/incoming payments that can be simultaneously sent to or received from the bank. In addition, these systems make it possible to deliver several types of payments at the same time. Apart from normal low-value payments – such as salary payments – that are usually sent in a batch, all sorts of electronic data interchange (EDI) payments, urgent payments and many other kinds of payments can be delivered to the bank.

Direct link systems are constantly being improved and offer a growing number of applications. These include trade-related supply chain payments, electronic bank account management (eBAM) messages, billing files (CAMT086) and foreign exchange payments in exotic currencies or countries.

9.3.3   BENEFITS AND CONSTRAINTS OF DIRECT LINK SYSTEMS

No manual interaction

People can be a weak link in payment processes. Access tokens can be lost and mistakes in payment entries can be made. User access management must be managed within the control framework of the bank. The big advantage of direct link systems is that no staff are involved. In situations where companies manage payment and reporting functionality in internal ERP and treasury systems, the host-to-host connection avoids duplicating work.

Cost savings through economies of scale

If a company has extremely large numbers of payments processed by a single bank, it will generally be offered more favourable payment rates. Host-to-host processing will be a prerequisite for the best conditions. All payment orders can then be handled by means of straight-through processing, which is cheaper. In general, a bank will pass this cost benefit on to the company.

Bulk channels

Bulk channels are a key factor in achieving a high level of straight-through processing and automated payment and collection processes linked to a corporate's ERP systems. Growing numbers of corporates are looking for a non-bank proprietary multi-bank global solution (such as SWIFT for corporates; see next section) to support a single-channel solution for multiple banks.

Cost of ownership can be higher than internet banking

Banks generally apply higher fees for a host-to-host connection than for internet banking. The one-off IT effort to set up a direct link is also higher, and requires more dedicated hard- and software. The decision to use host-to-host connectivity is often part of a centralisation or shared services project, and thus part of a larger business case.

No manual input possibilities

In practice, there are very few examples where internal ERP and treasury systems cover all banking transactions in an automated way. As soon as there is a need for manual input or authorisation, a direct link system alone is not sufficient. This is why most corporates use online banking systems alongside host-to-host connections with their banks. The most common reasons why a direct link connection alone is not sufficient are:

- Global ERP roll-out is not (yet) covering all business and countries
- There is a need for local internet banking to process tax payments, salaries via local payroll bureaus etc.
- Online banking is used as a fall-back option for direct link systems

9.4
Multi-banking (Swift, EBICS, payment hub providers, APIs)

This section elaborates on the growing range of multi-bank solutions. Larger corporates with an international footprint will work with a number of banks. This is because one bank cannot cover all the required services of every region, or in order to spread the risk. In addition, on the financing side of the business, corporates have to work with a consortium of banks.

All these banks will have solutions for online banking and/or host-to-host connections. The proprietary solutions vary, creating an undesired complexity. Treasurers sometimes have to use more than 10 different tokens from various banks to approve payments.

Multi-banking providers look for solutions to reduce this complexity. In this section, we discuss the following options and trends:

- Swift Corporate Access
- EBICS
- Payment Hub Providers
- Open Banking and APIs

9.4.1 SWIFT CORPORATE ACCESS

The Society for Worldwide Interbank Financial Telecommunication (SWIFT) is an organisation owned by financial institutions around the world. SWIFT operates a private network infrastructure that is used by parties in the financial value chain to connect technically. The SWIFT network links more than 10,000 financial institutions, securities organisations and corporate companies in 209 countries in one secure cloud for financial messaging

SWIFT's main tasks are:

- To maintain a secure and resilient communications network for financial messaging
- To help create common standards for financial messages

Since access to the SWIFT network has been opened to corporates, major developments have taken place and new methods of using SWIFT are continuously being introduced. Nevertheless, the core themes have been consistent. Frequently recurring topics include FIN versus FileAct, personal signatures via 3SKey, contracts, connectivity options and benefits/costs. We provide more detail on these below.

9.4.1.1 SWIFTNet FIN (message-based)

The SWIFTNet FIN service is SWIFT's main store-and-forward messaging service. It includes message validation to ensure that messages are formatted based on the SWIFT messaging standards. MT messages are designed for a large range of purposes, varying from initiating payment transactions to cash management reporting. Well-known examples are MT101 'request for transfer' messages and MT940 messages for end-of-day reporting.

9.4.1.2 SWIFT FileAct (file-based)

Messages sent through the SWIFT network do not necessarily need to comply with the standard SWIFT MT formats. If a company uses the FileAct service, the file may adhere to other formats such as XML or local payment formats. FileAct is typically used for the exchange of bulk files in order to ensure secure file transfers.

9.4.1.3 Personal 3SKey signatures

3SKey is SWIFT's multi-bank digital identity solution. The user purchases a 3SKey token from a reseller. Typically, this will be one of their banks. This token is then activated and maintained through a central portal operated by SWIFT (which is also the interface for revoking or re-assigning tokens). The token is used to place a digital signature on the payload, which is then forwarded to the applicable bank.

The bank receives the file, checks the digital signature and automatically confirms with SWIFT that the signature is valid (whether the token has been revoked or is still active). Following positive authentication, the transactions can be considered to be correctly authorised and are processed.

9.4.1.4 Options for connecting to Swift

A company can decide to build and maintain an in-house connection to SWIFT. This requires installation of:

- SWIFT Alliance Gateway (SAG) for overall connectivity (including FileAct)
- SWIFT Alliance Access (SAA) for using FIN

Because the one-off investment and run costs of a direct SWIFT connection are not always cost-efficient, many corporates decide to outsource the connection to a third-party vendor or a service bureau.

The advantage of a SWIFT service bureau is that the cost for hosting the infrastructure is shared and the same applies to the cost for the knowledge and expertise required for building and maintaining the infrastructure. A service bureau may also provide additional services such as data transformation, reconciliation support or AML filtering.

SWIFT Alliance Lite is a third option that aims to simplify access to the SWIFT network. Alliance Lite has two main features of connectivity:

- Access through a secure website, which allows for simple manual creation of SWIFT messages.

- Installation of AutoClient software for automatic forwarding of messages or files through SWIFT. This software is required when connecting to FileAct through Alliance Lite.

9.4.1.5 Benefits and costs of SWIFT connectivity

SWIFT offers some clear benefits:

- Single interface – the major benefit of SWIFT is that it allows connection to multiple banks through a single network interface. This offers the improved management of operational risk, standardisation of processes and optimised documentation.
- High level of security – the SWIFT network is a closed system and is therefore more secure than purely internet-based communication systems.
- High level of availability – the SWIFT network is very reliable (SWIFT claims it has a 99.99 % service availability).

The cost of SWIFT connectivity is still relatively high in comparison with bank proprietary solutions. This is mainly because banks only charge a fraction of the total cost of ownership of their connectivity solutions. Channels for banks support a broader earning model while connectivity for SWIFT is a core business.

A third-party vendor may appear to be more attractive than direct connectivity to SWIFT. In developing their offerings, service bureau providers are extending beyond simple connectivity into areas such as risk management, standardisation, financial supply chain management and electronic bank account management.

Connectivity

SWIFT-based connectivity is particularly useful to multi-banked companies. It is a relatively expensive solution but the more banks that are connected through SWIFT, the stronger the business case becomes. SWIFT connectivity offers companies several ways to enhance communications with banks using multi-bank connectivity tooling. These include payment initiation and reporting messaging, as well as trade-related messaging. These solutions can be accessed through FIN and FileAct communication services – although not every bank will offer the full suite of solutions described here.
When using a SWIFT-based solution, most businesses will opt for a service bureau connectivity model because of the economies of scale and the benefits offered by additional value-added solutions achievable through a service bureau.

9.4.2 EBICS

The *Electronic Banking Internet Communication Standard* (EBICS) was originally developed as a multi-bank standard in Germany and has also been adopted in France as a standard method of bank connectivity.

Accelerated by SEPA, an increasing number of international banks have extended the country coverage of EBICS beyond Germany and France. Especially in Europe this multi-bank connectivity option has become an alternative for SWIFT Corporate Access.

The main difference between SWIFT and EBICS is that SWIFT connectivity, with more than 10,000 banks worldwide, is much broader. Particularly outside the SEPA zone, many banks will not support a similar range of countries, products and services compared to SWIFT.

On the other hand, the charging model of SWIFT is based on traffic and the one-off investment in SWIFT connectivity is substantial, while the onboarding of EBICS is cheaper, and after the one-off installation there are no additional messaging costs on top of the banking fees. With a growing number of banks adopting EBICS, also beyond the home markets in France and Germany, it is becoming relevant to assess this option in addition to SWIFT when looking for a multi-bank solution.

9.4.3   PAYMENT HUB PROVIDERS

The payments industry is continuously working to improve standardisation with, for example, the global implementation of XML, SEPA, common communication protocol and security standards. Despite these efforts, an international operating company that uses many banks will still be faced with a lot of differences between countries and banks. Even in the SEPA area we see specific implementations of standards per country. The XML standards of banks differ and balance and transaction reporting over many banks can be a burden. For example, the presentation of remittance details in the widely used MT940 format differ per bank and is sometimes not even consistent within one banking group.

All these differences create the business case for fintech companies, providing so-called hub solutions between corporates and their banks. In the section about SWIFT, we discussed service bureaus for SWIFT connectivity, but the services of payment hub providers are much broader. These third-party vendors can, for example, reformat the different payment standards of 10 banks into one file to be interfaced with the ERP system of a corporate. If one of these banks changes its standard, the payment hub provider can absorb this maintenance work without impacting the corporate interface.

Certain vendors extend their bank connectivity services to complete value chain solutions, sometimes specialised in specific industries. An example in the "order to cash" flow is that some fintechs digitalise invoices, manage the authorisations of payments, reconcile incoming payments against invoice data, etc. Bank connectivity is positioned by these vendors as a 'module' within a much broader solution package. The size and agile/entrepreneurial culture of fintechs enable fast responses to new requirements, in contrast with large banks where change can take more time.

When considering whether to make use of a hub provider between the bank's and the company's systems, it is important to assess the operational risk of this third party. In addition, small fintechs must comply with the minimal corporate cybersecurity standards (see section 9.5).

9.4.4   APIS AND OPEN BANKING

The previous section discussed the value of fintechs. The current services of these third parties only reflect the beginning of an era where corporates, banks, fintechs and consumers will find each other in so-called digital 'ecosystems'.

The problem of traditional internet banking systems is that they are developed for bilateral relationships between the account holding customer and the bank. In digital ecosystems, all kind of other parties require access to these accounts as well, in order to deliver multi-bank services. Corporates, private individuals and fintechs want banks to open their accounts in an easily accessible way. The technology to do this is based on so-called application programming interfaces (APIs). APIs were developed to enable open banking solutions.

An API is a set of commands, functions, protocols and objects that programmers can use to create software or interact with an external system. This published software can be used by developers of IT vendors but also by IT staff of corporates to gain direct access to bank accounts. In fact, the APIs provide the programming code for online banking functionality without presenting the web-based screens of the respective banks.

Today, the revised Payment Services Directive (PSD2) is introducing a legal framework for standardised access to bank accounts by third parties in the EU. PSD2 requirements will result in the introduction of APIs for initiation of payments and for receiving account and balance information. This is because banks will be obliged to offer access options and standardised APIs will be the preferred solution for the majority of banks.

Easy digital access to bank accounts by third parties via APIs will pave the way for many innovations in the financial transaction and information landscape. Open banking will change traditional banking, and will create new business models for banks and fintechs as well. It is recommended that the treasury function as well as other business lines of corporates investigate how the company can benefit from API technology in the future.

9.5
Security

Online banking has been a great success, but this success also has a downside. Criminals are increasingly targeting online banking and are trying to find ways to break into systems and divert funds, steal information or disrupt services. Along with cybercrime attacks, aimed at the applications and infrastructure of banks and their customers, fraudsters are increasingly targeting corporate customers using invoice fraud and impersonation. The large transactions handled by investment and wholesale banks make these banks and their corporate customers an attractive target.

Given the threat landscape and the nature of the products (financial information such as payment orders or electronic balances), security is one of the most important aspects of internet banking.

FIGURE 9.2

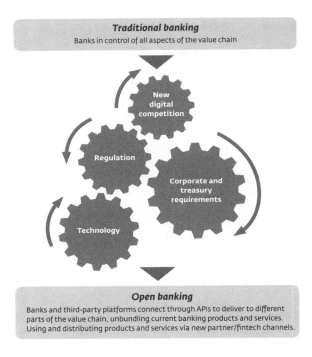

Unfortunately, the weakest link determines the strength of the overall security. If it is relatively easy to add fraudulent payments to an ERP system on the client side, the fully secured client-server direct-link system will not prevent this fraud from happening. Aside from the technological aspect, the human factor also plays a key role. Strengthening this part of the security chain by improving awareness is the first line of defence.

The entire financial and corporate ecosystem – including banks, corporates, regulators and others – must play their part in ensuring a safe environment. Knowledge sharing is essential to this approach.

This section will start by describing the basics of information security and the cybercrime and fraud landscape surrounding internet banking, followed by the measures to minimise these threats:

- Secure communication: the security of the connection between a company and a bank
- Authentication & signing
- Access control of the systems at a company and a bank

9.5.1 INFORMATION SECURITY

The relevant security measures are based on the information security building blocks and key concepts, as shown in the box below.

- **Confidentiality**
  Information is not made available or disclosed to unauthorized individuals, entities, or processes
- **Integrity**
  Protect data against unauthorised or undetected modifications, so the data remain accurate and complete
- **Availability**
  Information must be available when needed. This relates to the combination of the factors information processing, storage, protection and accessibility

  Other key concepts:
- **Authentication**
  The process to verify an identity (for example of a person or server)
- **Non-repudiation**
  Based on the authenticity and integrity, both the sender and receiver of a transaction cannot deny the sending or receipt of a specific transaction

Confidentiality and integrity are based on cryptography, which literally means 'secret writing':

- Confidentiality is ensured by encoding information with a key (this process is called encryption) so that only parties that possess the correct key can decode it and access the content.
- By hashing data and encoding the hash with a key (this process is called signing), the receiver can verify that the data has not been changed (integrity) and knows the identity of the party that sent the data (as only that party possesses the key to sign).

- **Symmetric systems** (secret key cryptography)
  In symmetric systems, the same key is used for encryption and decryption. Both the sender and the receiver have the same secret key. This key must be kept secret from all parties who are not authorised to read the messages. That's why symmetric systems are also called secret key systems.

- **Asymmetric systems** (public key cryptography)
  In asymmetric systems, a different key is used for encryption and decryption. In such systems, key pairs are used. One key pair consists of a private key and a public key. The private key is strictly bound to one party and must be kept secret. The public key is not secret and can be made known to all parties.

9.5.2 CYBERCRIME

As businesses and individuals become increasingly digitised and interconnected, new targets and methods of attack emerge almost daily. Exploits such as zero-day vulnerabilities, malware on mobiles and botnets using Internet of Things-connected devices are growing in magnitude and constantly evolving. It is a continuous struggle to stay one step ahead of cyber criminals, with both cyber defence teams and criminals sharing knowledge in their own communities to counter or take advantage of the most recently discovered vulnerabilities.

The increased importance of information security is apparent from the centralised role of the chief information security officer (CISO), which is increasingly being placed at the executive level in the decision-making hierarchy of larger organisations. The CISO must take an enterprise-wide view of risk management, working in collaboration with experts on legal issues, compliance, operations and finance, in addition to IT and with a focus on business products and services.

Computer emergency response teams (CERT) are being established to coordinate information sharing with the international security community, to continuously assess and scan networks and systems for vulnerabilities and anomalies and to be able to provide the required coordinated quick response to cybercrime events. Larger organisations often create a centralised coordination team (CCERT), linked to the CISO team, that coordinates the local CERTs.

While larger organisations have the capability to implement dedicated security teams and advanced cybercrime defences, such as intrusion detection systems, penetration testing, vulnerability scans, network analysis tools and more, smaller organisations must ensure that at least the application and system software is up-to-date, anti-virus and anti-malware is present and published critical vulnerabilities are solved as soon as patches become available. Keep in mind that when a supplier publishes a security patch, the vulnerability that is fixed by applying the patch is also communicated and common knowledge from that moment on. Critical vulnerabilities will be exploited almost immediately, as evidenced by the many reported cases of malware and ransomware, whereby cyber criminals even offered exploitation kits for sale to other criminals.

The growing number of internet-connected devices (such as domotics devices like webcams, smart doorbells, thermostats), which are in fact small computers that are often poorly secured, give cybercriminals an unprecedented number of machines for denial-of-service attacks (disrupting a service by flooding it with requests) and easy entry points to breach secured networks.

Just like in fraud cases, improving employee awareness is the first line of defence to avoid the infection of systems. This is described in more detail below.

9.5.3   CORPORATE FRAUD

Fraudsters are clever, very well-organised and masters in 'social engineering'. They use deception to manipulate individuals into executing actions or divulging confidential or personal information used for or resulting in fraudulent activities. Social media are used to map an organisation and the roles of the individual employees, a scam is often supported by cybercrime to install malware, obtain passwords and hack mail servers.

Common types of corporate fraud, affecting 75% of companies worldwide and causing billions in damage:

- CxO fraud: social engineering is used to profile the company and by posing as a senior manager or a third party acting on behalf of senior management, employees are manipulated into executing payment transactions or divulging confidential information. It is common in these scenarios that the fraudster explicitly stipulates that the transaction be made urgently and with the utmost secrecy.

- eBanking fraud covers phishing and malware infections. The cyber criminals will try to steal money by recovering the identification codes and electronic signature of their victim.

- Invoice fraud: the fraudsters will change the banking details of a company issuing an invoice into their own and, as a result, receive the invoiced amounts. To improve credibility, this fraud is often accompanied by a mailbox hack or by spoofing the email address of the sender.

The following employee awareness measures, accompanied by validation procedures, can prevent most such fraud cases:

- Ensure a company culture is created in which requests must be validated, even if they come from the top. Possibly appoint dedicated staff members to act as validators.

- Cybertrain all employees, including senior staff. Do not act upon unexpected emails, do not click on links or open attachments and report such events .

- Apply segregation of duties/access control: limit user access to what is required for their tasks, implement dual-control to apply (at least) a four-eyes principle. For more details, see the section below on access control.

- Enforce call-back procedures: whenever a supplier requests a change in details such as the account number, reach out (not using the details on the changed invoice) to the supplier to confirm this.

As a result of market demand and developing legislation, payment service providers increasingly apply transaction activity monitoring. Based on the historical behaviour of customers with regard to payment transactions, patterns are determined. When an incoming transaction deviates too much from the usual pattern, the customer will be contacted to verify the transaction.

The following sections will describe the security measures related to internet banking, with a focus on secure communication, authentication and signing (the basis for non-repudiation), and the importance of access control.

9.5.4   SECURE COMMUNICATION

The messages sent between a company and a bank include payment orders (from the company to the bank) and the transmission of balance and transaction information (from the bank to the company).

Secure communication is based on encryption and authentication. Encryption ensures that intercepted communication is unreadable for a third party. Authentication prevents attacks, like 'man-in-the-middle', by verifying that the connection is set up with the correct intended party.

For web-based systems (many-to-one), server authentication is applied. When setting up the connection, the identity of the server is confirmed based on a certificate verified by an independent certificate authority. For direct link systems, client authentication is also often used to effectively create a one-to-one connection where both the server and the client have verified each other's identity.

9.5.5   AUTHENTICATION & SIGNING

When a bank receives a payment order, it wants to be sure it originates from one of its customers. In other words, the bank wishes to verify who the sender is. Today, legal requirements tend to make two-factor or multi-factor authentication mandatory for manual payment entry and authorisation. This means it is often no longer possible to submit transactions with only a user name and password combination.

The elements of strong customer authentication can be categorised as knowledge (something only the user knows), possession (something only the user possesses, like a smartcard or smartphone) and inherence (something the user is). Two-factor authentication applies two out of these three elements.

Legislation

The legislative efforts of the European Banking Authority (EBA) in the area of payments and electronic money are aimed at ensuring that payments across the EU are secure, easy and efficient. The guidelines under the revised Payment Services Directive (PSD2) instruct the application of strong (two-factor) customer authentication for various types of payment service providers, only allowing exemptions (for example, contactless payments) under very strict conditions (maximum amount of the payment versus the fraud rate of the payment type).

For web-based systems, common two-factor security devices are smartcards, hardware tokens and mobile apps. Smartcards are usually connected to the user's work station and apply public key cryptography. While hardware security devices like smartcards and tokens are a safe way to store credentials, current technological developments also enable safe storage of credentials on mobile devices. This way the mobile device can function as a smartcard or token, without requiring a user to keep separate hardware devices on hand. Apart from the secure encrypted connection with server authentication, a signature based on the payload and the key is created to verify the identity of the sender and guarantee the integrity.

Direct link systems do not usually require human intervention to connect and send data, as the idea is that customers can connect their ERP systems directly to the bank servers. The knowledge and possession parts of strong customer authentication are stored in the software. This requires additional security measures:

- Client authentication: using public key cryptography, the identity of the client side is verified when the secure encrypted connection is set up between the client and the bank server. Contrary to web based systems, this means that the connection to the bank server can only be used by this specific customer system (one-on-one instead of many-to-one).

- Payload encryption and signing: an additional layer of security can be added by the customer encrypting the data so that only the receiver (bank) can decrypt the data using the private key. A digital signature is added to once again ensure the receiver of the sender's identity and guarantee the integrity.

9.5.6   ACCESS CONTROL

In order to restrict access to payment systems, users have to be identified and authenticated. Within a web-based online banking application, the system manager can usually define individual user profiles. A user profile defines the tasks each user is allowed to perform (for example view, create or authorise payment orders, download account statements), which data a user may access, signing permission configurations applying multiple signatures depending on the transaction amount and sometimes even detailed permission levels like whether a user is restricted for fund transfers to the existing predefined counterparties or has access to confidential payments like salary batches.

The segregation of duties and responsibilities that are applied at the company itself should also be configured when setting up users in the online banking system. This is a major factor when it comes to protecting the company from fraud.

For direct link systems, the segregation of duties and access for individual users must be applied in the ERP system as the credentials securing the client-server connection are specific for the one-on-one connection but cannot be used to distinguish different users.

9.5.7 IMPACT OF APIS AND OPEN BANKING ON SECURITY AND FRAUD

Open banking via APIs involves new challenges for banks concerning cybersecurity and fraud detection:

- API access means opening up a part of the bank infrastructure. The critical bank applications can no longer be hidden behind firewalls and elaborate security layers. This introduces a whole new field of attack for cybercriminals.

- When customers are using the application of the third party providers (TPP) instead of logging on to the bank applications, less information is available for the bank to detect anomalies in customer behaviour and transactions.

All participants in the API ecosystem will have to comply to strict requirements (including those for PSD2, the EBA Regulatory Technical Standards) and there must be a central registration indicating whether a TPP is verified and thus allowed to handle customer data and call bank APIs. In addition, the user needs to give consent to a TPP application to access an API on behalf of a user. This consent is stored in a so-called 'token', that enforces the correct level of authentication and authorisation without revealing the secret user credentials to the TPP. The API provider verifies the validity of the token (against an internal or external source, see box below) and allows access according to the authorisations included in the token.

Trusted identity

An open API environment creates the need for a federated identity. Without an identity that can be trusted by the parties in an API ecosystem, API providers will require that consent is given by the user based on the security credentials of that specific API provider. A TPP offering a multi-bank solution requires the user to use the specific security credential for each bank separately to allow the TPP to access the accounts and services at that bank, unless there is an identity provider that can be trusted by all parties involved.

The previously mentioned SWIFT 3SKey is an example of a trusted identity provider, which allows the user access to multiple banks using one set of security credentials (or one digital identity).

Another example is the EU eIDAS initiative. Starting in September 2018, all EU citizens and companies can use their own national ID (such as the Dutch DigiD) to communicate with every public (government) service provider in any European country.

9.6
Summary

The following table summarises the features, benefits and constraints of the different delivery channel types.

Delivery channel	Advantages	Disadvantages
Online banking sytems	– Access from anywhere – Wide range of cash management solutions (e.g. payments, collections, reporting, authorisation, client self-service, trade) – Ability to perform manual entries for ad hoc transactions – Ability to upload files	– Not fit for very large volumes – Not STP, manual action always needed. This involves additional security risk
Direct link systems	– Automated integration with ERP, no manual manual intervention needed – Fit for processing large volumes	– No online functionalities – Implementation requires IT development capacity
Multi-bank systems	– Bank independent solution – Standardisation – Can be used for both internet-based and direct link connectivity with banks. – APIs accelerate many open banking innovations	– Involvement of a third party creates an extra step in the value chain, and thus additional operational and security risk – More costly than bank proprietary solutions

Chapter 10

Treasury Management Systems

10 Treasury Management Systems

10.1
Introduction

Treasurers are facing turbulent and challenging times. This period of increasing volatility and challenging interest policies has led corporate treasuries to prioritise monitoring the financial markets, optimising cash flow and managing risk management. Considering the speed of developments, a comprehensive and real-time treasury management system is essential to proactively manage financial positions and risks.

Treasury management has become more automated through improved straight-through processing (STP) and further integration with corporate financial systems. This reduces the required number of manual activities, makes the process more efficient and – provided the system is implemented adequately – more secure. Ideally, this automation reduces time spent on repetitive activities, freeing up time to for tackling value-adding tasks. Because of this focus on process automation, corporate treasuries are paying increasing attention to the automation support offered by treasury management systems. The requirements placed on the system in terms of functionality, process transparency and security increase each year. Given the critical functionality provided, companies need to fully rely on the system and the support provided by the vendor which, like other key relationships, should be evaluated on a regular basis.

This chapter presents an overview of the different types of treasury management systems (TMS) and the TMS market, and provides an overview of a typical TMS software selection process.

10.1.2 MARKET OVERVIEW

Today's world of treasury management is marked by various changes as described in chapter 3 (Treasury Transformation). Treasurers are confronted with the question of whether their information systems can handle all these new developments and challenges, which include:

- The growing need to collect financial information from a group's entities
- The expansion and increasing complexity of the type of instruments handled
- Open Banking by making use of application programming interfaces (APIs) enabled in Europe by the Payment Services Directive (PSD2)
- The development of remote banking communication (elimination of the EDIFACT, the growing strength of SWIFTNet and the appearance of EBICS (electronic banking internet standard))

- Heightened expectations regarding the internal control of treasury activities
- Ever-increasing and changing regulatory requirements

Software vendors aspire to cover an ever broader spectrum of treasury management needs stemming from market activities, liquidity management and banking communication. In this environment, the key factors for success in choosing a TMS are:

- Selecting a tool that is adapted to the treasury's operational needs and that adds value to their operations, maximising straight-through processing
- Automating recurrent tasks, particularly reporting, in order to ensure the permanence and relevance of the information
- Integrating reliable internal control solutions directly into the application's processing flows

In the wake of the economic turmoil, treasury departments have refocused from crisis management back to the task of efficiently managing activities and are raising the question of what lessons can be learned and what opportunities can be leveraged from enhancing the organisations' access to information through the improved TMS. How can the organisation better employ technology to gain access to vital real-time information? For example, a well-implemented system will provide strong and automated functionality through automated payment solutions, real-time balance information, automated reconciliations and confirmations. It can also provide strong analytical tools to effectively measure and monitor financial risk positions and execute hedging of exposures to transparent pricing. It may also offer the functionality to manage the liquidity positions through integrating cash forecasts (with careful input), balancing foreign currency cash accounts, managing collateral, controlling banking authorities, monitoring credit, and enhancing the control environment.

Looking at the variety of software solutions to support treasury processes and the vast array of different operational processes throughout the different treasuries in the market, identifying and evaluating the available system solutions is paramount in order to reach a comprehensive vision on which system might be the best fit at the lowest cost both today and in future. While technological developments within the treasury landscape have been evolving, with a relatively stable state of providers, the focus has been on offering solutions tailored to the needs of treasury departments. As such, a 'single-system solution' that either is, or has the potential to be, fully integrated with the banking, trading or other portals (e.g., SWIFT) and ERP systems, has become paramount in achieving these cost reductions. This 'wall-to-wall' approach on system selection continues to be popular as companies try to save costs on interface support and system licenses in efforts to create a more efficient and visible financial value chain management.

10.2

Different treasury management system for different requirements

When looking at the TMS market, there are a variety of vendors and systems from which to choose. These range from straightforward entry-level systems to complex all-in-one solutions. As a rule of thumb, one could say that the more complex the treasury operation, the more complex the system needs to be, and therefore the higher the implementation and licensing costs. In addition, there are different hosting approaches (on-premise, web-based and vendor hosting).

FIGURE 10.1
OVERVIEW OF
TMS MARKET
SEGMENTS

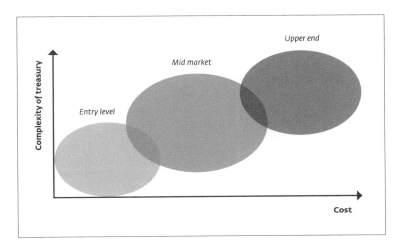

10.2.1   ENTRY-LEVEL SYSTEMS

Entry-level treasury management systems focus on the main treasury activities like cash position, management of basic treasury deals (like money market and foreign exchange) and basic payment functionalities, usually via EBICS or via integration into online banking tools. Most entry-level systems come with a standard definition for the most common treasury processes. The standardisation of the process flows usually allows for rather short implementation times with little implementation effort required. However, it usually requires the client to adjust processes to match those supported by the system. Therefore, the flexibility of these types of systems is limited.

Benefits

- *High degree of standardisation*
  Most entry-level TMS are very standardised, meaning that one or two common process flows have been designed in the software. With many stand-alone TMS, the client does not have much of a choice concerning how a certain process should be

implemented in the system. However, he will have to accept the solution that has been designed by the software vendor. Even though this high degree of standardisation limits the client to some extent, it allows for short implementation times as the setup of the systems is usually comparatively simple.

- *Little effort for functional enhancements*
  When a system vendor provides a system update to ship new functionalities to the client, or if the client chooses to implement functionalities that have not previously been implemented, efforts related to this task are comparatively minimal for entry-level systems. As these systems provide basic functionality, when enhancements are made to the system only limited regression testing is required. This will keep implementation efforts low and will put undue stress on the treasury department.

Challenges

- *Required modifications*
  Modifications to standard functionalities may be required to adjust the system to fit organisational requirements. If a client decides that the standard process setup of the TMS does not suit his business requirements, this will often lead to increased implementation costs for entry-level systems as the desired process flow must be specifically developed by the vendor or the implementation partner to meet the client's needs. If this is the case for a number of processes, the advantage of a quick and cost-efficient implementation is countered by efforts to take customer specific developments into account.

- *Integration into existing IT landscape*
  For many entry-level treasury management systems, the biggest challenge is the integration into the existing landscape. TMS require a lot of data from other finance systems (i.e. information about payables and receivables for exposure management) and need to provide data to finance systems (i.e. general ledger entries for treasury transactions) in order to be used efficiently. For every set of data that is required by the TMS, a separate interface has to be created in order to provide the data to the TMS. Many entry-level TMS do not offer standard interfaces to fully connect and communicate with ERP systems.

10.2.2 MID-MARKET TREASURY MANAGEMENT SYSTEMS

The mid-market treasury management systems are designed for larger multinational treasuries with a more complex process design and a higher level of functional requirements. They offer a wide range of functionalities, while maintaining reasonable licensing and implementation costs. These systems can be adjusted to a lot of different customer-specific organisational processes and contain more complex functionalities like in-house banking, tailored risk management and evaluation procedures. Often these systems have also standard interfaces to the most common ERP systems.

Benefits

-   *Wide range of functionalities*
    The functional capabilities of mid-market treasury systems range from basic
    functionalities, like cash management and basic financial instruments, to more
    complex functionalities like in-house banking, design of specific local payment
    formats, setup of payment factories, complex evaluation and risk management
    models as well as functionalities covering hedge accounting requirements.
    Because of their functional diversity, these systems allow for the support of most
    processes in multinational treasuries.

-   *Customisable to fit most clients' needs*
    In addition to offering a lot of functionalities that may be required by treasury,
    most mid-market systems offer a wide range of customisation options which allow
    the system to be adjusted to existing processes in the organisation without cus-
    tomer specific developments.

Challenges

-   *Implementation and licensing costs usually higher compared to entry-level systems*
    The functional diversity, as well as the high degree of customisability, comes at
    a cost. Not only are licensing fees usually considerably higher than they are for
    entry-level systems, but the high degree of process flexibility causes implementa-
    tions to be considerably more time-consuming and hence more expensive.

10.2.3   UPPER-END TREASURY MANAGEMENT SYSTEM

For highly sophisticated treasuries with complex requirements, the mid-market solutions
will most likely not provide all of the required functionalities. These clients will tend to look
at the most sophisticated systems in the market, knowing full well that these are also the
most expensive systems, both in terms of licensing and implementation.

Benefits

-   *High flexibility of process setup allows the system to be customised to the client's needs*
    Most treasury solutions incorporated in an ERP system are shipped with a certain
    set of standard functionality. All processes that are required by treasury need to be
    customised during the implementation of the system. This allows for a high degree
    of system flexibility but also causes increased implementation costs compared to
    most stand-alone solutions.

-   *Easy integration into the existing IT landscape*
    As most upper-end TMS ship with a wide selection of standard interfaces to dif-
    ferent ERP systems, the integration into modules like accounts payable, accounts
    receivable, accounting, etc. is usually a standard functionality of the solution. This
    means that data available in ERP systems is ready to be used in treasury and data

generated by the treasury solution, such as posting entries, can be directly transferred into the accounting solution of the ERP package.

–   ***Resources are available on the market***
    Whereas for most entry-level and mid-market TMS, implementations are usually done by the vendor himself, for most upper-end systems there are a wide variety of consultants available on the market. This gives the client the choice of who he wants to run the project with and also creates competition in the market, somewhat reducing implementation costs. In addition, when hiring IT or treasury personnel, the chances that they have worked with an upper-end treasury system are quite high.

Challenges

–   ***High implementation costs***
    As mentioned before, the high degree of flexibility results in implementation costs that can be significantly higher compared to other TMS. This is one of the main drivers for companies deciding on a simpler solution, even if this solution fails to cover the full extent of functional requirements.

–   ***Implementation of functional enhancements can be complex***
    Not only do implementation costs tend to be rather high, but implementation of functional enhancements or technical updates can require a lot of co-ordination. The more complex the system and its implementation, the more likely it is that errors will be made during or after a system update or enhancement. Therefore, a significant amount of regression testing is required every time changes are made to the system. As treasuries are usually always short on time, this can lead to very static update/enhancement processes that only allow for one or two update time slots per year.

–   ***Development of functional enhancements often later than market requirement***
    The more complex a treasury management system, the more interdependencies between different functionalities and the more complex the programming logic. Therefore, adding new functionalities is a labour intensive process, which requires a lot of design and testing on the vendor's side in addition to the actual development of the new functionality. As a result, treasury critical functionalities often reach the market later than required. And even if shipped in time, additional time is required to implement the solution and customise it to fit in with the setup of the client's treasury solution.

10.3
Various types of hosting for treasury management systems

In the past, data was the most valuable asset to most companies. This meant that the mindset that this asset could not be trusted to anyone else was predominant. Thus, treasury management systems were applications installed locally (on-premise installation), which allowed the company to control the IT security environment and data. This perceived data security comes at a cost, as internal IT resources are required to implement and operate the system. In many cases, no such resource is available within the company and needs to be hired specifically to operate the TMS.

With improved levels of network security and a changing mindset within organisations, more and more vendors are offering web-based or cloud-based solutions as well as solutions hosted directly by the software vendor. Web-based systems usually provide standardised processes, which lead to potentially simpler implementations. Since some companies are uncertain about the security and data privacy of web-based solutions, one alternative is to have the installed application hosted by the system vendor. In this case, the vendor supports the IT infrastructure and no training of internal IT resources is needed.

10.4
Selecting a treasury management system

10.4.1   MAIN DRIVERS FOR SELECTING A TMS

Looking at the selection process for treasury management systems, the main drivers need to be identified and prioritised. Is it the ability to effectively manage and monitor the trading risks in real time using a variety of complex instruments? Or indeed the ability to strengthen and improve cash management, cash visibility and access, as well as cash flow forecasting tools and processes? Or is it the ability to interface with the ERP and generate automated posting entries and payments? What needs to be considered in a TMS in order to make a sound choice between the most popular systems currently on the market and the system that might best fit the company's needs? There are several key drivers in evaluating the choices:

- Identifying and prioritising the needs for business-critical treasury activities
- Identifying and evaluating solutions that can adapt to a changing business environment
- Identifying and evaluating costs and benefits associated with integration
- Assessing the software delivery model that best meets the company's functional and economic needs
- Assessing the system vendor and developing that relationship before, during and after implementation to best serve the company's needs

10.4.2 IDENTIFYING CRITICAL BUSINESS REQUIREMENTS

Basic functionality of any TMS must always feature functionalities that:

- Allow for accurate capturing and monitoring of all required financial instruments
- Provide access and visibility to cash flows
- Support segregation of duties and enforce controls
- Generate confirmations (i.e. in SWIFT format, PDF, print, etc.)
- Allow for reconciliations and the execution of hedges and payments in a mostly automated process
- Have a user-friendly and flexible report writer
- Support interfaces to other systems

But what else can a strongly integrated system provide? How well does a system or process calculate and continuously provide accurate valuations and real-time management information? Recent changes in regulations as well as market volatility have now created demand for systems that:

- Allow for the flexible calculation of valuations for all financial instruments in use
- Allow simulations and scenario analyses to be run
- Can also provide useful real-time information to better control working capital levels
- Can make global cash balances visible and have the scope to robustly identify core, liquid and strategic levels of funding and liquidity

Every treasury function operates in a different risk environment and treasurers face a multitude of differing business drivers. With this in mind, the real differentiators for a TMS will centre on how a TMS package comprehensively covers the company's business requirements, its ability to adapt to the specific business or industry needs of the company as well as the flexibility to adjust the system to existing organisational processes. However, if the system does not meet the majority of the business requirements, should a company consider customisation or implementing the application in a way for which it was not intended? If yes, then what level of 'customisation' is appropriate and how can this be supported going forward? Will the customisation be too rigid to support new functionality as a company's needs and focus change? What is the risk that the vendor will eventually decline to support these customisations or 'unintended' uses?

10.4.3 SOLUTIONS FOR A CHANGING BUSINESS ENVIRONMENT

When selecting a suitable TMS, treasuries must be clear about the current system requirements, the treasury footprint within the organisation and what functionality will be required in the future. There is no doubt that cash is a top priority to treasuries. Therefore, a back-to-basics approach has been adopted. This means, for example, that cash management and forecasting, covenant management as well as monitoring and supporting local funding solutions have all been revisited, expanded or further embedded. With the right system selection and implementation, various assumptions related to commercial and economic environments may be flexed and analysed to provide further insight into how the balance sheet value can change.

Further advances are being made by treasurers to achieve more effective liquidity planning and management or, in essence, to expand the cash management footprint. This means treasury has more influence and impact on accounts receivable, collections and the order-to-cash cycle – with a particular focus on the time value of money and credit risk. But does the current TMS, on its own, offer greater visibility and control over this cash process? Does the TMS facilitate the reporting of all group bank account balances while supporting a robust forecasting process and escalation of variations? To what extent can the TMS assist in setting up a comprehensive system for cash forecasting for the company and its subsidiaries? And to what extent can treasury provide the resources with the necessary knowledge to facilitate this?

10.4.4   EVALUATING THE COSTS AND BENEFITS OF INTEGRATION

We have mentioned the ability of the system providers to deliver functionality for the more recent business developments. Is the company's vendor overly concerned about the problems the company has with connecting its treasury system to other system applications? It seems so, but how well does the company's system provider enable it to directly obtain the information required? For example:

- What is the system's ability to capture foreign exchange-embedded derivatives in contracts?
- Is it possible to extract the required level of detail (or provide the flexibility for accurate manual input or overlays) for a reliable short and medium-term forecast?
- How does the system allow you to interface directly with an internet dealing platform without the need of another application, web-based or not?
- Is it possible to integrate other, especially local payment, formats and at what cost?
- Can a multilateral netting program be easily run in the chosen system?
- Is the system able to generate general ledger entries for treasury transactions and send them to the ERP system?
- Can the system handle payment and collection factory processes?

These questions are sometimes ignored during the implementation of a treasury management system. Still, they are critical to achieving an integrated solution that provides visibility and access to information allowing the treasury department to analyse and take prompt action that benefits the organisation. Prioritising the connectivity between systems should be part of considering existing and future requirements, as companies begin the selection process, and certainly as implementation proceeds.

10.4.5   EVALUATING THE SOFTWARE DELIVERY MODEL

In the last 10 to 15 years, many well-known names in the treasury market have disappeared and others have emerged. Through consolidation, system vendors have become larger and have expanded their global presence. This expanded scale has the potential to enable these vendors to invest more in development towards improving their solutions, to meet the increased expectations of their global customer base and to provide better service levels. However, this consolidation is also associated with the risk that vendors will include functionality of acquired systems in their main system and cease supporting the other systems in order to further push their main product into the market. Additionally, many treasurers are rightly concerned about the lack of competition in this market if the consolidation trend continues. Nevertheless, we are happy to see new vendors emerging as this contributes to improved choices – installed, web-based, in the cloud or hosted – as well as competition and innovation in this market. In the past, most treasury management systems were locally installed applications and this led to numerous challenges, including the need for IT resources to provide support and operation as well as implementation.

To address these challenges, and thanks to the advent of improved network security, an increasing number of vendors are offering other software delivery models to meet these needs. Two models have increased their prominence and acceptance – the web-based/cloud-based solutions, software-as-a-service (SaaS solutions) or the hosting of your installed application. The SaaS model has the advantage of standardised processing, potentially simpler implementations and a per-user/per-function pricing model that is budget-friendly. However, some companies have struggled with security and data privacy concerns as dictated by their internal security policies. Another alternative is to have the company's installed application hosted by its vendor. Hosting the application has the advantage of having the hardware installed, implemented and hosted at the vendor's location. The vendor supports the company's IT infrastructure needs relative to the treasury application. No IT department training is needed to install the application and manage the database, and there is no need to schedule upgrades with the company's outsourced IT department – all this provided by the vendor.

10.4.6   ASSESSING THE VENDOR RELATIONSHIP DURING SELECTION

One area that seems to be very much in need of improvement is the support given to existing customers and control over apparent 'development' costs. Whether this is due to system providers focusing on new clients to drive revenue or customising existing developed solutions is unclear. However, this has become a constant source of frustration among many treasury departments.

If the company has a good working relationship and a high level of support from its TMS vendor, it is most likely that the company is large and has a substantial budget, or that it has a highly dedicated vendor.

An important part of the selection process focusses on selecting a vendor that will offer the most rewarding client relationship package. In addition to assessing system capabilities, there is a need to review the commercial risks and financial stability of the TMS provider, as well as the possibility that it may be acquired and/or that its TMS will no longer be supported. Moreover, the degree of emphasis the vendor puts on after-sale customer support is also an issue that requires confirmation during the selection process. The company should ask how else the system vendor can provide support. This is what is referred to as the 'soft factor'. Good examples of such soft factors are implementation support and that the vendor may also allocate development time (via invoices) to existing customers instead of focusing mainly on new business to drive revenue growth. The vendor may offer extended support once the company 'goes live' on the system as the team transitions to its new roles. The company may also expect its system vendor to have a vision on, and a solution for, the latest treasury business developments. Finally, one may expect that the system vendor not only focusses system developments on enhancing the core system, but also on enhancing the integration with other systems in the organisation.

10.4.7 ASSESSING THE VENDOR — IMPLEMENTATION AND POST-SALES SUPPORT

Some of the distinguishing features of a successful implementation are the level of engagement concerning implementation by the treasury team and the vendor as well as the quality of implementation resources available. However, resources are always stretched, especially during ongoing challenges in the financial markets. Companies seconding resources are often a critical factor in achieving a smooth and successful implementation project, but what level of resources and implementation support are offered by the vendor and are they independent enough to help ensure a smooth implementation?

Often, if vendor information is reviewed during the selection process, it is mainly the financial stability and geographical location that are assessed. Vendors understand that it is the client who has the least amount of experience. This has prompted conscientious vendors to redesign their implementation approach. The best way to shorten implementation time and effort is to eliminate choices. Choices need decisions and decisions take time. Therefore, some vendors have decided to sell their system with a set industry-standard parameter. This is based on the size of the treasury, the position in the organisation, the strategic goals, the complexity of the instruments, the transaction volume and the size of risk positions. The benefit is mutual. If the company's treasury is organised according to industry standards, the system can be implemented quickly. This is because many choices have already been defined that allow the company to achieve 'go live' in half the time usually needed for a full-scope implementation. In this regard, the vendor is more or less assured of a well-defined project with minimal risks. However, making educated choices is of paramount importance in implementing a TMS that offers an organisation the power to drive through efficiencies and improvements in the way its treasury thinks and manages its cash, funding and risks.

10.5
TMS selection and implementation approach

As described in the previous sections, there are many different TMS with different capabilities and delivery models, offered by a range of different vendors. This wide variety makes it very hard for companies to select the right system to fit their needs. This means that a structured approach for the system selection phase is required.

When working with clients to replace the current TMS, there is usually a fair amount of disenchantment with the client's present system or the realisation that the system has served its useful life. The reasons for the disappointment vary, from the realisation that the system was not a good fit, or that it was a poor implementation of a good system, or that the system is incompatible or unstable in their environment. However, the underlying theme appears to be a lack of clear expectations. To avoid this, companies should take a more pragmatic approach to system selection in order to help ensure the best system fit. Successful projects manage expectations by thoroughly assessing business requirements, focusing on project management during selection and implementation, and considering the capabilities and capacity of the chosen vendor.

A key element in selecting the right system is a thorough and detailed understanding of the business processes in place and the definition of business requirements. However, technological and data opportunities and constraints should never be ignored in the search for a system solution. When selecting a system, the following implementation should be seen as a separate phase from the selection process, as it largely depends on the vendor and the package chosen.

Project start-up and planning
Before starting a project, a project plan should be drafted. This plan should contain a description of the resources required, a clear timetable with deadlines and work products, and the responsibilities of each project member. Furthermore, it is important that the project management is in place before the project gets under way.

Phase 1: strategic framework and requirements specification
The first step in the selection process is to carry out an assessment to identify the client's strategic framework. The strategic framework provides the necessary setting and required parameters for the TMS. Taking or confirming previous decisions with respect to strategy, overall business processes, organisation and system philosophy lays the foundation for the requirements specification. The importance of this phase is often forgotten or considered irrelevant to the system selection. If this phase is omitted, however, the project runs the risk of being based on the wrong assumptions, which could result in fundamental and costly revisions late in the selection or implementation phase. Simultaneously, the treasury management processes, methods and techniques used should be reviewed and compared with market practice.

Key considerations concerning requirements at this stage may typically include:

- Accounting standards in hedge designations and valuations
- Customised reporting tools
- Cash management benefits and multilateral netting opportunities
- Forecasting tools
- Real time limit monitoring and risk management
- Security
- Robust interfaces with banking platforms, trading systems, accounting packages and market information sources
- TMS limitations and flexibility towards the changing needs of the business

FIGURE 10.2   SAMPLE PROJECT PLAN FOR A SYSTEM SELECTION

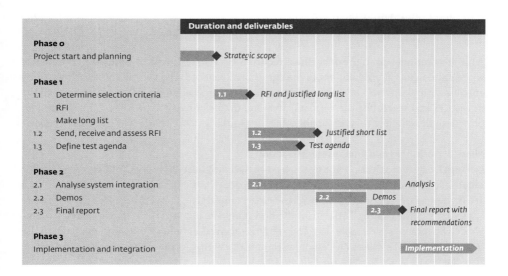

The requirements specification describes the organisation's requirements for the future TMS. The requirements specification is used as the basis for the request for information (RFI), sometimes called a vendor questionnaire.

FIGURE 10.3   SCOPE AND REQUIREMENT SPECIFICATION

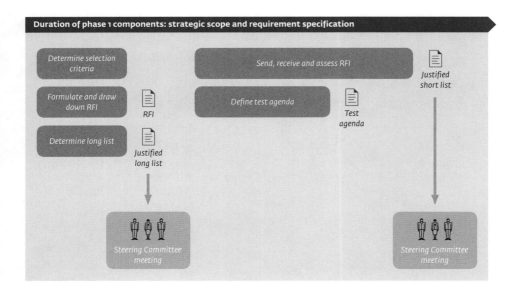

It is not advisable to start this phase by sending out a request for proposal (RFP). The contractual complexity of an RFP undermines the goal of this phase of the selection process, which is to gather information about the vendor(s) and the functional and technical specifications of the system(s).

A tailor-made questionnaire of business requirements geared to the complexity of the client's wishes and needs should be sent to the shortlisted vendors. The specificity of the questions enables a rapid analysis of the responses. Based on the weighting of the various questions in the RFI and scores for the vendors' answers, the responses to the RFI can be quantified, providing the client with a reasonably objective ranking of the vendors and their systems.

Phase 2: workshops and final system selection

During the system selection phase, the best and second-best choices of TMS and vendor candidate are identified. Two or three vendors that receive the highest scores in the RFI phase are invited by the client to demonstrate their systems during a workshop. Depending on the complexity of the desired TMS, this workshop should be planned for at least one day; in complex environments preferably two. The vendors receive a detailed workshop agenda with the invitation from the client and some examples of client-specific transactions or processes. The client will score the vendor demonstrations. These scores are compiled and compared to the RFI scores to illuminate the system's functionality and which system best meets the client's stated business needs. At the end of this phase, the client should know with some degree of certainty what their final choice of system and vendor will be. Their choice is supported through a combination of analysing the results of the RFI and the demonstration of the vendor's systems during the workshops.

FIGURE 10.4   SYSTEM DEMONSTRATION AND FINAL SELECTION

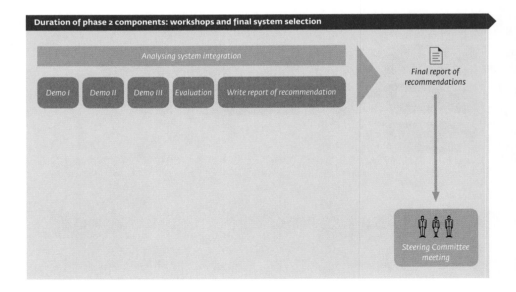

After the system is selected by the client, the next step is the contract negotiations. The importance of these negotiations should not be underestimated, as the selected system may be operational for a period of 5 to 10 years. It is also important that the contract with the vendor reflects not only pricing, but the level of commitment to be given by both parties, such as frequency of upgrades or patches to the core system and the level and length of support given to existing versions of the TMS package. During this phase, the implementation plan is drawn up. This plan should form part of the contract.

Phase 3: integration

Few projects will place as much burden on treasury, compliance and treasury accounting as a TMS implementation. Although much is written about how critical 'project sponsorship' can be, a lack of 'project ownership' can have disastrous results. Without well-defined, documented and understood business needs, the project will wear down because other business-critical initiatives will always take precedence. The best project managers bring a number of skills to the table. The project management methodology is in itself important, but an understanding of treasury practices, the company's business and treasury systems is crucial.

10.6
Conclusion

In the last 10 to 15 years, the market for TMS has seen a lot of changes. Driven by technological change, the treasurer's mindset has changed and he now accepts web-based/cloud-based and vendor-hosted solutions as equals to on-premise installations. This gives TMS vendors a degree of flexibility in product design that was unthinkable years ago. The increased flexibility allows for further acceleration of developments in the TMS market as web- and cloud-based applications in particular allow for rapid deployment of new functionalities. In the past, software updates needed to be shipped to and implemented by every client in order to have the newest version of the system available. Many treasuries and IT departments have opted against a frequent update and enhancement policy in order to reduce project workload. Web- and cloud-based solutions allow for central updating, configuration and testing by the system vendor. This provides the client with the newest functionality while keeping the workload comparatively low and the systems up to date.

Still, these developments have made it increasingly important but also increasingly complicated for treasurers to stay on top of market developments. It is of the utmost importance, especially for treasuries looking at selecting and implementing a new TMS, to take a structured approach to gain insight into the detailed capabilities of potential systems. This is because errors that were made during the selection process are very difficult to correct during implementation.

Chapter 11

The Payment, Clearing and Settlement Process

11 The Payment, Clearing and Settlement Process

11.1
Introduction

In the previous chapters, we provided an overview of transaction instruments and payment products. In this chapter, we explain how such payments are processed. The processing of payments is a complex matter. At the most basic level, a company sends a payment instruction to a bank, which enters it into its payment system for further processing. This ultimately results in crediting the account of the beneficiary (recipient). The complexity is linked to the multiple options available to a bank to reach the account of the recipient. These so-called routing options usually involve processing via 'clearing and settlement institutions'.

A basic understanding of payment processing and, more importantly, the characteristics of the various routing options will help to highlight why the instruments that banks offer differ. As not all banks have access to the same routing options, their capabilities and product offerings also differ. Furthermore, as payment processing is not identical in all countries, that is another factor that explains why there are differences in the products offered in each currency.

Processing payments across national borders in or between different currencies (foreign currency transactions) makes the process even more complex. In the case of cross-border processing, there are normally additional steps and more parties (such as payment service providers or PSPs) involved. In addition, cross-border transfers require special attention from a regulation and legislation perspective. In the Eurozone area, the creation of the Single Euro Payments Area (SEPA) has helped to harmonise domestic solutions and improve cross-border payment capabilities between euro countries on the basis of a pan-European scheme. However, the possibility of adding additional optional services for SEPA payments mean that some historically driven differences between countries are still reflected in the various processing options.

11.2
Participants and process

Making a payment would appear to be a straightforward process. After all, money simply needs to be transferred from the sender to the recipient. In practice, however, this is not always so straightforward. Several payment routing options are available, depending on the relationship of the participants. The model below shows a simplified relationship between the (potential) participants.

FIGURE 11.1   PAYMENT PROCESS

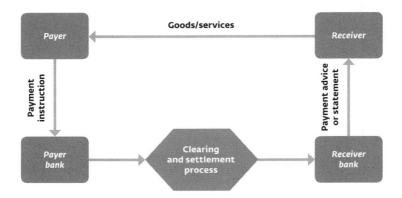

In the example above, the payer and the recipient exchange goods or services (and invoices) for which the payer needs to transfer funds. The payer instructs his bank to transfer these funds. The payer's bank will have various routing options, depending on where the recipient holds its account. The recipient bank will credit the recipient account and will advise the recipient.

Depending on the situation, there could be several participants involved in the process. For example, if the paying bank does not have a direct connection to a clearing and settlement process in order to reach the recipient bank directly, it will need to use another bank to obtain 'correspondent banking' services. This is often the case in foreign currency transactions. In this chapter, we will describe the various parts of the payments process in detail.

11.3
How the bank accepts and reads a payment instruction

Companies can choose various ways to send their payment instructions to a bank. This can be done on paper but is usually carried out electronically (directly into the bank's computer system or via electronic delivery). Whichever way the payment instruction is delivered, the format will be converted so that a bank's electronic payments processing system can read the payment instruction.

Before processing the payment, the bank checks the identity of the payer. This is called authentication. The authentication method depends on the payment instrument used. In the case of credit transfer orders on paper and cheques, the bank will verify the signature. With credit or debit card transactions at the point of sale, the payer's PIN (personal identification number) suffices. Where delivery of a payment instruction takes place via data communication, codes are used to check its authenticity automatically. Each instruction or batch of instructions must be accompanied by an acceptance code or transaction code. This serves as a kind of electronic signature. Customers use standardised software applications to generate the codes.

Before processing the payment, the bank will also check whether the payer's cash balance or credit facility is sufficient to make the payment. If it is not, the payment will be automatically refused and the bank staff will decide how to handle the payment request. They may decide to execute the payment order – in which case the bank allows an overdraft position – or decide to queue the transaction for later execution at a time when the account balance allows this.

A bank will also check further details of the payment in order to make sure these are all formatted correctly to allow further processing. In addition, banks are obliged by their regulators to complete checks against anti-terrorist files and anti-money laundering checks. These could cause a payment to be placed in quarantine for reporting and investigation before execution is allowed. In such a case, a bank is also not allowed to inform the sender of the payment instruction about the status of the payment.

11.4
Routing options

As soon a bank has received a payment order and the payment is found fit for execution, the bank may have several options to execute this payment. Although the various routing options differ according to the country and currency – as well as the market infrastructures – there are a number of core methods. The differentiation between the various routing options is based on the key characteristics of the clearing and settlement method, which play a role in the choice between these options.

Routing options
– In-house
– Real-time gross settlement (RTGS)
– Clearing
– Individual net
– Bulk
– Instant (or real-time payments)
– Correspondent banking

The following diagram shows several routing options: in-house, RTGS, clearing, correspondent banking and instant or real-time clearing and settlement. We will also review cheques as a payment option, although this is not a routing option a bank can choose upon the receipt of a payment instruction. Please note that not all routing options may be available for a specific currency. For example, where in Europe the EBA Clearing provides the EURO1 system for the individual clearing of payments, an equivalent system is not available in the UK.

FIGURE 11.2 PAYMENT ROUTING OPTIONS

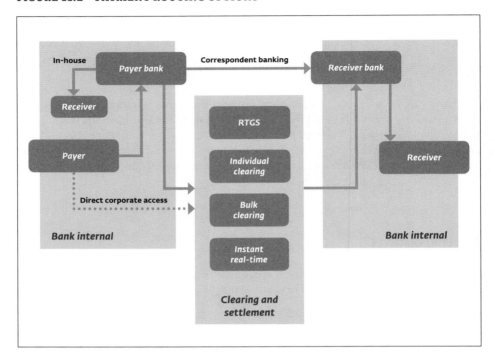

11.4.1   IN-HOUSE SETTLEMENT

Sometimes, the payer's bank and the beneficiary's bank are one and the same – in which case the routing of the payment can be done in the simplest way. We refer to this as an in-house settlement whereby all phases in the payment process occur within a single bank. This is often referred to as a 'book transfer' since the payer's account is debited and the recipient's account is credited within the books of the same bank. If possible, in-house settlement is usually the preferred routing option as it is quick, cheap, risk-free and the funds do not leave the bank (which is preferable from a liquidity management perspective). Usually, a bank will be able to offer preferable conditions for in-house settlement, such as longer COT for same-day value execution.

11.4.2   RTGS

RTGS stands for real-time gross settlement and is a system usually owned and operated by a central bank. As the name explains, an RTGS system is able to handle individual payments on a real-time basis. This makes it a particularly good fit for payments that need to arrive at the recipient within a limited time. An RTGS system passes each payment instruction individually to the central bank with the instruction to debit the paying bank's account at the central bank in favour of the beneficiary bank's account – regardless of any other payment instructions. If the balance of the paying bank is sufficient, the settlement takes place immediately and irrevocably within minutes (or even seconds). Otherwise, the payment might be put in a queue or is rejected immediately.

The settlement in an RTGS system is guaranteed by the central bank. Therefore, the settlement is final and irrevocable. In most RTGS systems, an overdraft is only possible if sufficient central bank eligible collateral (assets which can be used as collateral in order to obtain credit from the central bank) was provided. Some central banks accept collateral on a pledge basis (such as De Nederlandsche Bank), where the assets stay with the central bank for a longer period. Other central banks (such as the Bank of England) provide credit on the basis of repos (repurchase agreement or repo facility is the process of borrowing money by combining the sale of an asset with the subsequent repurchase of that same asset in the future). The Federal Reserve bank in the US relies on a risk management framework where the maximum over-draft depends on specific criteria and can be used with or (against costs) without collateral.

Many central banks in Europe, the US and, to a lesser degree, Asia operate RTGS systems for high-value payments. While the main features 'real-time' and 'gross settlement' are similar across the various RTGS systems, there are differences. Because of the size of the economy, monetary policy, number of direct participants, historical developments and the availability of alternative payment channels, the dynamics in the payment market are different for each currency.

RTGS systems	
– USD	FedWire
– GBP	CHAPS
– EUR	TARGET2
– JPY	BOJnet
– CHF	SIC

11.4.3 CLEARING

In order to process the millions of payments sent daily between different banks, the financial services industry has established specialised institutions known as multilateral clearing institutions, clearing and settlement mechanisms (CSM), clearing centres or automated clearing houses (ACH). These institutions work on a net settlement basis. Based on each bank's outgoing and incoming transfers, the settlement claims are calculated on a net basis. This is different from a gross settlement system (like an RTGS), where all transactions are processed individually and settled on a gross basis.

In general, such clearing institutions perform the following functions:

- Sorting payments and calculating ultimate claims for settlement
- Sending information on settlement claims to the settlement centre (RTGS)
- Exchanging relevant payment information for all individual transactions between the payers' and the beneficiaries' banks

With net settlement, the payer's bank will send payment instructions to the clearing institution. All incoming and outgoing payment instructions from all the participating banks are sorted and matched by the clearing system. This means that for each separate bank, all outgoing transfers are balanced against all incoming transfers and a net amount to be paid or received is calculated. The clearing institution forwards the information about individual payments to the participating (recipient) banks and information regarding the net transfers to the settlement institution (usually the RTGS system where the final exchange of funds will take place). The participating banks are only liable for the resulting net amount and therein lies the advantage of net settlement compared to gross settlement. Because of the netting effect, only a fraction of the total gross amount is required for settlement with the central bank. This saves the bank valuable and scarce central bank money (liquidity).

Note, however, that various providers have slightly different approaches to this process. One of the differences is the number of times during the day when they execute a clearing cycle. Other providers offer the possibility of pushing payments out to the recipient banks without netting in case the total amount has exceeded a certain limit. This will increase the speed by which the payment will reach the beneficiary, but the bank will not benefit from the netting effect and hence needs more liquidity to settle the payments.

In order to participate in a clearing system, participants have to fulfil certain entry criteria aimed at supporting the risk management framework of the clearing system (these can be financial or credit rating criteria). It is also required to have direct access to the local RTGS system to enable the net settlement process. For that reason, in order to obtain direct access to local clearing, a foreign bank will have to operate an expensive local branch with a bank licence and access to the local RTGS.

In principle, the clearing of credit transfers does not differ from the clearing of direct debits. However, the product requirements and rules surrounding refunds or payment rejections differ. Essentially, both types of transactions will result in a payment transfer between the paying bank and the recipient bank although in the case of a direct debit transfer, the recipient bank will initiate the payment order. Still, the clearing and settlement process is similar. In some cases, the clearing institute (such as Equens) will combine the net settlement of credit transfers and direct debits, whereas other clearing institutions (such as EBA STEP2 SCT service and EBA STEP2 DD service) choose to separate the two.

It is important to note that clearing works on the principle that the payment is following the money. The beneficiary's bank will only receive the payment order to credit the beneficiary after this bank has received the funds in its central bank account.

Clearing of individual payments

There are several net settlement clearing systems in the world that combine the processing of individual (real-time) payments with a net-settlement method. In these systems, individual payments are sent to the clearing institution, where the individual payment is checked against the bank's balance within the clearing system. If the balance is sufficient, the payment is executed within the clearing system and the payment order is forwarded immediately (on the same day) to the recipient bank.

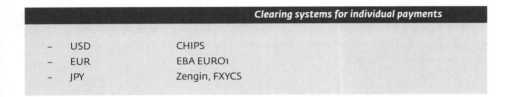

Clearing systems for individual payments		
–	USD	CHIPS
–	EUR	EBA EURO1
–	JPY	Zengin, FXYCS

FIGURE 11.3   CLEARING OF INDIVIDUAL PAYMENTS

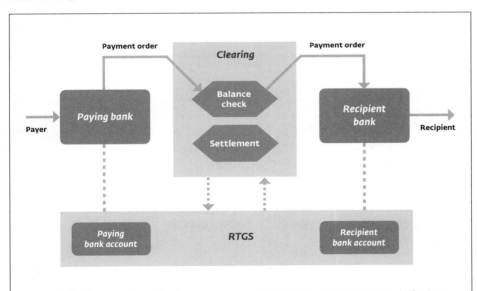

– Paying bank receives instruction from payer and after several checks, forwards the payment order to the clearing institution.
– Clearing institution checks the balance and limits (relevant to the specific risk management framework for the clearing institution) and if found acceptable, will execute the payment order, adjust the balances within the clearing system and forward the payment order to the recipient bank.

– The recipient bank can now apply the funds to the recipient's account.
– At the end of the clearing cycle (usually once a day), the settlement will take place in the relevant RTGS system. First, all debit positions are settled and then all long balances are paid. Sometimes, the debits and credits are done simultaneously via a settlement interface mechanism (such as the ASI settlement of EURO1 in TARGET2).

Payment finality

It is also important to be aware that as soon as a payment is executed within a clearing system and forwarded to the recipient, the payment will be irrevocable. Even if the net settlement of the clearing system has yet to take place (note the difference with a clearing payment, where settlement takes place before the payment execution). Sometimes these systems are referred to as deferred net settlement systems with payment finality. This finality must be based on a sound risk management framework which is accepted, monitored and approved by the regulator (usually the central bank) for the respective currency. As the finality is based on this risk management framework, the timing of the payment execution is dependent on certain checks within the system. Although the netting effect (or liquidity recycling) will usually result in execution within minutes, it could be that a payment is queued in the system for a longer period. Examples of deferred net settlement systems with payment finality based on various risk frameworks are:

Loss-sharing	EUR	EBA EURO1
Pre-funding	USD	CHIPS

Loss-sharing – EURO1

The payment finality in EURO1 is based on the single obligation failure structure (SOS) and the loss-sharing principle. In this framework, bilateral limits are set up between the participants on the basis of which each participant will have a maximum debit cap (based on limits assigned by others to this participant) and a maximum credit cap (based on the limits assigned to other participants).

The overall maximum debit cap is EUR 0.5 billion and for credit it is EUR 1 billion. Participants are obliged to deposit cash collateral at the European Central Bank (ECB) that will create a total cash pool of at least EUR 1 billion. This is sufficient to back up the failure of the end-of-day net settlement of at least two failing participants (as required in the rules set by the ECB for systemically important payments systems).

Via the flexible settlement capability, EURO1 participants are able to fund their EURO1 account if their balance is close to their debit cap. Banks close to their credit cap will see funds transferred from their EURO1 account to their TARGET2 (euro RTGS) account based on a system calculation several times per day.

If one or more participants fail, EBA Clearing will calculate the loss sharing amount for the remaining participants based on the limits they had assigned to the failing participants, and will be able to complete the end-of-day settlement on that basis. The loss-sharing will also make sure the collateral pool is replenished sufficiently for the system to open the following morning.

Pre-funding – CHIPS

The Clearing House Interbank Payments System (CHIPS) is the net settlement system in the US for the country's domestic currency. Like EURO1, every individual payment is checked against the balance of the participants. In CHIPS, the balance can never go below zero and participants have to pre-fund their CHIPS account in order to enable payments to begin flowing between accounts.

CHIPS works with a mandatory pre-funding amount based on the participants' recent payments traffic. During the day, it also defines a maximum credit cap that is a multiple of the mandatory pre-funded amount. And through the day, participants are able to increase their pre-funding and transfer funds (as well as withdraw up to the level of their mandatory pre-fund amount) from CHIPS to their Fedwire account. Towards the end of the day, the credit cap is released and calculations are made to establish the net settlement needed to settle all payments in the queue.

Clearing of bulk payment files

Because of the use of electronically transferred large payment files, bulk clearing systems are able to handle large volumes of payments. From a settlement perspective, the main difference with a clearing system based on individual payment transfers is that the payment orders (packed in files) are only forwarded to the recipient bank after the net settlement obligation is completed. On that basis, there is finality on the payments and the recipient bank can apply the funds to the account of the recipient. In some cases, such as with the older bulk clearing institutions (e.g. BACS), files may be exchanged before the final settlement. Where

FIGURE 11.4   CLEARING OF BULK PAYMENT FILES

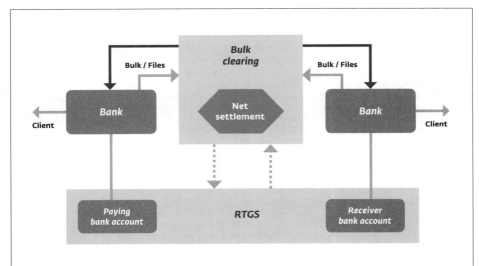

- Banks connected to the clearing send electronic payment files with multiple payment instructions for the other participants.
- The clearing institution performs technical checks on the files and at the end of the clearing cycle, calculates the net settlement requirement for each bank.
- After the calculation, settlement will take place in the relevant RTGS system. First, all debit positions are settled and then all long

balances are paid. Sometimes, the debits and credits are done simultaneously via a settlement interface mechanism (such as the ASI settlement of STEP2 in TARGET2).
- After settlement completion, the clearing institution will create and forward the bulk payment files for each participating bank.
- Some clearing institutions only have one cycle each day while others have several (in some cases, one an hour).

that occurs, there is usually a system of credit limits to support the settlement process and limit the credit risk in the system.

In many cases, transfers processed through a net settlement system are settled on the next working day (or in some cases after two working days). As payment systems develop and come under the pressure from regulatory requirements (such as the Payment Services Directive issued by the European Commission), more clearing institutions have started to work on a same-day basis. These clearing centres specify a cut-off time after which incoming payments are no longer processed for same-day settlement.

This cut-off time is usually linked to the cut-off time of the organisation responsible for settlement. Payments received too late for same-day settlement are set aside for processing on the following working day. The EBA STEP2 system is an example of a same-day system with multiple settlement cycles during the day.

Clearing systems for bulk payments
– USD   Fed ACH
– GBP   BACS
– EUR   EBA STEP2, Equens, STET, EMZ, etc.

Indirect participation
In many cases, it is possible for a bank to connect to a clearing institution as an 'indirect participant'. This means the indirect participant is able to send and receive payments files directly to and from the clearing institute, but the final net settlement is done via a direct participant. The indirect participant and the direct participant will have to set up an arrangement to settle the correct amount between themselves. Usually this is done to connect a branch or affiliate of the same company to a clearing institute but it is also possible that this service is provided to a third-party bank. If the service is provided to a third-party bank, it is obvious that there are risk management issues that need to be addressed.

Some clearing institutions also allow large corporate companies to participate in the clearing. In that case, the corporate is also permitted to send and receive files directly. The clearing institute will inform the supporting direct participant about the files sent by the corporate and the direct participant will have to approve these files prior to the settlement process. In that way, the direct participant can make sure the payment orders sent by the corporate stay within the balance or credit limit agreed.

Although the terms 'clearing' and 'settlement' are often used in conjunction, it is important to understand that both terms represent a different part of the payments process. Clearing is the part of the process where a clearing institution performs the gathering, sorting and calculation of the payment orders provided – individual or bulk – and prepares for transfer of the payment information between the participants in the clearing system. This is followed by the settlement process where the actual legal transfer of the payment obligation is settled and the underlying payments become irrevocable and final. Usually, this settlement takes place in so-called 'central bank money' in the RTGS system.

If an individual payment is processed in an RTGS system, the transfer between the payer and recipient is final and irrevocable and is also referred to as a settlement (although there is no clearing process). In an individual net settlement system with payment finality, we also refer to a settlement as soon as a payment is transferred with finality between the payer and the recipient (within the system rules and risk framework). In such a system, the clearing process will be completed at a later stage (usually at the end of day) where the final settlement of the payment obligation will ultimately take place in central bank money in the RTGS system.

Added-value services

Although the basic principle of the bulk clearing institutions is the same, the services they provide may differ due, for example, to specific domestic requirements. As a result, some clearing institutions provide various extended services (such as checks on payment details, adding account information or risk management services) whereas others only provide basic services (and are often referred to as a thin-service ACH).

Certainly in the Eurozone, all the original domestic clearing institutions are now part of a larger, multi-country area. The introduction of SEPA led to the development of clearing services. Some countries have moved away from their domestic clearing and make use of pan-European bulk clearing services such as EBA STEP2. Other clearing service providers expanded their services in Europe via mergers, partnering or by creating links between clearing services.

Systemic risk

In the clearing and settlement of payments, participants are exposed to systemic risk. There is a risk that one bank's failure to meet its settlement obligations (settlement risk) may have a knock-on effect where an individual participant problem can spread to a local problem in a clearing system, or beyond into a global problem.

For example, if one participant is not able to settle its obligation in a bulk net settlement system, the settlement obligations will have to be recalculated without taking the payments of this participant into account. These new settlement obligations could cause problems for other participants. However, many of the clearing institutions have been set up to help avoid settlement risk and reduce the possible spread of an individual failure into a systemic failure.

If large sums are involved, such a failure might cause significant liquidity or credit problems – and possibly even threaten the stability of financial markets. In 1974, the German Herstatt Bank caused just such a crisis when it could not meet obligations resulting from foreign exchange transactions. In the domino effect that followed, several other banks collapsed. Since then, systemic risk has also been known as the Herstatt risk. During the financial crisis following the default of Lehman Brothers in 2008, the various market infrastructures (RTGS and clearing institutions) have shown resilience with respect to systemic risk. Still, the importance of this issue is high on the agenda of the regulators, who are continuously looking for ways to further reduce systemic risk. Settlement systems, which are referred to as systemically important payment systems (SIPS), are obliged to adhere to the SIPS regulations applicable in their jurisdictions. Following the financial crisis of 2008, the number of rules have increased as well as their impact on the system providers and their users.

11.4.4   INSTANT OR REAL-TIME PAYMENTS

One could argue that the settlement of instant payments is just a variation of individual payment clearing (section 11.4.3). However, the characteristics of the instant payments services that have been emerging globally since 2015, differ substantially from the traditionally setup of clearing mechanisms for individual payments. This explains the choice to describe instant payment as a separate routing option.

The FPS (faster payment system) was introduced in the UK May 2008, and was the first payment system to provide a 24x7 service enabling bank customers to make payments at any time during the day with finality in a very short time frame. We also see these aspects of 24x7 service and finality in the recently introduced instant payment solutions. And similar clearing mechanisms have been launched in more recent years in various currencies with even more aggressive payment timelines (a number of seconds). This additional aspect means these are true instant payment clearing mechanisms. In Europe, the European Payment Council has created the SEPA SCTinst payment scheme, which defines the exact characteristics of the instant payment services. The aim of the scheme is to ensure a pan-European IP service which is similar across all Eurozone countries.

Instant payments largely follow the same logic as the settlement mechanism of individual clearings. Apart from the instant (seconds) character of the payment processing, the most important difference is the way in which finality of the underlying payment is provided. Instant payments need to be pre-funded by the sending bank. In this way, the beneficiary's bank is ensured, at all times, that the funds are available and on that basis, the money is booked on the beneficiary account. This is important, as the instant payment service is available 24x7 while the ability to settle at central bank level is limited to the opening hours of the RTGS system. This pre-funding can be done via a central bank eligible collateral buffer, or by separating cash in a specific account with the central bank.

Figure 11.5 provides a simplified conceptual overview of an instant payment clearing mechanism. An important part of the overall process is the messaging between the sender bank and the beneficiary bank, which ensures the transaction can be completed within the agreed time frame (e.g. 15 seconds). This is significant, as the payer and payee need confirmation of the payment within this period of time in order to complete their business. If, for whatever reason, the payment cannot be confirmed in time, a time-out mechanism will reject the payment and both sender and beneficiary bank will be notified.

FIGURE 11.5   INSTANT PAYMENT MECHANISM (SIMPLIFIED AND CONCEPTUAL)

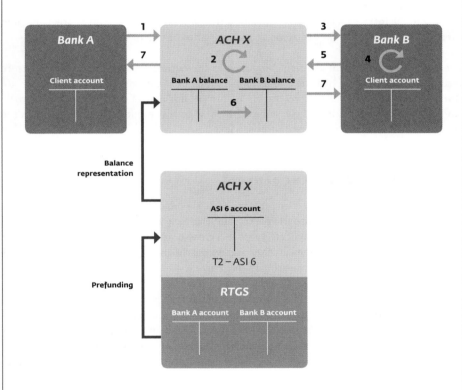

- Bank A and Bank B both provide pre-funding of liquidity to the account of the ACH X with the central bank. This prefunding will ensure finality of the underlying payment. The ACH will reflect the pre-funded amount on the balance of both banks with the ACH.
- Bank A will submit (1) a client payment to ACH X, ACH X will reserve (2) the amount of the payment on the account of Bank A and will forward (3) the payment instruction to Bank B. Bank B checks (4) whether the funds could be applied to the beneficiary account, and informs (5) the ACH X accordingly. If the reply is positive, ACH X will transfer the funds from A to B (6) and inform both banks of the transfer (7), after which the sender will be debited and the recipient credited.
- Please note that there may be different providers and models involved. As such, the above must be seen as a general and simplified description.

While most instant payment solutions make use of a clearing mechanism, whereby settlement finally takes place at central bank level, some jurisdictions (e.g. Australia) choose to create the instant payment mechanism directly in the central bank system. That way, there is factually no difference between clearing and settlement, as each individual payment is cleared and settled (in central bank money) in the same process. In such a case, the RTGS system will apply longer opening hours (24x7) for this service. It is important to note, however, that not all RTGS services will automatically be available for these extended services. Banks are still limited to normal business days with respect to monetary policy operations (open market operations, standing facilities, minimum reserve requirements for credit institutions and, since 2009, asset purchase programmes) and for managing their balance sheet. As result, banks need to understand their payment profile for instant payments in detail in order to be able to provide sufficient pre-funding for periods during which they cannot add funding to the instant payment mechanism. At the same time, banks want to prevent a high overcapacity of their pre-funded amount, as the pre-funding comes at a cost.

There are several different clearing companies in the European market. In order to ensure reachability across these clearings, an interoperability model needs to be in place. As we are still on the forefront of the IP development in Europe, it is not yet completely clear how the landscape will develop. Most likely, some of the first developments will be focussed on the domestic level, rather than the Pan-European level.

11.4.5 CORRESPONDENT BANKING

In many cases, the paying bank is not able to reach the recipient bank directly via the RTGS or a clearing institution, because the paying and the recipient bank are not both direct or indirect participants. This is usually the case in a cross-border situation where the payment is not in the paying bank's home currency and where the paying bank does not have direct access to the local RTGS or local clearing in that currency.

In order to be able to service its clients' needs to make such payments, the paying bank will set up various correspondent banking relationships that enable them to reach the possible recipient banks. Usually, there are several banks in a country that offer correspondent banking services. There are also large network banks with an extensive network of branches around the world with direct access to RTGS and clearing institutions that are able to provide these services for multiple currencies.

Most large banks have an extensive network of correspondent banks in order to offer a wide range of payment services to their clients in all currencies. Often, a correspondent banking relationship involves two banks holding accounts with each other that are denominated in the currency of the country where the correspondent bank is located. An account held by a local bank with a foreign correspondent is usually referred to by the local bank as a 'nostro account'. The same account is known to the correspondent as a 'loro account'. Whether an account is called a nostro account or a loro account depends on the point of view of the bank in question.

FIGURE 11.6   CORRESPONDENT BANKING

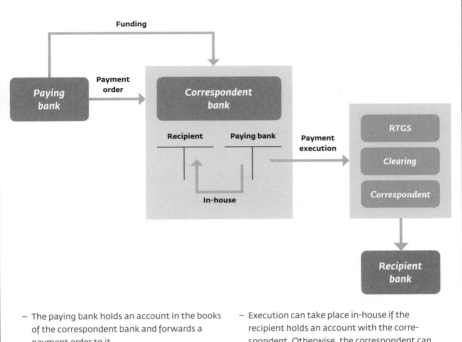

- The paying bank holds an account in the books of the correspondent bank and forwards a payment order to it.
- The correspondent bank performs necessary checks (balance and regulatory) before executing the payment order.
- Depending on product requirements (see paragraph 12.5) and where the recipient holds the account, the correspondent bank has various options.

- Execution can take place in-house if the recipient holds an account with the correspondent. Otherwise, the correspondent can process via the RTGS or the available clearing institutions. The correspondent may even use its own correspondent banking network to execute the payment.
- As an overnight balance on the paying bank account with the correspondent bank is a risk as well as a cost (interest), the paying bank has to fund the account before the end of the day. This is usually done via a money market transaction.

Non-US banks hold their USD accounts with US banks. A German bank's USD account is a nostro account to the German bank and a loro account for its US correspondent. If the German bank wishes to make a payment in USD, it will ask its US correspondent to debit its USD account for the amount in question. Conversely, US banks will hold their EUR accounts with banks in one or more EUR countries. If a US bank wishes to make a payment in EUR, it will ask one of its correspondents in the euro countries to debit its EUR account. Nostro account holders will have to manage the balance on their nostro account on a daily basis and need to ensure they fund the position created on this account.

11.4.6 CHEQUE CLEARING

Alongside credit transfers and direct debits, many customers still have the option to pay by cheque (please refer to chapter 8). Overall, there has been a decline in the use of cheques for payment and in some countries the use of cheques has completely vanished (for example, in the Netherlands). The use of cheques is still quite common in some European countries (e.g. France, the UK).

When a recipient presents a cheque to its bank to cash, the recipient bank will start the collection process in order to obtain the funds from the bank that issued the cheque (i.e. the payer's bank). The collection process differs in each country and sometimes several collection options are available.

The simplest collection process is the 'on-us' collection, whereby the recipient bank and the paying bank (cheque issuing bank) are the same. In that case, the cheque can be cleared within the books of the bank.

For any other situation, the recipient bank will have to collect the funds from the paying bank in another way. This can be done via bilateral agreements, whereby the paying and recipient bank have agreed on a process to settle the cheques between themselves. This is comparable to a correspondent banking settlement. In many countries – such as the US, the UK and Japan – cheque clearing has been set up alongside other methods, whereby a central cheque clearing system enables the collection (and settlement) of cheques between the recipient bank and paying bank. Usually, this is based on net settlement techniques that are the same as those for the settlement of credit transfers or direct debits.

11.5
Which routing is used?

One key question is on what basis the paying bank makes its choice between the various routing options. As every routing option has its own characteristics, the bank must consider various aspects in order to make the most effective and cost-efficient choice.

Factors for consideration include:

- Product requirements
- Reachability
- Transaction costs
- Risk
- Liquidity efficiency

Routing option	Examples	Transaction types	Advantages	Disadvantages
In-house	N/A	All.	Fast, cheap, no risk, no liquidity impact.	Limited reach.
RTGS	TARGET2 CHAPS Fedwire BOJnet	High-value, predominantly for settlement of high-value inter-bank financial transactions but also capable of handling low-value/urgent commercial transactions, settlement of ancillary systems such as net settlement systems.	Fast, same-day, real-time, low-risk, reach, ability to control the settlement time (if sufficient credit capacity is provided).	High transaction costs, relatively high use of liquidity.
Individual net settlement	EBA EURO1 CHIPS FXYCS ZENGIN	Systems are usually designed to handle a certain part of the payment market. They fill the gap and partly overlap with RTGS and bulk settlement systems. This could be either: inter-bank and commercial transactions, (high and low-value, urgent and non-urgent).	Cheap compared with RTGS, liquidity-efficient, same-day, intra-day finality, reach.	No control over settlement time due to queuing mechanisms, transaction value limited depending on the risk framework, possible risk between direct participants or the system. Note: FPS is an exception and does not queue transactions.
Bulk net settlement	EBA STEP2 BACS Fed ACH EQUENS STET	Low-value commercial transactions, credit transfers and direct debits.	Cheap, liquidity efficient, low risk, reach in the domestic area. Note: if the number of settlement cycles increases, the liquidity efficiency will decrease as the netting effect will decrease.	Reach can be limited for cross-border transactions in Europe, low speed, settlement depending on settlement cycle (which can be as long as two days or as short as several times per day).
Instant payments	EQUENS STET EBA RT1 Straks-clearingen InstaPay FPS	Low-value commercial transactions, person-to-person, credit transfers. Note: The definition of which use cases are included in Instant payments varies per jurisdiction.	Fast, immediate availability of funds for re-use, no-risk, 24x7.	Threshold on amount, liquidity inefficient due to pre-funding costs, high peak processing capability needed.
Correspondent banking	N/A	All – depending on the agreements made between the banks.	Provides the possibility to extend services in currencies where the bank has no presence, no direct liquidity costs (dependent on arrange-ments with correspondent bank).	Expensive, less competitive service offering (for example COT) compared with the local providers, credit risk against correspondent bank.

11.5.1   SERVICE REQUIREMENTS

Part of the strategy of a bank involves defining a certain number of services / products that can be offered to clients. The requirements with regards to the payments process will differ for each product, while the product suite offered will differ for each bank. As a result, each bank will have a certain set of requirements which it needs to fulfil to service its clients. Based on those requirements, a bank will set up internal systems to provide products and services but it will also make strategic choices with respect to an ability to connect to various routing channels (such as RTGS, clearing institutions or the correspondent banking network).

A bank is not always free to choose a certain settlement method based on the various requirements and routing options available. An example is SEPA (Single European Payment Area), which obliges the bank to process payments via the available SEPA-compliant clearing mechanisms whenever a payment was initiated as a SEPA payment.

Speed
One of the requirements could be the speed with which the transaction has to reach the recipient. If there is no specific requirement to reach the recipient within a certain time frame, other aspects of the payment requirements will drive the choice for the payment channel. If there is a specific requirement to deliver the payment before a certain time on a specific day (or even the same day), special arrangements can be made to route the payment through a channel so this can be guaranteed.

This is often facilitated by direct participation in the RTGS system. There are also examples where an individual net settlement system can be used for urgent payments. For example, the large Dutch banks use the EBA EURO1 system for processing their urgent payments up to an amount of EUR 11 million. If the underlying payment was initiated as an instant payment, there is a specific requirement to deliver the payment to the beneficiary within seconds and with all required messaging etc. The payment order can only be executed within a compliant instant payment mechanism.

Please note that even in cases where speed is not a specific requirement, there are often regulatory requirements to process payments within a certain time frame. The European Payments Service Directive (PSD2) (see Chapter 22) requires banks to process incoming payments within one day and the recipient bank has to book the funds to the account of the recipient on the same day (with same-day value) that it received the funds in the clearing and settlement process. The local bulk clearing system is usually the slowest routing channel available but is – at a minimum – able to comply with the regulatory requirements.

Cut-off time
Another aspect to consider is the latest possible time by which a payment can be accepted in order to be transferred to the recipient on the same day. For some companies, it is important to have the ability to deliver payment instructions for same-day execution later in the day. They will look for a bank that is able to give them a late cut-off time (COT) for sending payments.

The COT for processing payments depends partly on the routing channel. Every clearing and settlement mechanism has a deadline by which a bank can send payments to its system. Only participants that are sending payments directly to such systems will benefit from this. As a result, they are able to offer a better COT to their clients compared with those that depend on the correspondent banking services of other banks. In all cases, access to the RTGS system offers the best possible COT capabilities.

Another aspect driving the COT is the ability of the bank to fund its position. If the paying bank executes a payment for a client, it also must be able to fund this payment before the end of day. In certain markets, this funding ability can be restricted for foreign banks but is also determined by the bank's own operating hours across various time zones. A purely European-based bank with no access to the local RTGS or clearing in the US, and which only operates during European office hours, will not be able to process USD payments after those hours. Meanwhile, a European-based global bank with direct access to the Fed and CHIPS will be able to process payments until the end of the day in the US.

Amount of payment
Not all payment channels are able to handle all sizes of payments. Some payment channels restrict the maximum amount of a payment. That includes the UK FPS, where a maximum amount was agreed between the participants. Other systems' settlement models make them less fit for processing payments beyond a certain size. The EBA EURO1 system is limited because of its maximum debit and credit cap. Still, due to the use of sophisticated algorithms, EURO1 is able to process payments of amounts that substantially exceed the caps. In practice, however, such a payment could stay in the queue for a while. For that reason, most banks will only send payments up to a certain maximum amount (e.g. EUR 300 million) to EURO1.

Please note that the amount and the speed of a payment are often linked. Although the importance of a payment and the need to process it quickly increase when the payment size increases, that may not always be the case. A USD 1000 payment can be just as critical for a company (perhaps because it is linked to a new building lease contract) as a EUR 50 million payment (perhaps because it is needed to pay for the delivery of a shipload of new cars). Although in the past, clearing systems were designed to either handle high (RTGS) or low (bulk) value payments, more and more clearing systems are able to handle a wide range of payments of low to high-value amounts.

11.5.2   REACHABILITY

Before making a choice between the available routing options, a bank will have to determine via which route the recipient bank is reachable. For this purpose, a bank maintains routing tables where it can see which routing channel or channels can be used to reach the recipient bank for a specific currency.

Banks exchange information on how they can be reached. In addition, the clearing institutions usually provide routing tables where they state which banks are reachable via their system. If a European Bank A informs the banking community they are reachable for USD payments via their (correspondent banking) account with Bank B, the paying bank can base its processing on this. If the paying bank has direct access to CHIPS or the Fed, it can reach Bank B directly, as it is also a direct participant. Otherwise, the paying bank can instruct its own correspondent bank for USD transfers to Bank B for the account of Bank A with the recipient as ultimate beneficiary.

11.5.3   TRANSACTION COSTS

Ultimately, a bank will try to minimise the costs of payment processing. If all other aspects are taken into account and possible payment routing options are defined, the bank will almost certainly choose the most cost-effective routing channel available. A bank must take all costs of a specific routing channel into account rather than just the individual transaction costs. A direct connection to a clearing institution will usually also result in annual fees, possible shareholder costs, connection costs, costs for maintenance and costs for testing. Whether or not to connect directly will be part of the strategic choices a bank must make and depends on the number of transactions it expects to process and the products it decides to offer its customers. Often, clearing institutions and RTGS systems work with tiered pricing models. The more payments sent, the lower the average transaction price. That means larger players in the market are able to process at lower prices than smaller players. As a result, some market participants choose to send their payments through a larger player in the market rather than to become a direct participant in the clearing. For these participants, that option is ultimately cheaper. The choice also depends on whether the service level of the correspondent bank is sufficient.

11.5.4   RISK

There are various perspectives to consider with respect to the risks of payment processing. For example, one can look at the reputational and financial risk involved in not being able to process a payment according to the agreed terms. Usually, this aspect of risk is covered sufficiently by choosing the adequate channel based on the product requirements. There is another risk element a bank needs to consider when choosing between the various routing channels, namely that of processing via a correspondent banking network or participating in clearing institutions. Processing via a real-time RTGS system does not involve any risk for the paying or recipient bank.

Correspondent banking and risk
It's obvious that if a paying bank is processing via a correspondent banking network, the fact that it holds an account with the correspondent bank does involve a certain risk. A positive balance on the account is basically a claim on the correspondent bank which could be at risk if the correspondent bank runs into trouble. When the account is in debit, however, the correspondent bank has a claim on the paying bank, which could be at risk if the paying bank is not able to fund that position.

For that reason, a correspondent banking provider will control the debit balances on loro accounts by assigning and managing credit limits. Usually, these credit limits are uncommitted and sometimes they are required to be offset by collateral. A paying bank will also have to consider alternative payment routing options when using a correspondent banking network. If it is relying on a single correspondent, there is a risk that it will not be able to service its client if the correspondent, for whatever reason, is not able to provide services. A paying bank will have to ascertain how quickly an alternative correspondent banking relation could be put in place or whether, as an alternative, it needs to hold a second correspondent banking relation in the same currency.

Risk related to clearing institutions

The set-up of the various clearing institutions varies. For bulk net settlement systems, the direct financial risk is limited as the settlement will only take place after the net settlement is completed. In such a system, the main risk in relation to payment traffic is that underlying payments to and from a specific participant will not be settled if the participant fails to fulfil the net settlement obligation and payments sent are returned to the paying bank. The paying bank will then need to assess alternative methods to settle those payments.

For individual net settlement systems, the risk for the participants depends on the specific risk framework. As the individual payments settle intra-day with payment finality, there is no financial risk involved with the payment itself. However, in a system based on a loss-sharing principle (such as the EBA EURO1 system), the failure of a participant to meet its end-of-day net settlement obligation will result in loss-sharing up to the amount of pre-agreed bilateral limits for the remaining participants. In systems where the risk framework is based on full collateralisation or pre-funding, there is no financial risk between the participants. Finally, there is a financial risk for direct participants in clearing institutions where they are also obliged to become shareholders of the clearing system. As a shareholder, they could be forced to cover the clearing institution's costs or losses.

11.5.5 LIQUIDITY EFFICIENCY

The recent financial crises have highlighted the fact that the entire market had underestimated liquidity risk (the risk that you cannot settle short-term obligations because of insufficient liquid funds (cash) and the inability to turn assets into liquidity). This awareness and the introduction of various regulatory requirements has increased the pressure on liquidity and subsequently increased the costs as well. Whereas in the past, liquidity efficiency was not the most important aspect to take into account when considering payment routing, the increased costs as well as the increased scarcity of liquid assets has pushed this factor higher up on the list of considerations. The cost and availability of liquidity are increasingly becoming the driving factors in the selection of a payment channel or when considering participation in a clearing institution. A lack of access to liquidity can also guide banks' strategic choices as it can affect their ability to offer certain products.

Liquidity efficiency in clearing and settlement should be compared between the various payment routing options within the same currency. As dynamics in the payments markets for various currencies are different, it does not make sense to compare the liquidity efficiency between clearing institutions of different currencies. Meanwhile, from a development point of view, the various clearing institutions are learning from each other in order to improve the liquidity efficiency of the clearing mechanism.

Broadly speaking, RTGS systems are less liquidity-efficient compared to individual clearing systems that allow a certain amount of netting. An end-of-day net settlement system is the most liquidity-efficient clearing mechanism, as it maximally benefits from the netting effect by netting across all payments during the day. However, when (bulk) net clearing is settled in a number of cycles during the day, the netting efficiency decreases. An imbalance between the cycles can dramatically decrease the liquidity efficiency. And because the settlement cycle is very time-sensitive, the liquidity efficiency may decrease up to the level of RTGS settlement.

Due to the requirement of pre-funding for the settlement of instant payments and the fact that no delay is acceptable for the underlying payment, this IP settlement method is the least liquidity-efficient. If the use cases for which the IP is applied remain restricted to small retail payments, the liquidity impact is limited. However, if IP settlement develops towards 'the new normal', the liquidity costs for payments will dramatically increase.

Please refer to figure 11.6 for a comparison of the EUR clearing and settlement market from a liquidity efficiency, speed and cost perspective.

FIGURE 11.6 COMPARISON. EUROPEAN EUR CLEARING AND SETTLEMENT MARKET

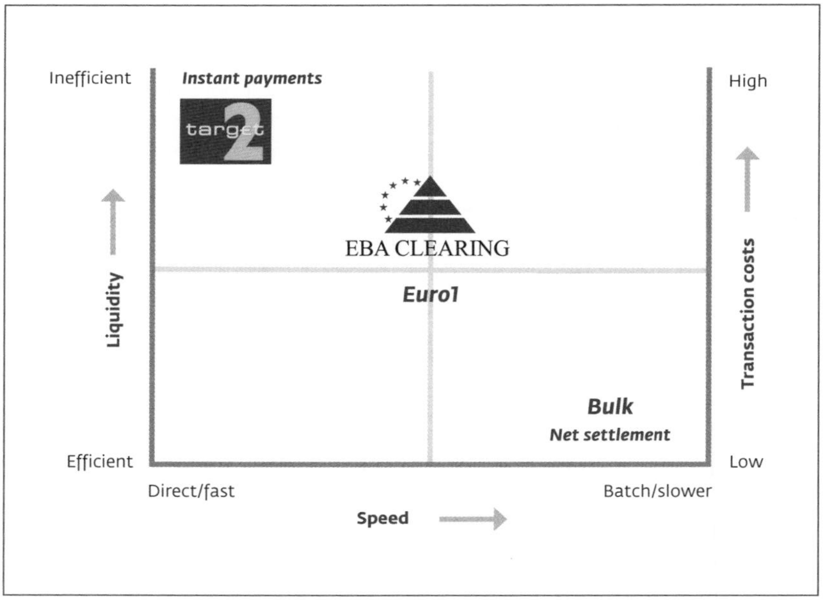

11.6
Local and cross-border transfers

The processing of payment orders across international borders also varies from country to country. In banking practice, the routing of transfers is primarily determined by the location where the accounts are maintained. For this reason, banks make a distinction between:

- Local transfers
- Cross-border transfers through a correspondent bank
- Cross-border transfers through remote local payments
- Transfers via international clearing systems

11.6.1 LOCAL TRANSFERS

A local transfer is a transfer between two accounts in the same country and in the local currency. The account holders may be residents or non-residents. In every country, the national clearing institutions only settle transfers in the local currency. For example, USD transfers are settled in the US, transfers in GBP are settled in the UK. Currently, clearing institutions for EUR transfers in Eurozone countries mainly handle domestic transfers in EUR. With the establishment of the Single Euro Payment Area (SEPA), EUR transfers between Eurozone countries are now regarded as local transfers.

Some countries are divided into separate regions where each has its own affiliate of the central bank and a clearing centre. In the US, there are 12 different regions that each have their own regional central bank (or Federal Reserve Bank (Fed)) and automated clearing house (ACH). All ACHs are connected and act as a single clearing house for inter-regional transfers. Settlement for inter-regional transfers takes place at the Federal Reserve Bank in New York and the settlement between the ACHs and different regional Feds is transparent to the sender and recipient.

11.6.2 CROSS-BORDER TRANSFERS THROUGH A CORRESPONDENT BANK

A cross-border transfer is a transfer between two accounts held in different countries or a transfer between two accounts in the same country but in a non-local currency. Cross-border transfers can be executed via correspondent banks or international clearing institutions rather than local clearing institutions.

The routing of a cross-border payment using a correspondent bank is a relatively costly and time-consuming procedure. As a result, banks have explored ways to speed up the correspondent banking system while reducing costs. This upgrading process is commonly referred to as enhanced correspondent banking. Enhanced correspondent banking systems all make use of special – or preferential – relations between banks and are based on agreements between the participating banks on common formats (or formatting arrangements) for file transfers between different countries. The club arrangements described in the next section are an example of this.

11.6.3 CROSS-BORDER TRANSFERS THROUGH REMOTE LOCAL PAYMENTS

Larger multinational corporations (MNCs) may also choose to open non-resident accounts abroad, often at a foreign bank. Suppose, for example, a France-based MNC opens a USD account at Bank A in the US, a GBP account at Bank B in London and a EUR account at Bank C in Germany. An MNC can now send payment instructions directly to these banks and make use of each bank's electronic banking packages. The payments they make directly from these accounts are fed directly into the local clearing system. However, the accounts are controlled remotely (which is why we refer in them as 'remote local payments').

One disadvantage of this procedure is that the MNC needs separate electronic banking packages for all non-resident accounts. International banks have found the following solutions for this:

- Network banks
- Club arrangements or partnerships

Remote local payments through international network banks

Another variant of this model is the 'in-house' arrangement. That is where a large network bank with international branches or subsidiaries becomes a member of relevant local clearing and settlement systems in different countries. In this way, the bank can route international transfers through its in-house network and enter them into the country of destination's local clearing system. Large global banks use this model. Clients of these network banks can open accounts at relevant international branches rather than at various local banks. The network bank's electronic banking package can gain access to these accounts and make either local or remote local transfers. Although setting up these direct connections is costly, network banking does offer advantages compared with a club of banks (see below) or partnerships. Such advantages can include one electronic interface, one service level agreement, uniformity in pricing, later cut-off times and the option of global liquidity management though global pools. Please refer to section 13.5 for more information on payment routing options.

Remote local payments through club arrangements or partnerships

One type of enhanced correspondent banking is the 'club' arrangement or partnership. This consists of agreements between a group of banks (one or more in each country) that provide one another with indirect access to the domestic clearing system in which each participates. Sometimes these arrangements operate in real-time and use proprietary harmonised standards. That way, the club banks can transfer funds directly between their customers' accounts. An example of this model is IBOS, in which several European and American banks participate. Banks participating in such partnerships offer clients the opportunity to open accounts at their partner banks. Companies can operate these accounts using the electronic banking package of their own (local) bank.

11.6.4 CROSS-BORDER PAYMENTS THROUGH AN INTERNATIONAL CLEARING SYSTEM

The processing of cross-border payments through an international clearing system is unique to the euro. It is the only currency that is cleared in several countries via several clearing mechanisms and via several central banks. The EURO RTGS system TARGET2, EBA EURO1, STEP1 and STEP2 are examples of clearing systems that are able to process cross-border payments. With the development of SEPA, a number of originally domestic automated clearing houses (ACH) developed capabilities (via links or partnerships with other ACHs) to process EUR payments across borders.

In essence, the EUR payments market is developing towards a domestic market where the difference between domestic and cross-border processing among the EUR countries will diminish. In some respects, the EUR situation can be compared with the US, where several Federal Reserve Banks are also linked with regional ACHs. But whereas the US payment market developed as a domestic market, it will still take some time before we can really look at the Eurozone as a domestic area from a payment, clearing and settlement perspective.

11.7
Differences between local and cross-border payments

Besides the differences in clearing and settlement arrangements, there are several practical differences between local payments on the one hand and cross-border and remote local payments on the other. That explains why a non-local (i.e. cross-border or remote local) payment is generally less easy to process and settle than a local payment. Key factors for consideration include:

- Reporting obligations to the central bank
- Exchange charges and foreign exchange risk
- Float
- Exchange control regulations
- Other risks associated with cross-border payments

11.7.1 REPORTING OBLIGATIONS TO THE CENTRAL BANK

Monetary authorities use international payments data to calculate their national balances of payments. These balances provide an overview of a country's imports and exports. The monetary authorities make a formal distinction between domestic and foreign payments when preparing the national balance of payments. They distinguish between:

- Domestic payments – where both the paying and the recipient parties are residents of the same country
- Foreign payments – where either the paying or the recipient party is a non-resident of a country

All foreign payments are included in the balance of payments on a cash basis. This includes outgoing foreign payments for imports and incoming foreign payments for exports. If an individual or a company is not officially registered in the country in question, the term 'non-resident' is used. In other words, resident status does not depend on the nationality of the parties but on their place of permanent residence. A resident of a country is either a natural person (consumer) registered in the register of births, deaths and marriages, or a legal person (company) registered in the public register.

Consumers and most small and medium-sized companies operate primarily within their own countries. Consequently, they tend to use the international payment services offered by their domestic banks. However, many internationally active corporations will either hold foreign currency accounts at their local bank or local currency accounts at banks in countries where they are active. There are two types of accounts – resident accounts and non-resident accounts.

Resident accounts

A resident account is an account held by a resident of a country at a resident bank in the same country. A resident account may be denominated in local currency or in a foreign currency. Holding a resident account in a foreign currency at a local bank has the benefit that the company does not need to buy and sell the currency in question each time it pays or receives funds in that currency.

Non-resident accounts (offshore accounts)

A non-resident account – or offshore account – is an account held by a non-resident with a resident bank. A non-resident account is almost always denominated in the local currency of the resident bank, such as a USD account with a bank in the US. Such an account gives the company direct access to the US clearing system.

In many countries, transactions between residents and non-residents have to be reported to the central bank. Reporting obligations differ from country to country. Some countries, such as the US and the UK, do not require any central bank reporting. Others, including Germany and France, require all international transactions above a certain amount to be reported.

11.7.2   EXCHANGE CHARGES AND FOREIGN EXCHANGE RISKS

When a local payment takes place, the parties involved mainly use the local currency. In the case of non-local fund transfers, payments are often made in a currency that is foreign to at least one of the parties. Either the payer will exchange the amount payable from its own currency, or the beneficiary will exchange the amount received into its own currency. Sometimes the currency used is foreign to both parties, so both will have to make an exchange to, or from, their own currency at some point. These currency exchanges obviously incur costs. In addition, parties exchanging currencies also run foreign exchange risks because exchange rates may fluctuate between the date of the contract agreement and final payment (please refer to chapter 19).

11.7.3   EXCHANGE CONTROL REGULATIONS

When international transfers are executed, the parties involved have to take account of the exchange control regulations both in their own country and the other party's country. In many countries, international transfers are still subject to restrictions. A common rule in many countries is that funds may not be transferred out of the country unless they relate to an underlying trade transaction. Moreover, currencies in some countries cannot be freely exchanged against other currencies.

11.7.4   FLOAT

Sometimes, the book date on which the payer's account is debited is one (or more) day(s) earlier than the date on which the beneficiary's bank account is credited. In other words, the banks involved retain the amount of the transfer for processing during a short period of time. This is called 'banking float' or more commonly 'float'. Generally speaking, banking float is more common with cross-border payments than with local payments. In countries with less developed financial infrastructures, banking float may also occur with local payments. Generally, banking float does not exist with credit transfers between two accounts held with the same bank (as is the case with network banks).

Banks may also generate additional income by applying a different value date from the date on which they make the entry on behalf of the customer's account in their bookkeeping system. The payer's bank may cease to pay interest one or two days before the book date and the beneficiary's bank may only pay interest one or two days after the book date. This practice – called value dating – differs from country to country and is subject to arrangements made between banks and their clients. Please note that in some countries, the application of float on book date or value date is restricted by regulation. For example, in Europe this restriction on 'taking float' was included in the Payment Services Directive (PSD).

11.7.5   OTHER RISKS ASSOCIATED WITH NON-LOCAL PAYMENTS

Apart from foreign exchange risks, parties involved in non-local payments run other risks such as debtor risk and banking risk. For example, there is a risk that the debtor or the debtor's bank will fail to pay on time. These risks also exist with local payments but they are more difficult to manage if the parties are located in different countries and are subject to different legal systems. Also, creditors sometimes run a political risk, i.e. the risk that the authorities will delay – or even prohibit – payment because of political upheavals or financial problems. Banks have developed special products to mitigate against such risks. These include documentary credits and export credit insurance.

11.8
Standards and SWIFT

As a result of the huge growth in international payment volumes since the 1960s, banks have been facing rising costs as well as difficulties in processing payments rapidly and efficiently. In response to this challenge, several European and US banks decided to set up an automated message transmission system linked to the banks' own computers. This led to the foundation of the Society for Worldwide Interbank Financial Telecommunication (SWIFT), which was created to establish a network for inter-bank communications. This so-called SWIFTNet network is commonly used by banks. The main service they employ is called SWIFTNet FIN. The messages in relation to this standard are called MT messages. An MT202, for example, represents a fund transfer between two banks, an MT103 represents a customer credit transfer and an MT940 an account statement.

The development of standards has become increasingly important over the years and is not restricted to the so called 'inter-bank space'. Today, the development of standards is organised within the International Organization of Standardization (ISO). In this way, the financial industry as a whole is looking to develop true global standards based on the ISO 20022 standards development method. SWIFT continues to provide network services for the transmission of messages in these new ISO 20022 standards. Of course, banks or other participants in the financial industry can also select a proprietary network to exchange financial messages. The newly developed standards are different from the 'old' MT messages. In ISO 20022, the most commonly used syntax is extensible mark-up language (XML) (please see chapter 10 for more information). In the payments industry, the vast majority of messaging is still based on MT messages. In some specific cases, a switch has been made to messages based on XML formats. The most obvious example is SEPA – where the scheme is based on ISO 20022 XML messages. In order for banks to become SEPA-compliant, they must be able to send payments in the new formats to the SEPA-compliant clearing mechanisms.

While the development of standards continues, it is expected that in time, the financial industry will have to migrate from the old MT messages to the new ISO 20022 – XML-based messages. It is essential that such a migration is coordinated on a global basis as global payment, clearing and settlement relies on the ability of banks to communicate with each other in a standardised way.

11.9
Developments in clearing and settlement

Although the world of clearing and settlement is constantly developing, this is not a world characterised by revolutionary change. However, one can certainly see that new technology has been introduced over the years as well as new ways of working and new cooperation models, resulting in an ever increasing speed of payment processing and processing efficiency (from multiple days to intraday to instant).

The main reason why this part of the financial industry is developing along evolutionary rather than revolutionary lines is because clearing and settlement can be seen as the plumbing of the financial eco-system. All financial products which ultimately result in a movement of cash depend on the efficient functioning of the clearing and settlement between banks. The systemic stability of the various providers (e.g. banks, clearing houses, central banks) is essential to ensure a stable clearing and settlement environment. As such, the central banks, in their role as supervisor, closely monitor these systemically important participants and systems. New technology or other enhancements (e.g. functional, rules, standards) are carefully reviewed in the industry, discussed, aligned and ultimately planned and tested before introduction.

Looking back at the financial crisis, we can conclude that the aim of creating a stable clearing and settlement function has been very successful. Despite the significant stress in the markets leading to unusual volatility and peaks in processing (number of transactions as well as value), we have not seen any disruption in processing as a result of the crisis. One can imagine that hampering clearing and settlement processes would have had a severe impact on the stress situation itself and would most likely have made the situation worse.

Nevertheless, we do see a constant stream of initiatives to improve the clearing and settlement space. In addition to the most recent emerging instant payments services, it is also clear that a number of central banks are reviewing (or have already planned changes to) their RTGS system with the aim of enhancing these to drive efficiency, align services to changing client needs and lower costs. Furthermore, we see that the introduction of ISO 20022 message standards is on the agenda of several market infrastructures.

The industry is also looking at the application of distributed ledger technology in the clearing and settlement space. In many different countries and areas, banks and sometimes central banks cooperate to explore the possibilities, often with FinTech organisations. However, it is still 'early days' in this respect. As mentioned previously, the stability of the clearing and settlement space is crucial and, as such, much work still needs to be done to prove the soundness of the legal underpinnings, robust governance structure, technological stability and effectiveness of the solution to address client needs. For the time being, these initiatives are limited to investigations, sandboxing or proof of concepts. It can be expected that if these initiatives lead to practical applications, the introduction will be in incremental steps.

Liquidity Management

Chapter 12

Cash Balances Management

12 Cash Balances Management

12.1
Introduction

As we have seen so far, liquidity management can be broken down into two main activities – cash balances management and (short-term) investment management and funding. Both tasks need to be performed each day by the cash manager. Cash balances management must be completed before starting investment and funding activities. Deficit and surplus balances should be offset and net balances have to be moved into one centralised location from where the cash manager can initiate investment or funding transactions.

Therefore, effective balances management is a fundamental requirement for successful liquidity management. To execute balances management effectively, the cash manager requires accurate information about the available balances in all countries and across all currencies. In addition, the cash manager must have the instruments to move these balances into a central location either manually or by using automated cash pooling techniques.

In this chapter, we will provide a high-level overview of cash balances management including its definition, objectives and – most importantly – the basic tools, such as automated cash pooling. A more extensive overview of cash pooling techniques can be found in chapter 13. Meanwhile, in this chapter we will highlight some of the organisational aspects as well as key trends in cash balances management.

12.2
The basics of cash balances management

Large international companies typically have various current accounts with different banks in many countries and currencies. These accounts are used by the company's operating entities to collect receivables and disburse funds to settle their obligations. The continuous flow of funds into and out of the company generates daily fluctuations in balances. Treasurers need to manage these balances in such a way as to avoid a large overdraft position on individual accounts, and the aggregation of current accounts as this would likely incur high interest costs.

Similarly, they seek to avoid large surplus balances because these funds can better be used to reduce overdraft positions, pay down external debts or invest in the money markets where they can potentially yield a higher interest income. In order to avoid these adverse effects, the company should centralise the surplus balances every day to offset deficits on current accounts in the same currency and move residual balances to the cash concentration bank for investments or redemption of outstanding loans.

Before cash movements are initiated, the cash manager will first collect up-to-date information about all balances and identify 'value balances' per value date. These are the balances that are used by the bank to calculate interest. In most countries and for most currencies, banks will pay interest on credit balances and allow overdraft positions on the current account while charging debit interest. Credit interest is generally much lower than the yield generated on short-term investments in the money market. And debit interest is generally much higher than short-term loans in the money market.

Cash balances management: definition and objectives

The daily movement of value balances or available balances between bank accounts in order to:
- Offset debit and credit balances
- Maximise interest income on net surplus balances
- Minimise interest charges on net debit positions
- Reduce outstanding debt

Cash balances management is quite easy and straightforward when the company has operations in only one country and one currency, and when only one bank is used. In that case, the bank is able to manage the balances automatically. When balances are held with various banks in different countries, the movement of balances will consist of more steps and subsequent processes because funds have to be transferred through local or international clearing. That means the transfers must be initiated well before cut-off time. It also means that the cash manager, when striving for optimisation, must forecast incoming payments through clearing and take these expected inflows into account before initiating balance transfers.

All of the above activities and objectives will apply to operations in one currency. For example, this means that one single balance position should be created for all EUR accounts and for all USD accounts. However, the above strategies can also be applied across various currencies. So companies will seek to avoid opposite balances – such as surplus balances in EUR and deficits in USD – at the same time. This can be achieved by using currency swaps to convert EUR into USD for a short period of time.

It is clear that an accurate balance forecast is critical. However, in practice it is difficult to predict the expected balance position precisely. Therefore, this amount is left on the 'master' (central) account without being invested in (surplus) or funded (deficit) from the money market. Having a net residual balance is not a problem. Which side is most beneficial depends on the differences in interest margins on the current account. Usually, the margin from the bank on debit balances is much larger than the margin on credit balances. That means the company can save costs by steering the overall balance into a surplus position.

12.3
Tools for managing cash balances

The current account is the main vehicle for managing cash balances. In addition, companies will need various instruments to efficiently move the balances across these accounts and achieve the objectives described above. Next we will discuss two types of instruments: balance information and cash concentration.

12.3.1   BALANCE INFORMATION

The first step in cash balance management is to determine the balances on all accounts and – to be more precise – to identify the expected (value) balance at the end of the day. It is the expected end-of-day balance that must be moved (surplus balance) or funded (deficit balance) in order to achieve the intended optimal position. To determine the end-of-day value balance, the cash manager will start by identifying the opening balance. This balance is usually equal to the previous day's closing balance. Both the closing and opening balance are generic items in standardised end-of-day balance reports. In addition, incoming and outgoing payments during the day will have to be taken into account in order to calculate the expected end-of-day value balance.

This kind of information is usually needed early in the morning, because the treasurer will have to plan and execute the required balance transfers as well as the funding and investment transactions. At that time, many of the incoming and outgoing payments cannot be reported by banks because they still need to be processed. This means that the treasurer will need accurate forecasts of expected inflows and outflows of the upcoming day. These need to be provided by the company's accounts receivable and accounts payable departments.

Online and offline bank channels are used to show the opening balances as well as the payments and collections (thus far) executed by the banks through intra-day transaction reports. Together with the internal forecasts of expected transactions, a calculation can be made of the anticipated end-of-day balance. These balance calculations can be made manually or by using the bank channel. It is also possible to use an in-house treasury system, connected with the bank channel, as a platform for making the necessary balance calculations.

> *Expected end-of-day balance =*
>
> *Closing balance of previous day*
> *+ receipts of current day*
> *– payments of current day*
> *+ expected receipts of current day*
> *– expected payments of current day*

12.3.2   CASH CONCENTRATION

For simplicity's sake, the optimal structure for many companies would be to have only one account with one bank. This scenario would enable the cash manager to oversee the cash position without having to aggregate the positions of multiple accounts. In the past, this was a utopia for most cash managers. However, the development of virtual cash management may create new possibilities in this area (see chapter 13). Today, however, figures show that even within a single country, most companies operate with various entities and accounts for organisational, tax, and legal reasons. This makes the assessment of the total cash position more cumbersome. To be able to achieve one position per currency and ensure access to financial markets, the company may choose to move the funds into a single physical location in its home country or another country with a preferential legal and tax environment.

There are different ways to move funds into the centralised location:

- Manual solution – initiate credit transfers
- Automated solution – use automated cash pooling offered by banks

Companies often use a bank channel to initiate a payment transfer for moving funds between accounts held with different banks. High-value or urgent payment instruments are typically used for this purpose. As we have seen in chapter 8, these payments ensure immediate processing and settlement, thus providing certainty and immediate information on the intended new balance position. This requires manual action and attention for initiating the payment well before cut-off time. Another downside of these in-house initiated payments is the operational risk that is inherent to the manual entry of payment details, which could mean the wrong amount may end up on the wrong account.

Alternatively, automated cash pooling is used to concentrate and offset cash balances. These solutions do not require any intervention by the corporate treasury staff. They enable the company to outsource daily cash balance movements to the bank. Usually, cash pooling is applied to accounts with one single bank. However, cash pooling is also possible between accounts held with different banks. Corporates can decide which bank they want to instruct to initiate the transactions; normally, both the sending and the collecting bank can initiate the required actions. It is often possible to automatically pool balances from accounts in all of the main currencies in almost every country that is not restricted by regulations.

Different types of cash pooling are available

- Mono and multi-bank
- Mono and multi-currency
- Sweeping and notional pooling

Cash pooling can be done through physical sweeps or 'notionally'. Physical sweeping means that the bank will move balances to a central account or move balances from the central account to a sub-account in order to fund the debit balance on that sub-account. This can be done during the day at a fixed time, at end-of-day as the very last booking of the day, or early in the morning based on the closing balance of the previous day.

In the case of notional pooling, no physical sweeps occur. In this case, the bank will treat all the balances in the notional pooling structure as if they were on one account. This single balance position can be used to calculate interest and/or to authorise payments. Regulation generally dictates if and how these balances can also be netted in the books of banks and corporates. With that, the detailed functionalities and pricing of these notional products are also determined. In Chapter 13, we provide a broad overview of the different cash pooling techniques.

12.4
The day-to-day operational activities of cash balances management

To achieve the primary objectives of cash balances management, the cash manager carries out the following daily activities:

- Compiling a cash position statement
- Leading and lagging of outgoing payments
- Performing cash concentration transactions

12.4.1   COMPILING A CASH POSITION STATEMENT

To determine the required balance transfers, the cash manager draws up a forecast of the end-of-day balances of all of the company's accounts. To this end, a cash position statement is prepared for each account. The cash manager compiles the cash position statement on the basis of:

- Electronic bank statements of the current accounts (electronic balance and transaction reporting)
- Forecasted payments and receipts

In most cases, the cash manager reviews the bank statements of all current accounts as the first activity of the morning. A sample bank statement of a centralised master account in euros is shown in figure 12.1.

FIGURE 12.1   BANK STATEMENT OF EURO MASTER ACCOUNT – 9 JUNE

	(EUR)	Book date	Value date
Opening book balance 8/6	1,000,000		
Value balance 8/6	800,000		
Accounts receivable	+900,000	9/6	10/6
Accounts payable	−400,000	9/6	8/6
Retransfered deposit	+1,000,000	9/6	9/6
High value payment	+800,000	9/6	8/6
Settlement forward transaction	+2,000,000	9/6	9/6
Cheque payed cashed under usual reserve	+600,000	9/6	12/6
Closing book balance	5,900,000		

For interest-related purposes, the cash manager will look at the value balance. In the above example, the value balance on 8/6 is EUR 800,000. However, the cash manager now wants to forecast the value balance for the current day (9/6) in order to determine what amount should be invested in or funded from the market. The value balance is calculated using the following components:

1. Value balance on 8 June.
2. Items on the bank statement of 9 June with a value date of 9 June.
3. Items previously entered with a value date of 9 June.
4. Items that are entered on or after 10 June with a value date of 9 June or before (forecast items).

Items on the bank statement of 9/6 with value date 9/6
The bank statement contains the following items with a value date of 9/6:

 – Re-transferred deposit EUR 1,000,000
 – Forward transaction settlement EUR 2,000,000

Forecasted items entered earlier with value date of 9/6
In addition to the bank statement, the bank channel provides information on items entered by the bank before 9/6 with a value date of 9/6. This could include the following items:

 – Incoming receivables from debtors of EUR 1,000,000, entered on 8 June with a value date of 9 June
 – Cheque income settled by the bank on 4 June for EUR 400,000 with a value date of 9 June

Forecast transfers with value date of 9/6
Finally, the cash manager must take into account transactions created during the day that will influence the value balance. The cash manager collects information about the outgoing and incoming payments with a value date up until the current date but which are not yet shown on the bank statement.

For instance, the cash manager may receive information from the accounts payable department about creditor payments with entry dates one day later but value dates of the current day. Or the controlling department may provide information on large investments that are to be paid later on the current day by means of a high-value payment. In their planning for that day, the cash manager also includes transactions originally scheduled for the previous day but not yet carried out. Finally, as noted, the operating companies may also communicate transactions during the course of the day.

In our case, the cash manager is confronted with the following income and expenditures with a value date of 9/6:

- Unreceived non-recurring urgent incoming payment of EUR 500,000 – expected on 8/6
- Outgoing creditor payments by electronic transfer of EUR 500,000 – entry date 10/6
- Outgoing creditor payments by cheque of EUR 300,000 (sent 1 June)
- Tax payment scheduled on June 9 of EUR 1,500,000
- Outgoing high-value payment in connection with purchase of a printer of EUR 900,000.

In addition, the following transactions are reported during the day by two operating companies:

- Operating company A – tax payment of EUR 1,000,000 with a value date of 9 June
- Operating company B – salary batch of EUR 400,000 with an entry date of 10 June and a value date of 9 June

The above transactions result in the forecast of the value balance for 9 June as shown in figure 12.2.

FIGURE 12.2 END-OF-DAY BALANCE FORECAST FOR 9 JUNE

(EUR)		Book date	Value date
800,000	**Value balance 8/6**		**9/6**
	On balance statement 9/6:		
+1,000,000	Retransfer of deposit	9/6	9/6
+2,000,000	Settlement of forward transaction	9/6	9/6
	Booked earlier:		
+1,000,000	Accounts receivable	8/6	9/6
+400,000	Incoming cheque payments	4/6	9/6
	Not yet shown on account statement:		
+500,000	'Overdue' high-value payment	9/6	9/6
−500,000	Accounts payable by electronic transfer	10/6	9/6
−300,000	Accounts payable by cheque	11/6	9/6
−1,500,000	Tax payment	9/6	9/6
−900,000	Company A International / hvp	9/6	9/6
−1,000,000	Tax payment, operating company A	9/6	9/6
−400,000	Salaries, operating company B	10/6	9/6
1,100,000	**Forecast end-of-day book balance**		**9/6**

For the cash manager's purposes, the value balance is much more important than the book balance. In the above example, the book balance of 9 June was EUR 5,900,000. However, if the cash manager was to deposit an amount of EUR 5,900,000 in the money market, the value balance would be – EUR 4,800,000. The account would then be heavily overdrawn for interest calculation purposes and the cash manager would have to pay debit interest accordingly.

12.4.2 LEADING AND LAGGING OF OUTGOING PAYMENTS

Timing is crucial for a cash manager. When compiling the cash position statement, the cash manager should look at least one day ahead. If a liquidity deficit is expected on any of these days, the treasury can try to delay outbound payments to a later date. Bank loan repayments or tax payments cannot be postponed. Salaries must also be paid on time. However, there may be some creditor payments that can wait a day or two. The cash manager will have to explore the opportunities for postponing payments in consultation with the purchasing and accounts payable departments.

296 International Cash Management

12.4.3 PERFORMING CASH CONCENTRATION TRANSACTIONS

After a cash position statement has been drawn up for all current accounts, and leading and lagging has been done where possible, the balances must then be moved. One of the primary objectives is to optimise the overall interest result for all of the company's current accounts. The cash manager can achieve this by manually transferring credit balances (from low interest accounts) into accounts with debit positions – achieving a self-funded position in an effective manner. The cash concentration transactions can also be performed automatically. This is done by moving surplus balances to a centralised master account and by moving balances from this centralised account to the sub-account with deficit positions. These transfers must be done on a 'same-day value' basis and the net effect should be that the net value balance in each currency is concentrated on the centralised master account.

In the case of automated cash pooling, balances held with one bank and within one country are swept to a local master account using single-currency mono-bank cash pooling. Balances held with one bank in various countries are concentrated using cross-border mono-bank cash pooling, whereas balances in one currency held at different banks can be concentrated by means of multi-bank cash pooling. As a result, one balance in each currency will remain – very often in a series of accounts in one country. The corporate treasurer can now focus on managing these single currency balances (surpluses as well as deficits) to further optimise liquidity and interest results. In practice, we see companies using different account structures and cash pooling techniques depending on the financial structure, the core business model, the funding position and the trade flows of the company.

The centralised liquidity position is the starting point for the next activity – funding net deficits in the financial market and using net surplus liquidity to reduce outstanding loans or investing excess cash in the money markets. These activities are explained in chapter 15.

12.5
Evaluation of cash balances management

Each company should periodically evaluate the performance of its cash balances management activities. Such a review focuses on this essential question: to what extent have overall interest results on all current account balances been optimised? Most importantly, the treasurer should investigate if the following situations could have been avoided:

- Simultaneous debit and credit positions (without notional pooling) across a group of companies. If one operating company has a credit balance and another has a debit balance, then there are opportunities to improve the consolidated balance sheet and reduce interest costs.
- Credit positions on local accounts and accounts with low credit interest rates.
- Debit positions on accounts with high interest margins.

To establish whether any of these situations have occurred, a treasurer should review the value balances over a period of time, such as every six or twelve months. One way to do this is to identify the daily balances for each cash pool and for each individual account outside a cash pool. To do so, all positive balances should be added to a gross positive balance each day, and all negative balances should be added to a gross negative balance each day. These two daily balance positions can now be compared to assess the interest costs that could have been avoided by matching simultaneous debit and credit positions. This is illustrated in figure 12.3.

FIGURE 12.3   UNMATCHED VALUE BALANCES IN EUROS

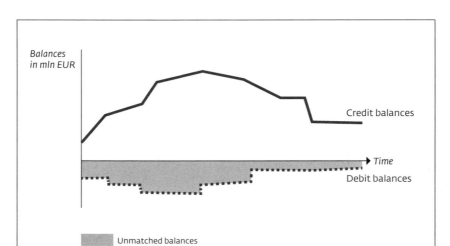

As illustrated in figure 12.3, the company has a continuous surplus balance. However, on all days in the period under review, there is also a (smaller) deficit balance that could have been avoided. The opportunity costs can be determined by multiplying the daily unmatched balances by the interest margin differential between the deficit accounts and the surplus accounts. Additional opportunity costs can be assessed on the residual balances that could have been invested in the money market.

An exercise like this will provide a view of the benefits of making further improvements. These benefits can be achieved by enhancing the company's account structure, by perfecting the balance information and – possibly – by executing the balance transfers and the cash pools. These topics are typical items that are included in KPIs related to cash balances management. A checklist is provided on the next page.

- Can the number of banks be reduced?
- Can any of the accounts be closed without hindering operations?
- Where possible, have all accounts been incorporated in a cash pool?
- Are the interest rates on current accounts still competitive?
- Do we receive timely and accurate information from our banks on movements on the accounts?
- Does treasury receive timely information from internal business partners about (large) receipts and disbursements?
- Are we using the right instruments to move balances instantly?
- Which additional cash pooling services can be used to improve interest results and reduce manual operating costs (i.e. cross-border pooling, cross-currency pooling, multi-bank pooling, virtual cash management)?
- Are we using the right products for our payments and collections?
- Can our bank give us a better cut-off time for our payments and receipts?

Chapter 13

Cash Pooling Techniques

13 Cash Pooling Techniques

13.1
Introduction

Companies operating in several countries have cash balances on different bank accounts, at different banks, in different currencies and often even in different time zones. As we have seen in chapter 12 on cash balance management, different tools are required to manage these balances effectively. One of these tools is automated cash pooling. There have been major innovations in the products and services banks offer – especially in terms of cross-border or cross-currency solutions. These instruments are critical in enabling companies to gain full control of their cash balances across countries and currencies. They enable international companies to rationalise and fully centralise liquidity management operations at a regional or global level. More recently, we witnessed the introduction of virtual cash management as a new tool.

In this chapter, we will provide a comprehensive overview of the various cash pooling techniques provided by some of the major international cash management banks. We will also explain the basic concept of cash pooling and discuss the different instruments involved in physical cash concentration, notional pooling and virtual cash management.

13.2
Concept of cash pooling

The basic idea behind cash pooling is to gain full control of cash balances and to offset the debit and credit balances of all accounts in the cash pool. A cash pool is often comprised of a group of current accounts in the name of one or more companies or subsidiaries, and a master account. The master account is usually in the name of the central treasury, and the other accounts are called 'operating accounts' or 'sub-accounts'. A cash pool with all accounts located in the same country is called a 'domestic' or 'in-country' cash pool while one that includes accounts held in multiple countries is referred to as a 'cross-border' cash pool. One of the most obvious advantages is that cash pooling achieves an optimised interest result. In addition to the interest benefits cash pooling offers, there are other benefits that depend on the various techniques used. The example below shows the impact of cash pooling on interest results.

EXAMPLE

Account	Balance	Credit interest rate	Debit interest rate	Interest amount (annual basis)
Operating company A	+600	2%	8%	12
Operating company B	−200	2%	8%	−16
Operating company C	+400	2%	8%	8
Operating company D	−100	2%	8%	−8
Total				−4

The debit and credit interest rates are identical for all accounts. Two accounts are in credit and two in debit. The bank charges 8% debit interest and pays 2% credit interest.

The total interest expense on an annual basis for the company is -4. What would be the interest result if the company was able to 'pool' all balances and the same interest conditions were applied to the pooled amount? This is shown below.

Account	Balance	Credit interest rate	Debit interest rate	Interest amount (annual basis)
Operating company A	+600	2%	8%	12
Operating company B	−200	2%	8%	−16
Operating company C	+400	2%	8%	8
Operating company D	−100	2%	8%	−8
Total	+700	2%	8%	+14

The interest expense of -4 now turns into an interest income of +14, a very significant difference of 18.

Why does the interest income in our example increase by 18? Before the balances were offset against each other, the company's total credit balance was +1000 (operating company A plus operating company C), and the total debit balance was -300 (operating company B plus operating company D). By offsetting the balances, the debit balances are completely eliminated. This means the company is no longer required to borrow 300 from the bank at a rate of 8% and lend the same amount to the bank at 2% (effectively losing a margin of 6% on debit and credit balances). By pooling all balances, the company realises 6% more on the offsetting balance of 300 (which is exactly the interest gain of 18).

In the example above, we have assumed that the rates for all accounts are the same. This is usually the case when the cash management department of the company negotiates these rates on behalf of all operating companies. Due to centralised negotiations and economies of scale, these rates can be more favourable than when the operating companies negotiate them individually with the bank.

There are three main categories of cash pooling techniques – physical cash concentration, notional pooling and virtual cash management. While in their purest forms all techniques yield the same interest benefits, they are achieved very differently.

From time to time, credit interest rates on current accounts can turn negative. In these circumstances, too, concentrating balances makes sense as offsetting the balances between accounts will minimise the interest due on those accounts.

Physical cash concentration
With physical cash concentration – referred to as 'sweeping' or 'physical pooling' – balances are actually transferred (swept) between the sub-accounts and the master account of the cash pool.

Notional pooling
With notional pooling, the balances of the participating accounts are not physically moved but mathematically combined for the calculation of the interest result.

Virtual cash management
Virtual cash management helps corporates manage their balances from a minimum number of accounts, by instantly concentrating individual transactions via virtual bank accounts into a master current account, while offering local subsidiaries autonomy in managing their balances on so-called virtual ledger accounts.

13.3
Physical cash concentration

In this section, we will discuss various physical cash concentration instruments (see overview in the box below).

Summary: physical cash concentration

Timing aspects
- Intra-day
- End-of-day

Cross-border physical pooling
- Intra-day payments-based
- End-of-day-based – cross-border zero balancing

Multi-bank funding and sweeping

Advanced sweeping solutions
- Target balance return sweeping

Interest aspects
- Bank interest
- Inter-company interest
- Inter-company loan administration

Credit facilities aspects
- Overnight limit on the master account
- Intra-day limits on the sub-accounts

The goal of physical cash concentration techniques is to concentrate cash held in the sub-accounts into the master account of the cash pool. In most cases, the sub-accounts are set in a zero position and all value balances are booked on the master account. This can be illustrated as follows:

FIGURE 13.1

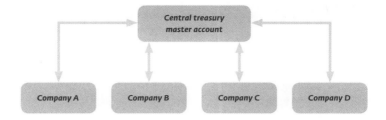

The transactions in a physical cash concentration scheme are usually referred to as 'sweeps'. Sweep transactions can occur in two ways: upstream and downstream. Upstream transactions transfer (or 'sweep') the credit balances from sub-accounts to the master account, while downstream transactions transfer (or 'fund') debit balances from the sub-accounts to the master account. The latter actually represents a funds flow from master to sub and is therefore sometimes referred to as a 'funding sweep'.

There are two categories of physical cash concentration solutions:

1. Intra-day – automatically initiated by the bank during the business day
2. End-of-day – automatically initiated at the end of the business day ensuring a zero or predefined balance on the sub-accounts

Features of physical pooling

Fixed amounts versus balance-based
- Sweeps may be based on a fixed amount or on the balance of the sub-account. When based on a fixed amount, this means that the payment is one-way, sweeping a fixed amount from sub to master. If the sweep is based on the balance of the sub-account, this means that two-way sweeping is possible. When the balance of the sub-account is in credit, the transfer is from sub to master. When the balance on the sub is in debit, the transfer is from master to sub (to fund the debit balance on the sub).

Residual amounts
- With sweeping, it is possible to leave a certain balance (a residual amount) in the sub-account and only sweep the excess over the residual amount. When two-way sweeps are used and the balance of the sub-account is less than the residual balance, the sweep will fund the sub-account to the residual balance.

Min/max transfer amounts
- It is possible to indicate a minimum or maximum on the transfer amount. A minimum amount can be used to avoid transfers of relatively insignificant amounts. A maximum amount can be used to limit the amounts that may be funded to the sub-account.

>

Sweep frequency
- Sweeping can occur on a daily basis (perhaps even multiple times during the day) or on a weekly, monthly or quarterly basis. Deciding what frequency is optimal is done in a trade-off between the benefit of concentrating the balances and the costs of the transfers. In general, if the balances on the sub-accounts are relatively small, daily transfers may not be needed.

13.3.1 TIMING ASPECTS

With end-of-day sweeping, sweeps are carried out at the end of the business day after all other transactions have been executed for the operating accounts. This means the zero-balancing sweep ensures that a closing balance of zero is achieved; the last booking of the day is the sweep. End-of-day zero balancing is typically completed between accounts held in the system of a single bank.

With intra-day sweeping, balances are transferred during the business day and before the end of the day. The main reason why companies would opt for this is to ensure that cash received during the day is concentrated and can be used for the investment and borrowing activities of the company's treasury department on the same day. Intra-day sweeping is also used in situations where end-of-day sweeping is not possible. This may be the case when a true cross-border zero-balancing solution is not possible because of time-zone limitations.

Timing of daily intra-day sweeps

There are three general categories for the timing of daily intra-day sweeps:
- Early in the morning – this sweeps the previous day's closing balance
- Sometime during the day – if the requirement is to concentrate the balances before investment or borrowing decisions are made
- As late as possible during the day – for most situations, the goal is to execute the intra-day sweeps as late in the day as possible to come as close as possible to a 'zero balance' at the end of the day

It is up to the company to decide which option fits their treasury operations.

Note that some banks also offer intra-day, book-to-book sweeping solutions that sweep funds on a continuous basis in real time. Whenever a transaction is booked to or from a sub-account, it is immediately swept to the master account. The sub-accounts are therefore always in a zero position. This requires additional measures to ensure that normal payments will be executed, such as balance compensation or intra-day credit facilities. Continuous sweeping leads to a very large number of transactions that may all need to be tracked, booked and reconciled.

End-of-day versus intra-day sweeping

The optimal form of physical cash concentration is end-of-day zero balancing. Intra-day sweeping is used in specific situations:

– To tailor the concentration process to other time-critical treasury processes – such as investment and / or borrowing activities
– When the bank cannot offer end-of-day zero balancing for certain countries or currencies
– For sweeps between accounts in different currencies

Frequency

Most companies use zero balancing for daily sweeping. However, there may be reasons why a daily sweep is not required or even desired. When the transaction activity of certain accounts is very low, a weekly or even monthly sweep might suffice. There is also an option of tailoring the sweeping in such a way that it ties in with the treasury or accounting activities of the company. This may, for instance, mean that a sweep only occurs on the last business day of the month. Most cash management banks can offer flexibility in the frequency of the sweeping process.

Variations

There are several possible variations and features of zero balancing that ensure the process is tailored to the company's requirements. We discuss some of these below.

Variations

Zero balancing
– Sets the sub-account balances to zero.

Constant balancing
– Sets the sub-account balances to a predefined amount by either sweeping the excess over the constant balancing amount or funding to the constant balancing amount.

Target balancing
– Sweeps the entire sub-account balance to zero and returns a 'target' amount back to the sub-account with next day value.

Trigger balancing
– Determines whether the sweeping process for a sub-account should be done (yes or no). If the balance of the sub-account is outside a range specified by an upper and a lower trigger amount, then the sweeping process for that particular sub-account is continued.

One of the subsidiaries of company A has complained that every time the zero balancing sweep occurs the opening balance of their sub-account is zero, preventing them from making any payments before the daily collections have been booked to their account. Typically, the collections were booked later in the day – leading to a timing issue between the payment operations and the booking of the collections. The solution for company A was to combine the trigger balancing with a target balancing setting. This then ensures that:

- the subsidiary has a balance on its account at the start of the day enabling payments to be made
- the benefit of concentrating the balances is maintained
- relatively small sweeps are avoided, reducing the reconciliation effort

13.3.2   CROSS-BORDER PHYSICAL POOLING

Companies operating in multiple countries often want to concentrate their cash balances from those countries into one location. The main cash management banks offer cross-border physical pooling solutions. In these solutions, the accounts are physically held in different countries. A distinction can be made between those that are intra-day, payments-based solutions and those based on end-of-day, book-to-book transfers (i.e. 'true' cross-border zero balancing).

Intra-day payments-based – cross-border physical pooling
As previously discussed, automated balance transfers and standing orders can usually also be applied to cross-border solutions. The execution is the same but because of the different countries and potentially different currencies involved, the cut-off time and value date implications can become more complex. This is certainly the case if the countries involved span different time zones.

End-of-day-based – cross-border zero balancing
The principle of cross-border zero balancing is the same as for domestic or single country zero balancing. It is guaranteed that the end-of-day value balance of a sub-account in a cross-border zero-balancing cash pool is set to zero and the funds will be interest-bearing on the master account (thereby offsetting the individual debit and credit balances of the subsidiaries). Most features available to single country zero balancing (such as constant balancing, target balancing, trigger balancing, sweep frequencies) can also be used for cross-border zero balancing.

13.3.3 SINGLE BANK OR MULTI-BANK

Single: network bank offering

When companies are looking for cash concentration solutions in multiple countries, the question about whether to choose a local bank in each country or use a single network bank in the region is an important one to consider. There are pros and cons to both options depending on various factors such as the company structure, the countries involved and the specific requirements for the domestic services required in each country. A solution based on a local bank in each country might be preferable when the number of countries involved is relatively small and very specific local services are required. A solution based on a regional network bank can be considered when the bank has branches or fully operating subsidiaries in multiple countries and can offer an integrated variety of advanced cash concentration capabilities.

Benefits network bank
The benefits of using the services of a network bank are: – Harmonised capabilities, reporting and services across the region – Coordinated and harmonised documentation – a simpler implementation process – More efficient negotiation with the bank – True end-of-day-based cross-border zero balancing is possible – Hybrid solutions are also possible where in-country single banks are used for the local services (such as payments and collections) while a network bank is used for the cash pooling services

Multi-bank offering

From an operational point of view, companies might want to use one bank as their cash concentration bank. In reality, they are likely to use other banks as well (whether in the same or in different countries) for payments, collections and other local services. In an optimal cash concentration situation, the balances that are held with these 'third-party' banks are also concentrated in the central treasury account held in the cash concentration bank. Some banks have reacted to that demand and developed sweeping services that move balances automatically between accounts held at a third-party bank and the cash-management bank. This service – known as 'multi-bank sweeping' or 'multi-bank funding and sweeping' – is discussed below.

Multi-bank funding and sweeping

With this service, the cash concentration bank traditionally keeps track of the balances on sub-accounts held with the third-party banks using SWIFT MT940 and/or MT942 messages (refer to 1 in the picture below). It then creates a transfer request using a SWIFT MT101 message (2) to move the funds to the master account. The payment instruction is executed by the receiving bank and, as a result, the funds are transferred to the cash concentration bank via a domestic or international transfer (3). New ways of sharing information on balances are entering the market. These include ISO20022 reporting messages (CAMT 52 and 53) and application programming interfaces (APIs), and are expected to be used for multibank aggregation of balance information and payment initiation and could replace the MT messages.

FIGURE 13.2   CASH CONCENTRATION MODEL

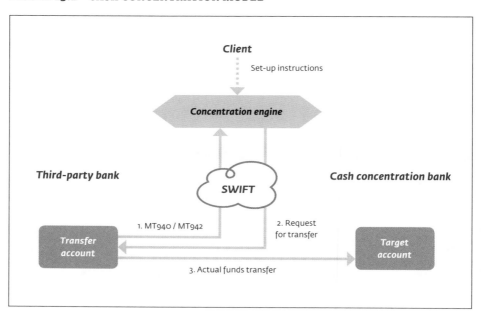

This service can be offered as a one-way (sweeping only) or a two-way (funding) service, where sub-accounts are funded by the master account when in debit, hence avoiding overdraft costs on the sub-account.

As we have seen with the intra-day payments-based cash concentration techniques such as the automated balance transfer, various sweeping options can be used. These include residual balances to maintain a working balance on sub-accounts, and minimum and maximum transfer amounts to avoid the sweeping of small amounts.

Multi-bank sweeps are executed through the local clearing process or, in the case of crossborder transfers, through the correspondent banking process. This means that the sweeps will normally be initiated before the end of the day, so it will be more difficult to achieve a zero balance on sub-accounts.

Achieving a zero balance is generally not possible when balances are swept between different banks. However, there are a few exceptions to this in situations where different banks work closely together.

Emerging multi-bank aggregation services

With the introduction of Payment Services Directive 2 (PSD2) (see chapter 22), banks are obliged to provide payment service providers (PSPs) with access to bank accounts, more specifically payment initiation services and account information services. In the case of corporates, this means that any bank and all registered payment service providers may offer these services that bring together information on their accounts, insight into their balances and even initiate payments.

PSD2 creates opportunities for banks and other payment service providers to develop and offer new multi-banking based, integrated digital financial services for corporates. The expectation is that new and innovative services will emerge that will help treasurers gain better real-time insight into their balances at multiple banks, as well as transfer balances between the banks, potentially supported by automatic calculations using robots, artificial intelligence and advanced data analytics.

As balances will still be held at the account holding banks, it is anticipated that interest benefits on those balances will continue to be determined by the account holding bank. Aggregation and payment initiation services may lead to new dynamics in moving the funds to the account holding bank with the best conditions.

New payment service providers that are not account holding institutions are not expected to be able to offer real end-of-day settlement as sophisticated orchestration within the banks' systems is required.

13.3.4   WHICH BALANCE TO SWEEP?

We now know that sub-accounts can be swept in different ways but which of the two types of balances are transferred – book or value balances, or both? The book balance represents the legal relationship between the bank and the customer whereby the cash held on account belongs to the customer and is at the customer's free disposal. The value balance is the amount on which the bank pays or charges interest.

Sweeping the book balance

If the book balances of the sub-accounts are swept, the sweeping operation includes all items stated in the book balance at the time of sweeping, irrespective of the value date. In other words, items with a value date in the future are also swept such that both the value and book balances of the sub-accounts are always zero. This is referred to as 'zero balancing with forward sweeping'.

Sweeping the value balance

When the value balance is swept, the sweeping operation only includes those items with the value date of 'today' or earlier. With this form of sweeping – known as 'zero balancing without forward sweeping' – the value balance on the account is always equal to zero. Items with a value date in the future remain on the sub-accounts and will be swept when the actual date has reached the value date. As a result, the book balance is not always equal to zero.

13.3.5   INTEREST ASPECTS

There are two aspects related to interest that are connected to the physical cash pooling techniques:

- Interest settlement between bank and company (bank interest)
- Interest settlement between different entities of the company (inter-company interest).

Interest settlement between the bank and the company (bank interest)
Physical cash concentration techniques aim to concentrate the value balances (the interest-bearing balance) on the master account of the cash pool as efficiently as possible. With end-of-day zero balancing, the interest settlement between the bank and the company is generally simple: the value balance on all sub-accounts is zero, so the interest accrued on the sub-accounts is also zero. The concentrated value balance on the master account (the pool balance) will not be zero so interest will be accrued and settled at the end of the interest settlement period on the master account. The same applies to target balancing – cash balances are maintained on the sub-accounts but the value balance on these accounts is always zero. Consequently, the bank does not need to pay or charge any interest on these accounts.

With trigger and constant balancing and other types of non-daily sweeps, there will generally be value balances on the sub-accounts. In these cases, interest will also be accrued and settled on the sub-accounts.

**Interest settlement between different entities of the company
(inter-company interest)**
As a result of achieving a zero value balance on the sub accounts, the bank only settles interest on the balance of the master account. That is the sum of the interest due on the balances originating from the sub-accounts. If all accounts in the cash pool are held by the same legal entity of the company, this is all that has to be done. However, if there are multiple legal entities involved in the cash concentration, then each and every sweep between two accounts held by different legal entities creates a so-called inter-company loan. As the master account is often held by central treasury and the sub-accounts by the operating companies, this means that inter-company loans are often encountered in physical cash concentration.

As discussed in chapter 19 on cross-border tax implications, interest must be settled at 'arm's length rates' when different entities engage in inter-company loans. Therefore, for tax reasons, the company must keep a record of the internal inter-company loans that take place between the treasury and the operating companies. This places an administrative burden on central cash managers and constitutes one of the main disadvantages of physical sweeping.

Most companies' internal interest policies dictate that operating companies are entitled to receive interest on the credit balances they have provided to the central treasury and are obliged to pay interest on debit balances. Next, we will focus on how the central treasurer re-allocates the interest that the bank pays or charges in respect of the master account to the various operating companies.

13.3.6   INTER-COMPANY LOAN ADMINISTRATION

The inter-company loans process can be divided into three sub-processes:

1. Keeping track of the inter-company loans created through physical cash concentration
2. Calculating the inter-company interest based on inter-company loans
3. Settlement of the inter-company interest

Cash managers can relieve the administrative burden in various ways. First, many modern treasury systems can administer internal loans by making use of electronic transaction reporting from banks. This can either be achieved by:

- Downloading the sweep transactions from the bank's channel
- Marking sweep transactions with a sweep code in the electronic banking reports that allows treasury systems to identify and select entries as sweeps and export them to the company's inter-company loan administration

As an additional service – often referred to as 'inter-company loan administration' – some banks can perform some or all of the tasks related to the inter-company loans process. The bank will keep track of the sweeps and report the inter-company balances electronically via their electronic banking system. At regular intervals (usually once a month) the 'inter-company interest' (which is the interest based on the inter-company balances) can be calculated, reported and in some cases even booked. The inter-company loan position can be checked on a daily basis through a bank's channels and the periodic reports can be made available through a bank's portal.

What rates to apply to the inter-company interest?
It is a company's responsibility to ensure that inter-company loans are tracked and inter-company interest is settled between the participants of the cash pool. If the bank provides these services, it must know what rates it should apply in calculating the inter-company debit and credit interest. It is the company's responsibility to select the rates the bank should apply, but the company is not fully free in that. The tax authorities will insist that internal interest rates are in line with the commercial market interest rates (the rates which an operating company would have received from a local bank). This is known as pricing 'at arm's length'. More on this can be found in chapter 19 on cross-border tax implications.

Example: inter-company loans
Let us continue our zero-balancing example from section 13.3.2 and focus on the inter-company loan aspects. The first example shows the results when the inter-company interest rates are the same as the bank interest rates.

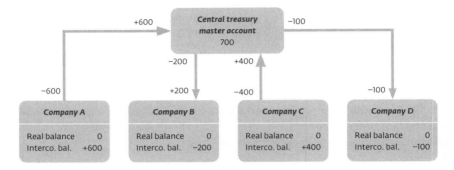

The figure above shows the sweeps that represent inter-company loans. The master account is held by the central treasury and there are four operating companies (OpCos), A, B, C and D, holding the sub-accounts. Despite the fact that the real balances of the OpCo accounts are zero after the zero balancing, the accounts do have inter-company balances. When the inter-company balance of the OpCo account is positive, it means that the OpCo is lending funds to the central treasury account – i.e. the OpCo provides an inter-company loan to the central treasury. When the inter-company balance of the OpCo is negative, the OpCo is borrowing from the central treasury – i.e. the central treasury provides an inter-company loan to the OpCo.

If we take the same inter-company interest rates as we would have applied to the real balances, the inter-company interest results are as follows:

Account	Inter-company balance	Inter-company credit interest rate	Inter-company debit interest rate	Inter-company interest amount (annual basis)
Operating company A	+600	2%	8%	12
Operating company B	−200	2%	8%	−16
Operating company C	+400	2%	8%	8
Operating company D	−100	2%	8%	−8

The interest on the real balances is paid or charged by the bank. This is the bank interest and in this example is only applicable to the master account as this account is the only one with a real balance. The OpCos have inter-company balances and the corresponding inter-company interest results are not paid to or charged by the bank but booked between the central treasury and the operating companies. The inter-company interest is calculated based on the inter-company balances of the OpCo accounts and counter-booked on the central treasury account. The figure below shows the bank interest and inter-company interest bookings.

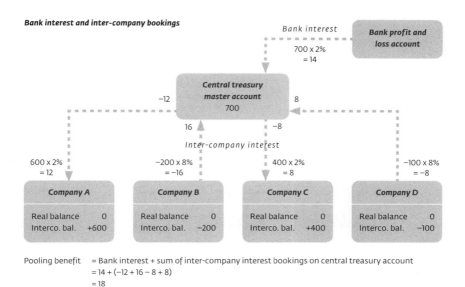

Bank interest and inter-company bookings

Bank interest

Bank profit and loss account

700 x 2%
= 14

Central treasury master account
700

−12   8

16   −8

Inter-company interest

600 x 2% = 12	−200 x 8% = −16	400 x 2% = 8	−100 x 8% = −8
Company A	**Company B**	**Company C**	**Company D**
Real balance 0 Interco. bal. +600	Real balance 0 Interco. bal. −200	Real balance 0 Interco. bal. +400	Real balance 0 Interco. bal. −100

Pooling benefit   = Bank interest + sum of inter-company interest bookings on central treasury account
                  = 14 + (−12 + 16 − 8 + 8)
                  = 18

We have seen that the central treasury benefit in the above example was +18. This is the sum of the bank interest (+14) and the sum of the inter-company interest bookings to the central treasury account (+4).

If the company wants to (partly) distribute this benefit to the participating companies, it is possible to determine better inter-company interest rates (shown in the following example). Note that these rates should comply with the 'arm's length' principle. With the choice of the rates in this example, there remains a benefit for the central treasury department which can be classified as a fee for the management of the pool.

EXAMPLE

Here, we use slightly improved inter-company interest rates compared to those used in the previous example to redistribute the pooling benefit to the operating companies

Account	Inter-company balance	Inter-company credit interest rate	Inter-company debit interest rate	Inter-company interest amount (annual basis)
Operating company A	+600	2.5%	7%	15
Operating company B	−200	2.5%	7%	−14
Operating company C	+400	2.5%	7%	10
Operating company D	−100	2.5%	7%	−7

The benefit on the central treasury account is now reduced to 10.

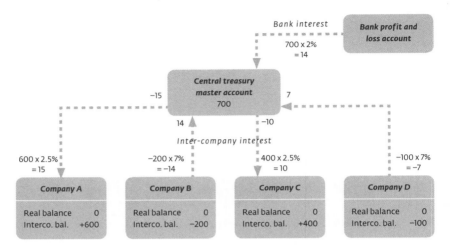

Pooling benefit = Bank interest + sum of inter-company interest bookings to central treasury account
                 = 14 + (−15 + 14 − 10 + 7)
                 = 10

13.3.7   CREDIT FACILITIES ASPECTS

As a result of the physical cash concentration techniques, all balances on the sub-accounts are concentrated on the master account, leaving the sub-accounts with a zero or predefined balance. In order to facilitate the normal daily business of the participants in the cash pool structure, this usually requires the following facilities:

- Overnight limit for the master account
- Intra-day limit for the sub-accounts

Overnight limit for the master account
If the company and the bank have agreed on a credit facility for the master account, it is allowed to be overdrawn up to a certain amount on an overnight basis. When the debit balance exceeds the overnight limit, the bank will contact the customer and ask for replenishment of the deficit during the day or agree on a temporary limit excess. The company is then allowed to replenish the debit balance the next day or even later. In daily practice, however, sweeps based on book-to-book transfers are executed even when it results in a higher debit position than allowed under the overnight limit. This introduces a risk to the bank and hence the need for a broad guarantee.

Intra-day limit for the sub-accounts

When a bank assigns an intra-day limit to the participating accounts, these accounts may be overdrawn up to a certain amount during the day. This is generally needed when the sub-accounts are zero balanced or when the constant or target balance does not provide enough headroom. As we have seen, sub-accounts will start the day with a zero balance. With an intra-day credit facility, the participants can make payments provided that the intra-day limit is not exceeded. An overnight limit is not necessary because all sub-accounts always have a zero balance at the end of the day. Note that if trigger balancing or a non-daily sweep frequency are used, this could mean that debit balances on sub-accounts are not swept. In that case, an overnight limit might be required on the sub-account as well.

13.4
Notional pooling

Another cash pooling technique is notional pooling. Contrary to physical cash concentration, in the case of notional pooling account balances will not be physically moved or 'swept' between participating accounts. Instead, they remain where they are on the various participating accounts. The bank mathematically combines the balances on the participating accounts and agrees to calculate interest on the overall net pool balance. The interest calculated on the pool balance is also referred to as pool interest. The pool interest can be settled on one of the participating accounts or on a designated 'pool settlement' account, usually held by the central treasury. This account is often referred to as the master account of the notional pool.

FIGURE 13.3   CASH CONCENTRATION MODEL

While in their purest forms, zero balancing and notional pooling lead to an identical improvement of interest results, there are some significant differences between them.

Balance compensation is the capability to allow payments to proceed as long as there is sufficient credit balance in the pool of accounts. It allows certain accounts in the pool to have a debit position as long as there are other accounts whose credit balances compensate for this debit position, leaving the net pool balance above 0 (zero). Balance compensation has no influence on the interest calculations but does have an influence on the process that allows or rejects payments from the accounts involved. Some banks offer solutions that can limit the utilisation of participants' credit balance or the overall limit by capping individual debit positions. Some banks also offer reversed caps. These systems can limit the contribution of credit funds from individual accounts.

Interest compensation is the capability to calculate interest on the net balance of a pool of accounts.

Notional pooling is often referred to as the combination of interest compensation and balance compensation.

13.4.1   WHEN BANKS OFFER NOTIONAL POOLING

Cash pooling achieves a benefit for the customer in offset between debit and credit balances. With zero balancing, this offset is automatically reached by physically moving the balances to one account. In notional pooling, the bank gives the company the benefit of the offset but the balances are not physically combined. Banks want to ensure 100% right of set-off for two reasons: 1) to protect against the risk of bankruptcy of one of the participants in the structure, and 2) to create the possibility of netting the positions for solvency reporting to the central bank as it would otherwise incur solvency costs over the gross debit and credit position.

Central banks have strict rules specifying when netting of debit and credit balances is allowed for the solvency reporting. One of the most important rules is that the bank must be able to ensure a '100% right of set-off' from the company. In other words, if one of the operating companies goes bankrupt while it has a debit position on its account, the bank has an undisputed right to claim a credit balance equal to the debit balance from any other customer account in the agreement. Whether a bank can effectuate a 100% right of set-off is dependent on a variety of factors such as the:

- Law of the country where the accounts are held
- Law of the country under which the cash pooling contract has been documented
- Law of the country where the account holder resides/is registered (this may not be the same as the country where the account is held)

The right of set-off is generally obtained and documented in security instruments such as pledges or joint and several agreements (usually combined with parent or inter-company guarantees). All these factors play a role in the bank's decision on whether it offers notional pooling in a certain country or to a certain account holder in a certain jurisdiction.

See chapter 22 for the impact of Basel III on notional pooling.

Most banks are strict in applying the rule of not allowing the company to participate in a notional pool if they are not able to obtain the benefit of reporting the client balances net to the central bank. Nevertheless, there are different forms of notional pooling that allow companies to receive a certain benefit even if the bank cannot achieve 100% offset (this will be discussed in the next section). In general, more restrictions and legal requirements apply to notional pooling with full offset than to physical sweeping techniques.

13.4.2 FULL OFFSET VERSUS PARTIAL OFFSET

Full offset
Full offset notional pooling means that the credit balances in the notional pool are used to offset the debit balances (or the other way around) and the spreads on the compensated balances are returned. This is the most beneficial form of notional pooling and usually only applicable to notional pooling where all accounts are held in one country.

Partial offset
If the bank cannot obtain the 100% right of offset, there are solvency costs associated with the debit balances for the bank. There are therefore alternative forms of notional pooling that do not apply the full offset but a partial offset instead. This means that 100% of the spreads on the compensated balances are not returned, but instead only a certain percentage. Partial offset solutions are usually applied for cross-border and cross-currency notional pooling solutions and are also referred to as 'interest enhancement'.

Let us look in greater detail at the differences between full and partial offset notional pooling. We shall use the same accounts, balances and rates as in section 13.2. To better highlight the working of the notional pooling techniques, here we show the interest rates that are applied as a base rate plus or minus a spread. Note that there are various ways to calculate and settle the notional pooling results, all leading to the same end results. In the example below, we show one of those possibilities.

EXAMPLE

SITUATION BEFORE NOTIONAL POOLING

Account	Base rate	Debit interest spread (bps)	Effective debit rate	Credit interest spread (bps)	Effective credit rate	Balance	Interest amo (annual basi
Operating company A	3%	+500	8%	−100	2%	+600	12
Operating company B	3%	+500	8%	−100	2%	−200	−16
Operating company C	3%	+500	8%	−100	2%	+400	8
Operating company D	3%	+500	8%	−100	2%	−100	−8
Total							-4

The total interest expense on an annual basis for the company is -4.

The table below shows the situation with notional pooling and assumes that the interest results of the participating accounts based on their 'own' balances are also settled by the bank:

SITUATION WITH NOTIONAL POOLING

Account	Base rate	Debit interest spread (bps)	Effective debit rate	Credit interest spread (bps)	Effective credit rate	Balance	Interest am (annual bas
Operating company A	3%	+500	8%	−100	2%	+600	12
Operating company B	3%	+500	8%	−100	2%	−200	−16
Operating company C	3%	+500	8%	−100	2%	+400	8
Operating company D	3%	+500	8%	−100	2%	−100	−8
Notional Pool Balance & Interest	3%	+500	8%	−100	2%	+700	+14[1]
Benefit Settlement							+18[2]

Notes

1. Fictitious notional pool interest amount. This represents the net interest the company earns on the notional pool. In this example it is fictitious as the bank has also settled individual participants' results and these therefore need to be taken into account to asse the final settlement (see also note (2)).

2. Through the individual participants' settlements, the company paid -4 to the bank. The net result for the company on the notiona pool is +14, so the bank will settle the difference between those two – an amount of 18 that represents the notional pooling bene compared to a situation without notional pooling. This pooling benefit is the same as obtained in our earlier zero-balancing exam

In this example, the compensated balance is 300. The total debit balance of 300 is fully offset by a credit of 300. With full offset, the bank fully returns the spreads applied to the compensated balance. In this case, it is 100 bps on the credit balance and 500 bps on the debit balance – a total of 600 basis points (bps).

On the credit balance: 300 at 100 bps = +3
On the debit balance: 300 at 500 bps = +15
The total benefit is therefore 18.

If we used a partial offset of 80%, this would mean that rather than 100% of the full spreads being returned, only 80% are returned. This will result in a notional pool benefit of 80% x 18 = +14.4.

13.4.3   SINGLE COUNTRY VERSUS CROSS-BORDER

Notional pooling whereby all accounts reside in one country is referred to as single country notional pooling. If the accounts are spread across multiple countries, it is referred to as cross-border notional pooling. Single country notional pooling solutions are common while cross-border notional pooling solutions are not. One of the reasons for this is that in order to actually manage a notional pool properly, credit facilities are required that cover all participating accounts as well as balance compensation capabilities that work across multiple countries. Only a few banks have these cross-border credit management systems that provide credit facilities on the pool accounts and include the payment and limit monitoring capabilities that allow them to report a net solvency position to the central banks.

Another inhibitor that prevents many banks from offering cross-border notional pooling solutions is that required pledges or securities for cross-border notional pooling will be documented under the legislation of the countries where the balances are held. In case of an insolvency of one or more of the notional pooling participants, this results in extremely complex situations from a legal point of view.

In practice, it means that true full offset cross-border notional pooling solutions are very rare and usually only cover a few countries. Most cross-border notional pooling solutions are therefore based on partial offset.

13.4.4   SINGLE-CURRENCY VERSUS CROSS-CURRENCY

So far we have discussed notional pooling of balances in a single currency but some banks also offer notional pooling of balances in different currencies. This service – called 'cross-currency notional pooling' – generally works in the same way as single-currency notional pooling but interest results are affected by two additional factors: daily movements of currency exchange rates and varying interest rates on different currencies.

This is similar to single-currency notional pooling in that there are multiple ways of calculating the cross-currency notional pooling results. The following is just one example. To make its notional pooling calculations, the bank notionally converts the balances in each currency to a chosen base currency. This calculation is made daily, based on current exchange rates. The bank then calculates the compensated balances in the pool. These are used to calculate the pool benefit using interest spreads for each currency. We can illustrate this by using a simplified example based on full offset:

EXAMPLE

A company has accounts in euros, USD and GBP:

Total balances in EUR:	8,000 credit
Total balances in USD:	4,800 debit
Total balances in GBP:	1,600 credit

Credit interest rate:	EUR:	EONIA – 100 bps
	GBP:	SONIA – 120bps
Debit interest rate:	USD:	Fed Funds Effective + 150 bps

The base currency is euros.

Exchange rate:	EUR-USD = 1.20
	EUR-GBP = 0.80

The bank makes its notional pooling calculation in three steps:

Step1: Notionally calculating balances in base currency (euros)

Balances in EUR	8,000 credit
Balances in USD (euro equivalent)	4,000 debit (4800 / 1.2 = 4,000)
Balances in GBP (euro equivalent)	2,000 credit (1600 / 0.8 = 2,000)

Total credit balance	10,000
Total debit balance	4,000

Step 2: Calculating the 'offset ratio'
The offset ratio is calculated for both credit (CR) and debit (DT) and is defined as the compensated balance divided by the gross CR (or DT) balance:

Offset ratio credit balances = Compensated balance / Gross CR balance
= 4,000 / 10,000   = 40%
Offset ratio debit balances = Compensated balance / Gross DT balance
= 4,000 / 4,000   = 100%.

Step 3: Calculating interest benefit using interest spreads by currency

Interest benefit EUR credit balances:	8,000 x 100 bps x 40% = €32
Interest benefit USD debit balances:	4,800 x 150 bps x 100% = $60
Interest benefit GBP credit balances:	1,600 x 120 bps x 40% = £7.68.

This example shows that –similarly to single-currency notional pooling – the benefit is calculated by fully returning the spreads on the compensated balances of the currencies involved. As previously mentioned, some banks do not include all credit balances in the calculation but only allow a percentage of the total credit balance. This is referred to as interest enhancement.

It is apparent that there is a direct relationship between the interest benefit and the offset ratio. The higher the offset ratio, the higher the benefit. It is for this reason that cash managers actively managing the notional pool will try to steer the net pool balance as close as possible to 0 (zero) as this ensures an offset ratio close to 100%. Cash managers usually use one account to steer the net pool balance by either taking funds out of the account and investing this cash into (potentially) higher yielding instruments, or placing funds into the account by borrowing.

13.4.5 INTEREST RATE AND SETTLEMENT ASPECTS OF NOTIONAL POOLING

Interest rate for the total cash pool applied to the net balance
The bank and the company agree on the interest rate for the entire pool. The interest income or charges are calculated daily, based on the total pool balance and settled at the end of the interest period. How this pool interest is allocated to the participating accounts is then determined by the company.

Interest rates for the sub-accounts
The company determines the debit and credit interest rates for each participating account. The bank pays interest on each account (in the case of credit balances) or charges interest (in the case of debit balances) based on these rates. The central treasury can set the rates so that the local managers of the participating accounts are encouraged to manage their liquidity for the good of the company as a whole. For example, relatively high credit and debit rates can be applied to encourage local cash managers to increase credit positions and avoid debit positions. Much like the situation with zero balancing where inter-company loans are created, tax authorities require that arm's length pricing is used. Let us consider what amount the bank will pay into the master account if interest is also paid or charged to the participating accounts:

1. First, the bank calculates and pays (or charges) the interest to each participating account based on its individual interest conditions
2. The bank then calculates the total amount of interest to be paid on the entire pool based on the net pool balance

3. The amount to be paid to the master account is then determined by taking the net pool interest from step 2 and deducting (or adding) the interest already paid (or charged) to the participating accounts from step 1

The resulting interest payment into the master account is referred to as the pool benefit settlement. It is equal to the margin on the offset between the credit and debit balances. For a numerical example, see section 13.4.2.

The company may decide to pay out this benefit to the participating companies using a certain allocation key – such as the profit contribution of the operating company. In some countries, depending on local tax requirements, it is also possible to enhance the interest rates paid or charged to the participating accounts. The most appropriate solution will also depend on tax requirements.

13.4.6   PARTIAL OFFSET NOTIONAL POOLING SOLUTIONS

Cross-border cash optimisation (CR balances only)

Cross-border cash optimisation is a technique offered by some banks to 'reward' a customer for holding credit balances with the bank in different locations and different currencies. Based on the size of the credit balances, the country where they are held and the currencies involved, a discretionary bonus is calculated by the bank that is paid to the company.

Cross-border interest optimisation (DT and CR balances)

Essentially, the interest optimisation product is a discount given on the debit interest rate and a premium on the credit interest rate that is calculated with reference to the offsetting balance and paid out centrally. The benefits are generally less than with full offset notional pooling or sweeping solutions but the following benefits apply:

- Accounts can be located in countries which are solvency netting-restricted
- No need for security or forms of inter-company guarantees
- No need for sweeping or administering inter-company loans

13.4.7   CREDIT FACILITIES

Overnight limit

An overnight limit can be attached to the notional pool as a whole (a 'group' limit) and the bank will allow the net pool balance to be in overdraft up to the agreed maximum amount. This means that an individual account can be in overdraft up to this maximum amount plus the net credit position on the other accounts in the pool. In order to control the use of credit by individual operating companies, an additional 'sub-limit' (also referred to as 'maximum debit amount' or 'compensation limit') can be attached to an operating account or a group of participating operating accounts. This is an overnight limit for each individual account. The bank will check credit positions on individual accounts against the 'sub-limit' as well as the overall pool limit.

Intra-day limit

As with a zero-balancing pool, intra-day limits may also be set for all participating accounts. Because the balances of the participating accounts in a notional pool remain on the accounts (they are not swept) the need and/or size of the intra-day limits is generally less than with zero balancing. In some cases, banks offer intraday limits on top of the entire pool. This allows central treasury to invest funds from a central account in the notional pool when the markets are still open. It is the client's responsibility to ensure the notional pool is within the agreed limits overnight.

13.5
Virtual cash management

A recently developed cash balance management tool is virtual cash management. Virtual cash management was developed to help corporates take the next step towards optimising the management of their balances using the latest technologies, while minimising the number of 'real' bank accounts. Virtual cash management is the term used to describe both virtual bank accounts and virtual ledger accounts.

Interest results on virtual bank accounts are the same as for physical cash concentration or notional pooling. Balances are concentrated on the central master account and the interest benefit is calculated over the balances held centrally.

Virtual bank accounts

Virtual bank accounts (VBAs) are basically a stripped-down version of a traditional bank account. Every VBA is linked to a current account with the bank (see Figure 13.4) and has a unique virtual bank account number (VBAN), which helps to segregate funds in the current account. VBAs do not hold a balance, as all incoming payments are automatically swept to a linked current account. As a result, any outgoing payments need to be pre-funded. As the account does not hold a balance, it does not attract interest. Control over the account is held by the signatories that are authorised on the linked current account, hence reducing the risk of fraud.

In this sense, the use of VBAs is a new form of physical cash concentration, but whereas in traditional cash concentration structures the *balances* are swept to the master account, with a VBA the *individual transactions* are swept from the VBA to the master account. As a result, unlike in a traditional sweeping or pooling structure, in the case of a VBA sweep the details of all payments & collections are fully visible in the master account. This has the benefit of easier reconciliation at the master account level than with traditional cash concentration.

Used appropriately, VBAs offer treasurers a number of benefits, including:
- The possibility of significantly reducing physical accounts, which lowers account management costs
- Central control over the operation of the VBA, which reduces the risk of fraud
- The ability to centralise incoming and outgoing transactions and cash concentration, which optimises interest results
- Enhanced visibility and control through improved reconciliation compared to physical pooling
- Reduced manual post-processing of unmatched items, which saves time
- The capability, like a regular account, to make typical local payments that require a local IBAN

Nevertheless, VBAs do have their limitations. For example, they are currently restricted to single bank usage, and are only available on a cross-border basis from select banks. VBAs are always in the same currency as the master account to which they are linked.

FIGURE 13.4

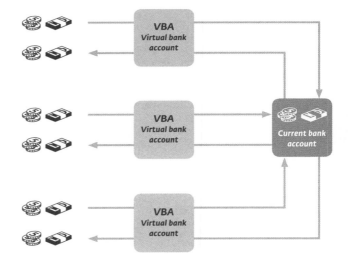

Virtual ledger accounts

Virtual ledger accounts are essentially administrative sub-accounts that enable the treasury function to allocate cash without segregating it physically. This allows treasurers to gain an overview of cash positions as well as deeper insight at any desired level, including managing their intercompany loan administration.

Unlike virtual bank accounts, virtual ledger accounts do hold balances and can generate interest, but only as a subset of the 'real' bank account balance and interest result.

Virtual ledger accounts enable treasurers to set-up an in-house bank, thereby eliminating the need for expensive in-house banking software. By creating virtual ledger accounts as a subset of the real bank account, the in-house bank can allocate incoming funds to (or implement collections on behalf of) specific entities or business lines, calculate intercompany loans and interest as well as execute payments (or payments on behalf of entities/business lines). With an advanced invoice matching and funds allocation module, the in-house bank is better able to match incoming and outgoing payments to the relevant business unit.

Corporates may choose to maintain a virtual ledger account structure and the related in-house bank in their ERP/TMS systems, in a dedicated software package, or to buy this as a service from their banks.

In addition, the virtual ledger account solution helps optimise reconciliation. Incoming transactions are automatically recognised and allocated to the appropriate virtual ledger Account, based on the solution's self-learning capability and its ability to facilitate one-on-one matching with outstanding invoices. In situations where a customer doesn't provide remittance information, the system proposes allocation of the funds based on historical data and mimics recurring actions, thereby reducing day sales outstanding (DSO).

FIGURE 13.5

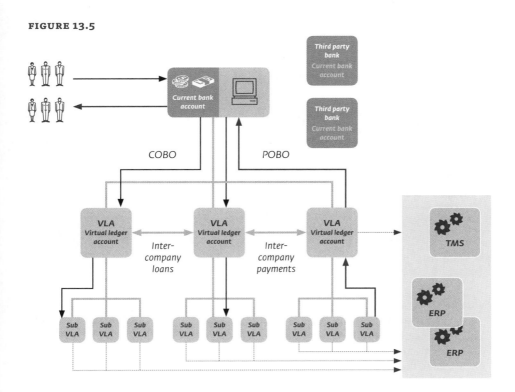

Optimising interest using virtual cash management

Interest results on virtual bank accounts are the same as for physical cash concentration or notional pooling. Balances are concentrated on the central master account and the interest benefit is calculated over the balances held centrally.

13.6
Hybrid solutions

The cash pooling techniques described in this chapter can be seen as the tools in the cash manager's toolbox. Many of these tools can be combined to construct a solution that fits a particular company structure or requirement. There are situations where the different forms of cash pooling are combined. One popular solution is a cross-border zero-balancing structure with a notional pool on top:

FIGURE 13.6

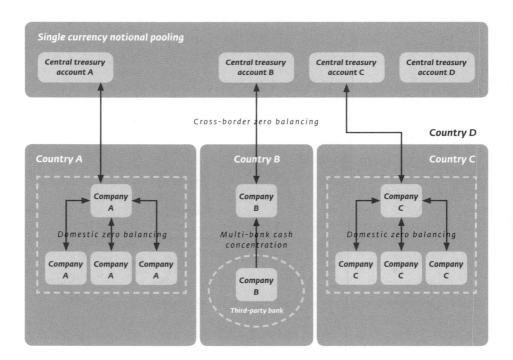

Some characteristics of this example:
- The treasury department of the company manages the cash pooling structure with the central treasury account D in the notional pool.
- Domestic zero balancing is combined with a cross-border zero-balancing sweep. First, the domestic zero balancing is executed, followed by a cross-border zero-balancing sweep.

- In country B, the company has an account with another bank than the company's cash management bank. Multi-bank funding and sweeping is used to ensure the balances of the account with the third-party bank are also included in the cash management solution.
- Fund flows are separated for each legal entity. The funds that end up in the accounts in the notional pool are still separated for each legal entity. That makes the administrative management of the inter-company loans relatively simple – as long as the interest rates applied to the participants in the notional pool are at 'arm's length'.

Another solution is to combine virtual bank accounts with virtual ledger accounts, as per the figure below. Integrating virtual bank accounts with virtual ledger accounts allows full cash concentration and visibility to be realised right across the group, no matter how the company's treasury function is organised, or how sophisticated and harmonised its technology infrastructure.

As a result, treasurers can free up time for more value-added tasks, such as deciding how best to put cash to use. Through the enhanced reporting capabilities of virtual cash management, and its sophisticated invoice matching engine, treasurers can also concentrate on optimising the company's working capital position by streamlining order to cash and purchase to pay processes.

FIGURE 13.7

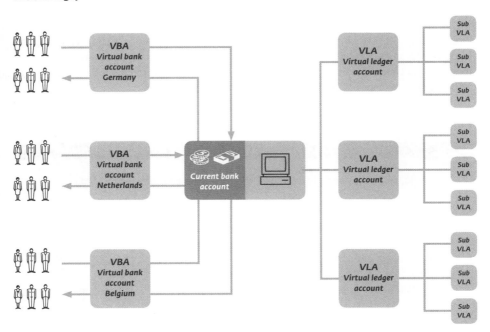

13.7
Implementing international cash pools

In order to decide whether there is a good business case for a cash pooling structure, a treasury must first define the purpose of such an undertaking. Broadly speaking, cash pooling can serve two purposes:

1. Providing central treasury with better visibility and control of the balances of each operating company
2. Improving a company's interest results

In today's treasury environment, many companies are more concerned with cash control than improved interest results. In times of economic uncertainty, it is important to show all financial stakeholders that treasury has full control over the cash available in a company. For obvious reasons, this is easier to achieve when all the company's cash is swept to a single master account than when the cash is spread over a series of operating companies across the world. Through multi-bank reporting, corporates can maintain an overview of balances in their accounts. With virtual ledger accounts, a consolidated view can be created in a multi-bank dashboard.

Almost all the cash pools are fully automated solutions. Bank systems are set up so that sweeping can be executed without human intervention. After the initial set-up, the company can leave the management of the balances to the bank with only periodic evaluation of the pooling settings. As a result, cash pools enable treasury departments to focus less on the operational workload and more on the strategic items.

When setting up a cash pool, a treasurer must decide which accounts will be included in the structure. It is not always necessary to include all the company's accounts in the pool, especially if the accounts have relatively small transaction volumes and balances. The costs of including such an account may be greater than the benefits.

Inclusion criteria

The following elements are relevant in the decision-making process concerning inclusion of an account in the structure:
- Cost of setting up a sweep (the implementation costs)
- Cost of executing the sweep – fixed fee per month or a fee per sweep (the so-called 'maintenance costs')
- Interest earned or charged on the local account
- Interest benefit of using the local balance on the central master account
- Costs when no sweep will be set up – the monitoring of and the manual transfer of the cash from or to the local account

---

Table 13.1 compares the characteristics of physical cash concentration, notional pooling and virtual cash management.

TABLE 13.1   COMPARISON

	Physical cash concentration	Notional pooling	Virtual Cash Management
Ownership of balances	Operating companies lose ownership of their balances	Operating companies retain ownership of their balances	Operating companies lose ownership, but retain control over their balances
Intercompany positions	Inter-company loan administration required	No inter-company loans occur	Intercompany loan administration inherently part of the product
Fiscal consequences	Many fiscal consequences	Minimal fiscal consequences	Many fiscal consequences
Cross-border availability	Cross-border solutions widely available	Cross-border solutions less common or more expensive	Cross-border solutions available with a limited number of banks
Legal complexity	Legal documentation relatively easy	Legal documentation complex because of security required by banks	Legal documentation relatively easy
Accounting treatment	Accounting treatment straightforward	Could lengthen the balance sheet	Accounting treatment straightforward
Number of accounts	Fewer accounts required	More accounts required	Fewer accounts required
Currency	Only single currency	Single and cross-currency available	Single currency for VBA, cross currency for VLA
Benefit to central treasury	Visibility of balances in one account	Visibility of balances across accounts	Visibility of balances in one account & improved reconciliation

Chapter 14

Cash Flow Forecasting

14 Cash Flow Forecasting

14.1
Introduction

All corporations, and treasurers in particular, are being affected by multiple forces outside their influence, including the financial crisis, the current low-to-zero interest rates, major economic and political surprises and new geopolitical dimensions. These are shaped by four factors: volatility, uncertainty, complexity and ambiguity (or VUCA for short). Treasurers must currently navigate unclear waters, with FX market volatility adding fuel to the fire. This changing environment requires more time and dedication to managing cash, and that it needs to be treated as a corporate asset. The market volatility and the continuing trend towards treasury centralisation require greater visibility, more financial control across the group, and reducing opportunity costs of idle cash balances. Having a proper cash flow forecasting is paramount to achieve these goals.

The complexity of forecasts will depend on the underlying business of a company, with different life cycles of products, currencies, treasury and treasury-related systems. Also the set-up with respect to cash pooling or netting, foreign currency and interest rate exposure management will impact the complexity and accuracy of the forecasting. The objective is to keep format and content as pragmatic as possible, without diluting their relevance and the ability of treasurers and senior management to make well-informed decisions.

In this chapter we will discuss the objectives of accurate cash flow forecasting, describe the concept and the challenges companies are facing. Finally, we will discuss potential solutions supporting the process and critical aspects to be considered in their implementation.

14.2
Effective cash flow forecasting

Effective cash flow forecasting is a critical function to any business. However, while it is a very important area in treasury, a number of surveys indicate that cash flow forecasting – together with liquidity management – are still among the top two focus areas for improvement within corporations. The reasons for this are the lack of accuracy and manual efforts in the process of forecasting.

The reliability of the cash flow forecast is fundamental in many ways as it enables a company to ensure liquidity, maximise investment income and/or minimise borrowing costs, identify potential financing requirements, manage currency exposures and anticipate financial risks. It is crucial to accurately fund a company's business operations and to ensure that potential shortfalls in liquidity are identified at an early stage and corresponding measures can be taken. These may include (re)negotiation of credit lines, attracting additional funding through financial markets or improving working capital management.

14.3
Objectives of cash flow forecasting

Cash flow forecasting can have various objectives within the wider finance function and in the treasury organisation of a company, whereas the importance of these objectives can vary. The main objectives are listed below.

14.3.1   CASH BALANCE MANAGEMENT

The goal of daily cash management is to optimally allocate the cash across the company. Cash balance management refers to the process of ensuring that all current accounts are sufficiently funded and that cash balances are centrally available if possible and required. Therefore, it is crucial to have daily visibility of the cash balances in all currencies and accounts. This is usually one of the first tasks of the day, whereby the cash manager checks the closing balances of the accounts from the previous day. Based on the very short-term cash flow forecast (one to five days), the cash manager initiates transfers between the accounts to ensure that at the end of the day, all current accounts are appropriately funded and access cash is centralised and available for investments. If cash pooling is used, the more accounts are part of the cash pool, the less they have to be checked and transferred. In addition, no cash buffer must be left on the sweep accounts. Only the master account is required to have a certain balance to cover the potential daily movement.

14.3.2   SHORT-TERM LIQUIDITY MANAGEMENT

As cash balance management relates to the very near term, short-term liquidity management copes with a time horizon of up to roughly six months, depending on the predictability of the cash flows. Therefore, forecasting is key for a treasurer to understand what actions he needs to take in terms of short-term funding and/or short-term investments. If a company has excess cash, a decision must be made as to whether the cash will be invested and if so, the duration. Companies that are not in an excess cash situation have to consider which funding instruments are to be used, in what currency funding shall be provided and which time horizons are to be covered.

The chart below (figure 14.1) provides a schematic illustration of the potential issues concerning inaccurate forecasts. If actual liquidity is higher than forecasted, opportunity costs arise due to missed investment opportunities. Vice versa, if the cash position is below the forecasted situation, a company faces excess costs for borrowing.

FIGURE 14.1   MISSED INVESTMENT OPPORTUNITIES

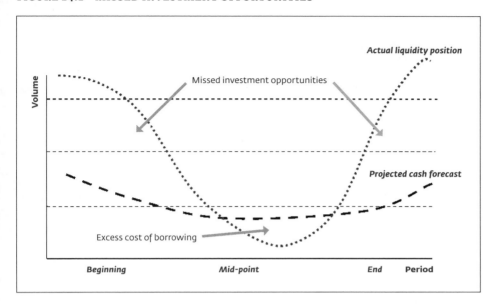

Often, forecasts are prepared in the currencies that correspond with the cash flows and then converted into the functional currency of the company. Depending on the flows, it might make sense to make short-term investments or funding in non-functional currencies in order to avoid swapping currencies.

14.3.3   FX EXPOSURE MANAGEMENT AND HEDGING

Another crucial objective of cash flow forecasting is to understand future flows in foreign currencies. As mentioned above, most companies forecast in the same currency as the cash flow. The treasurer can use this information, combined with the current foreign currency balances, to gain an understanding of which currencies would need to be hedged. In addition, natural hedging can be detected with one legal entity having outgoing cash flow in one currency and another entity with collections in the same currency and during the same period.

This way cash flow forecasting strongly supports the hedging of future cash flows (off-balance sheet).

14.3.4   LONG-TERM FUNDING

For decisions regarding a company's long-term funding and capital structure, the above-mentioned forecasts will not suffice. The requirement here is different, as a longer time horizon of one to five years is required. However, the level of detail can be significantly reduced. Usually, forecasts are only performed on a monthly or even quarterly basis and only separated into cash flows originating from operations, financing and investments.

The importance of cash flow forecasts depends on different factors. Below are examples of some key drivers:

- *Size of the company*
  The bigger the company, the more important it is to have a strong process and governance around forecasting. In smaller companies, chief financial officers (CFOs) often have a good sense of the cash situation and expectations on sales, costs, investments etc., so the collection of data might not lead to much more insight. However, in a larger company involving more divisions and/or legal entities, a CFO cannot have full insight and more data-based facts and information are required.

- *Core business model*
  Different business models and industries have different levels of volatility and uncertainty concerning their expected cash flows. For example, a company generating sales primarily through long-term contracts with licence fees will have more stable cash flows than a company in the machine-building industry selling big projects with uncertain cash flows, or entities in the retail business affected by seasonality. When there are stable cash flows, a forecast will be less important than in an environment with volatile cash flows due to a different business model.

- *Global footprint (in terms of currencies)*
  To be able to properly hedge forecasted cash flows in foreign currencies, an accurate forecast is clearly vital so as not to over- or under-hedge. The importance of forecasting therefore increases with higher percentages of cash flows in foreign currencies and higher numbers of currencies.

- *Financing of the company*
  However, the most important influencer is the structure of the financing. The company will have to focus to a greater or lesser extent on accurate cash flow forecasting depending on whether it is mainly equity financed or financed by long- or short-term third-party debt. Basically, the more a company is financed on a short-term basis via external funding (credit facilities or short-term overdrafts), the more it will focus on the cash flow forecasting. Cash-rich companies with a buffer to compensate for short-term fluctuations in cash or companies that are backed by, for example, strong private equity might not be as dependent on a highly accurate cash flow forecast. Highly leveraged entities with limited committed credit lines need a more accurate forecast to be able to take action in time before a shortfall occurs.

14.4
The concept of cash flow forecasting

Having listed objectives and described the importance of cash flow forecasting, it is now time to cover the basic concept of forecasting and how companies cope with this strategically important but difficult task in practice.

The starting point of every cash flow forecast is the current liquidity position to which the expected and forecasted cash inflows and outflows are added.

Liquidity position

The liquidity position is the sum of all cash balances on current accounts, including short-term investments and short-term loans (committed) from banks. It goes without saying that all currencies have to be taken into consideration.

Given this basis, future liquidity positions can be forecasted, potential shortfalls identified or investment opportunities recognised. The time horizon the forecast covers must be defined. This decision depends, on the one hand, on the requirements and objectives of the forecast and, on the other, on how experienced a treasury and a company is in forecasting. The horizon can be longer if there is better data and a more predictable business (and therefore also better cash flows).

Typically, a company populates different forecasts with different time horizons. For daily cash management operations, a rolling 13-week time horizon with monthly, weekly or even daily updates is often used. The first one to two weeks are forecasted on a daily basis and for week two to 13, weekly cash flows are populated. Using this basis, the forecast can cover the objectives of daily cash balance management and short-term liquidity management.

The way the forecast is structured and formatted varies from company to company and is dependent on the objectives. What most forecasts have in common is that the cash flows are separated into cash flows from operations, financing and investments. Further drill-downs make sense to provide transparency, increase understanding of the origins of deviations and to give guidance to the people forecasting so as not to omit certain flows.

FIGURE 14.2   EXAMPLE 13-WEEK FORECASTING STRUCTURE

Cash flow planning - daily view, 13-week forecast
based on individual legal entities
in kCHF

	2017/21					
Year	2017					
Week	21					
Date (ISO Week)	22.05.17	22.05.17	23.05.17	24.05.17	25.05.17	26.05.
Weekday	Full week	Mo	Di	Mi	Do	Fr
Liquidity status - Start of period (Actual)						
Thereof: Cash pool						
Liquidity status - Start of period (Forecast)						
Surplus / Deficit						
Cashflow from Operations						
Operating inflows (+)						
External inflows (+)						
Intercompany inflows (incl. netting) (+)						
Operating outflows (-)						
External outflows (-)						
Intercompany outflows (incl. netting) (-)						
Salaries and other personnel expenses (-)						
Corporate tax payments (-)						
Cashflow from Investments						
Divestments (+)						
CAPEX (-)						
Mergers and acquisitions (-)						
Cashflow from Financing						
Change in external loans (+/-)						
Change in internal loans (+/-)						
Interest and dividends paid / received ext. (+/-)						
Interest, dividends and mgmt. fees p/r int. (+/-)						
Cash flows due to equity financing external (+/-)						
Cash flows due to equity financing internal (+/-)						
Liquidity status - End of period (forecast)						

	2017/24	2017/25	2017/26	2017/27	2017/28	2017/29	2017/30	2017/31	2017/32	2017/33
	2017	2017	2017	2017	2017	2017	2017	2017	2017	2017
	24	25	26	27	28	29	30	31	32	33
	12.06.17	19.06.17	26.06.17	03.07.17	10.07.17	17.07.17	24.07.17	31.07.17	07.08.17	14.08.17
	Full week	Full week	Full week	Full week	Full week	Full week	Full week	Full week	Full week	Full week

For FX exposure management and mid-term liquidity planning, a longer time horizon of 12 months and even beyond is required. Usually, such forecasts are populated on a monthly basis. In addition, a long-term cash flow forecast is populated jointly with supporting investment and divestment decisions as well as long-term financing strategies (derived from the three- to five-years company budget). Such forecasts are typically made on a monthly or even quarterly basis and are often populated based on the indirect cash flow method (see chapter 15).

14.5
Predicting future cash flows

There are two different methods in cash flow forecasting which are in line with the techniques used in accounting and controlling to calculate a cash flow statement: the direct method and the indirect method.

	Direct method	Indirect method
Description	Forecasts are directly populated by treasury and the business to predict cash flows, where treasury provides a standardised template (see figure 14.1)	Forecasting is based on the planned income statement (e. g. starting with EBIT), adjusted for non-cash relevant movements on the balance sheet (e. g. changes in A/P A/R). This method is typically used by the Controller to perform longer-term forecasts
Advantages	– Easy to understand – Accurate and detailed in the short-run – Flexible and can be tailored to treasurer's needs – Business is responsible for forecasting – All available information from the business and local legal entities is used – Business has responsibility for forecasting its own cash flows	– Aligned with financial planning – Less effort required and not dependent on business
Disadvantages	– Relatively time-consuming – Treasury relies on business delivering accurate forecasts	– Accuracy is not very high – Lower level of detail – Only possible on a monthly or even quarterly basis (depending on planning interval) – No responsibility for forecasts for the business

While for the indirect method, balance sheet movements have to be forecasted, the direct method is based on directly predicting cash flows. It is important to understand the patterns of cash flows, whether they are daily, weekly or monthly. In addition, seasonality is often a factor that needs to be taken into account.

Some cash flows are easier to predict than others:

Certain cash flows	- Interest payments
	- Repayments of financing
	- Taxes
Predictable cash flows	- Payroll disbursement
	- Vendor payments (short-term)
	- Direct debit collections
	- Dividend payments
Less predictable cash flows	- Collections of sales
	- Vendor payments (long-term)
	- Unexpected flows
	- Legal litigations

For the direct method to be successful, it is important to involve the department or company that originates the cash flows. Therefore, direct cash flow forecasts are mostly a joint effort whereby treasury coordinates and consolidates together with various stakeholders using different information. For example, the sales and/or account receivable (A/R) department will be able to predict incoming operating cash flows using the sales forecast, the defined payment terms and average DSO (days sales outstanding). In addition, the sales department will know if a new product will be launched or when a special campaign is running to promote a product, which might have an impact on the cash flows.

The A/P team will be able to support predicting outgoing operational cash flows. Usually, payment files for creditor payments are produced and sent to the bank some days before execution. Using this information should lead to a very accurate forecast of the short-term outgoing vendor payments. The human resources or human capital department (HR) will be able to provide an accurate forecast of the payroll figures each month. Tax departments should also be involved because while tax payments or returns might not occur very often, their values are relatively high.

In addition, treasury itself holds a lot of cash flow-related information which needs to be included, such as interest payments on financing, maturing investments, FX settlements etc.

- How has the company's overall turnover changed compared to the previous year?
- What does the planning indicate?
- Have there been any peaks over the last year due to special events (e.g. new big client acquired)
- Have payment terms changed, whether on the part of the vendors or the company?
- Have there been any other changes in the way working capital is managed e.g. implemented factoring or dynamic discounting?
- Etc.

14.5.1 HISTORIC FIGURES

Often historic figures are used in the forecasting process of operational cash flows. Companies at a lower maturity level in treasury and minor experience in forecasting, might use this data as a starting point for their predictions. Due to seasonal fluctuations, often previous year's figures are used, but it is required to challenge these figures and adjust accordingly.

14.5.2 PREDICTIVE ANALYTICS

Recent developments in technology, including the strongly increased capacity of calculation engines, have paved the way for sophisticated data and predictive analytics. With sophisticated software, well-defined algorithms and intelligence, predictive analytics have and will further revolutionise cash flow forecasting (see chapter 23). Below are some examples of how predictive analytics can support the process of achieving a highly efficient way of producing the most accurate cash flow forecasts:

- Cash flow forecasting is usually a very labour-intensive process which can be highly automated using predictive analytics
- Modelling of payment patterns of clients and/or client groups can increase accuracy to predict incoming operational cash flows. In addition, it supports management of the credit risk
- Due to automated processes, forecasts can be performed on a more regular basis and without much effort from the business, so a treasurer can act sooner
- Predictive analytics allows a treasurer to learn from the past by spotting patterns and identifying whether such patterns can happen again, and taking action if required
- Certain solutions also include external data sources to model future cash flows. For example, long-term weather forecasts or political risks in certain regions

However, all these advantages can only be realised by using sophisticated software and the software can only be effective if the data used is correct. Often data is a big challenge for companies as multiple systems are in place with multiple sources. Data quality, availability and different structures make it difficult to implement predictive analytics tools. In addition, implementation costs are often significant and a clear business case should be worked out (cost-benefit analysis).

14.6
Process and organisation of cash flow forecasting

As mentioned above, cash flow forecasting is normally a joint effort between different departments and legal entities within the same company or group. Below (figure 14.3) is a very simplified forecasting process, including responsibilities.

FIGURE 14.3   SCHEMATIC CASH FLOW FORECASTING PROCESS

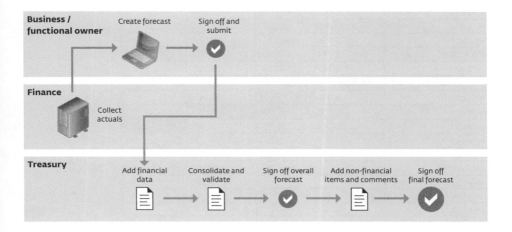

In general, it is important that the business and/or legal entities delivering data as input for the forecast understand the importance and take on responsibility for their forecast. It is therefore required that a clear governance structure is in place. Treasury policy supports the process and defines roles and responsibilities as well as ensuring treasury is mandated by the management.

14.7
Deviation analysis

To constantly improve or maintain forecasting quality, it is important to perform a deviation analysis to identify potential quality issues with the forecast. For this purpose, incentives could be created by defining key performance indicators (KPIs), against which treasury and input providers for the forecast can be measured.

The most straightforward approach involves comparing the forecasted liquidity position with the actual liquidity position. In a 13-week rolling forecast, the same week is forecasted 13 times and it is expected that the closer the forecasted week to the actual week, the lower the deviation.

We now show a simplified example of what such a deviation analysis could look like in practice. Every forecast must be copied into a data table or database so that it can be used for analysis.

FIGURE 14.4   EXAMPLE DATA TABLE WITH SAMPLE FIGURES

Date	ACTUAL	-1 W	-2 W	-3 W
week22	55,000			
week23	57,324	57,154		
week24	87,400	55,382	63,508	
week25	59,002	132,988	140,393	...
week26	137,800	133,987	122,442	...
week27	120,896	145,254	146,827	...
week28	123,444	134,902	130,409	...
week29	135,789	120,387	140,292	...
week30	141,300	133,991	144,238	...
week31	98,746	148,455	150,478	...
week32	40,000	33,098	86,490	...
week33	48,272	36,587	34,829	...
week34	35,700	43,091	35,774	...
week35	44,298	32,487	44,389	...
week36		46,789	48,972	...
week37			57,893	...
week38				...
week39				
week40				
week41				
week42				

The figure above shows an example of a potential deviation analysis. In order to ensure readability, only actuals and the forecast from the last three weeks are shown. For example, in week 30 the cash balance for the coming 13 weeks – up to week 42 – are forecasted. The table shows actuals in week 30 of EUR 141,300 and then the first two forecasted weeks (red boxed cells). This way of structuring data leads to the possibility of showing how one specific week has been forecasted. Again, looking at week 30 we can see that one week before, the cash balance was forecasted at EUR 133,991 and two weeks before at EUR 144,238.

Based on this data, graphs can be drawn to illustrate the deviation in cash flow forecasting. For example, the chart below shows the average absolute deviation for every week forecasted. Actuals do not have a deviation but the further ahead the forecast, the higher the absolute deviation. The average deviation is calculated as follows:

$$\text{ø abs. dev}_j = \frac{\sum_{i=1}^{13} \text{abs } (FLP_i - LP_i)}{13}$$

ø abs.dev$_j$:   average absolute deviation in week j
FLP$_i$:   forecasted liquidity position in period i
LP$_i$:   actual liquidity position in period i

FIGURE 14.5   GRAPH ILLUSTRATING AVERAGE ABSOLUTE DEVIATION

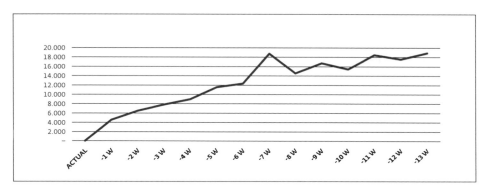

To further analyse the results, the standard deviation is calculated and populated in the chart below.

$$\text{std. deviation}_j = \sqrt{\sum_{i=1}^{13} (FLP_i - LP_i)^2}$$

ø std. deviation$_j$:   standard deviation of forecast to actuals in week j
FLP$_i$:   forecasted liquidity position in period i
LP$_i$:   actual liquidity position in period i

FIGURE 14.6   STANDARD DEVIATION

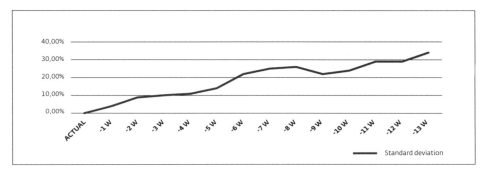

Often, the deviation analysis is more difficult than it might seem. Comparing the forecasted liquidity position with the actual liquidity position is fairly simple. However, if deviations are high and should be explained, forecasted cash flows must be compared to actual cash flows. These figures can typically be obtained from finance and accounting departments.

14.8
Systems needed for implementation

Having the right people and technology is key to effective forecasting and the obstacles are often both organisational and technical. Forecast data is typically held in different systems (see chapter 21) across the group, and often in quite different formats and templates. Even with effective technology there can still be issues where owners of data which are required for forecasting may not always be aligned with treasury. In addition, their timelines and planning are often outside treasury's direct remit. As a result, treasury is required to influence the behaviour and priorities of local finance teams or other departments in charge of data that directly contribute to the forecasting.

There are three main barriers to developing a robust and successful forecasting system and process:

- Lack of system(s) integration
- Overuse of spreadsheets or other e-mail reports
- Lack of support

If these barriers are not sufficiently considered and addressed, they may undermine treasury efforts to achieve more accurate forecast results. As mentioned above, these results are the starting point of an accurate cash management system, as well as investment decisions for the more optimal deployment of idle cash, optimisation of funding or utilisation of credit lines, and hedging decisions concerning FX, interest rates and possibly commodity exposures.

Depending on the IT strategy and sophistication of a company as well as the nature of business and geographic reach, sources may include:

- Enterprise resource planning (ERP)-integrated forecasting tools
- Specific modules of fully-fledged treasury management systems (TMS)
- Specialised or so-called best-of-breed treasury solutions for forecasting, or a mix of, for example, payroll, accounts receivable and payable, invoicing and inventory management systems

The graph below (figure 14.7) outlines the complexity of householding with the different data sources.

FIGURE 14.7 COMPLEXITY OF DIFFERENT DATA SOURCES

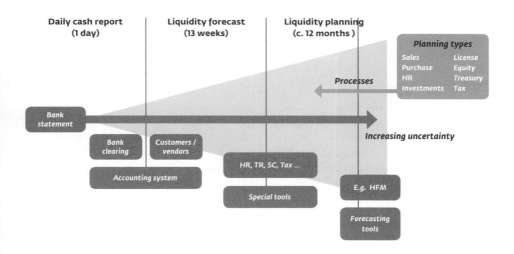

These solutions can interact with different systems, automate the collection, consolidation and reconciliation of data, and create standard or basic scenarios as well as reports.

Further explanations to the graph
- A medium-term liquidity forecast means predictable cash flows based on already booked data within accounting systems and further records based on available planning data.
- To create an informative cash and liquidity forecast, so-called planning types will be defined to cluster the company's significant cash flow positions such as sales, purchases, investments, tax, financing, divestments, salaries etc.
- By integrating the accounting system in a functional cash management tool, information regarding short-term liquidity is available as well as information concerning payables and receivables.
- In order to refine both the reliability and quality of the forecast for 13 weeks, it is recommended to include account payables and receivables, including intercompany.

Most companies have understood the importance of a stable cash flow forecasting process and its immediate impact on the treasury value chain. This is also demonstrated by several surveys executed over the last few months and years.

Despite company-specific differences (underlying businesses, jurisdictions and therefore currency exposures, funding needs, geopolitical influences etc.), a vast majority of companies deploy a robust cash flow forecasting system or application (ERP, TMS) but still rely on Excel spreadsheets for more flexible reporting, analytics, data input and, lastly, even for reconciliation purposes or deviation analysis.

There is still a lot of potential for more integrated approaches. Best-of-breed systems or even solutions from FinTech/start-ups are promising, but are often still at an early stage and lack maturity as well as a track record in the treasury area. Again, while a good system solution is one aspect, the governance and the process design are equally important for long-term success.

14.9
Critical success factors

Key success factors are discipline (strong governance in place), high organisational visibility (in treasury's remit) and a regular, detailed deviation analysis (including threshold of acceptance) with back testing. Cash flow forecasting should be seen as part of the DNA of an organisation, which is steadily and actively monitored by senior management.

An accurate forecast requires bringing together data from different internal and external sources, often in different formats as well as different levels of consistency and accuracy. Data analytics and business intelligence (BI) solutions cluster all those data, using them for statistical purposes such as variance / trend analysis or slicing and dicing of information for the user's needs. Such data analytics and business intelligence solutions integrate historical data patterns (e.g. accounts receivable and payable, inventories, salaries etc.) from internal ERPs, banking systems, market interest and exchange rates, purchasing and sales statistics, to build a comprehensive and more advanced forecast.

> *Leading practice approaches*

Role of senior management
The request for cash flow forecasting must originate from C-level or executive management with strong support for the implementation and long-term development (e.g. technology and IT progress) and maintenance (e.g. deviation analysis).
Furthermore, risk or treasury committees where senior management (e.g. CFO) and the (group) treasurer are present should be discussing and deciding on which economic, business or regulatory changes are impacting the forecasting process and may require change (e.g., new investments, divestments, change in functional currencies, new FX policies, new payment tools, implementation of a new TMS etc.).

Governance and policies
Cash flow forecasting and its principles, characteristics, rationale, roles and responsibilities, should be part of a group or a treasury policy document and this should also incentivise the operating entities involved for time commitment and accuracy.

>

It should not be forgotten that the process itself – which is a short-term view helping a treasury to manage its cash and liquidity – should be linked with the group forecasts and associated budget process (more from the controller and finance point of view, therefore beyond 18-month cycles).

Philosophy of a treasury

The role of a treasury department should be made transparent, acting as a value-adding service centre setting with its respective policies and rules.

Tools and technology

An understanding of the underlying templates and the positions to be reported in a forecasting process is essential and, as a result, the implementation of appropriate tools for data capturing, reporting and follow-ups (e.g., deviation analysis and incentivisation) as well. The objective should be to standardise consolidation and reporting of cash flows to treasury in a single system.

Performance measurement

The introduction of KPIs for cash, alongside all other metrics for treasury operations, is an important success factor and is often summarised in a treasury policy or framework.

Deviation analysis and improvements

Variances in cash flow forecasting should be monitored and receive follow-up on a regular basis, depending of course on the cycles chosen for the forecasting process. Less mature or cash-poor organisations have to update their forecasts on, for instance, a weekly basis (including e.g. covenants management required by the banks) or for other programmes in place such as factoring. More mature and cash-rich companies do their forecasts on a monthly basis, including respective deviation analysis.

Group treasury is responsible for defining thresholds of deviations, including the rightsizing of the acceptance levels (diminishing over time and gaining more maturity in the processes).

Role of operating entities

At an early stage, operating entities need to be involved and asked for their contribution to a successful cash flow forecasting and liquidity planning. KPIs can be a supporting factor.

Career path and job rotation / enrichment

The appointment of a dedicated person for this process helps to implement a process, including the authority to implement a methodology and system(s).

Such treasury personnel are also responsible for conducting regular trainings, including the on-boarding of new staff (job rotation) at operating entity level.

The rationale for a strong cash flow forecasting tool and mechanism is manifold, underpinned with some KPIs (as explained above):

No liquidity shortage or avoidance of drawing (un)committed credit lines due to misallocation of group-wide cash positions	The percentage of global cash positions visible to treasury on a daily basis or the percentage of cash under the control of group treasury but also the percentage accuracy of forecasts vis-à-vis actual or timeliness of forecast deliveries
Reduction of debt and interest costs and / or increase in interest income (opportunity costs)	Idle cash at operating entity level as percentage of sales
Better understanding and explanation of risks of certain cash flows and currency positions, also in taking hedging decisions	The percentage of foreign currency exposures hedged against the functional currencies vis-à-vis non-hedged items (free float) and its impact on the financial result
Early warning indicator for changes in business patterns, client behaviours (payment patterns), and its immediate impact on business financials	Regular reports / dashboard(s) for senior and executive management – depending on the maturity levels of the company, ranging from daily / weekly to monthly / quarterly reports

Corporates are making improvements to their cash and liquidity management practice, especially the forecasting processes. However, progress is not uniform across industries. Companies can perform a so-called maturity assessment with a great proportion of own assessment of where they stand in their processes. Maturity levels, as shown in the graph below, are ranging from early stages, 'Foundation', to 'Leading Practice':

FIGURE 14.8 MATURITY LEVELS

Leading practice

Systems	Real time monitoring of intraday cash and collateral requirements across the organisation
Organisation	Capability to measure intraday needs on a currency, legal entity and business line basis Clearly defined limits and management of explicit and implicit intraday liquidity risks across the organisation
Methodology	Established transfer pricing mechanisms for charging intraday liquidity costs to lines of business and customers Projected cash and collateral positions for all sources/uses
Management actions	Stress testing of intraday use across multiple dimensions Optimised payments release (throttling), credit lines usage and collateral management Maintenance of separate intraday liquidity buffer

Advanced

Systems	Capability to monitor intraday liquidity positions against expected activities and available resources (balances, remaining intraday credit capacity, available collateral)
Organisation	Board oversight and defined roles and responsibilities for functions that support intraday liquidity risk management
Methodology	Transfer pricing of intraday liquidity costs based on average usage Projected cash positions for all sources/uses
Management actions	Limit and trigger framework in place Back-testing and historical analysis of intraday liquidity usage for intraday liquidity buffer sizing

Foundation

Systems	Regulatory reporting of intraday liquidity metrics
Organisation	Intraday liquidity roles and responsibilities included in the existing framework
Methodology	Stress testing on aggregated EoD data and peak usages
Management actions	Manage the timing of liquidity outflows in line with intraday objectives, including those of customers who receive intraday liquidity from the bank

Maturity assessment

14.9
Summary

The requirements of banks (covenants reporting, Basel III and IV to come), capital markets and shareholders regarding the company's ability to effectively manage its cash positions have greatly increased. This is resulting in an increasing need for liquidity information and cash transparency, especially considering that debt, equity and divestments as well as lines of credit are no longer natural sources of capital.

By improving a company's ability to manage its cash by e.g. producing more detailed cash forecasts and improving technology to support the automation of forecasting processes, such efforts do result in higher certainty regarding the cash situation at individual entity levels and geographies.

A reliable cash planning process turns into a key source of competitive advantage for companies, which increase their degree of automation and integration with regards to the extraction and analysis of relevant cash information – from existing but not currently aligned data within a company.

There is great potential for corporates to increase financial performance by optimising their cash flow forecasting. A one-time effort spent in understanding, committing to, automating and also standardising the forecasting process is a wise investment in the business and resources. Helping the operating businesses to think in cash flows, focus on accuracy, reduce time and error-prone manual entries, can result in cash and non-cash savings.

In conclusion, and putting emphasis once again on the importance of cash flow forecasting, a robust cash flow forecasting process requires the following:

- A structure that is defined and adhered to, incorporating sufficient controls (e.g. deviation analyses), considering changes in the wider setting in which a company is operating and including procedures to meet increasing regulatory requirements.
- Integrated technology or systems that facilitate the sharing and protection of accurate and reliable data used in the entire value chain of a treasury operation (investment management, funding / financing matters, netting / pooling, risk management).
- Co-operation across the company is crucial, including operating entities but also finance / control department with its overarching budget process (beyond 18-month cycles).
- The attainment of a complete and realistic view of global cash positions, preferably on a daily basis, independent of whether a company is cash-rich or cash-poor.

Chapter 15

Investment and Funding Management

15　Investment and Funding Management

15.1
Introduction

The daily activities of a company mean that cash flows in and out of that company. Cash flow is generally the combined result of a company's operational activities, capital expenditures and investment activities. At the end of the day, its cash position can be in balance, but it is more likely that there will be either an excess or a shortage of cash. Moreover, the company might require long-term funding and/or strategic excess cash reserves for unexpected opportunities or downturns. The treasurer is responsible for managing the excess or shortage of cash under the best conditions and at the lowest costs, while minimising several risk. Following the financial crisis in 2008, there have been many changes in the objectives and practices surrounding investment and funding management as well as the day-to-day activities supporting this process.

While the key short-term investment instruments have remained the same, the focus of achieving the best possible return on invested liquidity has been superseded by a focus on managing both counterparty and liquidity risk. Today's treasurers focus on the return *of* principal rather than the return *on* principal.

In the years following the financial crisis, some companies faced additional challenges in attracting external funding from the market. During that time, most banks have been restricted in their lending capabilities by their governing bodies. This has forced companies to achieve a greater level of diversity in funding sources, which has meant that a shift to alternatives, such as asset-based lending and the more traditional cash optimisation techniques, has become far more important to the corporate treasury.

Reliable cash flow forecasting is the basis for enabling companies to minimise the funding cost of short positions and it is the starting point for companies' investment decisions. The ability to fund or recycle cash from cash-positive to cash-negative parts of the organisation has become and remains highly useful (for more information, see chapter 14, Cash Flow Forecasting and Reporting). An increased focus on optimising working capital variables also contributes to minimising funding needs and costs, as described in chapter 4 on Working Capital Management.

This chapter starts with a brief description of the different sources of cash flows within a company. The second part discusses the treasurer's options for investing the company's excess cash balances and what variables to take into account when investing. The third section addresses the elements determining credit risk and the funding alternatives. The chapter ends with a description of interest rate dynamics.

15.2
Sources and use of cash in a company

The starting point for proper management of a company's short-term positive or negative cash balances is a good understanding of the sources and uses of cash. Figure 15.1 shows a simplified balance sheet and profit & loss statement.

FIGURE 15.1

Balance sheet   **Profit & loss statement**

Assets	Liabilities	
Land & buildings	Equity	Sales
Machinery	Long-term debt	-/- Costs
Equipment	Short-term debt	-/- Depreciation
Inventory	Payables	+/+ Interest received
Receivables	Short-term liabilities	-/- Interest payed
Short-term assets		-/- Taxes
Cash		
		Net profit

Long-term fixed assets like land & buildings, machinery and equipment require cash when acquired by the company. If these assets are purchased from the company's cash reserves, a substitution on the asset side of the balance sheet takes place from cash reserves to land & buildings. In most cases, a company attracts external funding when acquiring long-term fixed assets. When they are in use, these assets indirectly generate cash by enabling the company to realise sales. The proportional part of the economic lifetime costs of the long-term fixed asset is allocated to the profit & loss statement as depreciation. Depreciation is a cost that does not require a cash-out, since the cash-out was made at the moment the long-term fixed asset was acquired. If insufficient liquidity is available, a treasurer can decide not to buy the long-term asset but to rent it. Common examples are real estate and rolling material like cars and trucks.

Inventory can be divided into raw materials and (semi-) finished goods. Raw materials are processed into a product and, when sold, converted into cash. (Semi-) Finished goods include cash-outs like raw materials, labour costs and attribution of proportional general costs. When sold, finished goods generate cash. How much cash a company's inventory requires depends on the absolute level and time the inventory stays in the company. The longer this period, the more cash is required to pre-finance inventory, resulting in higher borrowing costs (or lower investment rewards). This can be measured by the days inventory outstanding (DIO).

A receivable is the result of a timing difference between selling goods and receiving the payment. How much cash a company needs to finance its receivables depends on the duration of the receivable (so-called days sales outstanding). The longer this takes, the more cash is required to pre-finance receivables, resulting in higher borrowing costs (or lower investment rewards). Some companies receive advanced payments, for instance when a product is customised for a certain buyer or when the product is project-related (e.g. construction). Advanced payments are listed on the balance sheet under short-term liabilities and are a source of cash for a company.

Most costs do not have to be paid immediately when incurred. The difference between cost incurrence and cost payment results in a payable. Payables are a source of cash funding for a company and, thanks to the absence of interest on a payable, it is a relatively cheap funding source. The 'duration' of a payable can be measured in days payables outstanding. Among other things, the payment term depends on relative buying power, the industry standard and the country. Sometimes a discount is offered by a supplier/seller when paying in the very short term. Depending on the company's alternative funding sources, and the costs associated with these funding alternatives (e.g. bank overdraft interest rates), a treasurer can opt to benefit from the early payment discount.

The other components on the liability side of the balance sheet will be described in detail in section 15.9.

15.3
Liquidity forecasts

Having covered the different sources and uses of cash, we will now describe the methods of deriving the cash position of a company. Based on accurate and reliable cash flow forecasts of the operations and cleared balances on accounts, a treasurer should be able to identify the total balances accessible for a company to invest or fund. The level of administration and manpower needed for this activity will depend on the level of centralisation within the company. Companies with centralised treasuries often concentrate the same currency balances – automatically or manually – from a variety of group companies to form a single bucket of cleared balances for investment or funding. This can be achieved by employing cash concentration techniques such as physical sweeping or notional pooling.

Decentralised companies will manage their own local positions separately. This results in the management of a number of smaller balances in different locations, which can create execution risk and missed self-funding opportunities, while attracting additional reconciliation costs.

Armed with accurate and timely balance information from the bank and internal back offices, a cash manager should be able to make the appropriate decision whether to arrange (short-term) funding or how to use surplus funds. In nearly every instance, the goals are to reduce total borrowing costs and maximise interest income. A liquidity forecast is a best estimate of the company's future liquidity positions. It also provides a picture of the company's expected financial position. Establishing a cash position statement and liquidity forecast can be a complex and time-consuming process. However, technology can be harnessed to ease the burden, as is discussed in chapter 10 on Treasury Management Systems. After determining the expected balance, the cash manager should know the expected positions for each currency and whether there is an overall net liquidity surplus or deficit. The liquidity forecast should include an estimation of how long the surplus or deficit will remain.

Sometimes, the cash manager is not certain of the outcome or timing of the liquidity forecasts. Unexpected events often occur in the course of a treasurer's and cash manager's day. In such cases, the cash manager needs to make certain that there is an adequate level of flexible-term cash to provide a liquidity buffer of investments that allows for easy conversion to free cash. If, for example, some of the funds will be used for a dividend payment within six months, that amount can be invested for a matching term. This will only be done if it does not weaken the company's ability to meet its financial obligations. Unwinding a six-month deposit before the due date can be very costly and could generate a negative net return.

15.4
Cash categories

When a company has excess liquidity, the cash often comes from diverse sources and has multiple future uses. Generally, most of the cash results from the company's daily core operations. More may be generated from divestments or other corporate finance-related transactions.

Cash can be used for daily, less easily predictable activities such as supplier payables or more predictable purposes such as repayment of debt. It can also be used for more strategic but less immediate purposes, such as acquisitions or share buy-back programs. These different sources and uses of cash determine the characteristics of the different types of cash held and need to be considered when implementing the investment policy.

Typically, cash can be broken down into three categories:

- Operating cash
- Flexible-term cash
- Fixed-term cash

Given the different characteristics and uses of such cash, the investment activity and instruments selected will differ for each type of cash.

15.4.1 OPERATING CASH

Operating cash balances can be defined as those that result from daily operations and are volatile in nature. This type of cash is designated for daily cash management use and lends itself to investment instruments that allow instant access. Typical instruments used include current accounts, overnight time deposits and money market funds.

15.4.2 FLEXIBLE-TERM CASH

Flexible-term cash has a typical investment horizon ranging from one month to twelve months. It has a level of stability that allows it to be invested longer than overnight but is the type of cash that is held as a liquidity buffer against unexpected or unpredictable events where the company needs direct access to its cash. In the wake of the 2008 financial crisis, many companies were unwilling to commit their cash to fixed-term investments. Indeed, with most companies now using short-term liquidity as their primary source of working capital funding, corporates are eager to retain access to this liquidity. At the same time, however, companies are keen to find ways to put this cash to work. This creates a dichotomy between investing in products that grant instant access but a requirement to benefit from rates that reflect the longer-term nature of this cash. Consequently, typical investments may be a blend of time deposits with differing maturities, money market funds but also commercial paper or existing bonds maturing within one year.

15.4.3 FIXED-TERM CASH

Fixed-term cash can be committed for longer maturities. It is the type of cash balance that is used for strategic purposes and can be the result of more reliable forecasting. Typically, it is available for investment for twelve months or longer. These funds can be invested across a wider range of instruments. The following graph (see figure 15.2) shows how the three time buckets comprise the total excess cash position of a company. If clarity can be determined for the different time buckets, the company can deploy its operating and excess cash more effectively.

FIGURE 15.2 CLIENT INVESTMENT STRATEGY

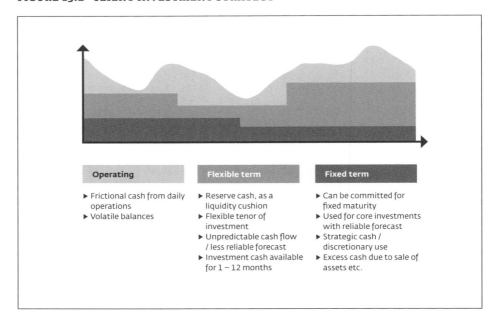

15.5
Developing an investment policy

This section describes the general outline of rules and procedures used by a corporate treasurer, namely the treasury policy. The treasury policy sets out the principles, rules and guidelines which form the basis for the daily treasury operations. Topics covered are foreign exchange risk, interest rate risk, liquidity risk, counterparty risk, bank and investor relations and funding methodologies. It includes the terms under which the treasury manages the financial risks the company faces. It defines the company's risk appetite and describes the way the treasury department interacts with the rest of the company. The policy translates the firm's liquidity, risk and return profile into a set of rules to be followed when investing excess cash or attracting external funding.

A treasury policy liquidity investment section should be specific enough to avoid misinterpretation but it should also provide sufficient flexibility to enable amendments as a result of changes in the market. Investment policies should have proper controls and be regularly reviewed to ensure that objectives and risk parameters remain accurate and meaningful as both the company and the environment in which the company operates can change.

Investing (excess) cash balances is a trade-off between liquidity, risk and return. In general terms, a firm has the potential to achieve higher returns if more risk is taken. This risk can be counterparty risk, liquidity risk or the risk associated with performance that is often inherent in more structured investment products.

FIGURE 15.3
LIQUIDITY
VS RISK
VS RETURN

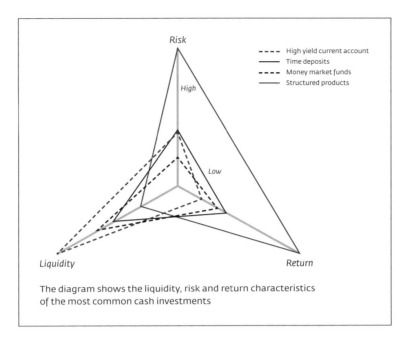

The diagram shows the liquidity, risk and return characteristics of the most common cash investments

As we have discussed, since the financial crisis in 2008 many companies are now primarily focused on the preservation of capital. This is followed very closely by an emphasis on liquidity – with an emphasis on keeping invested funds highly liquid. The company's assets and its ability to meet ongoing financial obligations must never be jeopardised for the sake of an improvement in return. The risk of having insufficient liquidity should be avoided at all costs.

Consequently, we have seen an increase in the size of liquidity buffers held by companies. Typically, these includes investments with a maturity of up to one year. Growth in balances in longer-term instruments has therefore diminished. In addition, significant yield enhancement has been difficult to achieve in the long-term, low interest-rate environment that followed the financial crisis.

Other practical factors that affect the development of an investment policy include:

- Determining how a company chooses an optimum mix of liquidity, risk and return
- Deciding whether an 'outsourced' or 'do-it-yourself' investment style is appropriate
- Categorising the excess cash positions into different maturity buckets with different investment parameters

It is also important to understand how investments are classified from an accounting perspective. Most likely they are classified as cash or cash equivalents, short-term financial assets or long-term financial assets. The different accounting treatment is determined by the minimal risk of the value changing over time during the investment period and the maturity of the investments.

Cash or cash equivalents
Maturity shorter than three months

Short-term financial assets
Maturity between three and twelve months

Long-term financial assets
Maturity longer than twelve months.

15.6
Balancing liquidity, risk and return

The corporate treasurer must consider three key factors: liquidity, risk and return. Each needs to be balanced against the others.

The ability to quickly turn at least some investments into cash – often within the same day – is crucial. Failure to do so can even cause the company to default when critical cash payments cannot be met. The need to consider how quickly an instrument can be liquidated if required (and the associated cost) is essential when choosing an investment instrument.

When choosing a strategy, appetite for risk is arguably the most important variable factor. Attitude to risk is based on the key objective underlying the investment policy: preservation of principal or maximisation of return. Adoption of one of these objectives will drive risk tolerance and, if appropriate, the different objectives could conceivably be applied to different elements within the investment portfolio.

Risk is not solely confined to counterparty risk where an assessment is made of the likelihood of return of the principal amount. Other elements that can be considered include:

–   *Duration/liquidity risk:* the length of the time horizon that one is willing to invest for (for example, up to twelve months) or the length of time to convert an investment to cash in the secondary market (such as when selling a certificate of deposit).

–   *Interest rate risk:* the risk that a change in the interest rate environment will alter an investment's value.

- *Operational risk:* the risk that arises from the operational activity surrounding the management of investments or funding. Conceivably, this could include a judgement as to whether the level of expertise present in the treasury department is sufficient to manage the portfolio effectively.

The level of expected investment return is generally linked to whether the objective is principal preservation or maximised returns. Different objectives can be applied to the different types of cash balances. Typically, these are operating cash, flexible-term cash and fixed-term cash. Which objective is chosen for which type of cash will drive the tolerance toward duration risk. Investment policies that seek to maximise returns tend to accept longer investment horizons as one way of boosting investment results. Additional considerations around return include:

- *Benchmarking:* to establish investment performance, it is important to establish benchmarks for comparison purposes that are measureable and relevant to investments held.

- *Accounting and tax implications:* it is important to understand the implications of these when booking gains (and losses).

When considering how to best execute and manage the investment policy and portfolio, there are two primary alternatives. The company can either execute the investment strategy itself without involving any external skills and resources or outsource the activity to a professional third party, such as an asset manager.

This second option means that, in return for a fee, the investor will benefit from the expertise of the market, economies of scale and the professionalism of the asset manager. If the company decides to execute the investment strategy in-house, there is the advantage of greater flexibility and intimate knowledge of the firm's day-to-day cash flows. However, this comes at the expense of maintaining a full investment team. Deciding between the outsourced or in-house approaches depends on many factors including cost, control, diversification, expertise and return.

15.7
Investment instruments

In this section, we will describe the key characteristics of commonly used investment instruments. There is a wide range of investment opportunities, which allow the company to achieve the optimum trade-off between liquidity, risk and return as appropriate within the boundaries of the investment policy.

15.7.1   DEPOSITS

The investing company deposits money with another party (usually a bank) for an agreed term and at an agreed interest rate. For the investor, this is clearly a deposit and shows as a cash asset on the balance sheet. The bank, as receiver of the deposit, is borrowing the money and records it as a liability on its balance sheet since it owes the balance back to depositor at the end of the term. The deposit is unsecured.

In the case of a fixed deposit or term deposit, the interest rate of the deposit is fixed at the outset. The interest rate is quoted on an annualised basis and the interest amount payable is calculated as:

> *Principal multiplied by annual interest rate / divided by number of days per annum (see note) multiplied by the number of days in the deposit period.*

Note: in order to be able to calculate the exact amount of interest, it is important to agree on which calculation methodology (convention) to use. Market conventions differ per currency, investment instrument and tenor of the investment. For most money market instruments, either the actual number of days/360 or the actual number of days/365 is used. The US dollar has a market standard of 360 days per annum (Act/360) while sterling has a market standard of 365 days per annum (Act/365).

EXAMPLE

Deposit principal = £5,000,000
Deposit term: 24 Jan to 23 April = 91 days
Deposit rate = 1.02% per annum

$$\frac{5,000,000 \times 1.02\%}{365 \text{ days}} \text{ multiplied by } 91 = £12,715.07 \text{ interest}$$

A company can place deposits with its bank in different currencies and for different terms. The minimum term for a deposit is one day (call deposit or overnight deposit). Typical deposit periods are one, two and three weeks and one, two, three, six and twelve months. Deposits may be 'broken' before maturity but there will be an adjustment to the interest result. Due to Basel III requirements, banks are less willing to allow breakable deposits as this will negatively influence the maturity and can have consequences for ratios such as the liquidity coverage ratio (LCR) and net stable funding ratio (NSFR).

Increasingly, banks are also offering account-based investments where deposits are placed in an interest-bearing bank account. The advantage of such accounts is that invested funds are not locked in for a specific period and can be withdrawn instantly. The appetite of banks, in particular, for such – on-balance-sheet – solutions will heavily depend on the regulatory treatment of these balances. In general, banks will welcome the company's cash that they could earmark as operational balances and will refuse balances which they would need to earmark as investment balances. Under the liquidity coverage ratio (LCR), which is part of the Basel III recommendations, the company's operational balances receive a more favourable treatment because they are, by nature, more stable. After all, they are required to run the company's daily operations. However, investment balances are less sticky because the company doesn't need them for daily operational purposes. Therefore, these balances could easily be shifted to other banks or institutions. Banks will have to reserve extra liquid assets if they want to keep these balances on their balance sheet. For more information on Basel III, see chapter 22, Regulations.

15.7.2 CERTIFICATES OF DEPOSIT (CD)

A certificate of deposit (CD) is similar to a time deposit in that the invested amount is placed with a bank for a fixed term over which interest is calculated and paid at maturity. However, it differs in that the bank accepting the deposit will issue the depositor with a 'certificate' showing the invested amount, the interest rate payable and the maturity date. This certificate can be traded on the secondary market, thereby allowing the depositor to liquidate the principal amount prior to the agreed maturity date. The price paid for the CD is the principal amount plus interest less an adjustment for the interest rate over the remaining period of time until maturity. At maturity, the bank taking the original deposit pays the principal plus the full interest amount to the bearer of the CD. In the UK, the issuing, trading and settlement of CDs and most other money market instruments is done electronically.

15.7.3 COMMERCIAL PAPER

Commercial paper (CP) is short-term debt issued by a company. Typically, CP is issued for a maximum period of twelve months, but practices may differ depending on the market in which they are issued. CP is issued at a discount and redeemed for the principal amount at maturity. Like a CD, commercial paper can be traded on the secondary market should funds be needed immediately.

When investing in short-term (or long-term) debt instruments, the investor is taking a credit risk on the issuer. Therefore, it is crucial that the investor has reliable information on the quality of the issuer. To meet the investors' information requirements, issuers of debt instruments generally apply for a rating at one or more of the well-known rating agencies (such as Standard & Poor's, Moody's and Fitch I.B.C.A.). Each institution assesses the company and expresses an opinion about its quality using a rating system. Companies often stipulate in their treasury policy that the treasurer or cash manager may only invest in securities of companies with a specified minimum rating.

15.7.4 REPURCHASE ORDER (REPO)

A repo is a short-term money-market instrument in which the investor deposits money with a borrower and in return, receives securities as collateral for the loan. It is a secured loan. The securities are often highly liquid in nature and have a strong credit rating. An example of such securities would be those issued by a government. In order to hedge against adverse changes in the market value of securities, repos are often over-collateralised. For example, the value of the securities may be 105% of the amount of the loan. Repos are commonly entered into on an overnight basis, where the investors lend the money in return for the securities, with the borrower agreeing to re-purchase them the following day. The term repo is applied to the party that sells the security and re-purchases it at maturity. For the party on the other side of the transaction who receives the security, the applicable term is a reverse repo. The price at which the securities are repurchased is greater than the original sale price and the difference is effectively in the interest rate. Repo rates are quoted in the same fashion as time deposits i.e. principal amount, applicable interest rate and maturity date.

15.7.5   BILLS OF EXCHANGE/BANKER'S ACCEPTANCES

In general, bills of exchange are instruments that result from an actual trade transaction between two parties. For example, in an export/import transaction, the exporter will draw a bill of exchange upon the importer which the importer will accept. Bills of exchange of this type are not payable at sight but at a date in the future and usually no longer than twelve months from the date of drawing. By accepting the bill, the importer agrees to pay the face value at the specified date. Bills of exchange become a money market instrument when they are accepted by a bank. This means the bank underwrites the obligation of the importer to pay on the due date, thereby guaranteeing payment. Once accepted by the bank, such bills can be sold in the money market to raise funds. Bankers' acceptances are sold at a discount based on interest rates prevailing at the time and redeemed in full at maturity.

15.7.6   MONEY MARKET FUNDS

Money market funds (MMFs) are collective investment schemes that invest in short-term, high-quality debt instruments. The primary objective of an MMF is to preserve the principal value of the invested amount while delivering investment diversification. MMFs offer same-day investment and redemption, thereby delivering a return commensurate with their instant access nature. Because MMF asset managers use the investor's cash to invest in different instruments from different financial institutions that are collectively owned by all the investors in the fund, they are able to offer a level of diversification of credit risk that individual investors would find difficult to match. With the principal aim being preservation of principal, MMFs only invest in the highest quality instruments in order to be able to achieve and maintain an AAA rating for their respective funds. It should, however, be noted that many fund providers also offer other funds such as 'cash plus funds' or 'enhanced cash funds' with a lower rating or no rating at all.

Investors will purchase a share in the fund, of £1.00 for example. In the case of constant net asset value (CNAV) funds, the face value of the share remains constant and income is accrued daily and either paid out at regular intervals or used to purchase further units. Variable net asset value (VNAV) funds do not distribute income but instead increase the value of the unit. Money market funds are commonly used in the US (where they are known as onshore funds) as well as in Europe (where they are known as offshore funds). There are a number of varieties according to the type of securities in which they invest:

- Government funds – investing in government securities
- Prime funds – investing in money market instruments of government and private issuers

Over the last five years, investments in MMFs have grown – particularly in Europe. However, measured over the shorter term and due in part to market conditions, assets under management (AUM) have dropped. During the height of the financial crisis, there was a re-balancing of the distribution of AUM. This was characterised by an outflow of balances held in prime funds in favour of investing in either government or treasury funds where the risk on the underlying investments is concentrated on government or treasury instruments. MMFs are regulated products. In the US, they are governed by the Securities and Exchange Commission (Rule 2 (a) 7). In Europe, such funds are regulated by the Undertakings for Collective Investment in Transferable Securities (UCITS), as well as the European Securities & Markets Authority (ESMA) and local regulators. In addition, many funds in Europe belong to the Institutional Money Market Funds Association, whose members operate funds under a voluntary code of practice. All these bodies have introduced new regulations to ensure continued investor confidence in MMFs. Such regulations differ by jurisdiction but often include:

- Minimum levels of assets with prescribed maturities (e.g. overnight)
- Maximum weighted average maturity of assets
- Maximum weighted average life of assets
- Maximum maturity period for any security held
- Concentration limits

During the 2008 financial crisis, the Reserve Primary Fund, a New York-based fund manager, was forced to reduce the net asset value (NAV) of its money market fund below $1 due to losses generated by failed short-term loans issued by Lehman Brothers. It was the first time a major money market fund had to break the $1 NAV. The fund lost two-thirds of its assets in almost 24 hours and had to suspend its operations and commence liquidation.

In 2014, the US Securities and Exchange Commission (SEC) issued new rules for the management of money market funds to improve the stability and resilience of such funds. Generally, the new rules enforce tighter restrictions on portfolio holdings and improve the liquidity and quality requirements of the assets. The most important change is the requirement that funds move from a fixed $1 share price to a floating NAV, which introduces the risk of principal where it had never existed with money market funds. In addition, the reform requires fund providers to use liquidity fees and suspension gates as a means of preventing a run on the fund. The requirements include asset level triggers for imposing a liquidity fee of 1 or 2%. If, for example, the weekly liquid assets fall below 10% of total assets, it triggers a 1% fee. Below 30%, the fee is increased to 2%. Funds may also suspend redemptions for up to 10 business days in a 90-day period. While those are the fundamental rule changes, there are several other factors corporates should know about the reform, however they are out of scope for the purpose of this book.

15.7.7 TREASURY BILLS

Treasury bills (T-bills) are short-term (maturity dates of less than one year) debt securities issued by governments. When investing in T-bills, the investor is exposed to the risk of default by the government concerned. There is no interest or coupon associated with T-bills as they are issued at a discount to the face value.

T-bills are issued through a competitive auction process with the discount to the face value reflecting the market interest rate.

EXAMPLE

Face value of T-bill = £1,000,000
Term = 91 days
Accepted bid price = £997,457.00

After holding the T-bill for the full term, the investor receives the face value of £1,000,000, which equates to an interest return of:

£1,000,000 minus £ 997,457.00 = £2,543.00

$$\frac{2,543}{997,457} \text{ multiplied by } \frac{365 \text{ days}}{91} = 1.02\% \text{ (day count convention T-bills: Act/365)}$$

T-bills can also be bought and sold on the secondary market.

15.7.8 LONGER-TERM INVESTMENTS

Many options exist for investing excess cash over longer terms. These range from simple time deposits with longer tenors to more sophisticated products, including structured deposits. A structured deposit offers a return dependent on the performance of an underlying market rate. Instead of providing a fixed interest rate, the return of a structured deposit is variable. The underlying market rate can reflect variables ranging from a currency rate to a commodity price and from a share price to an interest rate.

An example of a structured deposit is the tower deposit. A tower deposit is a deposit offering an above-market return if a particular exchange rate remains within a certain bandwidth and a lower-than-market return if it moves outside these bands. The rates depend on the term of the deposit, the range width and the minimum rate. The lower-than-market return can be as low as 0%. The investor decides on the term of the deposit and the expected range of the exchange rate. If the exchange rate falls on or outside the range, the client receives the minimum rate. These sophisticated investment products have become less popular due to the risks associated with such products and corporate treasurers' general shift from return on, to return of principal.

15.8
Executing investments

Having selected the most appropriate instrument, the next steps are to obtain interest rate quotes for the investment, make a choice of which financial institution to invest with, execute and settle the transaction. In most cases, this can be achieved either manually or electronically. Obtaining rate information and entering into an investment manually involves telephoning the investment counterparty. In order to ensure that a competitive quote is received, it is not unreasonable to contact more than one financial institution. The downside of manual execution is that it is operationally intensive, rates can change very quickly (potentially invalidating previously quoted rates) and it is open to error (which is why most banks record such conversations). Increasingly, transactions are being executed electronically. Providers are divided broadly in two groups:

- *Non-bank providers* – offering quotes over a range of products from multiple banks or other service providers
- *Bank providers* – offering quotes over a range of their own products

Regardless of which method is used, any transaction requires confirmation and settlement. Confirmation simply involves both parties confirming the details of the transaction (such as principal amount, maturity date and interest rate). Confirmations can be written but this is increasingly becoming an electronic process where the investor and deposit-taker's transaction record are matched and any anomalies are flagged. Investment transactions normally have two 'settlement transactions'. These are a) delivery of the principal amount to the deposit-taker and b) delivery of the principal amount plus interest back to the investor at maturity or when requested in respect of instant access investment products. Investment transactions are time-sensitive in that delivery of the principal amount must take place on the day of investment and the same can be said of delivery of the principal plus interest at maturity. Consequently, depending on the currency and location of the payer, these transactions take place using the local currency high-value clearing system or, for international transactions, are handled as urgent SWIFT payments.

At the start of an investing relationship, both the deposit-taker and the investor will exchange standard settlement instructions (SSI). These SSIs contain the bank account details concerning where to deliver funds on a per currency basis.

15.9
Market information and interest rate risks

The yield curve is a graphic representation of return set against investment horizon. It indicates the relationship between the various terms and the related interest rate yields. Normally, the longer the term the higher the yield, although there can be exceptions. The shape of the yield curve is open to change and includes:

- *Normal yield curve:* where longer-term instruments attract higher interest rates
- *Inverted yield curve:* where longer-term instruments attract lower interest rates than shorter-term instruments
- *Flat yield curve:* minimal difference between short-term and long-term rates
- *Humped yield curve:* where medium-term instruments attract higher rates than short or long-term instruments

FIGURE 15.4

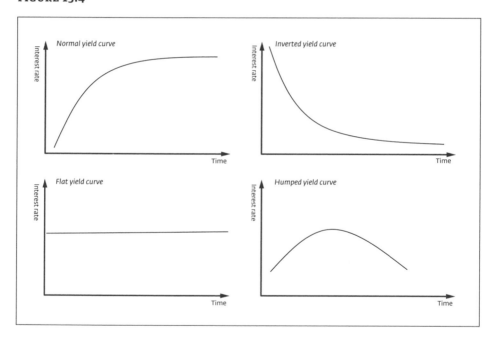

The short-term yield curve is driven primarily by the central bank's interest rate policy in the country in question. Expectations that a central bank will raise rates quickly will be reflected in the yield curve. For example, if the expectation is that the central bank will raise rates by 25bps in two months' time, the difference in yield of two and three-month rates will show that difference. The rate increases are – in this case at least – already priced into the market. Depending on market expectations of future interest rates, clients can select investments with longer or shorter maturities. In order to make such decisions, companies will need to have an understanding of the current interest rate market and a vision or expectation of where market rates are headed in the future. Often, companies will have an 'Investment Committee' or 'Treasury Committee' that will be responsible for setting the direction as well as formulating related treasury policy. A situation where no policy or guideline exists (or the policy is flawed) can lead to a negative impact on interest earned or potentially locking cash into term investments that are longer than necessary.

EXAMPLE

A cash manager sees that the company's liquidity position allows an opportunity to place a deposit for a period of six months. In addition, he knows that the current three-month interest rate amounts to 3.20% and that the six-month rate is 3.40%. However, the cash manager expects the central bank to raise interest rates in the very near future, which will push up the three-month interest rate to 3.75%.

In line with this interest outlook, the cash manager is likely to opt for a three-month deposit. The return on the first three months will then be 3.20%. The return the cash manager expects to generate over the following three months is 3.75%. The 'average' over the total period of six months is therefore 3.475%, while a six-month deposit would have yielded 3.40%. Of course in this case, the cash manager is betting against the market. If the market anticipated that the rate would be 3.75% in three months, this would be factored into the curve. If the cash manager is wrong and rates do not move, 20bps will have been sacrificed over the period.

Since interest rates can be affected by many factors, companies need to have good access to relevant information. At a practical level, this can mean gaining access to one of the many financial and business news provider services as well as receiving market commentary from a banking partner. Analysis of this information requires relevant expertise and a lack of such expertise can be a factor in deciding whether to adopt in-house or outsourced management of the investment portfolio. See also chapter 18 on Short Term Interest Risk Management.

15.10
Funding management

After having described the options for investing excess cash, we now will discuss the options available to a corporate treasurer to fund the company, as well as the main characteristics of these options. However, before we explore corporate funding alternatives, we will first cover the concept of expected loss. This concept is widely used by lenders (institutions that lend money to corporates) to assess the credit risk when lending money. Understanding the concept of expected loss helps a treasurer to make better funding decisions and it supports to positioning of the company with respect to future lenders.

15.10.1   EXPECTED LOSS

Expected loss is the financial loss a lender might occur when lending money to a company – the borrower – taking into account the probability that the borrower will default on the loan, times the financial impact of that default to the lender. A default means that the borrower cannot meet its obligations to the lender. Expected loss is calculated as:

> *Expected Loss = Probability of Default (PD) in % x Loss Given Default (LGD) in %*
> *x Exposure at Default (EAD) in EUR*

15.10.2   PROBABILITY OF DEFAULT (PD)

Probability of default (PD) is the likelihood (0-100%) that a borrower will not meet its obligations to the lender, leading to a partial or total loss for the lender. If a borrower has a 25% probability of default, it is considered a less risky company compared to a company with a 30% probability of default. Institutional lenders like banks and credit rating agencies use mathematical models to estimate probability of default. From a corporate treasury point of view, it is important to know what variables are used in the probability of default calculation. Many of these input variables are a result of the company's behaviour and performance. Although the probability of default is calculated as a percentage, it is often expressed as a score – the so-called credit rating score. Below is an example of a credit rating score used by global credit rating agency S&P, where AAA represents the best credit rating and C the worst credit rating. Figure 15.5 provides an overview of the main categories of variables used to calculate probability of default. All rating scores of BBB- and higher are considered investment grade. These companies can attract funding at far better conditions compared to non-investment grade companies.

FIGURE 15.5

S&P Credit Rating Scores		Key Variables Calculating Probability of Default	
AAA	Prime	Industry	Economic performance & outlook on an
AA	High grade		industry basis
A	Up medium grade	Structure	Ownership type, absolute size
BBB	Low medium grade	Financial	Analysis of historic & future financial
BB	Speculative		performance
B	Highly speculative	Internal Organisation	Track record management, financial
CCC	Substantial risks		reporting capabilities, audit quality
CC	Extremely speculative		
C	Prospect for nonpayment		
D	In default		

15.10.3   LOSS GIVEN DEFAULT (LGD)

Loss given default is the actual credit loss incurred by the lender when a borrower defaults. The loss is the result of the outstanding amount minus the recovery value of the securities pledged to the lender, such as real estate and receivables, plus the cost of recovery (e.g. auctioneer and legal costs) of the pledged assets. The recovery value is the value received by the lender when selling the asset to a third party. Loss given default is expressed as a percentage and calculated as follows:

Loss Given Default Calculation

Loan	100mln	Loss	= 90mln -/- 60.5mln + 0.5mln = 30mln
Outstanding	90mln		
Collateral recovery value	60.5mln	LGD	= 30mln/90mln = 33.3%
Recovery costs	0.5mln		

15.10.4   EXPOSURE AT DEFAULT (EAD)

Exposure at default (EAD) is the amount to which the lender is exposed when the borrower defaults. EAD is easily determined in case of a fixed loan, namely the balance outstanding of the loan. However, the overall credit facility might include revolving credit lines, such as bank overdrafts or acquisition facilities. Lenders use models to calculate (in fact, estimate) the total drawn exposure when a borrower defaults. The sum of balance outstanding of the loan, plus the estimated drawn exposures under the revolving credit lines are the exposure at default.

15.11
Funding alternatives

Having examined the dynamics in corporate lending from a risk assessment perspective, this section describes the funding alternatives and their main characteristics that are available to a corporate treasurer when attracting funding. The general rule of thumb is that the economic lifetime of the asset requiring funding equals the duration of the funding alternative chosen to finance the asset.

15.11.1   INTERNAL FUNDING SOURCES

As discussed in section 15.2, the cheapest funding sources for a corporate treasurer involve realising cash from adjustment of the key working capital drivers. A corporate treasurer can make cash available by decreasing stock levels, shortening days sales outstanding, and increasing days payables outstanding. In addition, companies are looking toward excess operating cash as a source of short-term funding by recycling funds from cash-positive parts of the organisation to cash-negative parts.

15.11.2 OFF-BALANCE FINANCING

Off-balance financing is, in fact, indirect financing. Both the asset that requires funding and the funding instrument itself are not on the company balance sheet. The company actually 'rents' the asset and pays a monthly or quarterly fee that is included in the profit & loss statement as a cost of operational lease. This fee includes interest, the instalment fee and a service fee. The biggest advantage to off-balance financing is that it does not impact the balance sheet and ratios, such as solvency. The most common examples of off-balance financing are:

- **Operational lease**
  For cars and special equipment: duration of five to seven years

- **Sale and leaseback**
  For real estate: a company sells its real estate to an investor (moving real estate off its balance sheet and renting back the real estate from the investor)

A method of off-balance financing that has gained popularity since the 2008 financial crisis is receivable purchase. In this case, a company sells its receivables to a financier and gets cash minus a small discount (namely the applied interest rate times the expected outstanding payment term in days). The receivable is converted into cash on the company balance sheet.

15.11.3 SHORT-TERM FINANCING

A company can borrow money from a bank and if the term of this loan is short, the loan is referred to as a money market loan. The interest rate is fixed during the term of the loan and is usually much lower than the interest rate a bank charges on a current account overdraft. The interest rate is quoted on an annual basis and the interest amount payable is calculated as:

> *Principal multiplied by annual interest rate / number of days per annum**
> *multiplied by the number of days in the loan period.*

Overdrafts and money market loan facilities can be arranged on both an uncommitted and committed basis. An uncommitted facility means that the bank has no obligation to advance funds to the borrower. Under a committed facility, the bank is obliged to advance funds during the life of the facility. Given this commitment on the part of the bank, it is required to hold additional regulatory capital against such a facility, which will make the cost to the borrower greater than an uncommitted facility. The cost normally takes the form of a commitment fee.

---

*   The number of days per annum follows market standards – the so-called day count convention – for the currency in question. For example, the USD has a market standard of 360 days per annum and sterling has a market standard of 365 days per annum.

15.11.4   ASSET-BASED LENDING

Asset-based lending is predominantly about the 'loss given default part' rather than the 'probability of default part' of the risk calculation. An asset-based lender is specialised in realising very high recovery values when a borrower defaults. Asset-based lenders are very knowledgeable about the assets they finance and have distribution channels to quickly dispose of the asset at a relatively high price. The advantage of asset-based financing is relatively high loan-to-value (LTV) percentages. LTV is the percentage of the value of the asset that is being financed. The most common asset-based lending alternatives are:

- *Inventory finance*
  Short-term financing of inventory (50% - 70% LTV) (mainly involves commodities with higher LTVs)

- *Factoring*
  Short-term financing of receivables (75-90% LTV)

- *Financial Leasing*
  Most common for medium-term assets like cars, trucks, equipment and machinery (80% - 100% LTV)

A variation of factoring is so-called reverse factoring or supply chain finance. The idea behind supply chain finance is to arbitrage between credit risk (expected loss) of a seller (supplier) and a buyer. Credit is allocated to the best credit-rated company in the supply chain. Supply chain finance programmes are attractive for investment-grade companies, in order to attract cheap funding. In return for accepting extended payment days of its client (e.g. paying in 90 instead of 60 days), a supplier receives immediate cash when invoicing the buyer from the bank(s) funding the supply chain finance programme of the buyer. The bank will charge an interest rate to the supplier based on the expected loss of the buyer (which is generally better rated than the supplier). The buyer pays the invoice amount to the bank on the pre-agreed (extended) payment date. In fact, the bank has a credit risk on the better rated buyer instead of multiple suppliers / sellers with relatively worse ratings. The advantage for the buyer is that by extending its payment terms (days payable outstanding) it creates an internal source of relatively cheap cash (see section 16.10.1). The advantage for the supplier is that it borrows money at cheaper interest rates (based on the better credit rating of its buyer) compared to what a bank would offer the seller on a stand-alone basis. Part of that advantage is diluted since the seller needs to fund itself for a longer period (e.g. 90 days instead of 60 days).

15.11.5   TERM LOANS

A term loan is a loan predominantly offered by banks with a maturity of at least two years. The loan can be either amortising (between two and 10 years) or a (partial) bullet loan (full repayment of the principal amount at the end of the commitment period). Interest rates vary from floating to equal to the full commitment period. Term loans are often used to finance medium / long-term assets and acquisitions. When a term loan is offered by an institutional investor other than a bank, this is called direct lending. Increasingly, professional investors like pension funds and insurance companies lend money directly, predominantly to corporates with good credit ratings.

15.11.6 COMMERCIAL PAPER

Commercial paper was discussed earlier in this chapter from the perspective of an investment product. The issuer of the commercial paper raises funds from the investor, which means the paper can also be used as a funding source. In order to do this, the company must set up a commercial paper programme. Banks operate as the arrangers of commercial paper programmes. As such, they prepare prospectuses and notify the central bank of their programme. A prospectus must not only contain information about the company but also about the maximum amount that may be issued. In addition, the bank plays the role of broker (issuing and paying agent). In this capacity, the bank is not exposed to debtor risk, which lies with the buyer of the commercial paper. Once a commercial paper programme is set up, the issuer can ask the bank to look for investors. The amount of the issue, the term and the yield are set by the issuer. The reason a company issues commercial paper is to diversify its funding sources and to reduce its dependence on bank financing alone.

15.11.7 CORPORATE BONDS

A corporate bond shares all the characteristics of commercial paper. In addition, most corporate bonds can be traded via an external exchange. A majority of publicly traded bonds have an external credit rating. Interest coupons are fixed and bonds are paid at maturity. During the lifetime of the bond, its value on the bond market fluctuates. However, the corporate treasurer does not benefit from a high or low bond price during its lifetime; the company receives cash at the moment the bond is issued. When there is substantial investor appetite, companies might issue a bond at a higher-than-nominal value. This monetary difference is called 'agio'.

EXAMPLE

Nominal:	EUR 1,000
Coupon:	2%
Issue price:	EUR 1,004
Bond numbers:	1 – 1000
Maturity	10 years

The company issues its 1000 bonds for EUR 1,004, realising EUR 1,004,000 in cash, of which EUR 4,000 is agio. At maturity, it only pays back the nominal value, namely 1,000 x EUR 1,000. The net yield for the bondholder is therefore (slightly) lower than 2%:

Net yield bond investor = [Coupon times maturity minus agio] divided by issue price divided by maturity [EUR 20 x 10 years -/- EUR 4] / EUR 1,004 / 10 years = 1.99%

15.11.8 SUBORDINATED DEBT

If the expected loss is relatively high due to weak financial performance, very high growth or a riskier project, the regular funding alternatives described above are not an option. Alternatively, a corporate treasurer can opt for subordinated debt. The difference between subordinated debt and 'normal' (or preferred) debt is the ranking in repayment in a default scenario. Subordinated debt is repaid only after the normal (or preferred) debt is fully repaid. In addition, the normal or preferred lenders may claim that interest and / or instalments to the subordinated debt lender can only be paid if the company meets certain financial key performance indicators. If not, the interest is accrued to the principal amount and / or the instalment is postponed. Therefore, a lender of subordinated debt accepts a higher risk and realises a higher return. Sometimes, subordinated debt is called junior debt, and normal or preferred debt is called senior debt, referring to the relative ranking in a default situation. Mezzanine is the most common form of subordinated debt.

15.12
Loan documentation

When a borrower and a lender agree on commercial terms, they jointly draft / negotiate a loan agreement, in most cases assisted by a lawyer. The loan agreement is a legally binding document containing all relevant characteristics of the loan including the terms and conditions, as well as stipulating the rights and obligations of the lender and the borrower. The document may contain other clauses, depending on the size and credit rating. Blue chip corporates have minimum terms and conditions, whereas highly-leveraged corporates need to sign loan agreements amounting to several hundred pages.

In principle, parties in the US and Asia (among other regions) are free to choose a legal format. In Europe, most institutional lenders, such as banks, apply a pre-agreed template. This so-called Loan Market Association (LMA) documentation template standardises legal clauses. The content of the clauses then needs to be adapted to the individual case at hand.

Aside from the loan agreement, other legal documents must be signed, such as security pledges. This so-called deed of pledge establishes the pledge of a certain asset. Together, the loan agreement, pledge agreement and other legal letters are referred to as the credit documentation.

15.13
Evaluation investment and funding performance

As with the other cash management disciplines, the cash manager must regularly evaluate the investment management and funding performance to ensure optimal results are being achieved. At an operational level, the cash manager needs to evaluate the effectiveness of his actions by examining such areas as:

- How successfully liquidity forecasting has met with actual liquidity positions

- Whether adequate liquidity has always been available to meet operational needs
- Whether an assessment of the current book balances confirms that all liquidity positions have been invested or funded and there are no significant idle balances
- Whether an analysis of the term and timing of investment transactions confirms that investments and loans have been effectively managed
- How the performance of the total investment portfolio compares to the pre-defined benchmark(s)

These analyses enable the cash manager to establish whether his forecasts and investment / funding decisions were correct. If the evaluation shows the following results, the cash manager knows he has done a good job:

- No material deficit or surplus liquidity positions in current accounts
- A good and balanced diversity in the investment portfolio which is in line with treasury policy and with the current liquidity risk and return profile

If the evaluation shows that one or more of the following situations have occurred, he knows that certain changes are required in the coming period:

- Large debit or credit balances in the current account
- Deposits and loan portfolio skewed toward long or short maturities
- Many deposits or loans with the same maturity date

In the event that such situations have occurred, a root cause analysis should be undertaken.

At a strategic level, a regular review of the composition of the investment and funding policy should be conducted. Such a review should have board level involvement and include:
- An analysis of whether the policy still has objectives and goals that are relevant
- Whether upcoming events or changes will require the policy to be amended
- Whether any changes in the external/economic environment will necessitate changes
- An analysis of whether the liquidity, risk and return profile are still appropriate.

Risk Management

Chapter 16

Foreign Exchange Risk Management

16   Foreign Exchange Risk Management

16.1
Introduction

International companies face financial market risks in relation to their income statement and balance sheet resulting from foreign currency fluctuations. The fear of significant losses is a sufficient reason for a company to identify all known risks in advance. Numerous fundamental and technical factors influence the exchange rate. Currency fluctuations are a natural outcome of supply and demand in the currency exchange markets. Daily currency pricing behaviour is both a complex and fascinating phenomenon. Most major currencies are subject to a floating exchange rate system that allows their rates to float freely as market purchases and sales influence the daily value. Other currencies are more controlled through a fixed rate managed directly by the central bank or a pegged (managed) rate. Currency movements can result in unexpected appreciation or depreciation risks that are difficult to address. Currencies themselves react with price changes in the foreign exchange market based on fundamental drivers such as the global supply of the currency and the associated monetary policy mandated by each currency's sovereign government. In this chapter we will describe in more detail the topic of currency risk and how it can be mitigated within the corporate treasury organisation.

16.2
Currency fluctuations

Many government decisions, external economic forces, and regional financial issues influence currency behaviours that can either result in favourable or unfavourable movements. During the past few decades, multiple currency crises have affected the income statements of multinational companies. A recent example is the outcome of the UK referendum to exit the EU. This caused the value of the pound to fall and sent currency markets into short-term volatility. Some multinational companies even prepared for this event by entering into forward contracts to manage their risk exposure. And in 1997, Asian emerging markets experienced a currency crisis when the Central Bank of Thailand decided to remove the currency peg to the USD (fixed exchange rate), which was previously held at 25.00. This Asian financial crisis provided accelerated market exchange rate correction, and the Thai Baht depreciated by more than 50% against the USD, even though it was pegged. Thailand's financial institutions and businesses were thus required to spend significantly more Baht to satisfy their USD-denominated debt commitments. The previous examples are reminders of why there is a need to improve global awareness of currency rate changes and effective financial risk management planning.

FIGURE 16.1

Currency	Average Spot Rate 2012-present	January 2017 Spot Rate	Current Spot appreciation/ (depreciation) vs. USD
Euro	1.23	1.05	(14)%
British GBP	1.53	1.23	(20)%
Canadian $	1.15	1.33	(15)%
Chinese RMB	6.29	6.93	(9)%
Japanese Yen	102.60	116.43	(14)%
Australian $	0.88	0.73	(17)%
Singapore $	0.76	0.69	(10)%

Source: Oanda foreign exchange rates

16.3
Currency risk management

Continuous fluctuations in foreign exchange rates present a number of currency risk management concerns and generate critical questions for traders, investors, and multinational companies. For instance, does the organisation assess the market as part of its foreign exchange risk management policy and framework? Has it been and does it continue to be within the predefined hedge limits? Is the organisation prepared for unforeseen instability or liquidity in currency markets? Determining the future behaviour of foreign currencies is a primary concern for treasury managers. Fluctuations and price patterns can be used to predict the potential future trends. However, all currencies are also exposed to non-economic political pressure and central bank decisions, which may be very difficult to foresee.

International companies face financial market risks in relation to their income statement and balance sheet resulting from foreign currency fluctuations. The fear of significant losses is a sufficient reason for a company to identify all known risks in advance. Companies can attempt to forecast the impact of these events through planning, methods and tools to identify what could go wrong, by evaluating risks based on priority and degree, and implementing strategies to mitigate those risks.

Selecting an appropriate risk management strategy is a complex task. It includes accurately assessing foreign currency risk exposures and then determining the degree of risk exposure to be managed. Furthermore, factors such as international free trade, financial transfers and foreign direct investment are creating more complexity as global economies are becoming increasingly interconnected. This chapter aims to provide tools and guidance that can be applied in real-life situations. It covers types of FX risks, recent currency crises, practical applications of foreign exchange risk measurements and FX risk management practices.

16.4
Understanding types of FX risks

Companies with an effective foreign exchange risk management policy framework, tools and strategy have a higher chance of succeeding in international market management. A company should approach foreign exchange risk management programmatically to evaluate transactional exposures, existing and future business activities and their operating environment. Establishing an effective policy framework is a step forward to clarifying a company's FX risk objectives and preparing a treasury team for fluctuations in foreign exchange rates that affect cost competitiveness, profitability and company valuation. The absence of such a policy framework can leave a company unprepared to manage the potential adverse effects of currency movements, which can lead to increased costs and reduced market share and profits. If companies frequently face these exposures, what can they do to develop an effective policy and framework that can be clearly communicated to the company's executive management and its shareholders?

The starting point for formulating an FX risk management programme is to identify the exposures and establish the risk profile of the company. Foreign exchange exposure can generally be classified into three types: transaction, translation and economic exposure.

FIGURE 16.2   THREE TYPES OF RISK

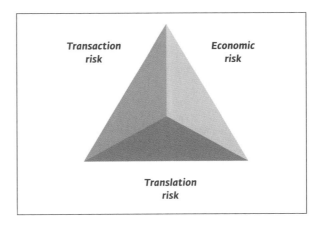

16.4.1   TRANSACTION EXPOSURE

Transaction exposures represent the company's risk for transactions denominated in currencies other than its functional currency. Examples of a transactional exposure would be when a company produces products in one country and sells them in another country in a different currency. The exposure starts when the company becomes aware of a non-functional currency transaction and ends when that transaction is settled through the receipt of cash. This risk can be split up into two categories: anticipated risk and book-to-pay risk. Anticipated risk is a risk that the value of 'anticipated' or expected non-functional currency revenues or expenses will be adversely impacted due to exchange rate movements. Book-to-pay risk exists when a receivable or payable in a non-functional currency is booked to the balance sheet and its value will be impacted by movements in exchange rates that occur during the period that the receivable or payable is outstanding.

EXAMPLE 1

Transaction exposure

A US company engages in DK and EUR transactions. It has the following projected cash flows for the next year:

Currency	Total inflow	Total outflow	Current exchange rate in USD
Danish krone (DK)	DK 50,000,000	DK 40,000,000	USD 0.12
Euro (EUR)	EUR 2,000,000	EUR 1,000,000	USD 1.20

Based on the projected cash flows for the coming years, the forecasted transaction exposure for the company is as follows:

Answer: The net exposure to each currency in USD is derived below:

Foreign currency	Net inflow in foreign currency	Current exchange rate	Value of exposures
Danish krone (DK)	+DK 10,000,000	USD 0.12	USD 1,200,000
Euro (EURO)	+EUR 1,000,000	USD 1.20	USD 1,200,000

The movements in DK and EUR have been highly correlated and both currencies have moved in tandem against the dollar. If these currencies remain higly correlated against the USD then these exposures will be magnified.

16.4.2   TRANSLATION EXPOSURE

Translation exposure risks occur when a companies' equity, assets, liabilities and income are denominated in a currency other than its home currency and change in value when converted into the functional or reporting currency. Depending on the exposure, offshore entities' balance sheets and income statements are converted into the home currency at either the average exchange rate or the period end rate. Since the rate generally moves, there are changes in the values between reporting periods. The more operations a company carries out that are denominated in a foreign currency, the greater the translation risk.

EXAMPLE 2

Translation exposure

An Indian company with a UK subsidiary.
Financial details of UK Subsidiary:

	Year 1 (GBP 1 = INR 85)		Year (GBP 1 = INR 70)	
	Value in GBP	Translated value	Value in GBP	Translated value
Real estate	GBP 1,000,000	INR 85,000,000	GBP 950,000	INR 66,500,000
Inventories	GBP 200,000	INR 17,000,000	GBP 250,000	INR 17,500,000
Cash	GBP 150,000	INR 12,750,000	GBP 160,000	INR 11,200,000
Total	**GBP 1,350,000**	**INR 102,000,000**	**GBP 1,360,000**	**INR 95,200,000**

16.4.3 ECONOMIC EXPOSURE

The third exposure that companies face is economic or market exposure. Compared to the other two, the impact and significance of this risk type tends to be significantly higher because it affects companies beyond single transactions and accounting translation issues. This exposure directly impacts the value of a company's business and its competitiveness. The greater challenge here is to identify and measure this exposure. The degree of economic exposure impact on a company varies based on its specific industry and business interests. For example, a retailer may import goods from Japan and sell them in the United States and is therefore affected by the changes in the exchange rates of those two currencies. If the Japanese yen increases in value against the USD, the goods from Japan become more expensive in USD terms. This economic change may hurt the margin performance of its business operations in the U.S. as that retailer may have constraints on increasing the USD price to recover the higher cost. To address this risk, the company could use the foreign exchange markets to protect the import pricing for a period of time and reduce the impact when the JPY strengthens. If there is a long-term functional change in the currency, the company may no longer be competitive in its pricing or it may lose significant margin.

Analysing these three types of potential exposures puts managers in a position to assess the impact of foreign currencies on a company's business and help the company make informed decisions.

FIGURE 16.3 FX EXPOSURE

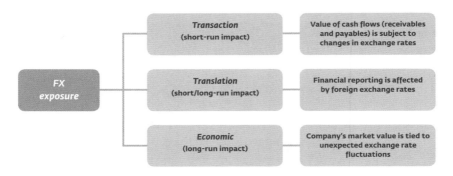

16.5
Market participants

16.5.1 CENTRAL BANKS

The most impactful, yet constrained, market participants are the central banks. Every single tradable currency is authorised by a sovereign government as a medium of exchange for the economy. As part of their charters, central banks are charged with overseeing the currency market along with monetary policy and regulation of commercial banks.

Central banks make the following decisions:

- How can we manage, promote, and possibly limit our currency flows?
- Should we allow foreign banks to hold our currency inside our borders? What about outside?
- Are other sovereign central banks allowed to hold our currency as a store of value?
- Should there be limits on the convertibility of our currency for transactions in our country?
- Should convertibility even be allowed outside the country?

16.5.2 COMMERCIAL BANKS

While central banks stand at the source of currency flows, every market participant must have a counterparty when acting in the market. Major participants are the commercial banks, which make markets in foreign currency. Commercial banks therefore both facilitate foreign currency flows on behalf of their clients and mitigate their own risk. A company would typically enter into foreign exchange trades with a commercial bank.

16.5.3 CORPORATES, INVESTMENT FUNDS, AND SPECULATORS

Corporates play the biggest role in this group as customers of the commercial banks that spur the FX market. They do this either by depositing currency at the bank or by requesting specific FX transactions to fulfil a business need to convert foreign currency flows or to protect transaction or translation exposures.

Two other market participants – namely investment funds and speculators – can enter the foreign currency markets, but for different reasons. These participants usually do not have an underlying risk they seek to mitigate or a business transaction they seek to execute. Rather they seek returns on their investment to facilitate other aims, either for themselves or their clients. Many currencies demonstrate long-term returns through appreciation of holding or selling currencies for the purpose of making a speculative profit.

16.6
Managing FX risks in modern times

Currency volatility often comes with unpredictable timing. Understanding the history of currency crises, government policies and its impact is key to being prepared to address FX issues.

Each currency crisis, the government policies that led to the crisis and the subsequent government response provide insights into the currency market and the need for constant review and preparation. Studying the past will help companies address specific FX risks.

Swiss franc market events

Switzerland has historically been a well-performing economy and the Swiss franc has been a stable currency that is effectively managed by the Swiss National Bank. That status quo started to change in the wake of the eurozone financial crisis in 2011. The country's exporters faced increasing competitive pressures as the CHF appreciated sharply against the EUR. Overvaluation of the CHF posed an emergent risk to the Swiss economy and carried the continued risk of deflation. The Swiss National Bank (SNB) authorities became concerned and, to address these issues, kept the currency from rising above 1.20 CHF to the EUR starting in September 2011.

On 15 January 2015, the Swiss National Bank surprised the FX markets by removing the cap on the CHF's value against the EUR. This allowed the CHF to begin floating freely but also accelerated months' worth of change into a single day as the CHF appreciated 40% against the EUR and 30% against the USD. Swiss manufacturers and other traders working their normal operations suffered significant losses. The peg had previously been credited for its role in protecting Switzerland's export-dependent economy from turmoil in the neighbouring eurozone and reducing the risks of deflation. Now the free floating exchange rate has returned the CHF to its economic core.

On 23 June 2016, British citizens voted in a referendum to answer this simple question: 'Should the United Kingdom remain a member of the European Union?' When a majority voted for a 'Brexit', the GBP subsequently sank to a decade's low against the USD and EUR. The British finance minister assured global markets that the country was prepared for either referendum outcome. However, the FX rates dropped again the following day and set a new normal for the value of the GBP in world markets. An FX risk lesson for multinational companies is to develop contingency plans using scenario analysis and advanced risk management techniques to prepare for market shocks and desired end states.

We know from various currency crises over time that they will repeat in the future. Treasury managers therefore need to examine what their company has done to address FX exposures since the last crisis. Companies may not have sufficient resources, guidance, or even a culture of motivation to minimise risks. Here are some potential reasons that may explain why some companies may fall short in managing FX risk:

- Companies may manage exposures without a defined risk framework and fail to extend risk assessment to the local managers
- Companies may ignore FX risks because they are not sure how to address them, do not know when they arise or what tools to use
- Companies may continue to manage FX risks using spreadsheets, rather than investing in new technology
- Currency exposures may be assessed individually because the cost of calculating risk correlations is unclear
- Currency risk management may be left to individual business units without coordination or communication between the units and upper management

Companies that already have an FX risk management framework in place and have addressed operational issues can feel more confident that they will not repeat past mistakes. At a more mature stage, they will be prepared to use their FX risk management framework to manage similar potential FX exposures in the future.

16.7
Approaches to FX risk management and strategies

A fundamental approach to foreign currency risk management involves first identifying inherent business risk. Every company has commitments to and from customers, suppliers and employees in their business model. Based on the business model, corporate treasury groups can analyse the income statement, supply chain and balance sheet to uncover business risk related to foreign currencies.

Treasury groups should ask: are revenues and expenses in the same currency? Are revenues in one currency driven by capital investment in another, and does a support centre provide services denominated in one currency for multiple business units in various other currencies? What is the functional currency of the business unit or the parent?

Centralisation and optimisation of the supply chain is a strategy for producing lower costs and improving margins. However, this strategy may create currency risk. Commodities are generally priced in USD, regardless of the country of origin, and this creates supply chain currency risks. Companies need to review currency pass-through risk from suppliers. This could be the case where a foreign supplier may be passing through their own foreign currency risk, even if they have fixed their prices in a single currency.

Global companies generally do business in a wide range of currencies, while their investors commonly view their earnings and returns in the home currency. Changes in currencies affect returns and create the need for a financing strategy which includes the currency risk of foreign operations and capital expenditures.

To directly address the underlying foreign currency risks, a company can redeploy assets and/or negotiate contracts to mitigate currency risk. By participating in decision-making on investments and pricing, the treasury group can include currency outlook and mitigation strategies as part of the business plan.

After a company looks at the changes in the deployment of assets, currency of financing and natural diversification, it can develop a hedge strategy that uses financial products and/or derivatives to address their foreign currency risk.

16.8
Management of foreign exchange risks

All companies face uncertainty, including the challenge of managing foreign exchange risks. Companies must determine how much volatility and risk they are willing to accept as they strive to grow stakeholder value. There are several questions that can help develop steps for leading risk management practices.

- What elements should be included in the FX risk management policy?
- What guidelines should be included for FX risk management?
- Who should be responsible for identifying and hedging FX exposures?
- What should be defined in terms of the hedging approach?

The value of a policy and framework can be maximised when management sets objectives and addresses foreign currency exposures, as discussed in section 16.4, to achieve a balance between growth and related risks. This process often leads to effective deployment of resources to help meet a company's objectives.

The general building blocks of a risk management policy are identified below.

Business exposure identification
Business mapping, identifying the origin and magnitude of risk

Risk and impact analysis
Value at risk, scenario analysis and stress tests, earnings and cash flow impacts

Policy, procedures and control development
Defining risk objectives and assumptions, controls, authorisations and oversight structure

Risk system evaluation
Reviewing existing data collection processes, evaluating systems, determining pricing and valuations capabilities

Development of risk mitigation strategy
Evaluating current and potential approaches, cost of strategy vs. risk element

Tax and accounting review
Assessing hedge accounting and / or mark-to-market treatment; reviewing hedge entities and tax consequences

For FX risks specifically, treasury managers can use the building blocks of risk management, as shown above, to develop an exposure management cycle that continuously addresses FX exposures over time. Policy and framework are essentially a testament to a company's objectives and risk approach. What is truly needed is a 'living' reflection of the policy and framework. The cycle guides managers and defines a company's policy and framework (see figure 16.4).

FIGURE 16.4 EXPOSURE MANAGEMENT CYCLE

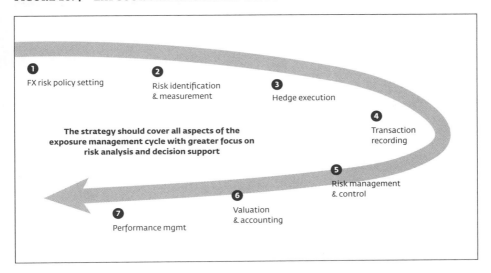

16.8.1 HEDGING TRANSACTION STRATEGIES

Mitigating FX risk and maintaining steady and predictable cash flows is generally beneficial to companies. When facing various foreign exchange risks, companies should employ an approach to minimise or 'hedge' their foreign exchange risk resulting from transactions in foreign currencies. It is possible to mitigate a risk in a specific time frame, but a company cannot remove all risks. A company can choose to accept and not manage currency risk, to attempt to manage nearly 100% of risk or to take a blended approach.

Philosophy on managing foreign exchange risk:

Determination of appropriate hedge accounting requires coordination with the controllership and tax groups, and potentially outside advisors, before entering into a financial instrument transaction.

Who needs to be concerned about transaction risk?
- Companies with significant business and cash flows in foreign currencies
- Companies with long-term contracts in foreign currencies

What is the impact of transaction risk?
- Uncertainty in pricing and margins
- Lower value for receipts and higher cost of cash outflows
- Volatile net income beyond operating income

What are the options available to manage transaction risk?
- Actively hedge transaction risks in the financial markets using derivative instruments
- Match cash flows from hedges and underlying exposures

Factors to consider
- Cost to enter into and execute hedge instruments
- Uncertainty of future cash flow projections
- Adoption of accounting principles that enable recognition of hedge cash flows during periods when underlying cash flows occur

Hedging individual transaction risk requires a solid understanding of the underlying transaction flows and the drivers of the FX risk as well as policies, processes and methods for identifying and hedging exposures.

Who needs to be concerned about economic risk?
- Companies with a business model in which purchases or sales prices are dependent on one or more foreign currencies

What is the impact of economic risk?
- The company's economic value varies due to currency movements not competitive performance
- Competitive disadvantages may result when competitors are in other countries with less expensive or more stable currencies

What are the options available to manage economic risk?
- Denominate all contracts in domestic currencies or adjust customer prices based on currency movements
- Redesign business model
- Incorporate foreign currency considerations into market growth plans

>

Factors to consider
- Ability to price competitively in the absence of currency considerations
- Link between pricing and margin management
- Impact of the hedging strategy on competitive position

Who needs to be concerned about translation risk?
- Companies with large investments in foreign operations with functional currencies other than the consolidated reporting currency
- Companies whose foreign operations are included in consolidated financial statements

What is the impact of translation risk?
- Value of assets and liabilities change in reporting separately from business operations
- Structural changes in foreign currency economics may permanently alter the value of investments in foreign operations

What are the alternatives available to manage translation risk?
- Where possible, borrowing in the functional currency of the foreign operations
- Closer management of repatriation and cash flows between parent entity and foreign operations
- Hedging the value of net current assets in foreign operations

Factors to consider
- Cost to enter into and execute hedge instruments
- Long-term strategy for earnings repatriation, local entity growth and eventual divestment
- Materiality of foreign operations to the consolidated financial statements

16.8.2 INTERCOMPANY RISK MANAGEMENT TECHNIQUES

Hedging techniques normally involve the use of financial instruments, known as derivatives, of which there are two types: internal and external. Internal techniques are tools that address FX risks based on the company's resources. These should always be considered before using external methods with a view to safety and cost. Below are several strategies that corporations use.

Invoice in functional currency
Companies encourage or requires foreign customers to pay in functional (home) currency

Matching
Receipts and payments are combined when company receives cash and makes payments in the same foreign currency at the same time

Leading and lagging
Companies speed up (leading) or delay (lagging) payment or receipts in a foreign currency because of an expected change in exchange rates

No action
A company can decide not to take any action by expecting to gain more than the losses it will incur

16.8.3 EXTERNAL TECHNIQUES

External techniques that are available in the broad FX market can be used for a variety of purposes. Below is a list of the major foreign exchange derivatives.

Foreign exchange derivatives

FX Spot
An agreement between two parties to buy one currency against selling another currency at an agreed price for settlement on the spot date (generally one or two business days in the future)

FX Forward
A deal between two parties to exchange currencies – to buy or sell a particular currency – at an agreed date in the future, at a rate – a price – agreed now. This rate is called the forward rate

FX Futures
A futures contract at a financial exchange to exchange one currency for another at a specified date in the future at a price determined by the exchange (exchange rate) that is fixed on the purchase date

>

FX Options
A financial instrument that gives the owner the right but not the obligation to exchange money denominated in one currency into another currency at a pre-agreed exchange rate on a specified date

Currency swaps
A simultaneous purchase and sale of identical amounts of one currency for another with two different value dates (normally spot to forward)

CCIRS (Cross-currency interest rate swap)
A product that provides the borrower the ability to switch their interest repayments from one currency to another on a fixed or floating rate basis

Money market hedge
This method uses the current day spot rate and money markets to lend or borrow for hedging instead of using a forward contract

16.9
Risk measurements

16.9.1   VALUE-AT-RISK CALCULATION

Value at Risk (VaR) is a widely used risk management tool in finance and treasury. Many companies employ this method through software application to calculate the volatility of a foreign exchange position resulting from a company's activities. VaR calculates the maximum loss expected or worst-case scenario over a given time period and specified degree of confidence.

Value at Risk

VaR has three main elements:
- Percentage of loss in value
- Time period over which risk is assessed
- Level of confidence with respect to the estimated risk

The practical use of this calculation allows treasurers to recognise the potential impact of a given change in exchange rates and also to identify how often it may happen. The calculation uses the past foreign currency price history, usually over a three-year period, and then applies that history to the current situation. Treasurers can become more confident with the sensitivity analysis that the company is less likely to lose more than a certain value given a range of movement in exchange rates. A company may also wish to invest in higher level analytics such as the covariance method, historical simulation, or a Monte Carlo simulation, but a thorough explanation of these methods is beyond the scope of this chapter. When doing a VaR analysis, a company must remain aware that it is doing a statistical analysis. As previously noted, major events such as Brexit or the Asian financial crisis do occur, and can affect a company's results beyond the range indicated in the analysis.

FIGURE 16.5 VALUE-AT-RISK ANALYSIS

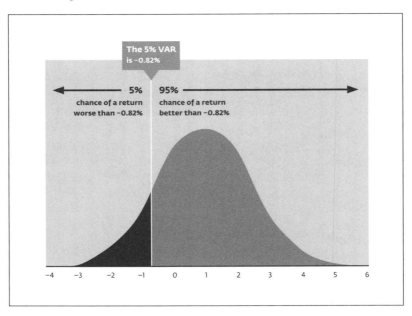

16.9.2   STRESS TESTING

Treasurers use stress testing techniques to provide potential risk exposure assessments, support capital planning and encourage liquidity planning. Stress testing provides a holistic view of FX exposures that a company has or might incur. A periodic application of stress test scenarios is a recommended risk management practice that can prepare the company for unexpected results from various types of risks and provides an assessment of the capital resources a company needs to cover the potential losses.

Identifying different types of scenarios is helpful for assessing all possible outcomes. The diagram below shows the overall process of developing scenarios.

FIGURE 16.6 TYPES OF SCENARIOS

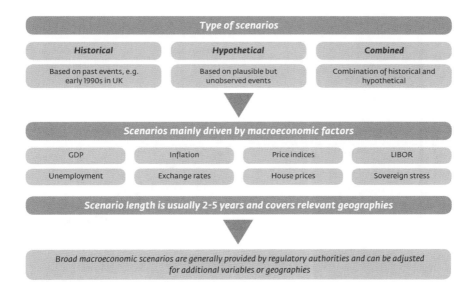

Companies use stress testing as a pragmatic approach to FX risk management. Hedging reduces currency risk in the short term, and creates a time for adjustment if there are significant movements in exchange rates. Stress testing identifies targets, stress buffers, recovery time, and resolution planning objectives. Exchange rates often move in relatively narrow ranges for periods of time. During these periods, a company is in the target operating zone as exchange rates will have a limited effect on sales, costs or margins. When the exchange rate moves beyond the target operating zone, the company starts to experience the effect of the movement. This stress buffer should be considered as an early warning indicator that the market movement may significantly change the company's business model. The next phase is the recovery time. During this period, a company that has hedged will have time to rethink its strategic risks with regard to pricing and production. Note, that a one-direction change in value of a currency will need to be absorbed after the hedge benefits have expired. Resolution planning requires a change in the business strategy, which may include pass-through of pricing, changes in sourcing or movement of facilities.

FIGURE 16.7   STRESS TESTING AND FX RISK MANAGEMENT

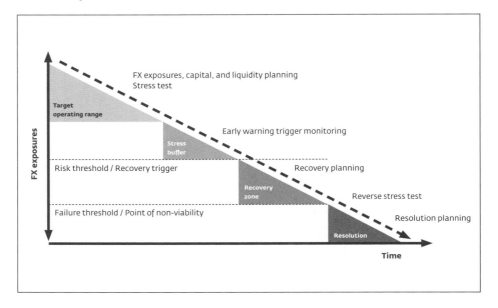

16.10
Summary

The business world is increasingly global and many companies are introducing new products and services to compete in foreign markets and expand profitability. Their pursuit of business opportunities inherently comes with a task, that of managing foreign currency exposures. Movements in exchange rates can cause instability in profit margins and generate other operational losses. As companies expand their operations and market influence around the world, the probability increases that they will face an impact from currency fluctuations. Currency risk management requires both resources and prioritisation. When managers recognise how different currency changes affect their business, they can more efficiently measure and manage foreign currency exposures using the practical tools and strategies discussed in this chapter. The volatility in previous currency crises is no measure of future volatility. The major challenge for many multinational companies is that volatility is everywhere. Managing FX risks in volatile markets is truly a team effort that requires effective collaboration across all levels of the organisation.

Chapter 17

Cross Currency Liquidity Management

17 Cross Currency Liquidity Management

17.1
Introduction

Corporate liquidity is at the forefront of a treasurer's mind and is a leading practice. Treasury management focuses on access to cash and funding to meet daily needs, contingencies, investments and unanticipated urgent situations. Chapter 16 has provided an introduction to foreign currency exchange risk and how it can be mitigated within the organisation. This chapter on cross-currency liquidity management presents an opportunity to build an effective process to enhance efficiency and take increased control of liquid assets.

What else should treasury operations groups consider when cross-currency cash flow exposures are identified? This chapter more closely examines major facets of cross-currency liquidity management and practices used by treasurers. The topics covered in this chapter are designed to be used as a basis for planning and responding to various liquidity situations.

17.2
Cross currency liquidity management

Cross-currency liquidity management involves:

- Using effective tools to manage business cycles across currencies, minimise interest rate differentials and maximise liquidity
- Assessing the impact of regulatory requirements on liquidity management practices and structures
- Establishing the level of liquidity risk that firms are prepared to address and tolerate
- Liquidity contingency planning
- Projections regarding available sources of liquidity

Companies across the globe seek to achieve visibility and control over their cash, reduce external borrowings, conserve credit lines for strategic activities as opposed to working capital, and maximise returns. In many countries, they face regulatory challenges, complex banking relationships and multiple accounts, which can make these objectives difficult to achieve. As companies continue to compete in foreign markets, many use liquidity tools such as multi-currency notional pooling or auto FX solutions.

Companies face a variety of tax and regulatory requirements when implementing cross-border liquidity management strategies and tools. The physical movement of funds requires collaboration in a decentralised organisation, as regional managers transfer their cash to other subsidiaries. Cross-border considerations also include withholding tax, replacing local bank financing with non-resident group entity funding, a need for accounting and tax review, and trapped liquidity (when regulatory restrictions limit the ability to send or receive funds from certain countries). Companies operating in various regions worldwide may have challenges related to trapped liquidity and non-convertible or restricted currencies. They seek to optimise liquidity and currency positions while also navigating regulatory or tax complexities in each country.

17.3
Approaches and strategies

17.3.1   FOCUS ON SURPLUS OR DEFICIT

Approaches to cross-currency liquidity management are similar to single-currency liquidity management. Treasury operations teams begin their day concerned with prior day balances and flows by counterparty compared to current day needs; additional currencies add an extra layer of decision-making. The decision process for liquidity management starts with a reconciled prior day activity that is compared with current day expectations. It assesses balances by counterparty to make buying, selling or transfer decisions primarily from money markets and liquid investments. Cross-currency liquidity management takes that same decision process, but separates the liquidity pools by currency. The experienced cross-currency cash positioner sets their position within each currency first, including any currency trades, then takes the necessary cross-currency action, finalising the cash position in the surplus or deficit currency of choice, most likely the corporate's domestic currency.

Developing the cash position

Areas of consideration in developing the cash position include the following:

- After considering transaction costs + overnight deposit / borrowing rate by currency and counterparty, focus on either eliminating deficits or investing surpluses in the following order:
    1. Cross-counterparty within a single currency
    2. Cross-currency within a single counterparty
    3. Across both if the two above are not satisfactory

- Complete trades and transfers to set the position and include the effect of these trades for the next cash position review

---

Using multiple iterations and historical analysis of the cash flows and necessary liquidity management transactions, a strategy can be created that both reduces the cost of daily transactions and the daily workload on the treasury operations staff.

17.3.2   SWAPS OR ACTIVE SPOTS

Building on the historical analysis of company cash flows and necessary cross-currency liquidity management transactions, an advanced treasury operations staff can improve their cross-currency liquidity management tactics to include anticipatory FX trades and FX swaps. However, before understanding more complex FX instruments and counterparty issues in capital markets, the treasury staff has to get more comfortable with their forecasted cash flows for each currency at least four weeks and ideally up to 90 days in advance. Standard business operations serve as guidance on temporary, seasonal, and even perpetual surpluses and deficits for a specific currency. For example, revenue streams may be denominated by a single currency due to the primary customers' market, while the cost structure needed to earn that revenue is denominated in a different set of currencies. This creates a perpetual surplus of cash from revenue streams with an ongoing deficit of cash in the cost structure required to generate that revenue.

Identifying the nature of the surpluses and deficits can allow for an advanced strategy such as anticipatory spot trades. Anticipatory spot trading strategy focuses on pre-defining the known FX trades that a treasury operations staff will have to make, allowing the decision process to focus on the most accurate amount to execute.

EXAMPLE 1

For example, a corporate with an identified natural surplus of GBP and a EUR deficit from one business unit and a EUR surplus and a SEK deficit from another can set their anticipatory spot trades to sell GBP and buy SEK primarily against the EUR. At the same time, they can consider their net EUR position such that they may execute one of three trades at any notional amount:

1.   Sell GBP to buy EUR
2.   Sell EUR to buy SEK
3.   Sell GBP to buy SEK

This strategy requires collaboration with the business units. Since the analysis of historic activities generated from business operations identifies natural surpluses and deficits, any changes to business operations that would disrupt this balance must be incorporated and ideally anticipated. From the example above, moving support operations from Sweden to Poland would both reduce to eliminate the need to buy SEK, while introducing the need to buy PLN. Conversely, altering the EUR cost structure that supports GBP revenue into GBP not only reduces the GBP surplus, but potentially switches a net EUR deficit to a net surplus depending on relative notional amounts.

When the anticipatory spot trading strategy reaches its maximum added value, many corporate treasury groups consider an FX swap strategy. This is especially popular when corporates have material international operations where natural surpluses and deficits may offset across currencies. FX swaps are financial instruments that have been introduced in chapter 16 as part of the suite of ways to manage foreign exchange risk. The difference when moving to this strategy is that the treasury operations staff evaluates the forward markets and future-dated contractual obligations.

Corporate treasury departments should weigh in on the design and implementation of this strategy – a practice used by many multinational corporates. FX swap strategies can reduce the level of volatility in the week-to-week cross-currency liquidity management efforts (something the anticipatory spot trading strategy accepts in trading day-to-day) and allow for flexibility when executing the trades used to manage cross-currency liquidity. Continuing with the same example, an FX swap is likely better for managing the net EUR surplus or deficit, setting the trades of sell GBP to buy EUR and sell EUR to buy SEK as FX swaps with a short-term maturity. This allows the treasury operations staff to take advantage of the offsetting position to buy and sell EUR, while at the same time potentially using the forward position of the FX swap to satisfy the future surplus or deficit of EUR.

17.4
Stress testing scenarios of liquidity strain

Companies can prepare themselves for potential situations by developing scenarios and conducting stress testing.

Below is a list of key objectives for liquidity stress testing.

- It should support risk management and identify any potential liquidity risk issues
- It should use a limit system
- It should define liquidity buffers available to absorb liquidity stress
- It should validate whether the risk profile is aligned with the risk appetite defined by the Board
- It should serve as key input into recovery and resolution planning

It is also imperative to identify liquidity sources and demands that a company may expect.

Liquidity sources	Liquidity demands
– Cash/contractual cash flows	– Liabilities falling due (actual and potential)
– Marketable assets unencumbered and eligible for secured funding	– Maturing debt/funding arrangements
	– Deposit withdrawals – retail
– Borrowing capacity, commitments and facilities	– Contingent liabilities and commitments
	– Unfunded facilities and guarantees (e.g., off-balance sheet vehicles, implicitly supported operations)
– Correct currencies or ability to swap	– Collateral/credit support
	– Payments and settlements obligations – direct participation, commitments to agent banks, CCPs

Companies need to prepare and outline their liquidity plan. Below is an overview of liquidity stress testing phases and approaches.

FIGURE 17.1   STRESS TESTING SCENARIOS

Creating a number of scenarios	Calculating cash flows	Liquid assets	Estimating survival horizon
▶ Creating regulatory scenarios	▶ Segmenting funding sources and creating behavioural assumptions	▶ Estimating realisable cash from liquid assets	▶ Compare cash outflows vs. stock of liquid assets
▶ Identifying individual risk drivers	▶ Forecasting asset cash flows		▶ Incorporate management actions
▶ Creating additional scenarios	▶ Incorporating other effects, e.g. collateral management		▶ Assess consistency with risk appetite

17.5
Summary

As new risks arise when companies expand into new markets, these risks compel companies to rethink liquidity operations and management. Strong and efficient liquidity management across currencies is needed to effectively facilitate treasury operations and provide continuous improvement. With cross-currency liquidity management comes cross-border concerns, and treasurers need to keep track of the latest regulatory and economic developments. They also will need tools to invest cash, minimise costs, and maximise yields. By using strategic products and the approaches described above, companies can improve their visibility and access to global cash, improving liquidity and reducing interest costs.

Chapter 18

Short-Term Interest Risk Management

18   Short-Term Interest Risk Management

18.1
Introduction

Interest risk is the risk that a change in interest rates may negatively affect a company's earnings or net worth. Every company is exposed to interest risk to some extent and one of the responsibilities of a corporate treasurer is to optimise a company's interest results and manage interest risk. With respect to short-term interest risks, the treasurer can use several financial instruments such as forward rate agreements (FRAs) and short-term interest rate futures (STIRs). This chapter explains how future liquidity positions generate interest risks and what instruments can be used to cover these risks. We will describe how interest rates can be fixed or managed for future periods.

18.2
The concept of short-term interest risk management

It helps to explain the concept of short-term interest risk by using an example. Suppose that in December, a treasurer prepares the following cash flow forecast for the coming year.

CASH FLOW FORECAST

Month	Jan	Feb	Mar	Apr	May	Jun	Jul	Aug	Sep	Oct	Nov	Dec
	€m	€m	€m	€m	€m	€m	€m	€m	€m	€m	€m	€m
Cash inflow	10	12	15	14	12	13	11	14	16	13	12	10
Cash outflow	-12	-15	-19	-15	-14	-16	-31	-37	-37	-17	-14	-11
Cash balance	-2	-3	-4	-1	-2	-3	-20	-23	-21	-4	-2	-1

In this example, the treasurer anticipates a major cash shortfall in the period from July to September. This could be due to high seasonal expenditures from July to September.

As a result, the treasurer knows that the company will have a substantial cash shortfall for three months during a specific period in the coming year. What the treasurer does not know, however, is what interest the company will pay on that deficit. If the controller asks the treasury department for an estimate of interest expense in the year ahead, the treasurer will need to prepare a specific forecast. Assuming the three-month money market rate is currently 3%, the treasurer could use this interest rate for his forecast. If, however, the three-month money market rate at the beginning of July is 6%, the actual interest expense will be well above his estimate. This means that the company will run an interest risk.

18.3
Objectives and tasks of interest risk management

Short-term interest risk management objectives and tasks
The objective of short-term interest risk management is to protect company earnings against the negative impact of interest rate fluctuations. Interest risk management involves the following tasks: – Determination of a policy in relation to short-term interest risks – Identification of short-term interest risks – Development of interest rate scenarios – Concluding hedging transactions

18.3.1 DEFENSIVE VERSUS OFFENSIVE STRATEGY

Some companies wish to avoid all risks and cover every position. When such a company is expecting a future liquidity shortfall, the treasurer may want to fix the interest rate applicable to that position. This is called a defensive strategy. Other companies may only want to cover future positions when they think they can avoid an expected loss or generate a potential profit. These companies typically compare different interest scenarios with the actual (forward) interest rates and use the outcome of this comparison for their decision to hedge the exposure or leave it open. If such a company anticipates a future cash deficit, and expects an increase in interest rates, for example, it may fix interest rates for the expected shortfall position. If it anticipates a decrease in interest rates, the company will want to leave the position open and wait until the moment that the liquidity position materialises and fix the interest at the decreased rate. This is called an offensive strategy.

18.3.2 IMPLIED FORWARD INTEREST RATES

The shape of the forward interest rate yield curve can provide information about the market's expectations about future interest rate developments. If the rates for longer maturity periods are higher than those for shorter periods, it may indicate that the market expects a rise in interest rates. In the case of a declining or inverse yield curve, the interest rates for shorter terms are higher than the interest rates for longer terms. In this situation, market participants may expect interest rates to fall. With a flat yield curve, interest rates for all periods are roughly the same. The (theoretical) market expectations are reflected in the so-called implied forward rates.

Forward interest rates are used for interest rate instruments for which the term lies in the future. Theoretically, forward interest rates can be derived from the interest rates for periods starting on a spot date (referred to as spot rates).

EXAMPLE 1

For example, if the six-month interest rate is 0.75% and the twelve-month interest rate is 1.00%, it can be concluded – at least in theory – that the market expects that interest rates in the period between six months and twelve months (referred to as the 6s v 12s implied forward yield) will be higher compared to the current rates, i.e. 1.25%. After all, the long-term rate (12 months) must be roughly the mean of the current six-month rate and the expected six-month rate after six months.

FIGURE 18.1   6S V. 12S IMPLIED FORWARD YIELD

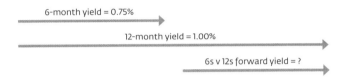

6-month yield = 0.75%

12-month yield = 1.00%

6s v 12s forward yield = ?

To indicate the level of the implied forward yield, the following simplified equation can be used:

$$\text{Implied forward rate} = \frac{\text{Long period x long-term interest rate} - \text{short period x short-term interest rate}}{\text{Future period}}$$

In the above example, the implied forward rate = (12 x 1.00% - 6 x 0.75%)/6 = 1.25%.

By using this equation, for each (short) period in the future, an implied forward yield can be calculated that the company can use to make informed hedging decisions, i.e. whether or not to fix its future cash position.

18.4
Instruments for hedging future short-term positions

To cover future short-term interest risks, a treasurer can use two products: forward rate agreements (FRAs) and short-term interest rate futures (STIRs). Essentially, these products are identical. The most striking difference is that forward rate agreements are over-the-counter (OTC) products, i.e. they are bilateral without the use of an exchange. Short-term interest rate futures are traded on an exchange such as the Chicago Mercantile Exchange or Euronext BV in Amsterdam.

- Forward rate agreements (FRAs)
- Short-term interest rate (STIR) futures

18.4.1 FORWARD RATE AGREEMENTS (FRAS)

A forward rate agreement (FRA) is an over-the-counter (OTC) interest rate derivative traded on the money market. In a FRA, two parties enter into a mutual obligation that – at a specified single moment in the future (the fixing date) – a sum will be settled that is based on the difference between an interest rate specified in the contract and the level of a reference interest rate on the fixing date. This rate differential is applied to a fixed principal sum (the nominal amount). A FRA is a product in its own right. From a contractual perspective, the investment and/or funding transactions for which the FRA is used as a hedge are entirely separate from the FRA.

The buyer of a FRA is the party that receives an amount of money from the other party if the reference interest rate on the fixing date is higher than the FRA contract rate. The seller receives an amount of money from the buyer if – on the fixing date – the reference interest rate is lower than the contract rate. The contract rate is usually set at the implied forward interest rate that corresponds with the relevant future period of the liquidity position. Companies generally either sell FRAs to fix the interest rate for a future short-term liquidity surplus, or buy FRAs to fix the interest rate for a future short-term liquidity shortfall.

The amounts involved in the settlement of a FRA are calculated on the fixing date. Settlement takes place on the corresponding spot date, which usually means two working days later, i.e. fixing date +2 (with the exception of FRAs traded in sterling, where the settlement usually takes place on the fixing date itself). Figure 18.2 shows the relevant periods for a 3s v 9s FRA.

FIGURE 18.2 TIMETABLE 3S V 9S FRA

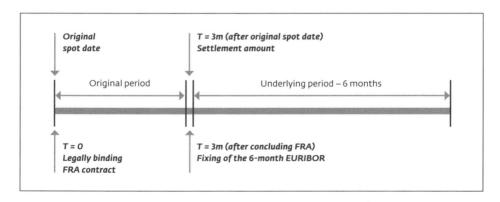

418   International Cash Management

- On the fixing date, the reference interest rate is compared with the contract interest rate
- The difference in interest rates is calculated as an amount over the underlying maturity period and over the principal amount
- Because the settlement date is at the start of the underlying period instead of at the maturity date of the underlying period of the FRA, the settlement amount is discounted against the money market reference rate that corresponds with the underlying period

As we have seen above, FRAs are typically used by companies wanting either to fix the interest rate in respect of a forecast liquidity surplus, if they expect that interest rates are likely to fall, or to fix interest rates in respect of a forecast liquidity shortfall (borrowing need), if they expect interest rates are likely to rise. When companies use a FRA to hedge their interest rate risk, they will always pay a fixed rate no matter what happens to the short-term yield curve. The overall fixed rate to be paid can be calculated by using the following equation:

> *Overall interest rate = interest rate on the loan + FRA cash settlement =*
> *fixing rate + credit spread + (FRA contract rate - fixing rate) =*
> *FRA contract rate + credit spread*

The following example shows how a company can use a FRA.

EXAMPLE 2

It is 15 March, and in four months' time – 15 July – a company will be faced with a liquidity shortfall of EUR 5 million that will last for three months. The '4s v 7s' FRA asking price is 3.75%. The company can borrow at EURIBOR with a credit spread of 30 basis points. According to the equation above, if the company concludes a FRA, the effective interest rate for the future period will be:

3.75% + 0.30% = **4.05%**.

If the fixing of three-month EURIBOR on the fixing date is above the contract rate of 3.75%, the company will receive the difference between the fixing rate and 3.75% as a cash settlement from the FRA contract. This compensates for the fact that the bank will use the actual higher EURIBOR rate on 15 July as the interest rate for the three-month loan. For instance, if on 15 July the three-month EURIBOR fixing rate is 3.95%, the overall interest rate for the company is:

3.95% + 0.30% + (3.75% - 3.95%) = **4.05%**.

If the fixing of three-month EURIBOR on the fixing date is below the contract rate of 3.75%, the company must pay the difference between the fixing rate and 3.75%. This compensates for the fact that the bank will use the actual lower EURIBOR rate as the interest rate for the three-month loan. For instance, if on 15 July the three-month EURIBOR fixing is 3.40%, the overall interest rate for the company is:

3.40% + 0.30% + (3.75% − 3.40%) = **4.05%**.

18.4.2   SHORT-TERM INTEREST RATE (STIR) FUTURES

Like FRAs, money market futures or short-term interest rate (STIR) futures are financial products traded in the money market that can be used to fix future interest revenues or interest costs of short-term future cash surpluses or shortfalls.

A STIR future is an exchange-listed future contract where the price is based on the forward interest rate for a specific future period – the so-called 'underlying forward period'. The term of the underlying forward period is fixed: one month (30 days, year basis 360) or three months (90 days, year basis 360). The cycle for money market futures is March, June, September and December. The table below shows examples of money market futures.

Contract	Value		Reference rate	
Short sterling	GBP	500,000	GBP	LIBOR
Eurodollar	USD	1,000,000	USD	LIBOR
Euribor	EUR	1,000,000	EUR	LIBOR
Euroswiss	CHF	1,000,000	CHF	LIBOR
Euroyen	JPY	100,000,000	JPY	LIBOR

The price of a STIR future is quoted as 100 minus the (implied) forward interest rate. For example: 100 − 2.25% = 97.75. Therefore, the price goes up if the forward interest rate for the underlying period goes down. This means that a company that wants to protect itself against rising interest rates must sell a STIR future. After all, if the interest rate increases, the price of the STIR future falls. This is the opposite of FRAs, where the company would have had to buy the FRA contract to hedge against rising interest rates.

If the price of a STIR future is known, the forward rate for the underlying period can also be calculated.

EXAMPLE 3

In January, the price of the March eurodollar future is 98.87. This means that the implied 2s vs 5s forward rate at that moment is 1.13%.

Because STIR futures are exchange-traded, the profit or loss on a STIR contract is settled on a daily basis during the contract period. This differs from FRAs, where the settlement takes place at the end of the contract period once the reference rate is fixed. Companies may use STIR futures for hedging short-term interest rate risks. This is shown in the following example.

EXAMPLE 4

A company has a short cash position in the three-to-six-month period. In order to hedge its interest rate risk, the company sells a STIR future. If the price of the 3s vs 6s STIR future is 95.50, by selling the future the company has ensured that the financing costs (ignoring credit spreads) are fixed at a level of 4.5% (30/360). If the fixing at the end of the contract period is exactly 95.50, no settlement has taken place, on average, during the term of the futures contract. However, for a loan the company must pay the market rate of 4.5%.

If the fixing at the end of the contract period is 94.50, then under the futures contract the company would have received the difference between 95.50 and 94.50 during the term of the futures contract (100 ticks or -1% on an annual basis) over the size of the futures contract. Since the company must pay the market rate of 5.5% for a loan, its interest costs – on balance – are 4.5%.

If the fixing at the end of the contract period is 96.50, then under the futures contract the company has paid the difference between 96.50 and 95.50 during the term of the futures contract (100 ticks or 1% on an annual basis). Since the company must pay the market rate of 3.5% for a loan, on balance its interest costs are 4.5%.

18.4.3   STIR FUTURES AND FRAS – A COMPARISON

A key advantage of STIR futures over FRAs is that the former are traded on a more liquid market and the instrument is fully standardised. This is true both for the product specifications and for the terms and conditions. Another advantage is that a STIR futures contract is settled against a market rate – set by supply and demand – compared to a FRA which is settled against a money market reference rate such as EURIBOR.

A disadvantage of STIR futures compared with FRAs is that profits and losses are settled daily during the contract period. This creates daily cash flows that must be tracked and administered. This is not the case with FRAs, where settlement takes place at the end of the contract period. Another disadvantage of STIR futures is that there are only four underlying periods per year, each with a term of three months (90 days) or 1 month (30 days) that starts on the third Wednesday of March, June, September or December. This means that companies often run an interest risk for periods that do not exactly coincide with one of the futures periods.

If the hedging period is slightly longer than the underlying period for a STIR future, a company can adjust the number of futures proportionately. When the hedging period starts slightly earlier than the contract period for a STIR future, the period until the start of the future is called the 'stub'. When the hedging period ends slightly later than the contract period for a STIR, the period after the end date of the contract period of the future is called the 'tail'.

EXAMPLE 5

A company wants to hedge a short liquidity position of USD 20 million with a start date of 15 March and an end date of 21 June using the March STIR future (97 days). The underlying period of the March future extends from 23 March until 21 June (90 days). Since the period to be hedged does not exactly correspond with the underlying period for the STIR future, it calculates the number of STIR futures to sell as follows:

Number of futures contracts: 97/90 x 20 contracts = 21.56 contracts
In order not to be under-hedged, the dealer has to sell 22 contracts

---

If the hedge period lies partly in the contract period of one STIR future and partly in the contract period of a subsequent STIR future, a company can choose to hedge the position using both STIR futures and set the number of contracts for each future in proportion to the part of the underlying period that overlaps the underlying period of each future. In total, the number of contracts must be of a size that matches the underlying position – for example 2/3 and 1/3 times the value of the underlying position.

EXAMPLE 6

It is December and a company wants to hedge a short cash position of USD 15 million from 22 May until 22 August.

The company is advised to hedge the position using March and June futures. The period to be hedged lies in the contract period for the March future for one month and in the contract period for the June future for two months. Therefore, the company is advised to sell March contracts for 1/3 of the exposure and June contracts for 2/3 of the exposure.

FRAs	STIR futures
– Non-standardised product	+ Standardised product
– Less liquid market	+ More liquid market
+ Flexible periods	– Only standard periods
+ Single settlement at end of contract period	– Daily settlement

18.5
Summary

A company's short-term interest rate risk can be managed by using either a FRA from, for example, a bank or a STIR entered into via a futures exchange like Euronext. Other products that can be used to manage short-term interest rate risks are caps or interest rate swaps. However, these are more commonly used to manage longer-term interest rate risks.

Part F

Regulations

Chapter 19

Tax Consequences of Cash Management

19 Tax Consequences of Cash Management

19.1
Introduction

The implementation of an international cash management structure presents treasurers with many challenges. One particularly significant challenge is the plethora of tax rules across the globe. When doing business in an international environment, a treasurer needs to be aware of the rules in that region. It is therefore advisable to consult with a tax specialist before the implementation of such a structure in order to avoid additional costs if changes have to be made or the company incurs penalties or fines for breaching tax regulations.

A regular review of the cash management solution with a tax specialist is also recommended since tax rules often change and company structures evolve (for example, through a change in ownership). Such changes can have serious consequences with respect to the tax treatment of a particular solution in a specific country. In general, banks are not in a position to provide tax advice as it is not their field of expertise. Banks can provide practical guidelines or share the experiences of other clients (while remaining within appropriate confidentiality rules). However, such information should not replace the advice of a professional tax advisor.

In this chapter, we will provide a high-level overview of the main tax considerations of international cash management structures, particularly with respect to the following areas:

- Withholding tax on interest
- Stamp duties
- Transfer pricing
- Thin capitalisation/other interest deduction limitation rules
- Controlled foreign companies
- Treasury centre locations

We will also highlight significant changes in the tax landscape affecting the treasury function, such as the Action Plan on Base Erosion and Profit Shifting (BEPS Action Plan) of the Organisation for Economic Co-operation and Development (OECD) and the EU Anti-Tax Avoidance Directive (ATAD).

It is worth noting that there may be additional tax consequences that apply in specific countries.

19.2

The basics of tax

To examine the potential tax consequences of a cash management solution, it is important to understand how taxation authorities look at such structures. Where companies and banks focus predominantly on the physical location of an account when setting up a cash management structure, taxation authorities will focus on the residency of the legal entities involved.

FIGURE 19.1   PHYSICAL VERSUS LEGAL STRUCTURES

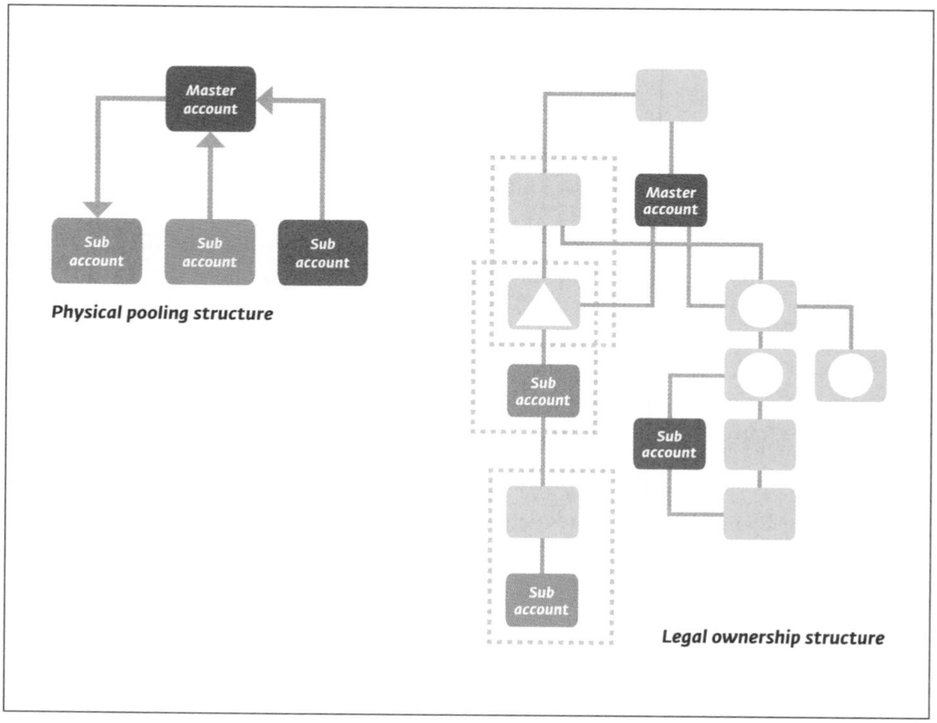

Physical pooling structure

Legal ownership structure

For tax purposes, residency is determined by that of the entities involved and not by the physical location of the account. For example, a Belgium-based company makes an interest payment from its non-resident bank account held (at their bank) in the Netherlands to a France-based entity's non-resident bank account held with that same bank in the Netherlands. For tax purposes, it is considered a payment from a Belgium-based to a France-based entity rather than a domestic interest payment within the Netherlands. In most cases, the country of incorporation or the effective place of management of a legal entity determines its residency.

There can be a significant tax impact from the physical movements of funds between the accounts of different legal entities. For example, an automated multi-bank cash balance transfer from a local subsidiary to a master account owned by central treasury will create an intercompany loan and a deposit. The majority of tax consequences arise from these intercompany loans.

With regard to notional pooling, balances are mathematically combined for the purpose of calculating the net interest result. Balances do not need to be moved physically as long as all participants reside in the same location. As a result, no transfer of ownership of funds occurs in that case, nor intercompany lending. However, this does not mean that notional pooling could not have tax consequences, as balance compensation often triggers inter-company (cross) guarantees. Nevertheless, although there is a material difference between the form of the two pooling methods, the level of interest rates on either inter-company physical balances (receivables and payables) or notional balances of group participating companies can ultimately be influenced by the group shareholders, and as such is subject to transfer pricing rules.

19.3
Withholding tax on interest

Many multinational corporates struggle with withholding taxes levied in several countries on interest payments between group companies (intercompany loans) and/or interest payments to banks. If not well managed, such withholding taxes can have a significant impact on interest earned. In countries where withholding tax is levied, it also involves an additional administrative burden.

Withholding tax is levied at the source. For example, take the case where central treasury has used cross-border zero-balancing to sweep funds to a bank account of a local group company that is resident in a country that levies a withholding tax. The credit balances swept from the central treasury to the local group company are the source that generates the interest on which withholding tax is levied.

Withholding interest is withheld from the proceeds (i.e. interest) being sent to the recipient. In this example, the central treasury is the recipient of the interest – as the provider of the inter-company loan – and receives a lesser amount than expected following deduction of the withholding tax.

19.3.1   IMPLICATIONS FOR PHYSICAL CASH CONCENTRATION

Withholding tax may be levied in domestic or cross-border situations:

- Domestic situations – where both recipient and payer are tax residents in the same country. It should be noted that they may not necessarily be tax resident in the same country where their bank accounts are located.

- In cross-border situations – where the recipient is a tax resident in a different country to that of the payer. It is important to be aware that the bank account of the recipient and the source (paying the bank deposit) can be physically located in the same country but for tax purposes are considered to be owned by tax residents of two different countries.

As explained above (see figure 19.1), the physical location of an account is not relevant when determining the tax implications. Residency for tax purposes is generally determined by the jurisdiction in which the account holder is incorporated.

An important step in determining whether a country will levy a withholding tax on interest is to characterise interest as bank or intercompany interest. The relevant withholding tax rate may differ for bank and intercompany interest. This distinction is also relevant for interest paid in cross-border situations, as tax treaties may treat bank interest differently from intercompany interest.

- Bank interest – withholding tax may be levied when there is a lending relationship between a bank and a corporate entity and one has made an interest payment to the other. For example, if a bank in Italy pays interest to a resident account holder (recipient) it will withhold the relevant withholding tax rate for bank interest and pay this to the tax collector in Italy.

- Intercompany interest – withholding tax may be levied when there is a lending relationship between two different account-holding entities and one party pays interest to the other. For example, if a resident in Italy pays interest to a non-resident of Italy, the Italian entity will withhold the relevant withholding tax rate on intercompany interest and pay this to the tax collector in Italy.

FIGURE 19.2
WITHHOLDING TAX
ON INTEREST

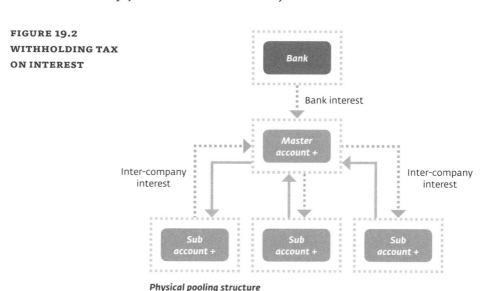

Physical pooling structure

- **Step 1**
  Identify the interest flow and direction
- **Step 2**
  Determine whether flows are 'bank interest' or 'intercompany interest'
- **Step 3**
  Check the tax residency of the entities involved
- **Step 4**
  Determine the relevant withholding tax rate
- **Step 5**
  Ascertain whether a treaty or the EU Interest and Royalties Directive allows for a more favourable tax rate

19.3.2   IMPLICATIONS FOR NOTIONAL CASH CONCENTRATION

With notional pooling, the parties to the bank accounts included in the notional pool are the bank and the company that holds the bank account. Any overdraft on an individual account continues to be a claim of the bank against the company (or vice versa in the case of a surplus position).

With most notional pooling structures, the central treasury receives or pays interest on the net pool balance from or to the bank. Withholding tax on bank interest is applicable to this interest settlement. The pool benefit will generally be considered as an increase of bank credit interest or decrease of bank debit interest and, as such, it would not necessarily be separated from the actual interest for withholding tax purposes. By identifying the expected interest flows prior to implementing the cash pool, a company will be able to establish in which countries a potential withholding tax issue may arise and identify potential solutions.

19.3.3   EXEMPTION OF WITHHOLDING TAX ON INTEREST

Withholding tax can be lowered or exempt in the following situations:

- ***Under bilateral tax treaties***
  A lower (perhaps even 0%) withholding tax on interest is possible if certain conditions are satisfied. The more bilateral treaties a country has, the more popular it will be as a treasury centre location (please see section 19.8).

- ***Interest withholding tax exemption based on the EU Interest and Royalties Directive***
  This directive provides for an interest withholding tax exemption between 'associated EU tax resident companies'. Associated companies under the directive are companies that have an indirect or direct holding of at least 10% of the shares.

The BEPS Action Plan provides 15 actions that equip governments with the domestic and international instruments needed to tackle BEPS. Countries now have the tools to ensure that profits are taxed where economic activities generating the profits are performed and where value is created. These tools also give businesses greater certainty by reducing disputes over the application of international tax rules (including transfer pricing) and standardising compliance requirements.

The Organisation for Economic Co-operation and Development (OECD) and G20 countries, along with developing countries that participated in the development of the BEPS package, are establishing a modern international tax framework under which profits are taxed where economic activity and value creation occur. Work will be carried out to support all countries interested in implementing and applying the rules in a consistent and coherent manner, particularly those for which capacity building is an important issue.

http://www.oecd.org/tax/beps/beps-about.htm

On 5 October 2015, the OECD released a final report with recommendations for addressing treaty abuse in connection with Action 6 of the BEPS Action Plan. The report includes model tax treaty provisions and related changes to the model commentary to address the inappropriate granting of treaty benefits and other potential treaty abuse scenarios.

After implementation, the changes may make it more difficult to apply reduced treaty interest withholding tax rates if obtaining treaty benefits is the main reason for routing interest payments through a certain country or if there is a lack of sufficient substance in the country of residence of the recipient of the interest. As a result the focus will increasingly be on the economic reality rather than merely looking at the contractual relationships.

What is to be considered sufficient substance differs for each country but includes having an office, employees, local resident directors, effective place of management, a resident bank account, etc.

On 3 June 2003, the European Council adopted Directive 2003/49/EC on a common system of taxation applicable to interest and royalty payments made between associated companies of different member states. The benefits of the Interest and Royalties Directive are only granted to companies that are:
- Subject to corporate tax in the EU
- Tax resident in an EU member state
- Of a type listed in the annex of the directive

For some member states countries, a transition period is applicable. For more information, please visit: http://ec.europa.eu/taxation_customs/taxation/company_tax/interests_royalties/index_en.htm

19.3.4 WITHHOLDING TAX AND CASH MANAGEMENT SOLUTIONS

Withholding tax can pose an additional cost burden or become an obstacle to cash management solutions. However, this does not necessarily mean that certain cash management structures cannot be implemented. There are many techniques to mitigate the effect of withholding tax. In most cases, withholding taxes are levied in advance of the final income tax liability of the company receiving the interest income. The company is therefore paying a tax before its annual corporate tax liability is known or due. In general, withholding taxes may be deducted from (or credited against) the domestic corporate income tax liability of the recipient (a credit is 100% tax relief and does not lead to an increased overall tax burden/cost).

EXAMPLE: TAX CREDIT

A company's taxable income amounts to EUR 50. Withholding tax of EUR 8 has been levied on that company's interest income. Assuming a corporate income tax rate of 20%, its domestic corporate income tax liability amounts to (20% x EUR 50) = EUR 10. An amount of EUR 8 may be deducted from the domestic corporate income tax liability of EUR 10, resulting in a residual amount of corporate income tax (EUR 2).

In this case, total tax paid = domestic EUR 2 + foreign withholding tax EUR 8 = EUR 10. If there had been no withholding tax, the company would have paid taxes equalling the same amount (i.e. EUR 50 x 20% = EUR 10). Please note that some countries may apply different ways of calculating a maximum limit to the tax credit allowed.

Alternatively, withholding tax can be offset against a recipient's taxable income as a deductible expense. Prior to determining its corporate income tax liability, the company can deduct the withholding tax paid as an expense. As a result, the corporate income tax liability is reduced by the amount of withholding tax paid times the applicable corporate income tax rate. Therefore, the deduction of withholding tax is not a 100% relief but only a relief at the applicable tax rate.

EXAMPLE: DEDUCTIBLE EXPENSE

A company's taxable income amounts to EUR 50. Withholding tax of EUR 8 has been levied on the interest income of that company. An amount of EUR 8 is deducted as an expense from the company's taxable profit, resulting in a taxable amount of 50 – EUR 8 = EUR 42. Assuming a corporate income tax rate of 20%, corporate income tax of 20% x EUR 42 = EUR 8.40 will be due.

Total taxes paid = domestic EUR 8.40 + foreign withholding tax EUR 8 = EUR 16.40.

Even in a situation where withholding tax is fully credited, there may be a timing mismatch resulting in an opportunity cost. This can occur in two ways:

- Withholding taxes are levied upon the settlement of interest, whereas the corporate income tax is normally levied (and the credit for withholding taxes claimed) after the end of the financial year.

- In cross-border situations, some countries levy withholding taxes at their domestic statutory rates that are higher than the tax rates allowed under tax treaties. As a result, the recipient of the interest income has to apply for a refund in the country of the interest payer. During the period between the withholding tax being levied and the refund being received, the company does not have use of the amount to be refunded.

In situations where a recipient is not able to fully utilise a credit or a deductible expense for foreign withholding tax on interest, the tax may represent an actual cost to the company. However, other solutions may be found in sub-pools of accounts making use of more favourable tax jurisdictions to reduce or avoid the withholding tax.

Cash pooling arrangements must first be characterised for US tax purposes as either intercompany loans or transactions with a third-party bank in order to determine the appropriate tax treatment. The arrangement, including any intercompany and third-party contracts or agreements, must be examined under the federal tax rules and regulations, and also under case law evaluating the potential application of common law re-characterisation concepts such as conduit principles and the substance over form doctrine. Application of such re-characterisation provisions to a cash pooling arrangement can mean the difference between applying the interest and withholding tax provisions to the provider bank or to one or more related parties that may be considered to have funded the bank loan.

19.4
Transfer pricing

In general, transfer pricing rules refer primarily to the pricing of intercompany transactions (including transfer of tangible goods, intangibles, services and financial transactions) within a multinational company, where the intercompany prices should be at arm's length. However, from a transfer pricing perspective it is also important to ensure that the actual transaction, viewed in its entirety, possesses the commercial rationality of arrangements that would be agreed between unrelated parties under comparable economic circumstances. Otherwise, adverse tax consequences may arise, including the risk of double taxation.

Related to physical pooling, transfer pricing principally refers to the suitability of the interest rates that are applied to intercompany receivables and payables in the case of physical pools. However, it may also refer to the interest rates that are applied to the notional balances of group companies, in the case of notional pools, as such pool interest rates are also generally up to the group's (and not the bank's) discretion. Alongside the arm's length nature of interest rates, there are also other transfer pricing considerations relevant for cash management solutions. These include, but are not limited to, intra-group risk assumptions (e.g., through guarantees and/or joint and several liabilities), remuneration for the services provided by the cash pool leader, potential allocation of the net interest rate advantage (i.e., the so-called pooling benefits) among the group companies and commercial rationality of those cash pool balances that are steadily growing and remain outstanding for long periods of time.

As money is mobile and fungible, tax administrations recognise that multinational companies may strive to achieve favourable tax results by adjusting the amount of debt and/or interest in a group entity, trying to take advantage of low tax jurisdictions.

While most of the countries around the globe have adopted and been following the arm's length principle, which is a universal tax principle, specific local transfer pricing regulations and/or the interpretation of the arm's length principle may vary across countries.

19.4.1   IMPLICATIONS FOR PHYSICAL CASH CONCENTRATION

Physical cash concentration raises a number of transfer pricing issues. For example, the following questions may arise:

- Are the debit and credit interest rates on the intercompany balances consistent with the arm's length standard?
- What is the arm's length level of compensations that the cash pool leader entity should receive for its activities, taking into account the functions performed, assets used, and risks assumed?
- Which entity / entities within the group should be entitled to the pooling benefit and how should such benefit be allocated?
- Are the contractual relations between the cash pool leader and the group participants aligned with the actual conduct and intent of those parties?
- Does the cash pool leader have adequate economic substance (both the people functions and financial capacity) to control the contractually assumed financial risks, such as counterparty credit risk, liquidity risk, FX risk, etc.?

The compensation of each group company and the cash pool leader entity should be based on a detailed factual analysis of the functions performed, assets employed, and risks assumed by the parties to the cash pool arrangement. The level of income for the cash pool leader entity ultimately depends on its functional characterisation, e.g. a routine service provider, an asset manager, or an internal bank. As already mentioned above, in order to ensure transfer pricing regulations are not violated, an arm's length interest rate should be charged and paid on intercompany loans in each country. An arm's length interest rate is an interest rate that a third party under the same circumstances and conditions would also have been willing to receive or pay. Furthermore, an arm's length remuneration should be established for other intercompany financial transactions and/or services performed by the cash pool leader entity and/or the central treasury, e.g., term loans, intra-group derivatives, hedging, payment factory, etc.

When determining arm's length interest rates for both debit and credit balances, the main questions concern the economic nature of the cash pool payables and receivables (e.g., demand deposit vs. mid-term deposit, intraday overdraft vs. short-term credit facility vs. revolving credit facility) and the level of the counterparty credit risk, which can be reflected by (proxy) credit ratings of the cash pool leader and the cash pool participants.

With respect to the functional profile of the cash pool leader, there is a wide spectrum varying from a routine service provider (cost centre) to an in-house bank (profit centre). For example, in cash management structures the following scenarios are often applied in practice:

1. In-house bank: all economic risks connected to the cash management structure are for the account of the central treasury / the cash pool leader entity (profit centre) and group companies interact with the central treasury / the cash pool leader as if it were an external bank.

2. The central treasury/the cash pool leader acts as a value-adding service provider (e.g., an asset manager) to the participating companies, and may also assume limited economic risks in this respect.
3. The central treasury/the cash pool leader acts as a routine service provider for the participants and assumes no risk at all (cost centre).

These three scenarios are further described below.

In-house bank
Where all risks are borne by the cash pool leader, the remuneration of the participants could be approached from the perspective of those participants. Taking as a basis the interest rates offered by the well-rated bank, one could argue that the interest rate on a credit balance held by a participant on the intercompany current account should be adjusted upwards to reflect any differentials between the credit rating of the cash pool leader and the credit rating of the bank. Using the same reasoning, the interest rates on debit balances held by group companies on the intercompany current accounts with the cash pool leader should reflect the creditworthiness of the individual cash pool participants.

With respect to commercial terms, if a bank – under normal circumstances – requires collateral for debit positions, then tax administrations may argue that the cash pool leader should also receive such collateral from the participants with a debit balance. If no collateral is provided, additional guarantees may be requested as an alternative (either cross-guarantees by all participants or by a parent company, if different than the cash pool leader). The spread between debit and credit interest rates (i.e., the net interest margin) will reflect arm's length remuneration for the credit and liquidity risks that the central treasury undertakes. For example, if on one side the credit balances are characterised as demand deposits and on the other side the debit balances are characterised as working capital facilities, the in-house bank is exposed to significant liquidity risk (due to the asset-liability mismatch), for which it should be compensated (provided that the internal bank has the appropriate economic substance to assume and control such risk).

Asset manager
Where the cash pool leader does not assume economic risks related to the cash concentration structure, but instead acts as a facilitator/asset manager to the participants, 'investing' the excess cash in accordance with the mandate given by group companies – for example within the boundaries of the group's investment policy and/or by borrowing to group companies with cash deficit – it is conceivable that the central treasury should be remunerated with a handling fee. That can be either implemented as a spread between interest income and expense or a separately charged handling fee. Such a handling fee should be sufficient to cover the budgeted costs of the arrangements and leave a reasonable profit to the cash pool leader for the activities performed. The central treasury still assumes the risk of inefficiencies of its own operations but does not assume the financial risks (such as liquidity, counterparty, FX risks) on the overall position of the cash concentration structure.

In this situation, the benefit of participating in such a structure should be allocated to those participants assuming financial risks. The allocation could, for example, be accomplished by enhancing the internal interest rates on credit balances versus what the participants would pay or receive from the local bank. In this respect, the interest rates on credit balances could be linked to the overall rate of return achieved by the cash pool leader, less a handling fee.

Routine service provider

This situation reflects the cash concentration structure as a joint venture agreement between the participants. The participants need to appoint a treasury cash pool leader that assumes no economic risks and performs primarily administrative functions. As such, the cash pool leader will receive a service fee from the participants. This service fee could be determined on a cost-plus basis whereby actual costs are charged to the participants with a profit mark-up of a certain percentage. For example, if all the cash pool participants provide cross-guarantees, the pooling benefit (net interest rate advantage) should be allocated to the participants (either on a periodic basis as a separate allocation or through enhanced cash pool rates).

OECD Transfer Pricing Guidelines
for Multinational Enterprises and Tax Administrations

Cash pooling arrangements must first be characterised for US tax purposes as either intercompany loans or transactions with a third-party bank in order to determine the appropriate tax treatment. The arrangement, including any intercompany and third-party contracts or agreements, must be examined under the federal tax rules and regulations, and also under case law evaluating the potential application of common law re-characterisation concepts such as conduit principles and the substance over form doctrine. Application of such re-characterisation provisions to a cash pooling arrangement can mean the difference between applying the interest and withholding tax provisions to the provider bank or to one or more related parties that may be considered to have funded the bank loan.

In addition to the relationship between the bank and the cash pool leader, and the relationship between the cash pool leader and the pool participants, there may also be a relationship between the bank and the parent company (in the event that the bank requires a guarantee from the parent company to cover the credit risk). Any claims lodged with the parent company under this guarantee will – in principle – result in a tax-deductible expense (provided the parent company receives a fee from its group companies for the guarantee). A practical way for the parent company to earn a guarantee fee would be to charge such a fee to the cash pool leader, while the central treasury could either absorb such a fee (under the in-house bank model) or charge a guarantee fee to the participating companies (under the routine service provider model).

19.4.2   IMPLICATIONS FOR NOTIONAL CASH CONCENTRATION

Although the form of notional cash pools is different from that of physical cash pools, the same transfer pricing considerations essentially apply to both scenarios. Despite the fact that notional cash pools do not result in intercompany loans, the decision-making with respect to debit and credit rates concerning individual balances of the pool participants, which are subject to the notional pooling, lies with the multinational group (and not with the bank, as the bank is only concerned about the group's overall balance).

Similar to the physical cash concentration, the functional, asset and risks analysis is critical to determine the level of remuneration (e.g., interest rates, guarantees fees, handling fees, etc.) to be paid/received by the respective parties. In a notional pool, credit balances of cash-rich participants usually provide a guarantee to the bank for debit balances of participants with cash deficits. Therefore cash-rich participants will need to assume a credit risk. Following the OECD transfer pricing guidelines the cash-rich participants would require an arm's length compensation (either in a form of a separate guarantee fee, higher interest rate, and/or allocable pooling benefit). Such an arm's length compensation should reflect a fee that would have been agreed between independent legal entities, whereby facts and circumstances were comparable. Meanwhile, the same approach would usually apply to the joint and several liability of the participating companies in the cash pool.

19.4.3   CONCLUSION

Where withholding taxes generally tend to be reduced, transfer pricing is the current major tax issue, particularly given the most recent BEPS developments. Many tax authorities are taking a greater interest in transfer pricing and have been developing their knowledge of the matter. In recent years, tax authorities have considerably increased their focus on cash management structures and there are multiple cases of double taxation.

Tax audit experience – cash pool loans and deposits
– Re-characterisation of structural cash pool debit and credit positions, respectively, into long-term loans and deposits; asserting higher interest rates
– Insufficient evidence to support commercial rationality of a participant in the pool maintaining an excess cash/liquidity buffer over a longer period of time
– Focus on netting/pooling benefits allocation – majority of tax authorities expect pooling benefits to be quantified and (at least) partially allocated to cash pool participants, even when intercompany cash pool deposit rates are higher than the local bank rates
– Low deposit rates, e.g., 0% or a few/several basis points are frequently challenged, in particular if they are lower than the local bank rates
– Credit and debit rates not being at arm's length and/or insufficiently supported by the transfer pricing documentation/benchmarks
– Cash pool rates should take into account the creditworthiness of the cash pool leader and the cash pool participants
– Terms and conditions of cash pool deposits or cash pool loans not considered commercially rational from the perspective of the cash pool leader or the cash pool participants

- Substance - focus on the functional and risk profile of the cash pool leader and the financial capacity (adequate equity) to assume risks
- Cash pool leader profitability not aligned with its functional and risk profile (e.g., too high or too low; in some cases cash pool leaders are in a continual loss-making position)
- Taking an isolated approach, rather than looking at the whole picture and the total profit in the cash pool system (or at the treasury centre's level) often leads to double taxation
- Lack of (written) transfer pricing policy and procedures
- No (or outdated) contractual agreements in place
- Lack of sufficient (written) evidence to support the commercial rationality of participation in the group cash pool. Ideally, some group synergies should be passed to the participants and local benefits should be well-documented
- Requesting transparency regarding the cash pool leader's profitability and how excess cash in the pool is used
- Credit loss on cash pool positions in case of the participant's default is not tax-deductible at the level of the cash pool leader
- (Cross-)guarantees and / or joint and several liabilities provided in respect of cash pooling transactions were not analysed by taxpayers in the context of the arm's length principle

In order to avoid transfer pricing issues and tax challenges, companies should have both the up-to-date legal agreement and the contemporaneous transfer pricing documentation in place. Also, the transfer pricing policy should ideally be in place and be well-supported by the actual agreements and reflect the functions performed, assets used, and the risks assumed by the various group companies that are part of the cash pool arrangements. It is strongly recommended to properly document the arm's length nature of the interest rates, guarantee fees, handling fees, etc., as well as the applicable transfer pricing methods. Proper transfer pricing documentation will provide for internal consistency as well as serve as a first line of defence against the tax authorities. In most cases, failure to produce local transfer pricing documentation will reverse the burden of proof and may also result in penalties. If properly documented, transfer pricing does not form an obstacle for cash management solutions.

19.5
Thin capitalisation/other interest deduction limitation rules

In principle, interest paid on a loan granted by one company to another company is tax-deductible as an expense for the paying company (while the recipient has to include the interest received in its taxable income). Therefore, by increasing the debt load and interest expense of a subsidiary in a high tax jurisdiction (by providing an intercompany loan from a subsidiary in a low tax jurisdiction), the corporation can reduce net taxable income in the high tax jurisdiction. Essentially, income is transferred (disguised as interest payments) from the high tax to the low tax jurisdiction. In an effort to mitigate the erosion of their tax bases, tax authorities have introduced thin capitalisation rules that set a limit on the level of deductible interest generating (group) debt. In essence, thin capitalisation rules are a special form of transfer pricing rules that aim at setting hard and fast (tax) rules for the deemed arm's length level of debt funding of a company.

19.5.1   THIN CAP LEGISLATION

To reduce the potential loss of tax revenue from their jurisdictions, several countries have introduced so-called 'debt to equity ratios' or 'thin capitalisation rules' that deny the deduction of interest if a company is considered to be thinly capitalised. In general, these rules only apply to debt towards owned by group companies (i.e. intercompany loans). Tax deductibility of interest paid to third parties (such as banks and outside investors) is normally not affected by these rules.

A company is considered thinly capitalised if its debt to group companies exceeds its equity by a certain percentage (i.e. the debt-to-equity ratio). The debt-to-equity ratios vary by jurisdiction. The portion of a company's debt that exceeds its equity by a certain percentage can be re-qualified as equity for tax purposes. The implications of debt being re-qualified as equity are as follows:

- Interest paid on the re-qualified debt is considered non-deductible for tax purposes
- Interest paid on the re-qualified debt is considered a dividend. In this case, not only is the interest non-deductible but a dividend withholding tax may be due on the amount of re-qualified 'interest' paid

EXAMPLE

> The total debt of Company X is EUR 500 on which it pays 3% interest. Company X's equity is EUR 100. Therefore, the debt-to-equity ratio of Company X is 5:1 whereas the allowable debt to equity ratio in its country of residence is 3:1. The excess debt is EUR 200 (maximum allowable debt is 3 x EUR 100 = EUR 300). The interest paid on the excess debt is EUR 200 x 3% = EUR 6. This interest is treated as non-deductible for tax purposes. It may even be considered as a dividend (in which case dividend withholding tax may be due).

19.5.2   OTHER INTEREST DEDUCTION LIMITATION RULES

Apart from thin capitalisation rules, some countries have also introduced other rules to limit the deduction of interest expenses. Especially with the developments under the BEPS Action Plan and the EU ATAD, more countries are expected to introduce rules to limit the deduction of interest to a fixed percentage of earnings before interest, taxes, depreciation and amortisation.

On 5 October 2015, the OECD released its final report on recommended limitations on interest expense deductions (Action 4) under its Action Plan on Base Erosion and Profit Shifting (BEPS).

The OECD recommends that countries implement a 'fixed ratio' rule that would limit net interest deductions claimed by an entity (or a group of entities operating in the same country) to a fixed percentage of earnings before interest, taxes, depreciation and amortisation (EBITDA). This ratio should be somewhere between 10% and 30% of applicable EBITDA.

The report further recommends that countries adopt a 'group ratio' rule to supplement (but not replace) the fixed ratio rule and to provide additional flexibility for highly-leveraged groups or industry sectors. Under the group ratio rule, for example, an entity with net interest expense above a country's fixed ratio could deduct such interest expense up to the level of the net third-party interest/EBITDA ratio of the worldwide group to which it belongs. Countries could also apply an uplift of up to 10% to the group's net third-party interest expense to help prevent double taxation.

Beyond this basic framework, the report also recommends that countries consider the following: (i) adopting an 'equity escape' rule, which allows interest expense so long as an entity's debt-to-equity ratio does not exceed that of its worldwide group; (ii) providing for carry forward and/or carryback of disallowed interest expense and/or unused interest capacity, within limits; (iii) providing for exclusions for interest paid to third-party lenders on loans used to fund public-benefit (infrastructure) projects and for entities with net interest expense below de minimis thresholds; and (iv) providing targeted rules that would close down any remaining BEPS opportunities.

The report leaves open the timetable for adopting new rules in response to Action 4, but acknowledges the costs associated with changing existing financing arrangements and recommends that countries introducing the fixed ratio rule and group ratio rule should give taxpayers a reasonable period of time to restructure such arrangements. Countries may wish to grandfather existing debt, but the report recommends that any grandfathering provisions should primarily apply to third-party loans outstanding on the date the new rules are announced.

The Economic and Financial Affairs Council of the European Union reached an agreement on the ATAD on 21 June 2016. The ATAD is intended to provide uniform legislative implementation of some of the BEPS recommendations by establishing minimum standards within the EU regarding five areas, including the limitation of interest deduction.

The ATAD limits the deduction of exceeding borrowing costs to 30% of taxable EBITDA. Taxpayers who are part of a consolidated group may be given (i) a full deduction based on the equity-to-total assets ratio compared to equivalent group ratio or (ii) a reduction based on a group ratio (third party exceeding borrowing costs divided by group EBITDA).

The ATAD should be transposed into member states' national law no later than 31 December 2018 and should take effect as of 1 January 2019. However, member states with national targeted rules for preventing BEPS, which are equally effective to the interest deduction limitation rule as suggested in the ATAD, may apply these rules until the end of the fiscal year following the date the OECD has reached an agreement on a minimum standard with regard to OECD BEPS Action 4, but not later than 1 January 2024.

19.5.3   IMPLICATIONS FOR PHYSICAL CASH CONCENTRATION

In the case of physical cash concentration, bank debt at the level of the participant is replaced by intercompany debt. Such intercompany loans must be taken into account when determining a participant's compliance with thin capitalisation rules (i.e. must be included in the debt/equity calculation) or other interest deduction limitation rules.

19.5.4   IMPLICATIONS FOR NOTIONAL CASH CONCENTRATION

In general, thin capitalisation rules and other interest denial rules do not apply to notional cash concentration structures since intercompany loans are not created. However, it is worth noting that this assumes a multiple legal entity notional structure. When a single legal entity notional overlay structure is being used, where funds are being transferred from the local countries and held in name of the local entities in the overlay, the thin capitalisation rules may be applicable. Furthermore, a tax authority can re-qualify a bank loan as an intercompany loan, thereby requiring that the loan be included in the debt/equity calculation for thin capitalisation purposes. A tax authority could possibly make this re-qualification when a cash participant (i.e. an entity with a credit balance) provides the bank with a guarantee to cover the position of a cash-poor participant (i.e. one with a debit balance).

19.5.5   HOW CAN THE RISK OF RE-QUALIFICATION BE MITIGATED

In general, there are some strategies a company can use to reduce the risk of having inter-company debt re-qualified as equity. These are:

-   Seek approval from the local taxation authorities prior to implementing such a structure. On a case-by-case basis they may approve of a more lenient debt /equity ratio if it can be proven that the intercompany loan would be provided under the same terms and conditions by an unrelated third party
-   In some situations, a notional cash concentration structure could be used instead of a physical cash concentration (unless an overdraft could be re-qualified as an intercompany loan)

The strategies above to reduce the risk of falling within thin capitalisation rules or other interest deduction limitation rules should be tested in each individual case and country against the local rules and practices at the time.

Interest expenses

Action 4 of the BEPS Action Plan and the ATAD are generally broader in scope and apply to all interest expenses, not just related party interest. In addition, the interest deduction is linked to a company's EBITDA, which changes year by year. Both may cause multinationals to rethink debt levels in various countries (on a yearly basis) and may impact the efficiency of existing financing arrangements, including notional pooling.

US tax considerations of non-US treasury centres

The US tax treatment of cash management activity may be significantly changed by several ongoing developments, including comprehensive tax reform and the expansion or revocation of regulations, including the extensive debt and equity re-characterisation rules of Section 385 of the Internal Revenue Code.

19.6
Stamp duties

Some countries levy stamp duties in relation to physical cash concentration. Stamp duties or transfer taxes are a form of taxation related to the cost of stamps that are required to be affixed to legal documents. Stamp duties are different from the other tax aspects discussed in that they do not relate to income. Stamp duties vary per country and only a limited number within the EU levy stamp duties (Poland and Portugal are good examples).

Instances where stamp duties may be relevant in physical cash concentration concern the:

- Intercompany loan created due to the sweeps of funds between the group accounts and the treasury account
- Bank loan relationship between the treasury and the bank
- Interest paid by the treasury to a bank or vice versa
- Interest paid by a participant to the treasury or vice versa

Stamp duties can be levied at a fixed amount but can also be a percentage of the nominal amount of a loan. In some cases, stamp duties can be avoided by not executing the documentation that supports the agreement in the countries that levy stamp duty (please note that in this case, the documents need to stay offshore during the entire duration of the agreement).

In general, stamp duties do not apply to notional cash concentration structures since intercompany loans are not created (assuming a multiple legal entity notional cash concentration structure. If a single legal entity structure existed and funds changed ownership during the process of centralising the positions into one jurisdiction, then stamp duties may be applicable).

19.7
Controlled foreign companies

Upon the implementation of a cash management structure, it should be decided which company will act as the treasury centre in the structure. In regard to physical cash concentration in particular, companies are inclined to locate the treasury centre in a country that levies little or no corporate income tax. However, the benefit of the low level of taxation at the treasury centre could be annulled by taxation at shareholder/group level because of controlled foreign corporation rules (CFC rules).

The tax laws of many countries do not tax a shareholder of a company on the company's income until the income is distributed as a dividend. If the shareholder/parent company of a group is located in a country without CFC rules, it could shift income (such as interest income) to subsidiaries in countries with low taxation. Only upon distributing a dividend could that income be taxed in the country of the shareholder/parent company. CFC rules are designed to limit such artificial deferral of tax by using lower-taxed entities abroad. The basic mechanism and details vary among jurisdictions but in general, certain classes of taxpayers must include in their income certain amounts earned by foreign entities that they or related persons control. A set of rules defines the types of owners and entities affected, the types of income or investments subject to current inclusion (as well as exceptions to inclusion) and the means of preventing double inclusion of the same income.

Prior to deciding upon the location of the treasury centre, it is important that it is carefully investigated to determine whether controlled foreign corporation rules at shareholder/group level apply.

Action 3 of the BEPS Action Plan relates to the use of CFC rules as an option to prevent profit shifting and long-term deferral of tax. The report discusses six building blocks for the design of effective CFC rules:

- Definition of a CFC (including the definition of control)
- CFC exemptions and threshold requirements
- Definition of CFC income
- Computation of income
- Attribution of income
- Prevention and elimination of double taxation

The report provides recommendations for the building blocks, except for the definition of CFC income for which it sets out a non-exhaustive list of approaches that could be used by countries.

The ATAD also stipulates that EU member states are required to introduce CFC rules to tax undistributed passive income of low-taxed entities.

A company qualifies as a Controlled Foreign Company if the following conditions are met:

- The taxpayer by itself or together with its associated enterprise holds, directly or indirectly, more than 50% of the voting rights, owns more than 50% of the capital or is entitled to receive more than 50% of the profits of that entity.

- The corporate tax paid is lower than the difference in tax that would have been charged in the taxpayer's member state and the actual tax paid under the applicable corporate tax system. In other words: a 50% criterion.

With respect to income earned by foreign corporations controlled by US persons, those results are largely determined from the application of extensive 'controlled foreign corporation' (or 'CFC') rules referred to as subpart F. The subpart F rules currently include almost all forms of passive income in the taxable income of a 'US shareholder' (as specifically defined). This generally encompasses the gains and losses from cash management activity, including dividends, interest, rents and royalties, as well as the net of gains over losses from derivatives and foreign currency. Importantly, net losses in certain categories of subpart F income cannot generally be used to offset income in other categories. Exceptions exist for certain cash and risk management activity, but such exceptions generally require activity that rises to the level of being an active trade or business. A hedging exception can apply to certain business risk transactions of active businesses, but most other treasury activity exclusions can be difficult for non-bank entities to meet. Of particular note is the treatment of foreign currency gains and losses. Because net losses cannot ordinarily offset other types of income under subpart F, the timing of gains and losses within the same tax year and the application of any early income recognition rules will be especially important. In addition, gross foreign currency losses must be specifically identified and separately reported if certain thresholds are met.

Recent US tax reform discussions have not generally focused on treasury activity, but proposals have included the possibility of vastly reducing subpart F of the Code applicable to controlled foreign corporations, allowing a one-time low-taxed dividend from overseas operations, and marking all derivatives to market (instead of only those under selective regimes).

Conclusion

As CFC rules are quite complex, they should be examined carefully prior to establishing a treasury centre and implementing a cash pool.

19.8
Treasury centre locations

A treasury centre is often set up to centralise all treasury and cash management activities of a group within one entity. The main advantages of a treasury centre are that it can deliver more expertise than individual operating companies can provide. In addition, it can make it easier for a group to control its treasury and cash management. Companies seeking optimal tax benefits will seek a treasury centre location that provides a relatively low effective tax rate on intra-group finance activities. A relatively low effective tax rate means:

- A relatively low corporate income tax rate on the income of the treasury centre
- A relatively low withholding tax on (interest) flows between the treasury centre and group companies

The optimal location for a treasury centre is not the same for all companies. It depends on each company's individual situation. Many tax and non-tax elements play a role. The following tax elements play a role when choosing the appropriate location to establish a group treasury centre:

- ***The tax jurisdiction of the parent company***
  The country of residence of the parent company that owns the central treasury may have implemented CFC legislation. As discussed in section 19.7, CFC rules can undo the tax benefits of locating the central treasury in a low-tax jurisdiction, or in a jurisdiction that is put on a so-called black list (such as a tax haven).

- ***The tax objective of the group – low tax or deferred tax***
  Where the objective of a group is to defer tax, the group may want to place its treasury centre in a country where taxation on currency exchange gains can be deferred.

- ***The tax jurisdictions of the group companies***
  This aspect is relevant for determining whether a withholding tax is levied on interest paid by the group companies to the treasury centre. This must be examined under both the domestic rules of the country of residence of the payer and under the tax treaty between the country of residence of the payer and the country of residence of the treasury centre.

- ***The scope of the activities of the treasury centres***
  Depending on the scope of the activities – whether involving group or third-party financing, or passive / active financing – it may be relevant for the treasury centre to be located in or near one of the world's financial centres. However, a more passive financing activity could be less bound by that consideration and could be more easily located in a tax haven.

- ***Financial position of a group company***
  Does the group have a group company in a loss-making position that could set up treasury activities and which could use the losses from its other activities to offset against the income out of the treasury activities?

The table below lists additional tax and non-tax considerations that should also be considered when deciding on locating a treasury centre in a particular jurisdiction.

Non-tax considerations	Tax considerations
Financial infrastructure	Absence of general withholding tax on interest
Availability of qualified staff	Absence of stamp duties
Overall costs	Tax treaty network
Exchange controls and central bank regulations	Corporation tax incentives (depends on whether the
Economic and political environment	treasury centre is a profit centre)
	Advance ruling practice
	Tax incentives for expatriates

Historically, some companies were inclined to set up a treasury centre in a low-tax jurisdiction or in a jurisdiction that levies no tax at all (tax havens). However, for cash management purposes, the use of a tax haven is generally not recommended. The reasons for this are:

1. Interest withholding tax may be levied on interest paid to a treasury centre resident in a tax haven by the tax authorities of the country of the payer. Tax havens do not tend to conclude many tax treaties. In the absence of tax treaties, domestic withholding tax rates are not reduced

2. The country of residence of the central treasury's parent company may have implemented CFC legislation. As discussed in paragraph 19.7, CFC rules can undo the tax benefits of locating the central treasury in a low-tax jurisdiction.

Many countries offer tax advantaged vehicles for companies wishing to establish a treasury centre in that jurisdiction. In Europe, most of the specialised vehicles have been put under pressure by the European Commission in order to harmonise regulations. With or without specialised treasury vehicles, common tax-driven locations for treasury centres are Belgium, Ireland, the Netherlands and Luxembourg. Those outside the EU include Switzerland, Hong Kong and Singapore.

US tax considerations of non-US treasury centres

Europe has traditionally been considered an appealing location for US corporations to establish a treasury centre because of the close ties among the European countries (and between those countries and the US), the open market policies of the central banks and the sophisticated banking infrastructure that exists, as well as the beneficial tax regimes offered by many countries for such activity. Relatively low rates of taxation, minimal withholding taxes, and the ability to centralise treasury activity where other group functions reside, make European treasury centres popular with US companies.

>

Although European treasury centres of US multinational corporations are currently taxed under subpart F of the Internal Revenue Code, if they are US 'controlled foreign corporations', local taxing regimes are an important part of the overall tax structure and impact the timing and amount of any US foreign tax credit (and therefore any additional US tax that may be due). In the US, a tax credit is generally provided for income taxes paid to other countries, but such rules are replete with limitations as to how and when those foreign taxes paid may be credited and thereby utilised. Therefore, before implementing a treasury centre, it is important to consider the local tax consequences of treasury activity, as well as the consequences in the country of the ultimate owner of that entity and how those two taxing regimes work together.

Considerations include, for example, the local taxes in the location of the treasury centre, whether treasury employees can reside there, and whether the location imposes its own withholding tax on certain payments or has any special regimes for treasury activities. Consider also whether the country has any beneficial tax treaties to reduce interest and dividend withholding, whether interest is deductible locally and whether any thin capitalisation rules may apply. Transfer pricing must also be considered with respect to any services between the treasury centre and its participating affiliates, as well as the rate of any interest paid or received. If the treasury centre is a 'controlled foreign corporation' for US tax purposes, the subpart F income must be assessed. Subpart F income includes most types of passive income, even when part of a treasury centre, and must be currently included in income by 'US shareholders'.

Chapter 20

Legal Considerations

20   Legal Considerations

20.1
Introduction

In this chapter, we will focus on the legal aspects of cash pooling and how related risks can be mitigated or avoided. We also discuss the important documents required to enter into a pooling agreement.

There are two opposing but not contradictory viewpoints to be considered. First, there is the perspective of the participating companies and their director(s) who represent the company and who will sign up the company for the pooling agreement. Second, there is the perspective of the service providers (predominantly banks) that are providing the pooling services.

It is essential for the company as well as the bank to comply with all legal and regulatory constraints in order to avoid being held liable by creditors, bankruptcy administrators or regulators.

Participants in international (cross-border) pooling arrangements are typically incorporated in different jurisdictions (countries). It is impossible to discuss the particular legal requirements in all relevant jurisdictions. After all, laws, rules and regulations may vary, sometimes significantly, per jurisdiction. Therefore, in this section we will focus on the most common legal issues companies will encounter.

It is advisable that a group of companies participating in a pool and its central treasury enter into a treasury management agreement, which should at least entail who in respect of the pool is responsible for daily management, authorisation and administrative processes. Such an agreement will ensure that all relevant group companies are aware of the implications of the pool structure and the role its central treasury has in that structure. In general, the bank is not a party to such an intra-group treasury management agreement.

20.2
Legal aspects pertaining to physical and notional cash pooling

The legal entity that participates in a cash pool, its director(s) and the bank providing the pooling services may be held liable for any losses resulting from participating in such a pooling structure.

20.2.1 PHYSICAL POOLING

Physical cash pooling may result in inter-company loans on an ongoing automated basis. This means that companies participating in a physical cash pool (i) *borrow* from the master account holder (often the central treasury) if the participant has a debit position on its participating account which is replenished (funding) by the master account holder or (ii) *lend* to the master account holder if the participant has a credit position on its participating account which is transferred (sweeping) to the master account holders' account.

The main risk for the individual participating account holders in a physical pool lies in the fact that the master account holder might not be able to repay the inter-company loan. To enable the daily payment operations in the physical pool to run smoothly, banks often grant the master account holder an overdraft facility (overnight) and each participating account holder an intraday facility (daylight facility to be repaid at the end of day).

Physical cash pooling can be offered with or without hard bookings. In the case of hard bookings, debit balances on the participating accounts will always be replenished from the master account, regardless of the balance on that account. This is the case even if this would lead to an unauthorised debit balance on the master account. In the case of soft bookings, debit balances on the participating accounts are only replenished insofar there are sufficient funds on the master account.

Inter-company loans may have tax consequences. Seeking tax advice before entering into a physical cash pool is recommended (see chapter 19 on Tax).

20.2.2 NOTIONAL POOLING

Notional pooling does not need to result in inter-company loans, as funds are pooled without changing the ownership of the balances (i.e. co-mingling). Please note that the concept of notional pooling can be interpreted differently. In most countries, notional pooling is only used as a tool for interest enhancement (partial notional pooling or interest optimisation). However, in some other countries it is used as a tool for calculating interest on the one hand and on the other as a means for allowing debit balances on participating accounts in the notional pool up to an amount equal to the aggregated credit balances in such notional pool (full notional pooling). By granting an overdraft limit on the notional pool as a whole (administered on the 'main' account of the pool, usually in the name of the central treasury) the available balance in the pool can be increased (extra headroom). This way, notional pooling not only works as a cash management, but also as a lending tool.

Depending on the jurisdiction, for a full notional pooling structure the bank will require (i) a legal right to set off a participant's debit balance on its account in the notional cash pool against the credit balance on the account of another participant in the notional cash pool (multi-party set-off), (ii) a pledge of credit balances on all accounts in the notional pool to cover for corresponding debit balances in the pool as well as to allow the bank to benefit from capital relief (risk-weighted assets (RWA)) and (iii) a cross guarantee/joint & several liability from all participants.

Notional and physical pooling entail legal risks for both the participating entities and the central treasury entity. To mitigate these risks, the directors should ensure that participation in a pooling structure is in line with the requirements as summarised below.

20.2.3   CORPORATE CAPACITY

One of the requirements which determines whether a cash pooling agreement entered into by a group of companies is valid and binding on these companies is each company's legal capacity to enter into that particular cash pool agreement.

Whether a company may enter into a cash pool agreement depends on a company's articles of association (and on the laws of the country of its incorporation). For instance, for entering into a *physical* pool the articles of association should allow for inter-company loans which are created by the sweeps. In case of entering into a *notional* pooling agreement, the granting of a cross guarantee, a pledge and a right of set-off to the bank should also fit within the boundaries of the company's articles of association. Therefore, it is essential to understand the company's articles of association prior to setting up a cash pool structure.

20.2.4   CORPORATE OBJECT (ULTRA VIRES, I.E. 'BEYOND THE POWER')

Participation in a pooling structure must proceed in accordance with the corporate object of the company. A corporate object clause is a provision in a company's articles of association stating the purpose and range of activities for which the company is carried on. The general rule is that anything not included in the company's corporate object, whether expressly or by implication, is ultra vires i.e. 'beyond the power' of the company and may be unenforceable. Please note that the interpretation of the wording of the corporate object, being expressed or implied, significantly differs per jurisdiction.

Wrongful exercise of corporate power directly relates to the authority of the directors who exercise the power on the company's behalf. Directors have a fiduciary duty towards the company on behalf of which they act. They must always act in good faith and in the best interest of the company. Breach of fiduciary duty could lead to personal liability of the relevant director and may result in a transaction being voidable.

Directors that do not comply with the appropriate legal requirements can be held liable for their (legal) acts and in some jurisdictions this can lead to criminal lawsuits which may even lead to a prison sentence (for example in France). Therefore, important questions to be answered before entering into a cash pool agreement are: does it fit within the corporate object and does each individual company benefit from it?

20.2.5   CORPORATE BENEFIT

Participating in a pooling structure must be for the benefit of the company and in the common interest of all participating companies in the pool from an economic, administrative and financial point of view. For instance, an individual company may not be solely a net contributor and its participation may not be in the sole interest of the dominant company (often the parent; sometimes the financial company) in the pool. In addition, such participation must result in overall benefits for the group as a whole and in more than the aggregate benefits that each single company could have realised individually.

The requirements relating to corporate benefit are especially clear when providing cross-guarantees in pooling structures. For example, a cross-guarantee in a notional pool agreement covering all the obligations which each participant in the notional pool has or may have under the notional pool agreement, including any obligations under a possible overdraft limit. The same goes for the pledge (reciprocal) of credit balances by account holders for their own obligations and for the obligations of all other account holders under a cash pool, including a possible overdraft limit and intraday limits.

The other requirements are:

- The guarantor (not being the parent company) must effectively and directly benefit from the underlying guaranteed obligations. In some jurisdictions, the amount of the guarantee may not exceed the financial capacity of the guarantor. Alongside a direct benefit, it can help to establish a benefit if there is some kind of consideration in favour of the guarantor (for example a fee or a discount).

- The cross-guarantees in a notional pooling agreement are usually unlimited. Such an unlimited guarantee may raise issues in some jurisdictions. For example, what you would see in a notional cash pool agreement governed by Dutch law with a non-resident participant from Germany for instance, is explicit German guarantor limitation language.

- The above also applies with respect to the pledge of credit balances and with respect to agreeing on (multi-party) set-off rights. However, the security (pledge) in a notional pool agreement in favour of the bank is limited to the credit balance on the relevant participating account.

Top-down guarantees (parent guarantees) are not often an issue. A top-down guarantee is what you would typically see in a physical pool guaranteeing the obligations from the physical pool agreement and the intra-day limits on the participating accounts.

20.2.6   GROUP COMPANIES

Most service providers will only offer pooling services to multiple legal entities if they belong to the same economic group and are under full 'control' of that group. Banks often assume 'control' if the company at the top holds the majority of the share capital – i.e. more than 50% (in some jurisdictions the majority would even mean two-thirds of the share capital) – and has the control over the participating entities. However, the ratios depend on each service provider's internal policies.

If the companies do not meet this requirement it could result in a void or voidable pooling agreement. Entities with less or equal share capital – for example joint ventures – or minority control, will make it harder to prove that it is in the company's interest to enter into a pooling structure. This could expose the directors and the bank to challenges in the case of bankruptcy of the relevant participating account holder or to conflicts between the shareholders. In such a case, creditors of that relevant participating account holder or even other participating account holders, if they are also affected, may challenge the directors and the bank.

Summary checklist

Companies can participate in a multi-legal entity pooling structure if they:
- Belong to a coherent group with actual commercial and economic ties
- Are under control (> 50% ownership) of the group
- Have a common interest in participating in the pooling structure

---

20.2.7 CAPITALISATION RULES

Capitalisation rules generally relate to the unlawful reduction of capital as a result of a pooling arrangement that causes a company to break the minimum capital requirement rules. This could happen when a reduction of net assets (i.e. assets minus liabilities) exceeds the amount of reserves that a company is allowed to distribute to its shareholders in the form of dividends. Any arrangement that would constitute such a situation would be void and recipients may be liable. The best protection against this is for the directors to consider whether the pooling arrangement could lead to a reduction in net assets and for them to determine the amount of profit available for distribution.

Such an analysis should take into account:

- The likelihood of loans not being repaid
- The likelihood of guarantees being called
- The market value of a loan or guarantee (depending on accounting rules)

Summary checklist

Directors should complete the following checklist if their company is entering into a cash pool:
- Corporate capacity – check the articles of association
- Corporate benefit – the pool must be to the benefit of the company
- Same group – more than 50% of share capital should belong to the group
- Fiduciary duties – no breach allowed

20.3
Liability risks of management and mitigation

If a director acts in breach of any fiduciary duty to the company in entering into a pooling arrangement, he may be personally liable to indemnify the company for any loss that occurs. However, there are some ways to mitigate the director's liability risks. These include the following:

- If the pooling arrangement is for the commercial benefit of the company and the shareholders have approved it, there is little chance that a director will be personally held liable
- In cases of a conflict of interest (for example if a director is a director of two or more companies that participate in the pool), it is prudent to obtain a shareholder resolution to authorise the participation
- Identification in the board resolution that commercial and economic benefits are expected
- Ensuring that an assessment of the solvency of the company and the other pool members is available
- Continual monitoring of the risks and benefits of the arrangement and reporting back to the participants on a regular basis
- In some jurisdictions, establishing the right that an individual company may resign from the pool without prior consent

20.4
Cash pooling documentation

There are two areas of documentation that affect a company entering into a cash pooling structure. First, the documentation provided by the bank to allow for pooling. Second, the documentation that the company must provide to the bank (such documentation is the first line of defence against the management risks mentioned above). Below follows an overview of the most common set of documents for each category.

20.4.1   DOCUMENTATION PROVIDED BY THE BANK TO THE CUSTOMER

Each bank will have its own approach when it comes to agreements but the aspects described below are commonly seen in all pooling structure agreements.

a.   The cash pool agreement
A cash pool agreement describes the way the cash pool structure actually works. It can be quite technical in stating how the funds move from one account to another in a physical pool or how interest or the available balance is calculated in a notional pool. There will also be elements that are common to all agreements such as liability, termination, power of attorney to the bank for physical pooling transfers and communications. The cash pool agreement often also includes the 'account schedules' (showing which accounts are part of the cash pooling

structure and the technical settings of the cash pool). In addition, it may also include service level agreements and pricing schedules.

b.   Credit facilities and guarantees in physical and notional cash pools

It is not unusual for the bank to grant an overdraft limit (overnight facility) on the master account and intraday limits (daylight facility) on the participating accounts in a physical pool. These credit facilities will usually be laid down in separate documents. However, intraday limits are often part of the cash pool agreement itself.

To mitigate the risk of non-payment of the intraday facilities, the bank will require a corporate guarantee from the master account holder. To this end, the master account holder often issues a corporate guarantee (top down) in favour of the bank, guaranteeing the obligations of the participating account holders under the physical pooling agreement, including the intraday limits. In most cases the master account holder is the parent company but it could very well also be the financial or treasury department. If the master account holder is not the ultimate parent company, the bank might want additional comfort in the form of a supplementary corporate guarantee from the ultimate parent company. In such a case, this also covers the non-payment risk the bank runs on the uncommitted overdraft facility granted to the master account holder.

On full notional pools a single uncommitted overdraft facility is often granted on the notional pooling structure in order to increase the available balance in the notional pool. In this case, all participating account holders in the notional cash pool qualify as borrowers since they can, in principle, all make use of the increased available balance created by the overdraft facility. The guarantee a company would typically see in a full notional pool is the cross guarantee/joint & several liability.

c.   Pledge and set-off right

In addition to the cross guarantee/joint & several liability, the bank will require a multi-party right of set-off across all the participating account holders in the notional pool. In certain jurisdictions, a cross-guarantee/joint & several liability may be a requirement from the central bank. Other central banks may require a pledge of credit balances on all participating accounts in the notional pool in order for the bank to benefit from capital relief (RWA). Ultimately, the type of security and/or guarantee/joint & several liability needed is determined by the law of the jurisdiction that governs the notional pooling agreement, which is by default the jurisdiction where all the accounts are held.

Providing securities can often be troublesome for companies and in many cases companies assume that they are restricted because of their participation in a syndicated loan facility. This is a common misconception as many syndicated loan facilities entail a 'carve-out' for securities granted for cash management purposes. These carve-outs are included because it is in the interest of the syndicate of banks that the company be able to improve its cash management position. This is beneficial to the company, which could therefore be at a lower risk of defaulting.

If there is no 'carve-out' in the syndicated loan facility, the bank (or the agent bank) should request the agent bank of the syndicate of banks to arrange for a waiver in order to make it legally possible for the participating parties in the notional cash pool to grant a first ranking pledge over credit balances.

d.   Country specifics

In cases where entities from certain countries are participating, there may be a necessity to include specific provisions. Such provisions are meant to ensure that a company complies with key aspects of laws of the jurisdiction under which it is incorporated.

20.4.2   DOCUMENTS PROVIDED BY THE COMPANY TO THE BANK

The bank that is providing pooling services will ask the company to submit certain documents to ensure that the bank is offering the service in line with local laws. These documents can also be useful for the company and its directors to demonstrate that they meet their own internal restrictions. Some of the requirements below may already be held by the bank for the initial opening of accounts and will not need to be provided twice. Meanwhile, others are specific to some jurisdictions and will not be applicable in all cases.

a.   Board resolutions / shareholders' resolution

The company's Board resolutions should indicate that it is entering into the pooling structure freely and that that Board of Directors acknowledges that the pooling structure and agreements are to the company's corporate benefit. In some countries, a company must obtain a shareholders' resolution. In that case, the corporate benefit should also be covered off.

Board resolutions
The most common items to be included in the Board resolutions include: – The pool must be to the corporate benefit of the company – It must cover all aspects of pooling – i.e. the cash pool agreement, set-off rights, securities and guarantees – No conflict of interest should be involved

b.   Articles of association

It is important that a bank be able to review a company's most recent articles of association to ensure that the directors entering into the agreements are authorised to do so.

c.   Extract of commercial register

An up-to-date extract of the commercial register is necessary so the bank can verify the incorporation of the company (existence), the place of incorporation and the power of representation.

d.   Power of attorney

As companies move more towards regional and global treasury structures, it is common that a power of attorney structure is put in place. This allows for greater control and a quicker and more efficient execution of documentation.

e.   ID documents

A bank will need to be able to verify that the person signing the agreement is who he/she says he/she is. Often, this is done using copies of the relevant passports.

20.5
Legal opinions

The bank needs to ensure that a cash pooling structure and the related guarantees and security rights are legally valid and enforceable. A legal opinion from an external law firm is one of the methods used to assess this.

The main purposes of a legal opinion are:

- To state conclusions of law as to the ability of a party to enter into and perform its obligations under a cash pool agreement
- To inform about the legal effect of a cash pool agreement and the related guarantees and security rights and
- To identify legal risks that the bank should further consider, evaluate and mitigate

> *Main items in a legal opinion*
>
> Basically, one can distinguish the following three main items in a legal opinion:
> - A capacity opinion: the company validly exists and has the necessary corporate power to execute and perform the cash pool agreement
> - An enforceability opinion: the cash pool agreement (including any guarantees and security rights) creates valid, binding and enforceable obligations
> - A choice of law opinion: the law that governs the cash pool agreement has been validly chosen.

A cross-border cash pool structure involves several jurisdictions. This means there will be several legal opinions, for example a legal opinion in respect of the jurisdiction of the governing law of the cash pool agreement itself and legal opinions relating to the jurisdiction of incorporation of each of the participating companies.

In some cases, the bank already has generic enforceability opinions for certain jurisdictions, so these are no longer required for a specific cash pooling structure. In such cases, only a capacity opinion (or internal capacity check by the bank, if possible) would be required.

In general, it is also good practice for companies and their central treasurers to consult their own internal lawyers to carefully assess local laws and regulations. However, when foreign jurisdictions are involved, it is recommended to seek specialised external legal advice before entering into a cash pool agreement. The level of comfort a company needs in this respect is dependent on its internal policies, the type of cash pool that will be implemented and the jurisdictions involved.

Chapter 21

Treasury Accounting and Control

21 Treasury Accounting and Control

21.1
Introduction

The general mission of the treasury department is to manage the liquidity of the business. This means that all current and projected cash inflows and outflows must be monitored to ensure that there is sufficient cash to fund company operations, as well as to ensure that excess cash is properly invested. While accomplishing this mission, most treasurers use financial instruments or financial structures that support their overall mission. However, these instruments will have an impact on the group's accounting treatment.

The treasury accounting activities therefore determine the accounting treatment of financial instruments in accordance with the accounting standards applied to the financial reports of the entity. Most of the listed corporates have a separate treasury entity. For the purpose of explaining the accounting treatment of financial instruments and, more specifically, the classification and measurement of financial instruments held by the treasury entity, the International Financial Reporting Standards (IFRS) issued by the International Accounting Standards Board (IASB) will be followed. IFRS covers the accounting treatment of financial instruments in a separate accounting standard covering the classification and measurement, impairment and hedge accounting of financial instruments. From 1 January 2018, the new Financial Instruments Standard, IFRS 9, will be effective and will replace IAS 39.

Accounting standards

IFRS Standards are now widely adopted around the world. Among 138 countries surveyed by the International Accounting Standards Board, 80% require the use of IFRS for all, or most, publicly listed companies. Over half (52%) of Global Fortune 500 companies use IFRS – more than use any other GAAP (generally accepted accounting principles). In addition, the European Commission has adopted regulations requiring all listed companies to present their financial statements using the IFRS standards. Therefore, all companies incorporated in one of the EU jurisdictions were obliged to migrate their external financial reporting from local GAAP to IFRS.

>

Some major economies have still not adopted IFRS, though there are encouraging signs in terms of convergence. For example, China has introduced standards similar to IFRS. And India is about to move to a new set of accounting standards based on IFRS, while Indian companies can currently apply full IFRS if they wish.

The US remains a major non-adopter. But the Securities and Exchange Commission (SEC) intends to provide greater clarity about its stance on IFRS, and the IASB is looking forward to working on this matter with the SEC's new chief accountant. Meanwhile, the US already has a significant interest in IFRS. Almost 500 foreign companies are listed on US markets, and the SEC oversees their IFRS-compliant filings. Convergence between IFRS and US GAAP has been achieved in many areas, such as segmental reporting, business combinations, fair value measurement and revenue recognition.

IFRS 9 makes a distinction between debt and equity instruments. The key characteristic to determine whether a financial instrument is an equity or a liability instrument is the substance of the contractual arrangement and not the legal form.

In order to understand the classification and measurement of financial instruments as part of treasury accounting, an example illustrative treasury balance sheet will be used to show the accounting treatment of the different financial instruments.

Balance Sheet	Description
Assets	
Cash and cash equivalents	Cash pooling is applied, whereas the cash balances from the group companies are pooled at group level. The cash balance is at the free disposal of the company.
Trade receivables	Payments due related to asset management activities for group companies. Payment is due within 30 days from the invoice date.
Non-current financial assets	Loans granted to group companies for periods exceeding a year consisting of the loan granted and the fair value of the related derivatives.
Liabilities and equity	
Share capital	Issued shares on a regulated capital market at par value.
Listed debt	Issued fixed coupon bonds on a regulated capital market.
Non-current financial liabilities	The company's long-term external debt (for a period exceeding one year) consisting of the debt due to third parties and the fair value of the related derivatives.

This illustrative balance sheet will be used as an example throughout the classification & measurement section to explain the implications for the different items on the balance sheet of a treasury entity.

21.2
Classification

Initially under IFRS 9, financial assets and financial liabilities are measured at their fair value (see section 21.4) on the date that they are initially recognised. The determination of the classification & measurement will be covered separately for assets and liabilities as the approach is different.

21.2.1   ASSETS ON THE BALANCE SHEET

The classification of a financial asset under IFRS 9 is determined based on two assessments:

- The entity's business model for managing the portfolio of financial assets (business model assessment)
- The characteristics of the contractual cash flows derived from the financial asset (contractual cash flow test)

The business model for managing the portfolio of financial assets
Under IFRS 9, the financial assets have to be classified based on the different business models under which the entity holds the financial asset. The business model is determined based on the entity's objectives for holding a particular financial asset or group of financial assets. The business model must be assessed based on the professional judgment of the entity and on a level which reflects how the groups of financial assets are jointly managed to achieve a business objective.

Applying the business model assessment to the illustrative balance sheet:

Balance Sheet	Business model assessment
Assets	
Cash and cash equivalents	If the company holds this current account for the collection of contractual cash flows, then the business model of cash and cash equivalents will be 'hold to collect'. According to the definition of cash and cash equivalents included in IFRS 9, this will generally be the business model in almost all cases.
Trade receivables	If the company intends to hold the trade receivables in order to collect contractual cash flows, then the business model will be 'hold to collect'. But if, for example, the intention of the company is to apply factoring on a regular basis (which is often applied by treasury entities) whereas the assets are derecognised from the balance sheet, then the business model will be 'hold to collect & sale'.
Non-current financial assets	If the company intends to hold the loans granted in order to collect contractual cash flows, the business model will be 'hold to collect.

21.2.2 THE CHARACTERISTICS OF THE CONTRACTUAL CASH FLOWS DERIVED FROM THE FINANCIAL ASSET

Under IFRS 9, the financial assets can only give rise to payments of principal and interest in order to be measured at either amortised cost (AC) or fair value through other comprehensive income (FVOCI). The principal is defined as the fair value of the financial asset, whereas the interest is defined as the return on a basic loan granted. The interest on a basic loan granted generally covers the time value of money and risk factors, such as liquidity risk and credit risk. When a financial instrument results in the sole payment of principal and interest then the characteristics test is passed and the financial instrument can be measured at AC or FVOCI. If, however, the characteristics test is failed, the financial instrument has to be measured at fair value through profit or loss.

Applying the contractual cash flow test to the illustrative balance sheet:

Balance Sheet	Business model assessment
Assets	
Cash and cash equivalents	This current account consists of short-term cash positions with only contractual cash flows, which is the principal as defined for the characteristics test.
Trade receivables	The trade receivables consist of payments which are due from group companies for asset management activities. There is no financing component and no interest, as these are also short-term positions. Hence, the characteristics test is passed and these financial instruments are measured at AC. If there is any factoring applied and the financial instruments are expected to be derecognised from the balance sheet, these financial instruments are measured at FVOCI (up until the moment they are sold and derecognised).
Non-current financial assets	When loans are granted to group companies, the treasury entity may not earn any interest. However, the principal is defined as the fair value upon initial recognition. Upon initial recognition, the fair value is calculated based on the effective interest rate (EIR), which covers the time value of money and risk factors. Therefore, the financial assets are solely held for collecting principal and interest payments. Hence, the characteristics test is passed and the financial instruments are measured at AC.
Derivatives	Derivatives always fail the solely payments of principal and interest (SPPI) test. This is because they do not result in payments of solely principal and interest as they include considerable leverage. Derivatives are therefore always measured at FVPL, except when certain forms of hedge accounting (cash flow hedging, net investment hedging) are applied and fair value movements can be (partly) reported through OCI.

21.2.3 LIABILITIES AND EQUITY ON THE BALANCE SHEET

The financial liabilities and/or equity are classified and measured at either FVPL or AC. This depends on the intention behind holding the financial liabilities and equity. When the financial liabilities are held for trading, the measurement is FVPL. IFRS 9 defines trading as actively and frequently buying and selling with the objective of generating profit derived from fluctuations in prices. If the financial liabilities and/or equity are not traded actively, then these financial liabilities and/or equity are measured at AC.

Applying the liabilities and equity classification to the illustrative balance sheet:

Balance Sheet	Description
Liabilities and equity	
Share capital	Share capital is measured at cost.
Listed debt	The issued fixed coupon bonds are typically measured at amortised cost. However, IFRS allows application of the fair value option for these instruments, in which case they would be measured at FVPL.
Non-current financial liabilities	This external debt is not actively traded and will therefore be measured at AC.

21.2.4 SUBSEQUENT MEASUREMENT OF FINANCIAL INSTRUMENTS

Based on the outcomes of the two assessments, the financial asset or the group of financial assets is classified and subsequently measured accordingly. The different classifications and the related subsequent measurements under IFRS 9 are the following:

Classification	Subsequent measurement
Hold to collect (HtC)	Amortised cost (AC)
Hold to collect & sell (HtC&S)	Fair value through OCI (FVOCI)
FVPL	Fair value through P&L (FVPL)

In addition, the financial liabilities and equity are either measured at FVPL or AC. This is dependent on whether or not the financial instruments are held for trading purposes.

21.3
Determining the fair value of financial instruments

Financial instruments held by a treasury entity are partly valued at fair value. The fair value accounting of these financial instruments is covered in IFRS 13 fair value measurement. The determination of the fair value is an important part of treasury accounting because it can be relatively complex. In order to create more comparability of the fair value measures used, the IASB issued IFRS 13. This standard defines fair value as follows: 'the price that would be received to sell an asset or paid to transfer a liability in an orderly transaction between market participants at the measurement date'.

21.3.1   THE FAIR VALUE HIERARCHY

IFRS 13 states that there is a fair value hierarchy. There are three methods to determine the fair value of a financial instrument. These are based on the input used in order to determine the fair value. The methods are as follows:

- *Level 1 input*
  Based on the directly observable market price of the financial instrument.

- *Level 2 input*
  Based on the directly observable market price of a comparable financial instrument, including events which affect the directly observable market price in such a way that the directly observable market price cannot be the fair value (e.g. financial crisis).

- *Level 3 input*
  Based on unobservable inputs to measure fair value to the extent that relevant observable inputs are not available, thereby allowing for situations in which there is little, if any, market activity for the asset or liability at the measurement date.

21.3.2   FAIR VALUE IN FINANCIAL STATEMENTS

The accounting standards require disclosures regarding the fair valuation of financial instruments. The IFRS rules on disclosure requirements have been laid down in IFRS 7. The higher the level of input, the more disclosures are required as the subjectivity of determining the fair value increases. When the fair value is determined based on level 3 input, the treasury entity is required to disclose the different variables included in the fair value model in such a way that the user of the financial statements understands the calculation.

21.4
Hedge accounting

One of the main responsibilities of treasurers is to manage the financial risks to which their company is exposed. The ultimate goal is to align the risk profile with the company's risk appetite. This risk management activity is often referred to as hedging, and almost always involves the use of derivative contracts, which are sometimes also referred to as financial instruments or hedging instruments. Whereas the derivative contracts reduce the risk to which an entity is exposed, they introduce another challenge: how to account for the derivatives that are used?

Under the accounting rules of IFRS, which we will focus on in this chapter, there are strict rules on how to classify and measure financial assets and financial liabilities. The different asset and liability classes for this purpose, as well as how they are measured and recognised, are summarised in the figure below.

Instrument	Measurement	Changes in value
Held for trading asset (incl derivative asset)	Fair value	Net profit or loss
Fair value option	Fair value	Net profit or loss
Loans and receivables asset	Amortised cost	Only if impaired
Held to maturity asset	Amortised cost	Only if impaired
Available for sale asset	Fair value	Equity
Held for trading liability (incl derivative liability)	Fair value	Net profit or loss
Fair value option	Fair value	Net profit or loss
Non-trading liability	Amortised cost	Not applicable

Example: normally, if a treasurer wants to protect its margin on highly probable or committed sales revenue in a foreign currency, a foreign exchange forward contract is traded. This contract is a derivative, whose measurement is fair value in the balance sheet, and whereby the movements in fair value need to be recognised in the profit and loss account (also referred to as P&L). IFRS 13 defines fair value as 'the price that would be received to sell an asset or paid to transfer a liability in an orderly transaction between market participants at the measurement date'. The highly probable or committed sales are not recognised. The consequence of this is an accounting mismatch and P&L volatility.

One of the solutions is to apply hedge accounting to match P&L recognition of gains and losses. Hedge accounting can therefore be best described as follows: hedge accounting is the application of special rules to account for the component parts of the hedging relationship. Hedge accounting involves recognising gains and losses on a hedging instrument in the same period(s) and/or in the same place in the financial statements as gains or losses on the hedged position.

21.4.1   RULES OF THE GAME & TYPES OF HEDGING RELATIONSHIPS

Applying hedge accounting is not mandatory, but is a privilege that must be earned. Entities can only use hedge accounting if they satisfy the requirements as set out in IAS 39 or IFRS 9. IFRS 9 replaced IAS 39 per 1 January 2018, but could be adopted earlier under certain conditions. Companies have the choice to continue applying hedge accounting under the rules of IAS 39. However, once a company has decided to adopt IFRS 9 for hedge accounting, it cannot go back to IAS 39. Macro fair value hedge accounting is carved out from IFRS 9, meaning that even if a company implements IFRS 9 for hedge accounting, IAS 39 will still apply for its macro fair value hedge accounting.

In order to qualify for hedge accounting, a company needs to set up and document a hedging relationship which consists of eligible hedging instruments and eligible hedged items. Only contracts with an external counterparty to the reporting entity may be designated as hedging instruments. Non-derivative financial liabilities may be designated as hedging instruments. A hedging relationship qualifies for hedge accounting only if all of the following criteria are met:

1. The hedging relationship consists only of eligible hedging instruments and eligible hedged items.
2. At the inception of the hedging relationship, there is formal designation and documentation of the hedging relationship and the entity's risk management objective for undertaking the hedge.
3. The hedging relationship meets all of the hedge effectiveness requirements.

An *eligible hedged item* is an asset, liability, firm commitment, or forecasted transaction that exposes the entity to risk of changes in fair value or future cash flows, and that has been designated by an entity as being hedged.

An *eligible hedging instrument* is a designated derivative or, in limited circumstances, another financial instrument whose changes in fair value or cash flows are expected to offset changes in the fair value or cash flows of a designated hedged item.

Hedge effectiveness is the degree to which changes in a hedged item's fair value or cash flows attributable to a hedged risk are offset by changes in the fair value or cash flows of the hedging instrument. There are both prospective and retrospective hedge effectiveness tests that need to be performed. To qualify for hedge accounting under IAS 39, the movements of the hedging instrument must be within 80%-125% of the hedged item in the retrospective hedge effectiveness test. The IFRS standard does not specify a particular assessment method, but the three primary methods adopted to assess hedge effectiveness are the critical terms match, dollar offset method and a linear regression method.

Using the critical terms match (CTM) method requires verification of whether or not the critical terms of the derivative match perfectly with the underlying hedged item. The CTM method is often used for prospective hedge effectiveness testing, but is not allowed under IFRS for the retrospective hedge effectiveness test as it does not include changes in credit risk.

The dollar offset method compares the cumulative fair value movements of both the hedging instrument and the hedged item. This method may be used under IFRS for the retrospective hedge effectiveness test, but has a major disadvantage, usually referred to as the small dollar effect. This is the case when the absolute value of changes being compared is small, which can lead to great relative changes. As a result, one might test outside the 80%-125% bandwidth in order to qualify for an effective hedging relationship.

The most refined method is the regression analysis to test the hedge effectiveness (correlation) in a hedging relationship. With this statistical method, one regresses the changes in fair value of both the hedging instrument as well as the hedged item to determine the regression line of best fit. Next, the slope of the regression line is assessed to determine if it falls within 80%-125% bandwidth, which in this analysis translates into negative 0.80 to 1.25. The regression analysis also considers the correlation of the regression (R-squared), which should be equal or greater than 0.8. Both periodic as well as cumulative regression analysis are generally accepted, whereas the periodic regression analysis is deemed to give the purest outcome.

Under IFRS, any hedge must be designated and formally documented at inception. This is also referred to as hedge documentation, and should cover the following requirements:

1. The nature of the risk being hedged
2. Identification of the hedged item or transaction
3. Identification of the hedging instrument
4. How the entity will assess the hedge effectiveness

Hedge accounting may only be applied once these four requirements have been met in full. The requirements must be expressed clearly and be date-stamped.

The above mentioned requirements apply to all three types of hedging relationships, which are:

1. Cash flow hedge
2. Fair value hedge
3. Net investment hedge

In the following paragraphs we will look at these three types of hedging relationships in more detail.

21.4.2   CASH FLOW HEDGING RELATIONSHIPS

A cash flow hedge is a hedge (CFH) of the exposure to cash flow variability that is attributable to a particular risk associated with a recognised asset or liability (such as all or some future interest payments on variable rate debt), or a highly probable forecast transaction. In addition to this, it could affect profit or loss.

A cash flow hedge offsets the cash flows generated on the hedged items against the corresponding cash flows of the hedging instrument. The hedged item is accounted for under normal principles, whereas the hedging instrument is measured at fair value each period.

The retrospective hedge effectiveness test will outline the extent to which the hedge is effective. The effective portion of any gain or loss on the hedging instrument is recognised directly in equity in the cash flow reserve, also referred to as OCI (other comprehensive income). Any ineffective portion of the hedging instrument's fair value is recognised immediately in profit or loss.

The amount taken to reserves remains until the hedged item affects profit or loss, at which time the amount held in the cash flow reserve is recycled to profit or loss to offset the movement.

EXAMPLE 1

In the example below, we focus on the impact on the balance sheet and P&L when applying/not applying cash flow hedge accounting for a variable interest loan and a hedging instrument.

In table 21.1, cash flow hedge accounting is not applied. The variable rate loan is held at amortised cost, whereas the hedging instrument is held at fair value. The fair value movements of the hedging instrument are recognised in the P&L. In table 21.2, cash flow hedge accounting is applied. The variable rate loan is held at amortised cost, but the fair value movements of the hedging instrument are now recorded in equity (OCI) for the effective portion and recognised in the P&L for the ineffective portion of the hedging relationship. As we assume the hedging instrument starts with a zero fair value, the effective portion of the hedging relationship is temporarily posted in OCI, whereas the ineffective portion of the hedging relationship is recognised in the P&L. Although the entity is economically hedged in both situations, applying cash flow hedge accounting results in limited to no accounting mismatch and P&L volatility during the lifetime of the hedge.

TABLE 21.1   CFH WITHOUT HEDGE ACCOUNTING

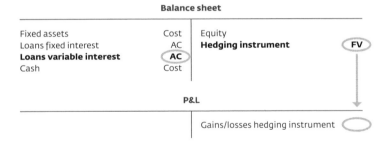

TABLE 21.2   CFH WITH HEDGE ACCOUNTING

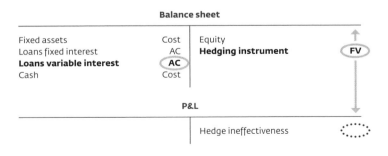

21.4.3 FAIR VALUE HEDGING RELATIONSHIPS

A fair value hedge hedges the exposure to fair value change of a recognised asset (liability), an unrecognised firm commitment or an identified portion of any of the above that is attributable to a particular risk and could affect reported profit or loss.

The hedged item is re-measured at fair value for the hedged risk, and the hedging instrument is measured at fair value with any gain/loss taken to profit or loss. Changes in fair value of any derivative instrument that is not part of a hedging relationship are recognised immediately in the income statement. The carrying amount of the hedged item is adjusted by any loss/gain attributable to the hedged risk ('basis adjustment'), with the other side of the entry taken to profit or loss.

EXAMPLE 2

In the example below, we focus on the impact on the balance sheet and P&L of applying/not applying fair value hedge accounting for a fixed interest loan and a hedging instrument.

In table 21.3, fair value hedge accounting is not applied. The fixed rate loan is held at amortised cost, whereas the hedging instrument is held at fair value. The fair value movements of the hedging instrument are recognised in the P&L. In table 21.4, fair value hedge accounting is applied. The fair value changes attributable to the risk being hedged of the fixed loan are recognised in the P&L, and the fair value movements of the hedging instrument are also recorded in the P&L. Although in both situations the entity is economically hedged, when applying fair hedge accounting the result is that there is limited to no accounting mismatch and P&L volatility during the lifetime of the hedge.

TABLE 21.3 FVH WITHOUT HEDGE ACCOUNTING

Balance sheet

Assets	Cost	Equity	
Loans fixed interest	**AC**		
Loans variable interest	AC	Hedging instrument	FV
Cash	Cost		

P&L

	Gain hedging instrument	

TABLE 21.4 FVH WITH HEDGE ACCOUNTING

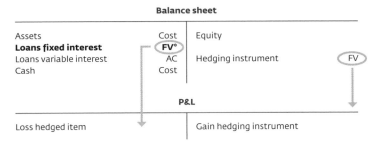

Balance sheet

Assets	Cost	Equity	
Loans fixed interest	FV°		
Loans variable interest	AC	Hedging instrument	FV
Cash	Cost		

P&L

Loss hedged item		Gain hedging instrument

° *Fair value changes attributable to the risk being hedged*

Having covered both cash flow hedging relationships and fair value hedging relationships, one could state that the main difference between these two hedging relationships is the type of risk being hedged. For instance, an interest rate swap can be used in a cash flow hedge to hedge (fixate) the floating interest rate risk, whereas the same hedging instrument in a fair value hedge intends to convert the fixed rate of a loan to a floating rate. In other words, cash flow hedging relationships intend to fix the exposure, where fair value hedging relationships try to cover the exposure to a floating rate.

21.4.4 NET INVESTMENT HEDGING RELATIONSHIPS

A net investment hedge in foreign operations is a way to hedge future changes in currency exposure of a net investment in a foreign operation. Although it does not fall within the definition of either a fair value or cash flow hedge, it can be best compared to a cash flow hedge. A derivative (or non-derivative) financial instrument can be designated as a hedge of foreign exchange movements on a net investment in a foreign operation. Similar to a cash flow hedge, the effective portion of any gains or losses on the hedging instrument is accounted for in OCI (equity). The amounts recorded in OCI remain there until the investment is sold or otherwise disposed of, at which point the amounts are transferred to the P&L.

EXAMPLE 3

In the example below we will focus on the impact on the balance sheet and P&L when applying/not applying net investment hedge accounting for a subsidiary and a hedging instrument. The parent company is a EUR company, whereas the subsidiary is a USD company.

In table 21.5, no net investment hedge accounting is applied, and the EUR/USD exchange rate is 1.00, meaning 1 EUR equals 1 USD. The net asset value of the subsidiary is USD 100, which translates into EUR 100 at parent level. The parent company also has a USD liability (loan) of USD 100 on its balance sheet.

Table 21.6 illustrates the impact of what happens when the USD declines in value by 10% against EUR, whereby no net investment hedge accounting is applied. The net asset value of the subsidiary is still USD 100, which translates to EUR 90. This leads to a cumulative translation adjustment (CTA) of minus EUR 10 in equity. The USD liability is also affected by the drop in value of the USD, which results in a translation gain of EUR 10 in the P&L, and therefore a profit for the year of EUR 10.

TABLE 21.5 NO NET INVESTMENT HEDGE ACCOUNTING, EUR/USD EXCHANGE RATE 1.00

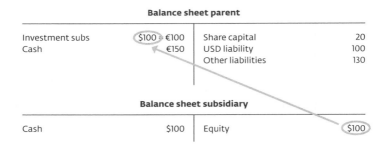

Balance sheet parent

Investment subs	$100 = €100	Share capital	20
Cash	€150	USD liability	100
		Other liabilities	130

Balance sheet subsidiary

| Cash | $100 | Equity | $100 |

TABLE 21.6 NO NET INVESTMENT HEDGE ACCOUNTING, EUR/USD 0.90

Balance sheet parent

Investment subs	$100 = €90	Share capital	20
Cash	€150	**CTA**	**-10**
		Profit for the year	10
		USD liability	90
		Other liabilities	130

Profit or loss parent

| Translation gain loan | 10 |

EXAMPLE 4

Table 21.7 shows the same situation as in table 21.6 but here, net investment hedge accounting is applied. The translation gain on the USD liability is offset by the translation loss of the net investment of the USD subsidiary. As such, there is no profit for the year on the back of the translation gain of the USD loan.

TABLE 21.7   NET INVESTMENT HEDGING, EUR/USD 0.90

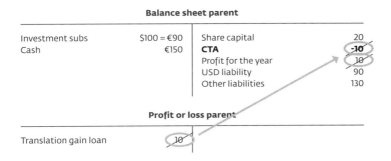

Balance sheet parent

Investment subs	$100 = €90	Share capital	20
Cash	€150	CTA	-10
		Profit for the year	10
		USD liability	90
		Other liabilities	130

Profit or loss parent

Translation gain loan	10

In the above example, a USD liability (loan) was used to hedge the net investment of the USD denominated subsidiary. Under the IFRS rules, it is also allowed to use derivative contracts such as foreign exchange forward contracts. In this example, net investment hedge accounting using a loan eliminated the accounting mismatch because the FX translation of the loan is recorded in the P&L, whereas the FX translation of the subsidiary is recorded in CTA. As such, the accounting mismatch is eliminated.

21.4.5   IFRS 9

As described in the introduction section, IFRS 9 has replaced IAS 39 per 1 January 2018 and has become effective for annual periods beginning on or after that date. Entities are permitted to apply the standard earlier but if they do, this must be disclosed and all of the requirements (including the classification and measurement, impairment and hedge accounting requirements) in the standard must be applied at the same time. IFRS 9 consists of 3 parts:

1. Classification & measurement
2. Impairments
3. Hedge Accounting

Whereas classification & measurement, as well as impairments are mandatory parts of IFRS 9, companies can decide if they wish to transfer hedge accounting to IFRS 9 or continue applying IAS 39 for this purpose.

Hedge accounting under IAS 39 is often criticised as being complex and rules-based, ultimately not reflecting an entity's risk management activities. Consequently, the objective of IFRS 9 is to reflect the effect of an entity's risk management activities on the financial statements. This includes replacing some of the arbitrary rules with more principles-based requirements and allowing more hedging instruments and hedged items to qualify for hedge accounting. Overall, this should result in more risk management strategies qualifying for hedge accounting and provide a better link between an entity's risk management strategy, the rationale for hedging and the impact of hedging on the financial statements.

Summary of the key changes:

- Hedge effectiveness testing is prospective only and can be qualitative depending on the complexity of the hedge. The 80%-125% range is replaced by an objectives-based test that focuses on the economic relationship between the hedged item and the hedging instrument, and the effect of credit risk on that economic relationship.

- IFRS 9 allows risk components of non-financial items to be designated as the hedged item, provided the risk component is separately identifiable and reliably measureable. Under IAS 39, this was only possible for financial items or when hedging foreign exchange risk.

- IFRS 9 introduces the concept of the cost of hedging. The time value of an option, the forward element of a forward contract and any foreign currency basis spread can be excluded from the designation of a financial instrument as the hedging instrument, and accounted for as a cost of hedging. This means that, instead of the fair value changes of these elements affecting profit or loss like a trading instrument, the amounts are allocated to profit or loss similar to transaction costs (which can include basis adjustments), while fair value changes are temporarily recognised in OCI.

- More designations of groups of items as the hedged item are possible, including layer designations and some net positions. IFRS 9 introduces more extensive disclosure requirements that are intended to provide more relevant information. Most of the basics of hedge accounting do not change as a result of IFRS 9.

Hedge accounting remains optional and there are still three types of hedging relationships: fair value hedges, cash flow hedges and hedges of net investments in foreign operations. However, IFRS 9 is stricter than IAS 39 when it comes to accounting for the amount accumulated in the hedging reserve. The treatment depends on the nature of the underlying hedged transaction. If the hedged transaction results in the recognition of a non-financial asset/liability, then the amount in OCI is required to be treated as a basis adjustment of the recognised non-financial asset/liability. In all other circumstances, the OCI will be reclassified to profit or loss as the hedged cash flows affect profit or loss.

21.5
Notional pooling

One of the biggest disadvantages of a notional pool (and one gaining increased attention over the past years) is that a notional pool can significantly enlarge balance sheets of both the banks offering notional pools and the corporates involved because debit and credit balances may not be offset. The implications of Basel III for notional pooling are still uncertain. (See also chapter 13 for further information on notional pooling and chapter 22 for further information on regulations.)

IAS 32.42 states the following with regard to offsetting financial assets and liabilities:

> 'A financial asset and a financial liability shall be offset and the net amount presented in the statement of financial position when, and only when, an entity currently has *a legally enforceable right to set off* the recognised amounts and *intends to settle* either on a net basis, or to realise the asset and settle the liability simultaneously.'

In 2014, some amendments were made to the offsetting principles under IAS 32, stating, among other things, that a 'currently' enforceable right must remain enforceable in all scenarios:

- Normal course of business
- Events of default, insolvency or bankruptcy (reporting entity and/or counterparties)

And for the criteria of simultaneous settlement, IAS 32:

- allows netting where transactions are cleared in batches during the day rather than in a single batch, provided that certain criteria are met such as the fact that settlements cannot be stopped once initiated

The IFRS Interpretation Committee (IFRIC) also shed light on the accounting treatment of notional pools. Although IFRIC mentioned that the set-up of notional cash pools was considered too diverse to be on the agenda of the Interpretation Committee, the Committee noted that – to the extent to which a group does not expect to settle its subsidiaries' period-end account balances on a net basis – it would not be appropriate for the group to assert that it had the intention to settle.

21.6
Debt management

Debt extinguishment versus modification

Companies engage in debt instruments via contractual agreements with counterparties. These debt instruments are recognised in the balance sheet of a company as financial liabilities, being long-term or short-term in nature. Subsequently, a financial liability is generally derecognised in the balance sheet when the contractual obligations are met, the contract is dissolved, or the contract has ended.

A common practice among companies is the refinancing of debt arrangements with counterparties before the contract has ended. Refinancing transactions may occur for multiple reasons, such as changes in funding needs and risk appetite, or taking advantages of favourable market conditions (e.g. low market interest rate).

The accounting standards set out specific terms for the treatment of the replacement of a financial liability by another financial liability, as is the case for refinancing transactions. An assessment is made as to whether the current financial liability should continue to be recognised (called 'debt modification'), or whether the current financial liability should be derecognised and a new financial liability should be recognised (called 'debt extinguishment').

The classification as debt extinguishment or debt modification depends on the facts and circumstances of the transaction. IFRS sets out that the key determinant in the classification is whether the terms of the new contract are substantially different than the original contract. If the terms of the new contract are substantially different, then the transaction should be classified as a debt extinguishment.

Given this, how can it be determined whether a new contract is substantially different compared to the original contract? The Application Guidance to IAS 39 (paragraph AG62) provides the answer, resulting in the execution of the '10% test', which focuses on the discounted present value of cash flows:

> 'For the purpose of paragraph 40 [IAS 39.40], the terms are substantially different if the discounted present value of the cash flows under the new terms, including any fees paid net or any fees received and discounted using the original effective interest rate, is at least 10 per cent different from the discounted present value of the remaining cash flows of the original financial liability. If an exchange of debt instruments or modification of terms is accounted for as an extinguishment, any costs or fees incurred are recognised as part of the gain or loss on the extinguishment. If the exchange or modification is not accounted for as an extinguishment, any costs of fees incurred adjust the carrying amount of the liability and are amortised over the remaining term of the modified liability.'

When performing an assessment of the classification of debt extinguishment versus debt modification, all facts and circumstances of the transaction should be taken into consideration. When the 10% test is met, this results in the extinguishment and derecognition of a financial liability. However, when the 10% test is not met, which would normally lead to a debt modification, other factors in the transaction may still lead to the overall conclusion of a debt extinguishment of a financial liability.

THE 10% TEST – ILLUSTRATIVE EXAMPLE

On 1 January 2011, HZK Treasury Services borrowed EUR 1,000,000 from Bank United to finance further expansion of the business. The term of the loan is 10 years, with an interest rate of 5%. The assumption is made that the contractual interest is equal to the effective interest rate.

Five years later, on 1 January 2016, HZK Treasury Services has achieved rapid growth and is using the bank for other services as well, such as cash management activities. HZK Treasury Services has renegotiated the overall package with the bank, resulting in a decrease in the interest rate on the bank loan to 4%.

Terms	Original debt contract	New debt contract
Principal	EUR 1,000,000	EUR 1,000,000
Interest rate	5.00%	4.00%
Maturity	5 years	5 years

Cash flow schedule – original debt contract

Years (remaining)	Principal payment	Interest payment	Total	Present value DCF
2016		EUR 50,000	EUR 50,000	EUR 47,619
2017		EUR 50,000	EUR 50,000	EUR 45,351
2018		EUR 50,000	EUR 50,000	EUR 43,192
2019		EUR 50,000	EUR 50,000	EUR 41,135
2020	EUR 1,000,000	EUR 50,000	EUR 1,050,000	EUR 822,702
Total	**EUR 1,000,000**	**EUR 250,000**	**EUR 1,250,000**	**EUR 1,000,000**

Cash flow schedule – new debt contract

Years (remaining)	Principal payment	Interest payment	Total	Present value DCF
2016		EUR 40,000	EUR 40,000	EUR 38,095
2017		EUR 40,000	EUR 40,000	EUR 36,281
2018		EUR 40,000	EUR 40,000	EUR 34,554
2019		EUR 40,000	EUR 40,000	EUR 32,908
2020	EUR 1,000,000	EUR 40,000	EUR 1,040,000	EUR 814,867
Total	**EUR 1,000,000**	**EUR 200,000**	**EUR 1,200,000**	**EUR 956,705**

Present value of discounted cash flows

Present value cash flows – original contract	EUR 1,000,000
Present value cash flows – new contract	EUR 956,705
Percentage change	−4.33%

The present value of the discounted cash flows of the new debt contract compared to the original debt contract changed in total 4.33%. This percentage is lower than the 10% test as set out in IFRS. In addition, no other facts and circumstances have been identified for this transaction due to which the refinancing should be classified as a debt extinguishment.

Conclusion: the refinancing should be classified as a debt modification.

21.6.1   INTERCOMPANY LENDING

Treasury departments engage in a wide range of intercompany transactions with related parties within the company. Funding is attracted from capital markets, which is subsequently lent to related parties which are in need of money for investments, operational expenses or other activities. In addition, treasury departments may function as in-house banks, where the liquidity needs of related parties are managed and settled on a daily basis. In practice, treasury departments normally have multiple intercompany accounts per related party, since transactions occur in multiple foreign exchange currencies. Furthermore, treasury departments may engage in derivative transactions on behalf of related parties, whereby the treasury department engages in derivative contracts with banking counterparties, and subsequently creates intercompany positions with such related parties.

Intercompany receivables and payables are recorded on the balance sheet as long-term or short-term assets and liabilities, depending on the facts and circumstances of the transactions (e.g. the contractual terms). In the event that intercompany balances are denominated in a foreign exchange currency, the revaluation of the intercompany balances will be recorded in the profit & loss statement.

However, intercompany loans may also be permanent loans, where the loan qualifies as an extension of the company's net investment. IAS 21.15 defines these loans as items for which settlement is neither planned nor likely to occur in the foreseeable future. For example, a related party has obtained a significant loan from the treasury department for the purchase of a large investment or take-over in the industry. The intercompany transaction was conducted to achieve strategic advantage or growth in the company, where a repayment in the foreseeable future is highly unlikely due, for example, to the liquidity forecasts of the related party.

For permanent intercompany balances, the foreign exchange revaluation will initially be recorded in other comprehensive income and reclassified from equity to the profit & loss statement on disposal of the net investment (IAS 21.32). Therefore, the accounting treatment of foreign exchange revaluations differs between permanent and non-permanent intercompany balances, since the foreign exchange revaluation of non-permanent intercompany balances is recorded on the profit & loss statement straight away.

21.7
Factoring

A corporate treasury function is typically responsible for managing funding and liquidity, and for monitoring the financial risk of a company and hedging that risk within a set mandate. As part of its liquidity management objectives, a corporate treasurer may enter into factoring arrangements. These will involve selling its accounts receivable (receivables from customers based on invoices sent) to a bank at a discount. As an alternative to selling accounts receivable, factoring arrangements can have the nature of short-term lending, secured by the accounts receivable.

Corporate treasurers enter into factoring arrangements in order to improve their cash and working capital position. Factoring is typically used by business-to-business companies to ensure they have the immediate cash flow in order to fulfil their current liabilities. Factoring will enable a company to directly convert accounts receivable, or its open invoices, into cash. There are three parties involved: the bank that purchases the receivable (the factor), the entity that sells the receivable (the seller) and the debtor with a financial obligation to make a payment to the owner of the invoice. The receivables are related to invoices for goods delivered or services performed, representing a legal right to collect money from the debtor. The seller will sell its accounts receivable at a discount to the factor.

21.7.1   FACTORING ARRANGEMENTS

Factoring arrangements can take different shapes and (legal) forms, varying from true sales of the accounts receivable to pass-through arrangements through secured financing. A factoring arrangement can be confidential, whereby the debtor is not notified of the assignment of receivable, and the seller may continue to execute the collection of cash on behalf of the factor. Additionally, there are factoring agreements with recourse and others that are without recourse. In an arrangement without recourse, the factor who purchased the accounts receivable bears the loss if the debtor does not pay the invoice amount. If the receivables were transferred with recourse, the factor has the right to collect (part of) the unpaid invoice amount from the seller.

When a treasurer enters into a factoring arrangement with a bank, the finance team needs to analyse the impact on the financial statements. Such accounting impact analyses typically focus on the question of whether accounts receivable that are part of a factoring agreement should continue to be recognised on the balance sheet of the seller. In the international financial reporting standards (IFRS), no specific guidance is provided in relation to factoring. However, there are detailed requirements in relation to recognition and derecognition of financial instruments in general. The following section sets out the applicable accounting standards and requirements relevant to factoring agreements.

21.7.2   DERECOGNITION OF FACTORED RECEIVABLES

Recognition and derecognition of financial assets, including accounts receivable, is set out in the international financial reporting standards (IFRS) in its sections on financial instruments. Both the former standard IAS39 as the new standards IFRS9 have similar requirements regarding recognition and derecognition of assets. With respect to factoring, the accounting analysis focuses on the question of whether or not the seller's accounts receivable should be derecognised from the seller's balance sheet. The seller receives cash in return for a transfer of its accounts receivable to the factor. The question is whether that cash consideration should be treated as sales proceeds or as a liability. IAS39 and IFRS9 answer that question by determining whether the accounts receivable should be derecognised (in which case the cash consideration is treated as sales proceeds) or should continue to be recognised by the seller, while recognising a financial liability towards the factor.

The requirements as per the accounting standards can be summarised in the following decision tree.

FIGURE 21.1 DECISION TREE

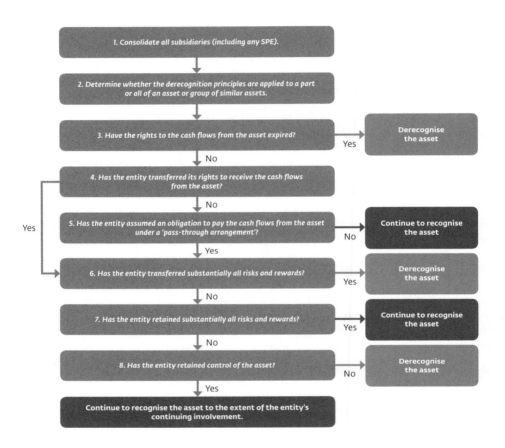

In relation to factoring, the relevant questions according to the above decision tree are 4, 5 and 6. Question 1 is not relevant as factoring arrangements do not typically result in the establishment of new subsidiaries or special purpose entities. Question 2 is irrelevant as factoring relates to the accounts receivable, related to goods and services invoiced in full. And question 3 is not applicable as the rights to cash flows from accounts receivable do not, in themselves, expire when a factoring agreement is created.

21.7.3   TRANSFER RIGHTS TO RECEIVE CASH FLOWS

A relevant question is whether the seller has transferred its rights to receive cash flows from the accounts receivable that have been assigned to a factor under a factoring agreement. In practice, some factoring results in the debtors being notified of the factoring agreement. In such situations, the debtor is often required (by means of statement on the invoice) to make payments to the factor directly. As a result, the seller has transferred its right to receive cash flows to the factor and step 5 of the decision tree can be skipped.

In other factoring arrangements, however, the debtors will not be informed of the agreements, nor of individual invoices being assigned to a factor. For the debtor, no change is observed at all, and payments of invoices continue to be made to the seller. The cash collected by the seller in relation to factored receivables, will then be paid through to the factor. In such a situation, the seller did not transfer its rights to receive the cash flows and the accounting analysis moves to step 5 in the decision tree.

21.7.4   PASS-THROUGH ARRANGEMENT

If the seller did not transfer the contractual rights to receive cash flows from its accounts receivable, it should be determined whether there is an obligation to pass on the cash flows under a pass-through arrangement. Such a pass-through arrangement arises where the seller continues to collect cash receipts from the accounts receivable but assumes an obligation to pass on those receipts to the factor that has provided finance in connection with the accounts receivable.

Under the accounting standards, an arrangement whereby the seller retains the contractual rights to receive the cash flows of a financial asset (the 'original asset'), but assumes a contractual obligation to pay the cash flows to one or more recipients (the 'eventual recipients') is regarded as a transfer of the original asset if, and only if, all of the following conditions are met (IAS 39.19):

a.   The entity has no obligation to pay amounts to the eventual recipients unless it collects equivalent amounts from the original asset.

b.   The entity is prohibited by the terms of the transfer contract from selling or pledging the original asset other than as security to the eventual recipients for the obligation to pay them cash flows.

c.   The entity has an obligation to remit any cash flows it collects on behalf of the eventual recipient without material delay. In addition, the entity is not entitled to reinvest such cash flows during the short settlement period from the collection date to the date of required remittance to the eventual recipients.

Whether the seller meets the requirement as per (a) above – namely, not to have an obligation to pay any amounts to the factor unless it collects equivalent cash amounts from the accounts receivable – depends on the specifics of the factoring contract. Some factoring agreements are 'with recourse', resulting in the factor having the right to collect unpaid invoice amounts from the seller. In such cases, the seller would have an obligation to pay certain amounts to the factor, even though it did not collect those amounts from the debtor. Similarly, there may be penalties for late payments by the debtors, which the seller must pay to the factor. If factoring agreements include such 'recourse' and late payment penalty features, the requirements under (a) would typically not be met and the seller should continue to account for the accounts receivable on its balance sheet.

Cash collected by the seller should be passed on to the factor 'without material delay', in accordance with requirement (c) above. The accounting standard setters have not expanded further on the term 'without material delay'. However, current market practice is generally that the seller is not required to pass through the cash collected from its invoices on an unrealistically frequent basis (such as daily). Payments are expected to be settled within a short timeframe, consistent with the normal routine of payment cycles by the seller.

If the seller is meeting the pass-through criteria as set out above, or if the seller had directly transferred its rights to receive any cash flows from the accounts receivable, an IFRS accounting analysis will then move to the next (and often the last) step in the derecognition decision tree: has the entity transferred substantially all risks and rewards?

21.7.5   SUBSTANTIALLY TRANSFERRING RISKS AND REWARDS

An accounting analysis of risks and rewards of the accounts receivable under a factoring agreement will focus on the financial risks in relation to the invoices sent. The risk of non-payment by the debtor (the default risk) and late payment risks are considered to be particularly relevant.

The common objective of factoring arrangements is to provide cash flow from trade receivables more quickly than would be the case from normal cash collections and to transfer default risk. However, in the case of factoring agreements 'with recourse', a part of the risk of non-payment of the debtor will be borne by the seller. This may be achieved by agreeing on a first loss amount: any losses related to non-payment by debtors up to the first loss amount will be borne by the seller, while the losses exceeding the first loss amount will be for the account of the factor. An accounting analysis of a factoring agreement will typically include an assessment of any recourse features and the expected significance of the losses that will arise from them. If it is concluded that the seller did not substantially transfer all risks as a result of the recourse features, the accounts receivable should continue to be recognised on balance sheet.

In determining the transfer of risks by the seller, the fee structure of the factoring agreement should be assessed. Typically, the fee paid by the seller to the factor will be a fixed fee, settled by means of a discount of the face value amount of the invoice (i.e. the factor pays a lower cash contribution to the seller than the original invoice amount). However, some factoring arrangements have fees that are variable, for example dependent on the duration of the collection process. In addition, the seller may owe late payment charges to the factor if the accounts receivable are not collected within a certain payment term. Variable fees or late payment charges may result in the seller remaining at risk in relation to the accounts receivable.

When factoring agreements are structured in such a way that the seller has transferred its rights to receive cash flows from accounts receivable, or the cash needs to be paid on under a pass-through arrangement, an accounting analysis will focus on financial risks of the accounts receivable. If those risks have been substantially transferred by the seller to the factor, the accounts receivable will be considered 'sold' under the accounting standards and derecognised from the balance sheet of the seller.

21.8
Governance & control

A system of internal control is one of the main tools for identifying and managing a company's risks and safeguarding the company's assets and shareholder investments. An internal control system will focus on financial controls and the detection and management of financial risks. This system has to be able to adapt to a constantly changing risk profile. This also means that demands on treasury departments change constantly, driven by shareholders, regulators and the organisations themselves. Requirements for increased transparency and better control mean that treasury leaders need to continuously refresh their technical knowledge, ensure clear lines of communication and a dedicated information system to support those challenges.

21.8.1   GOVERNANCE

Internal control systems are designed to detect, assess and manage the material risks a company is exposed to and not to avoid those risks. Management has a responsibility to establish policies and procedures governing internal control and the board has an oversight role.

Within treasury, a policy document should outline the mandate of the treasury departments and how the responsibilities have been shared among the different stakeholders.

Looking at a generic treasury policy, it usually consists of the following elements:

– *Overview of the relevant stakeholders* and their roles in defining, approving and executing the treasury policy. Regular stakeholders are the audit committee, CFO, director of treasury, treasury manager, treasury controller and operating company treasurers.

– *Financing.* Roles and responsibilities when it comes to attracting funding, what covenant guidelines apply, and the types of funding that may be used.

– *Interest rate risk management.* What percentage of the floating rate risk should be hedged, which tenors should be hedged and the types of hedging instruments may be used?

- *Cash management.* Who may open bank accounts, which banks may be used and should new accounts be linked to a pooling structure?

- *Currency risk management.* Which currencies, amounts and tenors should be hedged, which types of exposures should be hedged and which banks' hedging instruments may be traded?

- *Counterparty credit risk.* What is the profile a bank should meet in order to do business with the company and which banks are exempted in case there is no bank available that meets the profile?

- *Insurance.* If insurance falls within the realm of treasury, which risks need to be insured, what are the possible thresholds, and with which insurance companies can the treasury department do business?

In the event such matters are not stipulated per topic, an overview should be drawn up of the mandates given by the company's management concerning what the treasury department is allowed to do when executing its activities.

Another important element of a treasury policy is how frequently the policy is updated and when, as well as how exceptions to the policy are handled. Once finalised, the treasury policy should be translated into a single vision and strategy for treasury, which should be clearly communicated and implemented consistently. In order to get the buy-in of the management, it is important to have the topic of treasury risk management on the agenda of the board, which should define the risk appetite.

21.8.2 CONTROL

In addition to having a well-developed treasury policy, it is even more important to have its execution actively safeguarded by an independent treasury controller or treasury control team that has the backing of the CFO. Only when this is done can the governance and control around treasury also be well-managed. The way this is achieved varies per company, but usually leads to management reports on the adherence to policies and procedures, which are sent to the Board.

There are no EU or European national corporate governance codes dictating common principles and market practices with regard to internal control. Companies are free to decide the type of internal control framework they wish to implement. US Stock exchange listed companies are subject to section 404 of the Sarbanes-Oxley Act of 2002. This act, which was called into existence in response to accounting and financial scandals, requires companies to publish a statement on the effectiveness of internal controls over their financial reporting and to disclose any weaknesses they might have identified.

Control frameworks
There are several control frameworks that can be adopted when implementing an internal control system. The COSO framework is one of the most widely used frameworks, especially

in the US. In 1992, the Committee of Sponsoring Organisations of the Treadway Commission (COSO) issued the report 'Internal Control – Integrated Framework' in order to help businesses and other organisations assess and improve their internal control systems. The framework defined internal control and established standards and criteria companies can use to evaluate their own internal control systems. COSO is a non-profit organisation that was founded in 1985 with the objective of identifying factors that contributed to fraudulent financial reporting. It is sponsored and funded by five major professional accounting associations and institutes: the American Institute of Certified Public Accountants (AICPA), the American Accounting Association (AAA), Financial Executives International (FEI), the Institute of Internal Auditors (IIA) and the Institute of Management Accountants (IMA).

In order to benchmark the performance of the treasury department in terms of adherence to its policies and procedures, it is important to use key performance indicators for treasury processes. Doing so enables the management reports from treasury control to be measurable.

Chapter 22

Regulatory Implications

22   Regulatory Implications

22.1
Introduction

The cash management landscape is changing continuously. Alongside technological developments, financial regulatory reforms, mainly resulting from the financial crisis of 2008, are among the most significant factors affecting treasurers' activities both directly and indirectly. Notwithstanding the fact that most new regulations are bank-specific rules, they can have a serious knock-on effect on businesses in terms of higher costs, changing service models and new products. Indeed, the costs and risks associated with non-compliance have increased substantially.

In this chapter, we will describe a number of regulatory reforms, their implications for cash and liquidity management, and how treasurers can apply them to their activities. The main regulatory reforms we will describe include Basel III, the Payment Services Directive 2 (PSD2), and anti money laundering/know your customer (KYC). We will also look at how corporate treasuries currently approach risk management and regulatory compliance, how treasurers can best overcome the various issues and what role technology is playing in supporting compliance activities.

Corporate treasuries should be aware that there can be differences in interpretation and deployment across countries and organisations. This means that while the broad objective of the regulation remains the same, treasurers will need to understand the precise ramifications in each relevant jurisdiction.

22.2
Regulatory compliance challenges

The recent wave of regulations has made this area more pressing – and challenging – for corporate treasurers. They are currently facing a wide range of new and evolving requirements and are realising that, given the speed and complexity of regulations that are coming out of Europe, the US and other jurisdictions, they need to raise their awareness in this area.

Meanwhile, as corporations expand geographically, treasurers need to comply with multiple local as well as international regulations. As a result, compliance challenges will also vary from market to market.

While compliance is a challenge for treasurers around the world, the nature of those challenges – and the way in which treasurers address them – varies considerably between companies. And although there are many areas of compliance to consider, not all companies are affected in the same way.

22.3
Regulatory landscape and compliance requirements

Meanwhile, with so many regulations and variations to consider, it is important for corporate treasures to address any issues promptly. Different companies are addressing the regulatory challenges in different ways.

Coping with regulations requires a multi-step approach that every corporate treasure should follow: understand each regulation, determine how it affects their organisation (both in a direct and indirect way) and establish how and by when the organisation needs to make changes in order to comply. To that end, treasurers should also review their existing activities, identifying ways in which improvements can be made to their internal processes and workflows.

Multi-step approach

First, treasurers need to have a deep understanding of the regulatory landscape and their own compliance requirements, and they should be able to identify how potential regulatory changes affect the way their company does business.

Second, corporates not only need to understand their own compliance requirements but how different regulations affect their banks and financial service providers.

Third, wherever possible corporates will also want to improve the efficiency of internal operations and manage risk more effectively.

Fourth, where necessary corporate treasurers also should choose the right treasury technology and resources required for process reengineering.

Increased demands on treasury operations, and the expanding scope of treasury, has resulted in resource constraints for many treasurers. Because of these constraints, it has been all the more challenging to stay up-to-date with frequent post-recession changes in the regulatory environment.

22.4
Basel III

The Basel-based Bank of International Settlement (BIS) has adopted a series of capital accords designed to provide a minimum level of standards for member central banks to adopt in an effort to ensure stability within both national banking systems and the global financial system. This Basel III accord is a reaction to the financial crisis of 2008 and is the latest in a series of agreements. It includes measures to improve the quality and depth of capital and renews the focus on liquidity management. These measures are being introduced in a phased approach.

22.4.1   BASEL III REQUIREMENTS FOR BANKS

Basel III focuses on three core features of a bank's balance sheet and funding structure(s). It strengthens bank capital requirements and introduces new regulatory requirements on bank liquidity and bank leverage. Transition to the new requirements commenced in 2013, but banks have until 2019 to meet the full capital ratios.

Although banks were obligated to meet liquidity requirements by 2015, a calibration period was applied in order to investigate any unforeseen consequences.

			Comparison
	Basel I	Basel II	Basel III
Capital requirements			
Common equity	None	2%	4.5%
Tier I	None	4%	6%
Capital buffer	None	None	2.5%
Counter-cyclical buffer	None	None	0-2.5%
Total	None	8%	8%-10.5%
Leverage ratio	None	None	3%
Liquidity ratios	None	None	Yes
LCR	None	None	Yes
NSFR	None	None	Yes

Basel III includes three main measurable requirements:

(Minimum) capital requirements
The objective of the Basel III capital accords is to set minimum standards to be implemented by national regulators. Because the accords are implemented at national level, there are some differences between the rules applied among countries. However, the underlying

requirements are important and are already having a significant impact on corporate trea-suries.

At the centre of the Basel III capital accord is a requirement for all banks to hold 4.5% of risk-weighted assets in common equity or core tier one capital. In addition, some global sys-temically important banks will be required to hold an additional 1% to 2.5% (this value is determined by the relative importance of the bank) of risk-weighted assets in core tier one capital, as a mandatory conservation buffer. Finally, some regulators may require banks to hold up to 2.5% of risk-weighted assets in common equity as a discretionary countercycli-cal buffer. These additional capital buffers will be introduced to withstand future periods of stress and/or to curb excess credit growth. The Basel III capital requirements were intro-duced at the beginning of 2014, with full implementation by 2019. (The capital conservation buffer was introduced from January 2016.)

(Minimum) leverage ratios

The second requirement involves minimum leverage ratios for all banks. This leverage ratio is intended to constrain the banking sector from building up excessive on- and off-balance-sheet leverage. It requires a bank to hold Tier 1 capital in excess of 3% of their total asset exposure. In other words, under Basel III banks will be restricted to a maximum leverage of 33 times their core one capital. Leverage will be calculated without any risk weightings being applied and all exposures, including all off-balance-sheet items, will be included in the assessment.

Banking supervisors are tracking bank leverage and banks will be required to comply from January 2018. Because of the imminent disclosure of their leverage ratios, banks are already reporting these ratios and adjusting their behaviour to comply.

Liquidity ratios

The third requirement involves examining a bank's liquidity ratios, with a view to ensuring banks have sufficient liquidity to survive a short-term (30-day) or a longer-term (over a year) market stress event (without having access to external funding sources). Specifically, Basel III introduced two complementary metrics that are intended to 'encapsulate' banks' short-term liquidity and structural funding position. These include the Liquidity Coverage Ratio (LCR) and the Net Stable Funding Ratio (NSFR).

–   *Liquidity Coverage Ratio (LCR)*
    The first metric is the liquidity coverage ratio (LCR). This short-term liquidity met-ric is a standard intended to promote short-term resilience to potential liquidity disruptions over a short-term period. The LCR will require banks to hold enough high-quality liquid assets to cover any net cash outflows during a significant, stressed 30-day funding scenario specified by local supervisors.

    Banks were required to hold 60% of the required assets from January 2015, with the requirement rising by 10% each year until full compliance by January 2019.

– **Net stable funding ratio**

The second element is a net stable funding ratio, which will require banks to hold sufficient assets with a residual maturity of one year or more to finance longer-term, illiquid assets. This structural funding metric is designed to address liquidity mismatches and promote resilience over a longer period. The net stable funding ratio was implemented in January 2018.

Banks and Basel III: phased approach

Capital requirements

2013	Phasing-in of the higher minimum capital requirements
2015	Higher minimum capital requirements fully implemented
2016	Gradual phasing-in of conservation buffer
2019	Conservation buffer is fully implemented

Leverage ratio

2011	Supervisory monitoring – tracking the leverage ratio and its underlying components
2013	Parallel run I: The leverage ratio and its components are tracked by supervisors but not disclosed (not mandatory)
2015	Parallel run II: The leverage ratio and its components are tracked and disclosed (not mandatory)
2017	Based on the results of the parallel run period, final adjustments to the leverage ratio
2018	The leverage ratio has become a mandatory part of Basel III requirements

Liquidity requirements

2011	Observation period: Development of templates and supervisory monitoring of the liquidity ratios
2015	Introduction of the Liquidity Coverage Ratio (LCR)
2018	Introduction of the Net Stable Funding Ratio (NSFR)

22.4.2   BASEL III AND IMPLEMENTATION

The Basel III requirements are being implemented by all G20 countries, however the manner of execution varies by country. Corporate treasurers should be aware there may be significant differences in interpretation and deployment across countries and organisations. Although there are some significant variations in the way national regulators have implemented the Basel III accord, the underlying requirements are fundamentally the same.

Legislation is already in place in the key markets around the world. The translation of the Basel III requirements and standards into European rules is taking place through the Capital Requirements Directive IV (CRD IV) that was published in July 2013. Because it is a regulation, the CRR was immediately binding in all member states from January 2014 and requires no further legislation from those states. The UK FSA is responsible for implementing the rules in the UK. The translation of Basel III into US rules is embedded in the Dodd-Frank Act. Meanwhile, legislators and regulators face the challenge of trying to remove inconsistencies between national rules and Basel III requirements. For example, the US Federal Reserve has had to ensure that its implementation of Basel III is consistent with the Dodd-Frank Act, the US Congress's response to the financial crisis. Note that with the gradual implementation of Basel III, and national regulators' responsibility for providing much of the detail, the precise regulations will continue to develop and evolve over time, especially if unforeseen consequences become apparent.

22.4.3   BASEL III AND CORPORATE TREASURY

Though Basel III is a bank-specific regulation that will not have a direct impact on corporates, there will be a significant knock-on effect on corporate treasurers' cash management. Basel III has an impact on both banks' payments operations and on their liquidity management policies within cash management.

From a corporate treasury perspective, most banks evaluated the impact of the accord on their propositions, and in some cases adjustment was needed to meet the new requirements. These changes have important implications across the full range of cash management and trade finance activities. They might provide banks with an incentive to scale back activities which are most vulnerable to liquidity risks in periods of stress, such as documentary trade finance (L/Cs), and may encourage banks to pass (part of) the higher costs on to their corporate customers. As a consequence, Basel III is pressing not only banks but above all corporates to strengthen or adjust their cash management practices.

Notional cash pooling
Basel III rules as currently implemented may have a serious impact on banks offering notional cash pool arrangements. In its current form, notional cash pooling for corporate clients can have a significant impact on a bank's balance sheet.

Under Basel III, banks will be required to use gross amounts in calculating and reporting liquidity ratios. Overdraft balances, which are masked by notional pooling structures, may need to be reported. Netting loans with deposits will not be allowed, and the use of credit mitigation techniques will not be recognised to the same extent.

Basel III does not have significant implications for physical cash pooling. However, for notional cash pooling, where there is no physical transfer of funds between currencies, it might burden corporates with the requirement to significantly increase disclosure of their liabilities. Where currencies are managed separately but as part of a single master account, the liabilities associated with each currency position may have to be disclosed, and may have an equity capital allocation set against that position.

The current notional cash pool offering will oblige banks to keep more liquidity on their balance sheets or reduce the number of accounts, making it much harder to offer this service profitably. Indeed, banks may rethink their willingness to offer notional pooling due to the impact on liquidity and capital required. Some banks may even stop providing this service. Other banks are considering transforming their cash pooling offering into a single unit-of-account product based on one overall balance. This product would not require large amounts on the balance sheet.

Meanwhile the European Commission has proposed adjusting the leverage ratio regulations to conditionally allow for net treatment of cash pooling. New regulations (CRDv/CRR2), which are expected to be implemented in 2019, may well reverse the additional capital allocation imposed under Basel III.

Possible bank responses

First, banks may simply withdraw from offering notional cash pooling, either on a cross-border basis or altogether.

Second, they could increase the charges on debit balances, reflecting the additional cost of compliance. This would have the effect of making notional cash pooling uneconomic for most users.

Third, they may offer a similar product based on the use of mirror accounts to mimic the attributes of a notional cash pool, but where any cash movements are physical rather than notional. These products are already offered by a number of banks in a number of locations and are sometimes referred to as interest optimisation.

Fourth, they could alter the notional cash pooling such that the whole pool would be treated as one asset or liability.

Fifth, in view of the fact that further changes in the regulation have been announced, they may opt to weather the storm for now.

Centralisation of treasury activities

Corporate treasurers may also decide to centralise some of their own activities into in-house banks or similar structures. Regulators may require banks to hold additional assets against derivatives not traded on an exchange (if they are not cleared via a central counterparty). This could lead to additional costs for over-the-counter derivatives that treasurers use to hedge interest rate and currency positions. Centralising cash management allows the group treasury to offset any natural hedges within the organisation, thereby reducing the number and size of any external hedges required.

Bank lending

In the context of the new capital requirements, some banks have become more selective when extending credit to companies. In a number of cases, this has led banks to reduce lending or increase the cost of lending significantly in an effort to comply with both capital standards and, especially, the forthcoming net stable funding ratio.

Clients that manage daily operations through banks will be rewarded with credit facilities, as operating cash will be considered attractive from a regulatory perspective. This means corporate treasurers will need to understand how each of their banking partners has responded to Basel III. Companies that rely on particular banks for working capital finance will need to ensure they will continue to be supported by those banks.

Short-term investment

Basel III has a significant impact on depository relationships, short-term cash management strategies and financial services pricing. The introduction of the liquidity coverage ratio negatively impacts the availability and pricing of short-term investment products. Under the terms of the regulation, banks will have to characterise short-term cash deposits as either operational or non-operational cash balances. Operational cash that is used for working capital purposes, and includes cash held for transactional purposes, is mostly held with their cash management bank.

Corporates often choose not to place non-operational cash with their transactional banks, to diversify counterparty risk. Under Basel III, banks will have to hold assets against 25% of their operational cash balances and against 40% of non-operational cash balances from corporate clients.

Some banks will also need to hold more liquid assets to meet the liquidity coverage ratio. This means they will be competing with investors and asset managers (including money market funds) for the highest-rated short-term instruments, such as treasury bills and commercial paper issued by the best-quality issuers.

Impact on short-term cash investment

Banks may not offer short-term deposits

Banks may not offer short-term deposits for less than 30 days, as this will have a negative impact on their liquidity ratios.

Change in relative pricing of short-term assets

There may be a change in the relative pricing of short-term assets, with the increased demand driving up prices and therefore reducing yield. This will also affect the returns from asset managers, including money market funds, which are already subject to tighter restrictions.

Fewer options for placing short-term cash

As a result, treasurers may have fewer options when placing short-term cash. There will also be an impact on longer-term investments as the net stable funding ratio becomes a factor. However, this will be more of a concern for treasurers responsible for managing longer-term assets, such as the company pension fund.

Trade finance activities

Since the initial publication of the Basel III accord, there has been a hard lobby by trade finance practitioners to ensure that the collateralised nature of the instruments is adequately considered in any regulatory treatment. This lobby was successful and, as a result, in Europe CRD IV has exempted trade finance loans from the assessment of risk-weighted assets. This means banks will not have to set aside as much capital to cover any trade loans. Another result of this lobby was that European banks will only have to consider 20% of the value of letters of credit for the purposes of the leverage ratio, instead of the earlier proposed 100% (under Basel II).

CRD IV also recognises the guarantees of payment inherent in letters of credit and other guarantees, so these can now be relied upon when calculating cash flows for compliance purposes (previously, banks may have only been able to count on 50% of cash for inflow calculations).

All these changes mean that the relative cost of trade finance products is unlikely to change dramatically over the next few years. However, because the precise treatment is determined by national regulators, it will vary between jurisdictions and, as with other elements, will be subject to change.

Understanding Basel III

To understand the impact of Basel III more clearly, corporate treasurers should review three key elements in particular:

- **Provision of credit facilities**
  Treasurers should try to identify each bank's position on credit facilities. Is the bank going to continue extending the same level of financing, under the same terms and the same conditions? If necessary, would the bank provide additional credit facilities? And would the company have to provide additional business to the bank to obtain these facilities?

- **Investment opportunities**
  Is the bank (and other counterparty) changing its approach to attract short-term investment? Are these changes consistent with the company's short-term investment policy? If not, is it appropriate to amend the policy?

- **Liquidity management**
  Will the bank continue to offer the same liquidity management products? If so, will there be significant changes in pricing? Are there alternative ways of managing group liquidity?

22.5
The Payment Services Directive 2 (PSD 2)

The Payment Services Directive 2 (PSD2) will be incorporated into EU law on 13 January 2018. PSD2 is an extension of the original PSD, which was adopted by European legislators in 2007. The Payment Services Directive (PSD) provides the legal framework for payment services and payment service providers (PSPs) in the European Union (EU) and in the European Economic Area (EEA). This regulation was implemented by all 27 EU member states by 1 November 2009 as well as by the three non-EU EEA countries – Iceland, Liechtenstein and Norway. PSD2 is needed to take into account the development of technology that has led to the emergence of new payment types and new payment service providers that were outside the existing PSD.

22.5.1   THE PSD AND ITS OBJECTIVES

The purpose of the PSD is to establish a single payment market by removing legal barriers to the provision of payment services in the EU, and to allow citizens and businesses to make all kinds of intra EU/EEA cross-border payments 'as easy, efficient, secure and timely as national payments within a member state'.

The PSD aims to establish a modern and comprehensive set of rules that are applicable to all payment services in the EU and the EEA for all EU/EEA currencies. The PSD also seeks to improve competition by opening up markets to new entrants and fostering greater efficiency and cost-reduction.

In addition, the Directive provides the necessary legal platform for the Single Euro Payments Area (SEPA). However, the PSD that covers all 30 members of the EU/EEA, including Switzerland, is more extensive in scope than the SEPA initiative (which primarily covers the efficient processing of euro payments).

22.5.2   KEY PROVISIONS

The PSD stipulates the rights and obligations for both PSPs and users in intra-EU payment transactions in euros or other EEA currencies such as sterling or Swiss francs. All payment service providers in the EU/EEA area need to meet new conduct of business requirements. The Directive contains a number of protective measures that are applied uniformly across the EU/EEA on payment services offered to corporate customers. PSPs should meet key provisions of the PSD, including: faster (maximum) execution time for the banks' payment processes, strict rules on value dating, faster availability of funds, the level of charges that can be levied on customers for the service, transfer of full amount, full transparency to customers and defined refund periods.

Faster execution times

Since 1 January 2012, payments within the EU/EEA are subject to a D+1 execution time. That means that from that date, payments to EU member states and EEA countries in member state currencies should be transmitted to the payee within one banking day after the day on which the payer has given the payment order.

Strict rules on value dating

The value date – or the day specified for the PSP to debit and credit funds – is much stricter under the PSD. It puts an end to the practice of back value dating for debits and forward value dating for credits, which allows banks to earn float.

Transfer of full amount

The PSP or bank of the payer, the payee's bank and any intermediary bank must transfer the full amount and refrain from deducting charges from the payment itself. However, subject to an agreement between the payee and the PSP, the payee's PSP may deduct charges from the payment.

Information disclosure

The PSD mandates that an end user of the payment services be provided with all the relevant information. PSPs must provide full transparency to customers before and after a payment is executed. These rules apply where the payment service providers involved are located in the EU/EEA and also where the transaction is carried out in an EU/EEA currency.

The information required to be given depends on whether the contract is a single payment service contract or a framework contract. Fewer obligations apply to single payment transactions. Detailed terms and conditions must be given to corporate customers and any changes must be properly communicated (including all the charges payable (bank fees), maximum processing/execution time, spending limits, refund rules and confirmations of the exchange rate, if applicable).

BIC and IBAN

In order to comply with the new requirements under the PSD, PSPs need to ensure that if they accept an instruction to make a payment, they will be able to fulfil the contract to deliver the payment in accordance with the terms and conditions offered. It will be vital that PSPs capture all the information required from corporate customers in order to complete the payment successfully at the front end. As a result, they will need to be confident they capture accurate beneficiary account and routing code (sort code) details.

In the EU, this involves the capture of BIC and IBAN details. This is normal for quoting beneficiary account details for cross-border payments and domestic transfers. PSPs must ensure they are capable of validating BICs and IBANs as well as other local bank account and routing code details. This will help businesses and banks to maximise straight-through processing (STP) and reduce costs while complying with the PSD.

22.5.3 PRESENT SCOPE

The existing PSD has a particularly far-reaching impact on the way banks process payments. It covers the following:

- All banks and other payment service providers (PSPs) operating within the EU/EEA area
- Euro and non-euro currencies of all EU/EEA countries
- SEPA instruments as well as existing national payment instruments

Payment service providers (PSP)

Payment service providers (PSP) falling within the scope of the PSD include banks, building societies, e-money issuers, money transfer operators and mobile phone operators that provide payment services. The most significant categories of PSP are credit institutions (banks, building societies and e-money issuers). The PSD has also introduced a new category of firms called payment institutions (PIs), which will be subject to a new authorisation and registration regime.

Payment services

The regulations cover the provision of 'payment services' as a regular occupation or business activity. The PSD focuses on electronic means of payment. The annex to the directive sets out the payment services falling within the scope of the PSD.

Cheques and cash-only transactions (whereby only cash is acceptable) are explicitly excluded from the scope of the PSD (although any cash transaction involving movement to or from a payment account will be caught).

Payment services
– Services enabling cash to be placed on a payment account
– Services enabling cash withdrawals from a payment account
– The operations required for operating a payment account
– Debit and credit card payments
– Direct debits and credits
– Standing orders
– Issuing/acquiring payment instruments
– Money transfers
– Certain services through mobile phones or other digital and IT devices

22.5.4 ENLARGED SCOPE OF PSD2

The first part of PSD2 will extend the scope of the original PSD to cover two additional classes of transactions:

- Payments sent between a payment service provider (PSP) based in the EEA and a PSP based outside the EEA. These are sometimes referred to as 'one leg out' transactions
- Transactions executed within the EEA but denominated in non-EEA currencies, such as the USD

The second part of PSD2 will extend the scope to cover new types of payment service providers that simply did not exist when the first PSD was being negotiated. These are third party payment service providers. This change reflects the increase in mobile and internet-based payment and banking solutions, some of which are developed and provided by organisations outside the traditional financial services sector.

Third party payment service providers
PSD2 aims to open up the banking landscape and increase competition. PSD2 gives licensed third party payment service providers the opportunity to gain a significant role in the payment process by allowing them direct access to the payer's and payee's accounts, as well as to aggregate account information across banks, thus strengthening their offerings in areas such as merchant collection services. This will require banks to have strong authentication procedures in place.

22.5.5 PSD2 AND CORPORATE TREASURY

PSD2 will also have an impact on the corporate sector and on how a future treasury will function. This is especially relevant for corporate users, where transactions are triggered as single payments instead of bulk payments. The launch of PSD2 will allow corporates to better manage cash flows as it will create more certainty and transparency on the maximum cycle for payments, on value dating and on charging.

Cross-border services are more easily accessible to corporates, as the harmonisation of legislation concerning payment services across the EU/EEA makes it easier for PSPs to develop new products and services that can be offered to corporates at a pan-European level.

This generates opportunities for corporates to move into pan-European and EEA markets without the need to maintain local accounts in the countries where they do business. The PSD2 will also facilitate hassle-free entry into the region for non-EU payment providers (thereby increasing the scale of the market).

Increased competition and innovation
Under PSD2, increased competition between PSPs will force banks to offer corporates better deals on payments and cash management products within the EU/EEA and will drive the market to deliver a higher standard of products and services.

The biggest potential benefit for corporate customers may come from new value propositions, services and solutions. PSD2 creates opportunities for banks to develop and offer new multi-banking-based, integrated digital financial services for corporates.

This may be the result of banks and new entrants combining their individual strengths or banks becoming more innovative in the face of increased and agile competition.

PSD2 may also lead to cheaper, faster and more efficient payment solutions for corporates. The Directive will make charges more transparent and this, combined with new entrants, should drive down payment transaction costs for corporates.

Easier management and overview of cross-border accounts

For corporates, the main benefit of PSD2 is likely to be simpler management of cross-border accounts and transactions. New innovative offerings triggered by IT developments may also provide deeper integration possibilities of ERP functions into financial services, including multi-banking.

Consolidated account overview

Under PSD2, account information service providers (AISPs) will be introduced. This enables corporates to view all their multi-bank account details in a single portal. It will ultimately allow providers to consolidate a corporate's account information in one place and to permit the corporate to initiate better external payments and internal liquidity transfers (payments from one account to another). While such features are not new to cash management, these new access technologies may increase convenience, integration and efficiency.

22.6
Anti-money laundering and KYC regulation

Know your customer (KYC) and anti-money laundering (AML) requirements have been in place for many years and are aimed at stopping criminal elements from exploiting the financial industry to further their illicit goals. The proceeds of money laundering have been connected to human trafficking, the drugs trade and the funding of terrorism. Therefore, having robust KYC policies and procedures in place is fundamental, not just from a regulatory perspective but also from a societal perspective.

As criminals become more sophisticated in subverting the KYC processes, regulators have responded by pushing more rules and regulations onto financial institutions and increasing the penalties that can be levied where breaches are detected. These actions have meant that compliance with KYC and AML is a hot agenda item on the boards of all banks. The challenge for the banks is to comply with the regulations, while also protecting the customer experience and controlling costs in an environment where PSPs do not face equal regulatory pressures.

These challenges have inevitably had a negative impact on the customer experience, with most treasurers rating 'documentation' and 'onboarding' challenges among their top complaints in the transaction banking arena.

22.6.1   CLIENT ONBOARDING VS. PRODUCT ONBOARDING

There are two elements involved in starting a relationship with a financial institution: client onboarding and product onboarding. The aim of most treasurers is to procure a product (i.e. an account). In order to get that product, the customer must complete the client onboarding part of the process. However, this process has no added value to the customer and simply takes up a lot of time (it is not uncommon for client onboarding to take 30+ days to complete). Once this process is complete, the product onboarding can begin.

The pain points for customers in these processes are:

a.   Time – many banks struggle to onboard clients in a timely manner and, due to internal policies, it is often not possible to start product onboarding until client onboarding is complete.

b.   Lack of transparency – for many financial institutions, the internal processing times are difficult to predict as the time they take depends on the complexity of the customer, the countries where they do business and the products they will be using. Therefore, the whole process can feel like a 'black box' to the customer, with no way of getting a clear timeline for implementation or clarity on where they are in process.

c.   Differing requirements – each country where the customer is doing business with the financial institution will have an additional set of requirements that must be met in order to comply with local law. And while these requirements are based on local law, they will be interpreted by local compliance officers in line with bank policies. This can lead to differing requirements among financial institutions in the same jurisdiction (note: in some countries local bankers' associations give guidance on how to implement rules, which helps to standardise the approach in these countries).

d.   Two touch points – as noted above, the standard policy for financial institutions is that the KYC must be complete before product onboarding starts. This means that in terms of interaction with customers, there will always be two touch points. One at the KYC stage, where requirements such as ultimate beneficial ownership declarations (UBOs) or organisational charts will be collected. During the second, product onboarding requirements will be collected, for example the passport copies of authorised signatories on accounts. This second touch point is also the stage during which the contracting for the product will take place.

e.   Having to resend documents – this is a common complaint of customers. They have already submitted their corporate documentation and are then asked to resubmit the documentation again. There are different reasons for this. In some instances, the documentation will have a different standard for a different product, i.e. differing levels of certification or differing validation periods.

In addition to the initial onboarding, the KYC requirements are recurring, so that every one, three or five years (depending on their risk rating), customers will have to have their files checked again and, where necessary, remediation will take place.

With regard to product onboarding, customers can expect that they will have to provide additional documentation when they contract for a new product or service.

Furthermore, as a common standard, customers will always have a contractual obligation to keep the information held with the financial institution up-to-date. This obligation means that, for example, when an authorised signatory or legal representative leaves the organisation, the financial institution must be notified accordingly.

This all means that regulatory obligations cannot be seen as a one-off and should indeed be seen as an integral part of the customer/bank relationship.

22.6.2 TECHNOLOGY TOOLS

Banks have invested heavily in their online banking platforms and although at first this was aimed at facilitating the initiation of electronic payments and access to electronic reporting, banks have increasingly come to realise that these platforms can also be used to initiate service requests and as documentation repositories. These in-house solutions will eventually allow for a fully digitised solution for managing contracts and requirements, allowing straight-through processing and faster client onboarding. However, it is clear that for many banks, these ambitions are still in the works and a lot of groundwork needs to be done with regard to updating storage libraries and enhancing processes before these solutions and benefits can be fully realised.

22.7
Third-party service providers

Given the increasing costs that are incurred by financial institutions to be compliant with the various regulations, a new industry of third-party service providers has sprung up in the last few years. While the business model of these service providers varies, the idea remains the same. By specialising in KYC, they hope to reduce the costs to the banks compared to doing KYC checks in-house, while also improving the customer experience.

22.7.1 KYC UTILITIES

A KYC utility can either be a service centre shared among financial institutions or a standalone entity that performs the KYC checks on behalf of financial institutions. The main reasons why these KYC utilities have not been more successful are:

- It is difficult to gain market share. There are already at least 15 shared utilities in the market and, until there is some consolidation, they will struggle to realise the potential customer benefits.

- Banks remain liable for meeting their regulatory obligations, so they cannot out-source their regulatory liability.

- There are data protection challenges; where data are transferred between parties across borders, there will always be strict rules to adhere to.

22.7.2 ALTERNATIVE TECHNOLOGY SOLUTIONS

Blockchain

There has been much talk about the use of blockchain or distributed ledger technology (DLT) in the area of regulatory compliance because, at its core, the blockchain can provide an unassailable record of what has occurred. The areas that are of particular interest are:

a. *Authentication* – Allowing documents can be authenticated via the blockchain removes the need for copies to be certified. This could reduce fraud and increase reliance among financial institutions.

b. *Identification* – the first identification document has already been created via the blockchain but in order for this technology to take off, such advances would need to be adopted by local regulators.

c. *Storage* – there are a lot of interesting developments with respect to the storage of documentation via the blockchain. When documents are saved on the blockchain, they effectively become unhackable. Clearly, this has real benefits in the area of cyber security and data protection.

Application programming interface (API)

By integrating APIs into a customer-facing portal, customers can quickly and easily upload their customer information and contract for products in a fully digitised environment. It means, for example, that a customer can take a picture of their ID and have it authenticated in real time. The increasing development of such integrated interfaces means that for some banks, real-time client onboarding will become a reality in the near future. This means that the customer journey can be measured in hours instead of days and months.

Innovation

Chapter 23

Key Developments

23   Key Developments

23.1
Introduction

Corporate treasurers are facing waves of innovation across the payments and fintech areas. This is being driven by new technological capabilities and the various challenges many corporates are confronting in terms of increased need for efficiency, visibility and control over liquidity and risk.

These innovations may bring opportunities to improve, speed up and streamline a company's cash, liquidity, risk and working capital management and allow the treasurer to better react to the company's current cash and working capital needs.

There are a number of key game-changing technology innovations that will greatly impact the corporate treasury, including digitalisation, mobile banking, rise of cloud-based solutions, big data and analytics, and blockchain or distributed ledger technology.

23.2
Corporates and innovation

Corporate treasurers are increasingly exposed to credit, market, and operational risks caused by a complex and volatile market environment, globalisation, changed client behaviours and regulatory initiatives, among others. These have brought complexity in the traditional treasury management function. Existing system silos further complicate the need to adjust.

There is growing pressure for the corporate treasury to become more efficient. Pressure to use cash and liquidity efficiently and to deploy transaction banking and deal-hedging capabilities at key points in the corporate supply chain are a significant part of this dynamic. As a result, corporate treasuries are significantly increasing their spending on treasury technology and innovations.

Corporates are looking to take advantage of opportunities in innovation, where technology can carry out existing inefficient and laborious manual processes more quickly. They are thereby focusing on incoming tools that may meet the changing needs of corporate treasurers and risk managers, helping them gain greater visibility of their business-critical information and greater strategic control over their cash, to reduce risk and to strengthen internal controls.

Banks and other service providers are working increasingly hard on developing creative solutions to bring innovations into the corporate banking space. Both banks and specialised third parties are offering a wide range of solutions, including cost-efficient core functionalities of treasury management systems (TMS). The list of those innovation tools that add value is growing steadily, ranging from simple bank connectivity to cash forecasting, financial analysis and information. Together, these innovations will have a major impact on corporate cash management and wider operations, and may help to convert the role of the treasurer into a strategic position.

Key developments
– Digitalisation
– Mobile banking
– Cloud-based SaaS
– Big data and analytics
– Blockchain and distributed ledger

23.3
Digitalisation

A first key trend is the accelerated digitalisation of corporate banking services. This looks set to fundamentally change the way corporate treasurers operate. The driver behind this increased digitalisation is standardisation.

With increasing digitalisation and growing pressure to become more efficient, especially with respect to their cash management and payment structures, more and more decision-makers at corporates are attaching the highest strategic relevance to the digitalisation of entrepreneurial processes. This enables businesses to rethink legacy business models, to consider new opportunities, to redeploy excess capacity created through digitisation — not just for cost savings but also for sourcing new opportunities and revenue streams.

Today, corporates can call on a multitude of digital services provided by banks, vendors and other organisations that not only automate many core treasury processes but, in so doing, convert the treasury role into one that demonstrably adds value to the business. Banks and solution providers have enhanced their treasury tools across national and international payment schemes, collections, liquidity management, clearing and settlement. One common characteristic of these enhancements is the ability to centralise information seamlessly. This is achieved using consolidated account balances across multiple institutions to aid in cash forecasting, trade financing, escrow management, currency trading and other liquidity risk functions. This should enable treasuries to automate routine tasks, significantly improve the speed and efficiency of day-to-day treasury operations and reduce the operational burden on treasury departments.

These developments are allowing treasurers to spend more time providing meaningful insight and advice to C-Suite decision-makers, ultimately informing strategic direction.

23.3.1 DIGITAL TOOLS

Digitisation is increasingly manifesting itself in various solutions provided by banks, vendors and others in payments, the pursuit of working capital optimisation and mobile banking. These are designed to raise the speed, safety and efficiency of treasury operations. New tools such as virtual accounts, BPOs in trade finance, eBAM (electronic bank account management), digital personal signatories and digital disbursements can facilitate quicker and simpler execution of key techniques, including working capital optimisation.

Beyond this, these digital innovations can bring further benefits through efficient account management, strategic insights and fast, secure settlement. As new technology companies enter the transaction banking market, the emergence of competition in this market is triggering further new and more powerful innovations. With the guidance of providers and banks, corporate treasurers can select the tools they need.

Digital tools
– Virtual accounts
– Bank payment obligation (BPO)
– Virtual disbursements
– eBAM

23.3.1.1 Virtual accounts

An interesting innovative tool made possible by digitalisation is the virtual account (for a more in-depth description of virtual accounts, see chapter 13). Virtual accounts enable corporates to rationalise their disparate bank accounts into a single, digital account, which can then be divided internally into separate 'virtual' accounts to accommodate firms' corporate structures. These subsidiary accounts have their own funds, account numbers and administrators, but the funds they contain are notional allocations from the parent account.

Not only can virtual accounts help rationalise the number of physical accounts held by a corporate, but they also allow the company to gain superior visibility of its cash and liquidity. It affords corporates a big-picture view of their financial situation – giving them a clear idea of the risk exposures involved in informed strategic decisions. Virtual accounts may also minimise accounts receivable and reconciliation issues, without adding layers of complexity or expensive technology. Reconciliation with virtual accounts can help a corporate to increase the automation of customer receipts. It enables firms to automate their supplier onboarding and bookkeeping processes, thereby drastically reducing the amount of work created by new invoices for transactions.

23.3.1.2 Bank payment obligation (BPO)

Growing digitalisation is also evident in the increased adoption of the bank payment obligation (BPO), which provides some of the benefits of a letter of credit in a digital multibank environment. The BPO is a bank-mediated digital trade settlement method that removes the inefficiencies of paper-based letters of credit. The BPO combines rapid processing with invaluable cover against payment risk.

The BPO is facilitated by the Trade Services Utility (TSU), SWIFT's ISO 20022-compliant interbank messaging and transaction matching cloud application. Use of the BPO is set out in a dedicated International Chamber of Commerce (ICC) rulebook.

Processing can be done in a maximum of seven days, compared to the average of three weeks for paper-based letters of credit. Since BPOs are mediated by banks, corporates are able to offload any payment risk associated with the transaction, alleviating problems with open account settlement. It has the potential to improve trading relationships and resolve difficulties with payment terms.

23.3.1.3 Virtual disbursements

A third innovative tool made possible by digitalisation is virtual disbursements. Virtual disbursements enable corporate treasurers to send money straight to their bank account via an email address or mobile number. They thereby eliminate the need to obtain and store sensitive bank account information and remove the problem that prevented companies from simply making P2P payments directly into their customer's bank account.

23.3.1.4 eBAM

Another interesting digital tool is the electronic bank account management (eBAM). eBAM refers to the electronic exchange of messages with counterparty banks for opening or closing accounts, changing signatories, modifying spending limits and generating reports (as required by law or regulation). This tool, defined and offered by SWIFT, is a solution for enhancing the management of bank accounts and signatory information within the corporate organisation. eBAM could bring access and greater visibility across all the corporate bank accounts. It could also enable greater security and control, and give a complete picture of all these activities from beginning to end.

23.4
Mobile banking

A major key development in innovation for corporate treasurers is mobile including mobile banking. Wireless technology including iPhone, iPad and internet is changing the way corporates conduct business. Mobile banking enables banks and other financial service providers to offer more complex and sophisticated services to corporate treasurers via their mobile devices. It allows them to offer constant access to business-critical applications and data. In the context of a corporate treasurer, this translates to leveraging the power of mobile technologies to help a treasurer in their day-to-day operations and decisions.

23.4.1 MOBILE OFFERINGS

Although corporate treasurers have limited their adoption of corporate mobile banking solutions, their concerns about cyber fraud are encouraging notable advances in corporate mobile banking platforms and treasury management systems.

Banks are increasingly looking to offer targeted services to corporate treasury users via their mobile devices. These solutions are already in use for activities such as accessing reports and approving transactions through both bank systems and TMS. Other use cases are mobile-enabled consolidated dashboards and reports of real-time data around payments status, transactions, global cash positions, liquidity status and risk exposure, which enable and equip a corporate treasurer to make data-based decisions in real time and on the go. Existing service providers are broadening their offerings with additions such as tools to manage letters of credit and foreign exchange.

23.4.2 MOBILE BANKING PLATFORMS

Banks are now offering online platforms for executing various treasury transactions by integrating multiple services through a single channel, resulting in sophisticated integrated systems. Treasurers should seek out cash platforms that combine powerful, proactive analytic and multi-currency transacting capabilities with cross-bank decision tools, ERP-enabled analytics and visualisations to optimise cash, manage credit and market risk, and to maximise finance performance.

23.4.3 MULTI-BANK PLATFORMS

Meanwhile, other innovations, such as cross-bank bidding platforms, now enable corporates to let banks compete against one another in order to secure transaction services at better rates. Specialist technology companies are entering the transaction services space, offering their own platforms for corporate transactions – often faster and cheaper than previously available equivalents.

We are also starting to see some digital multi-bank platforms come to the market from independent providers so that treasurers with several bank relationships can manage them all from a single app or portal. As a reaction, a growing number of banks are now offering a comprehensive overview of all third-party bank account balances through a mobile application.

23.4.4 MOBILE CHANNELS

In the coming years, there will be considerable progress and innovations in the use of mobile phones and tablets for payments, cash, treasury and working capital. The future may see the mobile channel quickly emerge as the global channel of choice to meet certain control functions, allowing treasurers to manage liquidity more effectively and streamline their working capital cycles.

23.4.5   BENEFITS

The mobile channel offers huge promise as a way of enabling treasurers to remotely carry out complex and important operations that they may otherwise only be able to realise within limited environments. Mobile banking allows the consumption of time-critical information remotely and on demand – whether this is instantaneous access to balance information, status updates on the outcome of major financial transactions or alerts that enable decision-makers to affect corporate decisions.

Mobile access is important for internationally-oriented firms, which hold bank accounts in different countries and in a number of different national banks. Especially for treasurers on the go, being able to carry out treasury functions on a mobile device offers a great benefit in terms of convenience. Mobile technology provides treasurers with the ability to directly approve financial transactions, such as foreign exchange trading or wires, including those requiring multiple signatories. Approvals are probably the most important thing for banks to provide via a mobile corporate treasury app.

23.5
Cloud and SaaS

Another innovative development is the move in corporate treasury from locally installed systems to cloud-based applications. Cloud is an innovative concept that is changing the way IT is consumed. It works based on a 'sharing' model where IT services and solutions are delivered in a cost-effective manner. Cloud-based solutions are hosted outside of the corporate network, with all data stored and managed by the vendor in the cloud.

Cloud computing is an opportunity for treasury functions to leverage highly effective business solutions at low cost while adding more value to their businesses. Cloud addresses existing challenges by bringing optimisation through IT while cutting costs and freeing up management time for core business, i.e. treasury management.

23.5.1   CLOUD-BASED SOLUTIONS

Many professional service providers have been developing cloud-driven business solutions. These include cloud-enabled interfaces offering integration of multiple functions at various business layers: single view or workflow requiring much less investment; automatic reconciliation between the G/L and the bank statement; the ability to automatically generate reports and graphs based on data and automatic calculations.

23.5.2 SAAS OR SOFTWARE-AS-A-SERVICE

The cloud revolution is triggering increased demand among corporate treasurers for financial treasury management software-as-a-service (or SaaS) models. A growing number of vendors are offering cloud-based treasury management technology solutions for everyday decision-making around cash management, liquidity management, bank account management and financial risk management. Treasurers can now access more advanced tools without putting strain on internal sources.

These SaaS platform capabilities enable treasuries to improve the usability, flexibility and speed with which corporate treasurers can manage their cash, payments, risk and accounting. They also include functionality developed for various market needs, including integration tools with bank systems. This cloud-based software improves decision-making, control and security in corporate treasury and accounting operations.

Why corporate treasurers are moving to cloud-based systems

Scalability
Cloud software has the capacity to easily enable changes in size or scale, and to be deployed globally, over the internet, without subjecting the client to significant incremental cost increases or technical effort.

Simplicity
Standardised deployments, functionality and training help to simplify the initial implementation process and upgrades for ongoing use of the cloud solution for users.

Cost
The combination of subscription-based pricing and avoidance of upgrade costs, due to automated upgrade processes within cloud deployments, significantly reduces both one-time and ongoing costs for clients.

Visibility
Cloud computing provides management with an instant real-time cash overview of the organisation and guarantees information completeness (security and reliability). Management can have immediate access to the company's data from anywhere on all mobile devices.

Maintenance
Hosted ownership by the cloud provider helps minimise the IT resources needed to maintain all technical aspects of the solution and to streamline the installation and upgrade process.

23.5.3 CLOUD-BASED TMS

There is a strong uptake of cloud-based treasury management systems (TMS). These TMS systems provide treasuries with highly specialised technology, allowing for more flexibility in terms of features and access. Corporate treasurers can now go to the cloud for SaaS-based TMS solutions that offer complete ERP and bank function connectivity. These TMS typically cover the basic requirements of professional financial risk management, such as liquidity overview and planning, ensuring solvency, payment-related functions, hedging currency risk etc.

At the other end of the spectrum, banks are expanding on their ability to provide bank-agnostic offerings through cloud-based preparation and data aggregation.

23.6
Big data and analytics

A fourth key innovative development is big data and analytics. It is crucial that corporates embrace big data, advanced business intelligence and predictable analytics to keep their company agile, competitive and profitable. These days, corporate treasuries must cope with huge volumes of data that come from different sources in various formats. These data are becoming an increasingly valuable asset. Barriers to meaningful business analytics may arise from existing technology, resources and processes. Overlapping data sources and contradictory data versions often exist both within and outside the company.

23.6.1 STRUCTURED BIG DATA

With the large and disparate volumes of data being created, innovative and scalable technology is needed to collect, host and analytically process it. The treasurer needs to have accurate data/information around payment statuses and cash positions.

Treasurers are therefore looking for solutions that simplify the ability to acquire data from internal systems and external providers (including banks), as well as for software that provides aggregated data in a consistent, normalised industry format for loading into internal databases and other applications (e.g. financial and regulatory reporting systems).

23.6.2 DATA ANALYTICS

For the treasurer, however, the true benefits of being able to optimise liquidity positions in real-time come alive through the analytical tools being fostered by digitisation. There is increasing demand among corporate treasurers for advanced real-time business intelligence solutions and artificial intelligence capabilities to make effective use of these data.

Data analysis could offer significant value across a variety of financial and non-financial activities. It could derive useful insights for improved business operations and performance. And it could help corporate treasurers to get a much better, more integrated and more thorough analysis of liquidity, risk exposures, treasury performance and other treasury activities. Analysing these data may offer rich insights into the field of treasury management, such as asset and liability management, hedging of interest rate and foreign exchange risk, cash management, working capital management and compliance. These may enable the production of useful decision-making information for receivables, payables, FX options, exposure management and a host of transaction banking-based interactions.

This should enable treasurers to pre-empt (risky) situations and take preventive action, or draw actionable insights about liquidity and risk, and to be empowered to make decisions around strategic and operational parameters like investments, forex hedges, bank accounts, etc. Data analytics could also strengthen the CFO's ability to drive strategic decision-making and investment planning.

Leveraging big data and analytics in corporate treasury

Asset and liability management
Treasurers can leverage data related to foreign exchange, market value assumptions, mark-to-market (M2M), bank data, interest rate risk management and fund transfer pricing, balance sheet strategy and multi-factor behaviour models for consolidation.

Hedging of interest rate risk and FX risk
Treasurers can consult economic fundamentals for each country, and analyse currencies to determine the necessary time to hedge. Analytics allows a more efficient process to run simulations to test the effectiveness of hedges and to price complex derivatives.

Cash management
Treasurers can run detailed transaction analysis to institute cash culture programmes, compress payment terms, accelerate initial customer contact for collections and consolidate the number of collection paths.

23.6.3 BANK OFFERINGS

Corporates could also benefit from banks providing big data analysis that is built into established payment services. This would offer insights based on transaction data and other relevant material. These services could easily be integrated into existing arrangements. Many banks are looking to draw upon the large quantities of data already available to them to provide big data services to their clients. And banks are increasingly incorporating advanced analytics into their digital portals, providing corporate treasurers with an added layer of information that is only possible through digitisation – including reporting functionality. A majority of the effort has gone into beefing up most analytical capabilities, improving dashboards and providing better graphics and other visualisation tools. For example, treasury clients can receive big data analysis based on their regular transaction data – highlighting areas of risk concentration and other insights. This should allow them to take preventive actions.

Initiatives like the Common Global Implementation (CGI) allow corporates to collect information from their financial partners that is presented in the same way. This gives them access to the information at the level of detail they need and at the right time so they can make well-founded decisions about their global position.

23.7
Blockchain and distributed ledger technology (DLT)

Blockchain and distributed ledger technology are two very recent innovations that are probably among the most disruptive since the emergence of the internet. Blockchain has special qualities that makes it better than traditional databases: it is trusted, decentralised, shared, secure and automated. As a result, blockchain may fundamentally change the way corporate treasurers operate. Use cases of blockchain for corporate treasuries can be found in international payments, trade finance, supply chain finance, FX and data management & reconciliation.

Main characteristics of blockchain

Trusted
the distributed nature of the network requires computer servers to reach consensus, which allows for transactions to occur between unknown parties in a trusted way.

Decentralised
Blockchain allows for direct trade with any counterparty in a secure, fast and cost-effective way, without making use of a central authority or third party intermediaries (middlemen) to approve transactions and set rules.

Shared
Servers or nodes maintain the entries (known as blocks) and every node sees the transaction data stored in the blocks when created. Each counterparty has its own copy of the same ledger. It allows anyone to obtain an accurate view.

Secure
The database is built to be immutable and irreversible, which means that there is inherent security. Posts to the ledger cannot be revised or altered. The information is tamper-proof and visible for all parties involved.

Automated
Software is used to generate and record information about the transaction (when it took place, and the chronological order of all transactions). This results in a chain of information, stored in a so-called block – hence the name blockchain.

23.7.1   USE CASES

Cross-border payments in particular will become easier for banks to offer. Blockchain could also be integrated into a corporate supply chain. Trade finance may become a predominantly electronic business, as blockchain may enter the international supply chain. In addition to executing supply chain best practices, treasurers who use blockchain will have the potential ability to execute invoice discounting programmes. This, in turn, will help suppliers and customers as it will compel companies pay their invoices much faster.

Blockchain use cases in corporate treasury

International payments
Settlement time for international payments is shortened, transactions are carried out faster and the risk of fraud is reduced.

Trade finance
All parties – including banks, trading houses, seller and buyer, customer, freight forwarders – are able to see when goods have been shipped before releasing funds.

Data management & reconciliation
Providing rule-based standards on data could enhance the quality and auditability of any transaction. Blockchain can also make reconciliation of complex data easier and reporting more efficient, since a common ledger is applied.

FIGURE 23.1   BLOCKCHAIN AND PAYMENTS

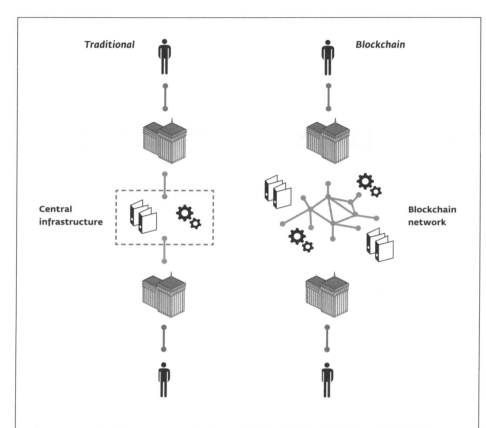

	Purpose	In traditional networks	In blockchain networks
Front-end	Interaction with end-user (untouched by blockchain technology)	Not affected: remains the same	Not affected: remains the same
Messaging	Technical connectivity with the network	Through central infrastructure	Peer-to-peer
Processing	Execution of transactions	▸ Centrally ▸ Batch or per transaction	▸ Decentral ▸ In 'blocks'
Ledger	Keeps track of participants' balances	▸ Central ▸ Closed (one trusted party)	▸ Decentral ▸ Public

FIGURE 23.2   BLOCKCHAIN AND TRADE FINANCE

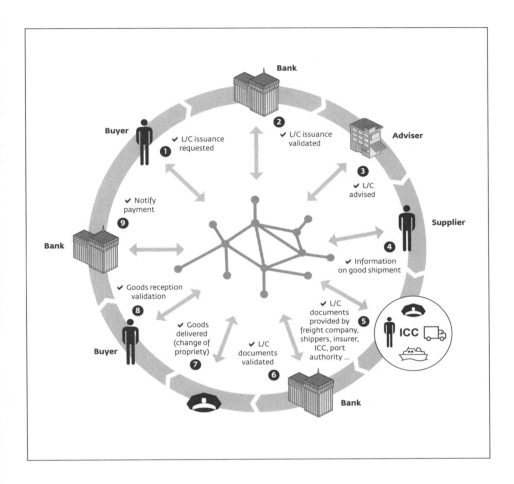

23.7.2   BENEFITS

Corporate use of blockchain will simplify corporate treasury operations and improve efficiency and security. Blockchain enables corporates to have real-time transparency with their customers, helping them to meet their payment terms and eliminating slack in the collection systems they currently use. Transactions will be quicker and cheaper, with the automatic creation of a full audit trial and easy push to straight-through processing. Reducing customer payment latency by even one or two days would increasingly improve the velocity of their cash.

23.8
Connectivity and integration challenges

Moving from manual to automated integration represents a major change in the way corporate treasurers work and has the potential to cut costs significantly and improve business efficiency. However, innovative changes on this scale will present significant challenges to the treasury community. Connectivity and integration will be key for the treasurer.

Corporates need to have a solution that automates their processes, from accessing and analysing bank data, to ensuring that data is correct and that solutions are integrated into ERP, investment and other cash management tools. Finding the right solution will be challenging, but the issue can be overcome with the right support.

23.8.1   SINGLE CHANNEL

The principle concern is working out the best way to integrate all these new services, innovation tools, and platforms through a single channel, into the corporate's cash management systems and processes while ensuring they maintain control over the company's data.

Automated channels in particular will usher in a new era of better integration for the information flowing from businesses to banks (and vice versa), and on to the likes of smartphones and tablet devices.

23.8.2   INTEGRATION TOOLS

Corporate connectivity continues to make steady progress regionally, using a business process integration approach to optimise the multistep process of service integration for payment instructions and entity collaboration. It is therefore wise to closely investigate corporate-to-bank integration.

The type of integration and related tools can take on different forms, including standard file feeds, improved APIs and more or less transparent vendor-supported integrated processes.

23.8.3   BANKS AND CONNECTIVITY

As a result of demand for cloud-based solutions, banks are demonstrating increased flexibility when it comes to connectivity solutions for corporate customers. It is now easier for corporate customers to take information in an automated way, and integrate it, with the banks handling the lion's share of this activity.

Banks are no longer dictating protocol, format or security procedures. Instead, they are looking at the customer environment and the technology investment that has already been made, and integrating with them accordingly. This enables (also smaller) corporates to take advantage of automated solutions, applying information to internal systems and getting the visibility needed to make mission-critical decisions.

Part H

Best Practices

Chapter 24

Cash Management Structures

A Roadmap for Centralisation

24 Cash Management Structures
A Roadmap for Centralisation

24.1
Introduction

In response to further globalisation, ongoing digitalisation and a strong focus on cost reduction, companies are taking steps to standardise and centralise their cash management operations through centralised cash management solutions and the set-up of payment factories, in-house banks and/or shared service centres.

In this chapter, we will take a closer look at international cash management structures and how they developed over time. First, we will review the key trends and developments behind this trend. For example, what are the main drivers for centralising liquidity and transaction processing and what steps are companies taking towards full consolidation? Next, we will provide a typical roadmap for companies to rationalise and centralise their cash management operations. We will discuss the most common structures and the way in which companies can move to the next stage of improvement. We will also explain the extent to which such structures can be applied in the different geographical regions of the world.

It is imperative that the cash management solutions and functions covered in this book be part of an integrated and holistic approach. Each company needs to select an operating cash management model that best fits within its ambitions, the maturity of the organisation and the infrastructure. As we will see, there are a wide variety of operating models that can differ according to the respective geographic scope, management philosophy or market practice. Therefore, there is no right or wrong structure.

24.2
Transformation of cash management

For a long time, companies traditionally operated their cash management on an in-country basis only. The local entities held accounts with a local bank – often selected by the local management – in the country of domicile. Every country was responsible for managing its own liquidity position and transaction processes. Since the 1980s, large companies have been starting to centralise funding and investment operations. In Europe, this development has gained substantial momentum since the introduction of the euro in 1999. The launch of the single currency has enabled large network banks in Europe to introduce cross-border cash pooling, delivering a single daily cash balance across multiple euro countries. In 2008, when the first components of the Single Euro Payments Area (SEPA) went live, and in 2009, when the Payment Services Directive (PSD) contributed to the legal basis for SEPA, further benefits could be achieved by the harmonisation and standardisation of the payment landscape in the SEPA area.

The financial crisis of 2008 increased the focus on the need for centralisation. As markets and banks struggled under unprecedented stress levels, companies realised that visibility of and control over liquidity are instrumental. Almost overnight, the availability of external short-term liquidity/funding, which was rarely an issue for healthy companies before this crisis, changed dramatically. The freeing up of internal cash became as important as the control over and access to the company's balances. The economic crisis that followed the financial crisis increased the pressure on the corporate treasury departments to show their added value in terms of their overall contribution to the company's general financial objectives. All of these trends accelerated the need for a more sophisticated treasury organisation.

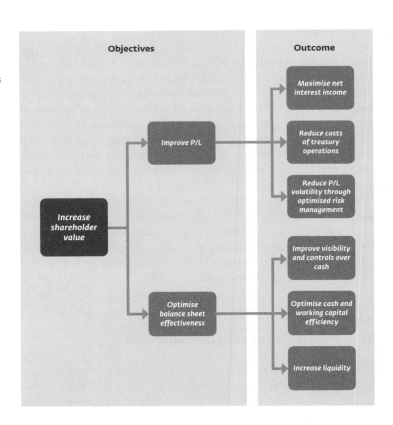

FIGURE 24.1 TREASURY OBJECTIVES AND OUTCOMES

In the years following the crisis, the cash management services provider landscape started to change. On the one hand, the international banks (the traditional providers of international cash management services) withdrew their operations from certain markets or stopped specific business activities altogether. This was largely driven by the introduction of Basel

III-related regulations, which make certain cash management solutions less attractive for banks (please also see chapter 22). On the other hand, new providers entered the cash management arena. These companies, often referred to as FinTechs, started providing services that fully leveraged the fast pace of digitalisation and the latest technology developments. They started competing directly with the banks, although most of them only offer certain services, while banks offer the full spectrum. Lower costs, user-friendly interfaces and quick implementations are differentiators of such service providers. Therefore, the current cash management service providers landscape has become a mixture of the traditional network banks and non-bank service providers.

24.2.1 CENTRALISATION OF LIQUIDITY MANAGEMENT

Many large companies have centralised their liquidity operations using a phased approach. Initially, a number of treasury responsibilities are centralised at country level, followed by centralisation on a regional and even a global level. Below (figure 24.2), we show a typical example of a migration path to full centralisation of liquidity operations that applies to most large companies.

FIGURE 24.2   MIGRATION PATH TO CENTRALISED LIQUIDITY MANAGEMENT

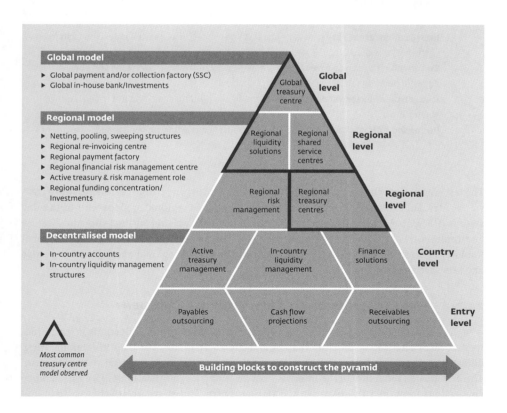

The first responsibilities that are often centralised in a multinational company are long-term funding and corporate finance. These are part of the minimum set of centralised treasury responsibilities – even for decentralised companies. Between 1980 and 2000, companies started centralising their liquidity operations. However, this was often limited to short-term inter-company loans and financial risk management.

Operating companies with excess cash were invited to place these balances with a regional treasury centre. Operating companies in need of cash could borrow funds from the centre against a favourable rate compared to what they would pay in their local market. In this initial stage of centralisation, subsidiaries were often allowed to continue their liquidity operations with local banks in the country of domicile. However, the cash pooling and netting centre was usually in a good position to compete effectively with the external banks due to internal matching of cash positions, centralised expertise and economies of scale. Companies started to concentrate their daily balances and centralise all investment and funding activity. By using automated cross-border cash pooling, companies were able to transfer all liquidity at a low cost into a regional treasury centre while still giving full flexibility to the local entities for the execution of day-to-day transactions. The main benefits of liquidity centralisation are summarised in the below table.

Key benefits of liquidity centralisation
– **Improved interest rates:** cash deficits can be funded internally using excess cash from cash-rich subsidiaries
– **Enhanced risk management:** this is achieved by centralised oversight and control over liquidity positions
– **Reduction of external debt:** this leads to lower funding costs and improved balance sheet ratios
– **Increased efficiencies:** these include yield enhancements from centralised investments

The last step in liquidity centralisation is to pool cash in all convertible currencies into a treasury centre. For example, by making use of fully automated regional or global end-of-the-day sweeps (the global sweeps are also known as 'follow-the-sun' and 'against-the-sun' sweeps) and multi-currency liquidity overlay structures. The benefits of such a regional or global liquidity centre will need to be balanced against the loss of regional and/or local expertise and access to the local markets.

24.2.2 CENTRALISATION OF CASH FLOW MANAGEMENT

A logical first step for optimisation of international payments and collections is the implementation of a netting system (see chapter 6, section 6.4). In the case of multi-lateral netting, all inter-company payments and receipts are processed through a central netting system. This results in a reduction of the internal cash flows and a centralisation of foreign currency conversions from the subsidiaries to the netting centre. This step is relatively easy to implement as it does not require a fundamental change of transaction processes. A possible next step – which is also relatively straightforward to implement – is to centralise all third-party payments and collections in non-domestic currencies into a multi-currency centre. In such a structure, the operating companies will still initiate their own payment instructions and process their own collections. However, all transactions are now routed through centralised multi-currency accounts that are often held in one of the financial centres (such as London, Amsterdam or Singapore). The company could negotiate more competitive rates with a single bank. Since all cash balances are centralised, the FX management and the off-setting of balances across currencies can be achieved relatively easily.

FIGURE 24.3 A CENTRALISATION JOURNEY

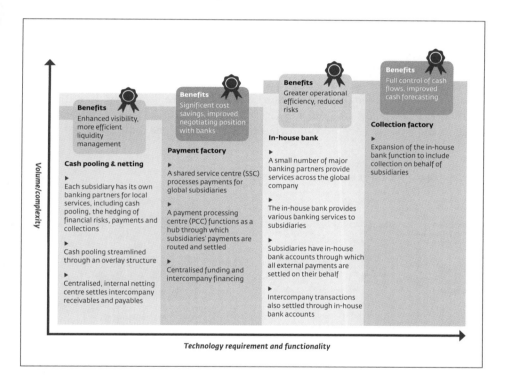

To create additional value for a company – in line with the key performance indicator for treasury as set out in figure 24.1 – the company can consider setting up a payment factory, in-house bank or a collection factory (see figure 24.3). These centralised structures can be challenging to implement and will therefore require considerable project resources and proper investments in dedicated resources, IT infrastructure and project management.

FIGURE 24.4   EXAMPLE OF A PAYMENT FACTORY

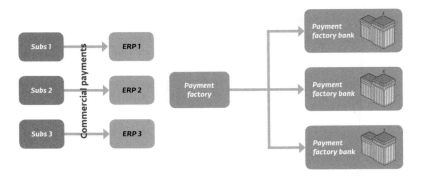

A payment factory (see figure 24.4) is a centralised entity that collects all outgoing payment instructions from subsidiaries, processes inter-company transactions in-house and sends one batch of payment instructions to the bank(s) through a single centralised electronic interface. The payments will be executed in the name of the centralised entity, on behalf of the operating or local companies. These are called payments on behalf of (POBO). The main benefits of a POBO model are a simplified bank account structure (no need to maintain local accounts and local currency pools) and a much better visibility and control over cash.

FIGURE 24.5   EXAMPLE OF AN IN-HOUSE BANK

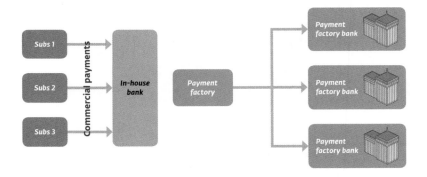

An in-house bank (see figure 24.5) manages the settlement of inter-company transactions on the in-house account and provides the subsidiaries with in-house account statements as a confirmation of the movements on those accounts – in the same way that an external bank would. All internal and external transactions in the group can be done through the in-house bank, which manages all intercompany relations between treasury and subsidiaries.

A collection factory could be seen as the mirror image of a payment factory. If the collection factory centralises the receivables on behalf of the operational entities, this scheme is referred to as collections on behalf of (COBO). Setting up a COBO structure can be very challenging and these challenges could easily outweigh the benefits. From an operational point of view, it is important to understand whether local collection instruments can be cleared from the centralised collection factory. Many local collections need to be cleared locally (i.e. from a bank account held in the local country). COBO could also add complexity with respect to the reconciliation process (i.e. the central collection account should show sufficient information in order to be able to identify the original creditor).

In addition to these operational challenges, a treasurer could also face legal and regulatory constraints. It is, for example, not always permitted to delegate the local collections to the in-house bank in a certain jurisdiction. It is therefore recommended that a country-by-country assessment be performed to determine the feasibility of a COBO scheme. The central treasury department should investigate whether it is feasible, efficient and cost-effective to clear local payments instruments from the jurisdiction in which the collection factory is set up. For further legal considerations, see chapter 20.

The further a company is on the road to centralisation, the more sophisticated its technology should be. For example, a payment and/or a collection factory can only be set up if a company has an internal communication network in place for exchanging payment and collection data (such as an enterprise resource planning (ERP) system). The benefits are the provision of centralised information for the treasury and a reduction in operating costs resulting from the decreased workload for the operating companies, as well as lower transaction fees and operating costs as a result of a single interface with the banks and other service providers.

FIGURE 24.6   TECHNICAL INFRASTRUCTURE FOR PAYMENT FACTORY/ COLLECTION FACTORY (SSC)

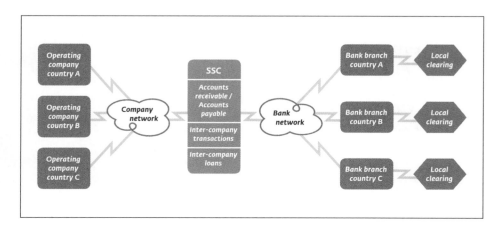

Setting up such a centralised treasury facility represents a fundamental change for a company's internal processes. Not only are payment and collection instructions centralised but all the end-to-end accounts payable (AP) processes and accounts receivable (AR) processes are also taken into account. More importantly, these processes are often rationalised and harmonised to ensure the highest possible efficiency. By separating the business support processes and consolidating them into a dedicated shared service centre (SSC) which can be measured on its performance, efficiencies can be increased substantially. Experience has shown that companies are able to reduce overall transaction costs by 50% thanks to reduced staff levels and improved economies due to the better negotiating position with the service providers.

Qualitative and quantitative benefits

Implementation payment/collection factory
- No cross-border payments/collections
- Reduction of currency payments/collections from/to local accounts
- Reduction of payment/collection transactions, dates, methods etc.

Implementation in-house bank
- Simplification of intercompany netting process
- Separate netting system removed
- Reduction of bank relationships and bank accounts

Process improvements
- Automated process for internal hedges (transaction exposure < 12 months) based on forecast
- Confirmations on internal deals based on workflow

Data quality improvements
- Cash flow forecast based on actual data
- Variance analysis to improve forecast accuracy
- Integration of financial and commercial flow
- Improved counterparty exposure information

IT costs
- Significant reduction of number of treasury related applications and interfaces
- Reduced dependency on end-user computing applications
- Bank connectivity costs

24.3
A roadmap for centralisation

So far, we have discussed a number of the liquidity-driven and cash-flow-driven operating models for companies to centralise cash management on a regional level. In reality, the two models are often combined or a liquidity model evolves into a broader model that includes transaction processing.

An operating model is a structure for the company's cash management that defines who is responsible for specific functions such as bank relationship management, liquidity management, cash flow forecasting, payment initiation or accounts receivable (AR) and accounts payable (AP) management. This structure should be supported by an infrastructure that includes a current account structure, typically one or more bank relationships and the electronic interfaces between the entities of the company and the transaction service providers.

Specific features of each operating model
– Allocation of financial responsibilities
– One or more bank relationships
– Current account structure
– Data exchange between operating companies, cash management centre and the service providers

Figure 24.7 provides a roadmap to optimise international cash management with a comprehensive overview of the operating models companies are currently using. We distinguish between four different types of operating models:

- In-country models
- Regional liquidity-driven models
- Regional cash-flow-driven models
- Global models

We have indicated how companies can migrate from one model to another. For example, by moving from in-country structures to a regional liquidity model or from a regional liquidity structure to a regional cash flow structure. In many cases, we see companies in Europe centralising liquidity before they start centralising cash flows. This is mainly because of the deregulated capital environment within the EU and the highly efficient euro cross-border cash pooling services available from service providers in that region.

Automated cash pooling can be implemented rather quickly and, as a result, interest benefits can soon be achieved against relatively low costs. Liquidity centralisation is often seen as a 'quick win'. The benefits of cash flow centralisation can be higher – particularly when establishing a payment factory – but implementation can take over a year with significant project and IT costs. In regions such as Asia, where in some countries cross-border capital transfers are restricted by exchange control regulations, regional transaction centres are often established first with liquidity centralisation following at a later stage. However, they are frequently more limited in scope and functions compared to their European counterparts because of the restrictions and controls present in several countries in the region.

FIGURE 24.7   INTERNATIONAL CASH MANAGEMENT ROAD MAP

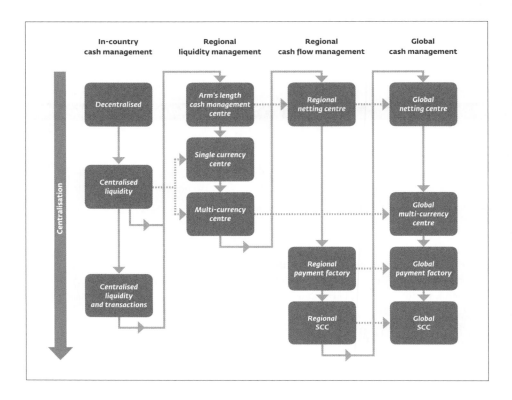

As illustrated by figure 24.7, companies can move vertically, to increase the level of central-isation, or horizontally, by extending the model geographically. How companies migrate in practice is dependent upon what is allowed from a regulatory perspective and the potential benefits the company can achieve in comparison with the costs of implementation and the costs of running the cash management centre. The process of centralising treasury func-tions, from an initial feasibility review and benefit assessment, to the actual migration of the local functions into the new central treasury function, is a complex process. This requires proper project management and buy-in from all internal stakeholders, including the local operating companies. See figure 24.8 for an example of a project plan.

FIGURE 24.8   EXAMPLE PROJECT PLAN

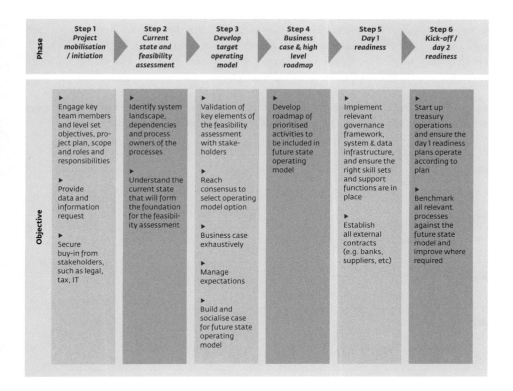

24.4
The role of the service providers

When choosing a certain operating model, a company must also choose the provider it will involve to run the structure. Should it be a single bank with local branches in the region that handles all cash management activities, several banks working alongside each other or a combination of a bank and a bank-independent service provider.

Traditionally, cash and liquidity management services were typically facilitated by the company's key banking partners (i.e. the most important lenders under the credit facility agreement). For in-country cash management, companies have historically been using local banks because they could offer local working capital funding and a complete array of domestic transaction services. When moving into the next phase of centralisation – regional liquidity management – one bank was frequently selected for the concentration of centralised liquidity.

Nowadays, with greater levels of standardisation and harmonisation (especially in Europe), local instruments are less important and local banks are less needed. For the centralisation of daily balances, most companies still involve pan-regional network banks, which operate as an 'overlay' on top of the local banks. The network bank has branches in all the countries and runs local 'overlay accounts' where all cash from local bank accounts is concentrated and subsequently swept into the master account maintained in the regional centre. Some cash management 'boutique' banks only offer a cash management overlay. New service providers frequently target specific parts of the cash management business. For example, foreign exchange, reporting/cash flow forecasting or payments.

Below, we have indicated how cash management services can be divided between the primary service provider and the other service provider that supports the cash management centre.

Operating model	Role of primary service provider	Role of other transaction service providers
Netting centre	Central settlement of accounts Netting system Optional: netting execution	Local service provider for all transactions
Single currency centre	Central accounts and cash pooling Local overlay accounts	Local service provider for all transactions
Multi-currency centre	Central accounts and cash pooling Local overlay accounts Optional: cross-border transactions	Local service provider for (local) transactions
Payment factory (through an SSC)	Central accounts and cash pooling Local overlay accounts All outgoing payments Single electronic interface	Local service provider for all collections and some local payments
Payments & collection factory (through an SSC)	Central accounts and cash pooling Local overlay accounts All incoming collections Single electronic interface	Local service provider only for cash payments and receipts that cannot be processed centrally

24.5
Centralisation strategies

Companies operating in one region and expanding into another have a number of options to improve cash management practices. Let us take the example of a large European company with a treasury centre in Europe and expanding business in the Americas and Asia. The treasury centre is responsible for group-wide long-term funding and FX management, for running a global netting system and the daily management of all liquidity positions in

Europe. How should they continue on the path of rationalisation and centralisation? They can choose among the following:

- *Option 1:* centralise the transaction processes in a European transaction centre
- *Option 2:* set up regional treasury centres in the Americas and Asia
- *Option 3:* consolidate liquidity from all regions into the European treasury centre

FIGURE 24.9   POPULAR TREASURY LOCATIONS FOR CENTRALISATION

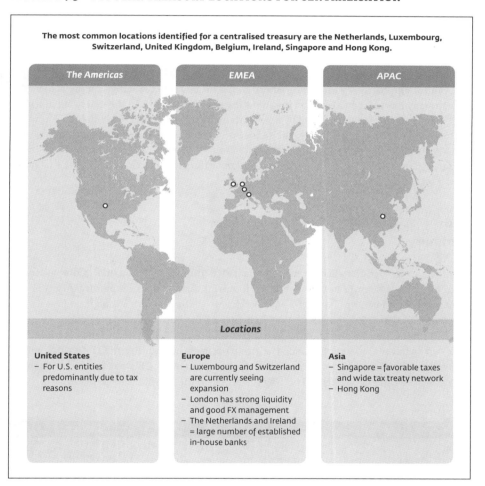

The most common locations identified for a centralised treasury are the Netherlands, Luxembourg, Switzerland, United Kingdom, Belgium, Ireland, Singapore and Hong Kong.

The Americas	EMEA	APAC

Locations

United States	Europe	Asia
– For U.S. entities predominantly due to tax reasons	– Luxembourg and Switzerland are currently seeing expansion – London has strong liquidity and good FX management – The Netherlands and Ireland = large number of established in-house banks	– Singapore = favorable taxes and wide tax treaty network – Hong Kong

As a number of considerations apply, we will focus on some of the main aspects.

Option 1. Setting up a European payment and collection factory requires considerable time and resources but the potential benefits can be tremendous. The savings will be bigger in cases where the current local transaction processes are inefficient with a low degree of straight-through processing. If the company already has a single ERP system in Europe, this will provide a basis to implement a payment and collection factory within a shorter time frame.

Option 2. A key consideration is whether there is already a treasury infrastructure in the Americas and Asia, or whether the cash management centre has to be built from scratch. The latter would require considerable time and investment. However, the benefits can be significant if the current local liquidity operations are inefficient with large opportunity costs due to unmatched balances and uncompetitive margins. Other questions include whether excess cash can be centralised or whether most liquidity is held in regulated countries, and whether the company has substantial FX balances – such as USD and EUR balances in Asia – or mainly local currency balances.

Option 3. Global consolidation should be considered when the company has large excess balances in foreign regions while being 'short' in the home region. Savings can be achieved if the company has external debt and is generating substantial cash in the emerging markets. The balance sheet can be improved by up-streaming cash and paying down debt. It is important to understand what capabilities the service providers have to sweep balances across time zones without losing value days and/or information. In addition, if the company is willing to use one global overlay bank, on top of the local or regional banks, this could have a negative impact on the local and regional relationships.

24.6
Summary

There is no 'one-size-fits-all' cash management structure for all companies. Companies differ in terms of their core business models, footprint, financial structure, organisation and management philosophy. Therefore, each will have to define its own strategic and cash management plan that offers the greatest net benefits and fits into the company's corporate strategy. It is important that the chosen approach is fully supported by senior management and reviewed by internal stakeholders such as group tax, legal accounting and IT. Drafting a business case and performing proper assessment is recommended. This will assist the company in making the right decisions and getting the buy-in of the internal stakeholders.

Conclusion

- Major efficiencies can be achieved by the centralisation and rationalisation of cash management operations across multiple countries or regions
- There is a wide variety of operating models from which companies can choose
- Regions differ in terms of restrictions and regulations
- Companies should define a clear strategy and plan for centralisation that is aligned with the underlying operating model, in order to get buy-in from all internal stakeholders

Chapter 25

Case Studies

25 Case Studies

25.1
Introduction

In this chapter we will discuss several illustrative cases of how various companies in different parts of the world have optimised their international cash management.

25.2
Centralisation: horizontal and vertical

As described in chapter 24, companies can centralise vertically to increase the level of centralisation, for instance per region or per business unit. However, they can also centralise horizontally, for instance by extending the model geographically. How companies migrate in practice depends on the potential benefits they can achieve in comparison with the costs of implementation and the costs of running the cash management centre.

Regional centralisation
Take the example of an IT company that is selling software to wholesale customers in more than 100 countries. The company is cash-rich and has a low net debt. It has a regional centralisation and because it wants to seize investment opportunities as they occur, including for tax reasons, the company maintains sizable cash balances in some regions. The cash balances also ensure liquidity at all times. Up-streaming of cash only occurs when cash levels exceed a certain threshold. Although some regions/currencies are currently in a low interest rate environment, the company has managed to negotiate competitive interest rates to keep credit balances on its bank accounts. Excess positions above the prescribed threshold are lent to corporate treasury at 'arm's length' rates. The company has also set up regional SSCs for all daily recurring routine functions as well as a global netting centre to optimise all inter-company cash flows.

Integrate horizontally
In another example, a global manufacturer of consumer goods has extensive external debt, used to fund production and product innovations. The company generates substantial cash in most countries where it sells and that cash is transferred daily into regional multi-currency centres (to the extent that it is legally allowed) in order to reduce external debt. After having established the multi-currency centres, the company has begun streamlining transaction processing and working capital operations, and centralising these into regional SSCs. As a next step, the regional SSCs have been integrated into one global supply chain process.

25.3
Global treasury centre

25.3.1   THE COMPANY

Our first case is a manufacturer of consumer goods in the personal care, cleaning and food sectors. The company is listed on European and US stock exchanges and operates in more than 100 countries, trading in a large number of well-known brands. The company operates in all the major trading regions of the world – including the Americas, Western Europe, CEE, Asia and Africa. It has production facilities in 25 countries. More than 50% of sales are generated in emerging markets such as Latin America, CEE, Asia and Africa.

Previously, the treasury operations were executed by four regional treasury centres that serviced the business in Europe, Asia, Latin America and North America. These treasury centres were tasked with executing the centralised funding, risk and liquidity operations in each region. For cash flow management, the company was using approximately 400 different banks to carry out its day-to-day cash management. It had established electronic banking interfaces with many of the banks in order to exchange payment orders and transaction information.

The company believes that the large number of bank relations is resulting in inefficiencies. It also lacks central oversight. For example, the company does not have a central overview of all current accounts and account authorisations. The situation is causing concerns, in part because the company was recently the victim of fraudulent payments.

25.3.2   OBJECTIVES

The company's ambitious commercial target to double the overall business in eight years was the key driver to get all stakeholders on board to change the company's financial organisation worldwide. The key strategic financial elements were:

- Flexibility to enable future acquisitions to be financed from current cash flows
- Centralised access to equity and debt capital
- Sufficient resilience to economic and financial uncertainty
- Optimal weighted average cost of capital

To facilitate these goals, the company was already working to implement one global supply chain. The next step was streamlining and centralising its transaction processes as well as integrating its treasury operations into a single global model. To this end, the company decided to establish a global treasury centre. The main objectives of this decision included:

- Higher level of standardisation
- More robust organisation with a better back-up structure
- More efficient communications within treasury

- Better interaction with key stakeholders
- Improved career planning and retention within the finance teams

25.3.3   THE NEW STRUCTURE

Financial risk management

At an earlier stage, the company had already centralised the following risk management activities into four regional treasury centres:

- FX hedging
- Interest rate risk hedging
- Commodity hedging

All operating companies were obliged to cover FX transaction risks internally via the regional treasury centre. The centre would offset FX exposures where possible, and cover their net exposures with other regional centres or externally with the banks. Interest rate risk hedging, closely connected to the company's extensive external funding, was also conducted by the regional treasury centres as was commodity hedging, which is closely related to the sourcing of raw materials.

Advancing technology meant the company soon saw no reason to keep many operations in the region. It decided to centralise all FX and interest rate risk hedging into the global treasury centre in Europe. For tax reasons, that treasury centre is based in Switzerland. Only commodity hedging remained in the respective regions. The advantage of having knowledge of commodity markets available in the regions outweighed the advantage of global centralisation. In this case, the global treasury centre is also responsible for the monitoring of all exposures and counterparty limits.

Cash flow management

So far, all operating companies are now managing their own accounts payable and accounts receivable operations. However, several years ago the company started implementing a corporate-wide IT platform to harmonise and centralise operations. This ERP system was implemented in all regions and allowed the company to centralise all of its payments and collections into a regional payment factory.

As a first step towards a global treasury, the company selected one core transaction bank in each region, all with a footprint matching the company's footprint and with a strong product offering in the region. The company only kept local bank relations in place in highly exceptional (niche) cases, where the regional bank was unable to provide necessary services. At this stage, an electronic interface was set up with each regional transaction bank to facilitate all types of transactions (such as individual vendor payments, batch payments and payroll payments).

Region by region, the company started to move transactions from the local banks to the regional transaction bank. Based on a common platform with uniform future-proof message formats, the company was able to achieve straight-through processing and reduce operating costs. The new structure allowed the company to reduce the number of local transaction banks involved and achieve cost savings by removing local interfaces based on local message formats. In addition, the company was able to reduce the number of current accounts used, and increased the transparency of its active bank accounts. To prevent unwanted account openings in future, the company's new policy is that local entities can no longer open new bank accounts without approval from treasury. Treasury considers the necessity of opening a new account, in a specific currency, as well as the best location for the account.

Ultimately, the company's goal is to concentrate as much of its transaction volumes with the regional bank. After having completed the centralisation of its transaction flows, the company's next goal is to centralise the administrative processes into regional SSCs.

Liquidity management and funding

Although long-term and short-term funding was mostly centralised into the regional treasury centres, cash balances management and short-term investments were organised differently in each region. The many bank relationships in each country made it more difficult to identify all products used, and services and agreements in place. In Europe, the company was using centralised in-country cash pools for local currencies and one regional cash pool for euros. In other regions, it was still operating on a very decentralised basis (using many local banks). Because treasury did not have an overview of positions on all bank accounts across the globe, positions were also managed based on internal cash forecasts and internal reporting.

At this stage, the company decided to centralise all of its funding and liquidity management operations into the global treasury centre in Europe. The aim was to take advantage of the newly available cash pooling techniques and implement global cash pools in all main currencies in which the company traded.

The company decided to open one header account for each pool in the name of the treasury centre, per currency needed and in the appropriate currency centres (for instance CHF in Switzerland, CAD in Canada, HKD in Hong Kong). All entity accounts were included in the cash pool and the positions were concentrated to the header account. These were mainly domestic cash pools (with some exceptions), except for the eurozone where multiple EUR accounts were held in various countries. These EUR accounts concentrated their positions towards one EUR header account in the Netherlands. The header accounts, held with the regional relationship banks, would sweep into the global multi-currency (and multi-bank) overlay pool. This pool was established with one of the company's liquidity management banks, providing it with one global balance in each of its currencies with the possibility to offset different currencies into the functional currency. Some of the currencies for which the company had lower exposure appetite were converted into USD, EUR or GBP.

The day-to-day cash management, e.g. low-value ACH transactions, are managed at the transaction banking level with the selected regional transaction banks. The high-value treasury transactions are managed at the top level of the multi-currency global liquidity overlay, with the global liquidity overlay bank.

The new structure allows the company to combine its funding operations with daily cash balances management, as funds are being provided to the local operating companies through the global cash pools.

FIGURE 25.1   GLOBAL TREASURY CENTRE – LIQUIDITY STRUCTURE EXAMPLE

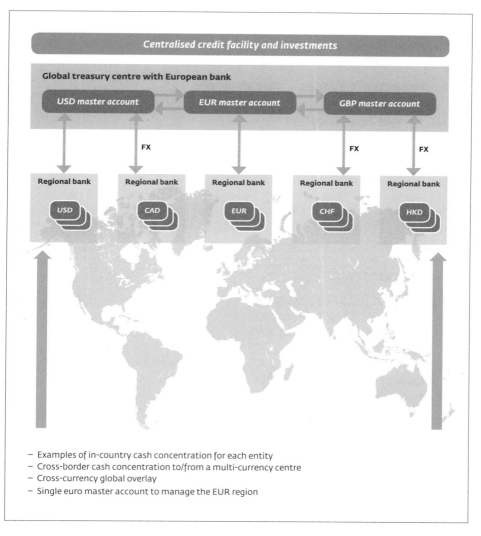

- Examples of in-country cash concentration for each entity
- Cross-border cash concentration to/from a multi-currency centre
- Cross-currency global overlay
- Single euro master account to manage the EUR region

25.3.4   THE RESULTS

Following implementation of the changes, the company has drastically reduced the number of bank relationships, bank interfaces and bank accounts, thus cutting banking transaction costs by an estimated 60%. It has also drastically reduced financial and operational risk by establishing a global structure for its liquidity operations and transactions that fit the business strategy and organisation, optimising visibility and availability of cash. Although the process of transaction centralisation is still ongoing, the company has already achieved significant benefits. It has increased control over balances, investments and daily transaction management and, at the same time, has achieved substantial cost reductions for cash flow management as well as liquidity operations. More than 80% of all third-party debt has been centralised as well as all of the inter-company loans and one-third of the external investments.

25.4
Treasury centre in Europe – case example

25.4.1   THE COMPANY

Our second case is a technology product and services company that is listed on a stock exchange in Asia. The company operates globally and has nearly 21,000 employees. In the recent past, the company has been very active and successful in acquiring new business. For this case example, we shall focus on its European business unit that is responsible for production, business-to-business sales and after-sales support to the distributors and dealer networks within Europe. Production is centralised in three major plants located in Germany, Poland and the UK.

25.4.2   OBJECTIVES

To reduce risk and optimise its cost of capital within two years, the European treasury organisation was assigned the task of decreasing the company's debt positions. Second, it was required to reduce cash management operating costs by increasing efficiencies.

Treasury's first and most important challenge was to achieve greater visibility and control over Europe-wide balances. The company had 27 operating subsidiaries across Europe – each with its own profit centre. There was a clear need to improve the existing in-country cash management approach. Following the market trend in Europe, the company decided to centralise its liquidity and cash flow management.

25.4.3   THE NEW STRUCTURE

Liquidity management
Whereas some subsidiaries were cash-rich, others required local bank financing. Key liquidity management priorities were the ability to gain central control over these cash positions and mobilise cash across the region. The company sought a liquidity management solution with a centralised approach to liquidity across the region.

The main goals were to:

- Increase the visibility and availability of cash: concentrate excess cash in Europe
- Reduce interest costs through better use of internal funds and reduce local external borrowing

- Reduce banking costs (including administrative costs, banking fees, system costs)
- Free up treasury staff

By being able to pay down debt in one part of the organisation using spare excess cash from elsewhere, the company could reduce idle cash balances and improve its working capital position. The company then adopted a regional multi-currency centre and needed a single bank with the geographical reach and automated, multi-currency solutions to help it achieve that goal. The company had formulated clear criteria for its regional cash management bank. Among the key factors that aided in the selection of the cash management bank were:

- A proven track record in international cash management solutions
- Proper implementation and services model to support both the local and central organisation
- Competitive pricing
- System capabilities and scalability
- Strategic advice on the solution and the regulatory environment

The regional currency centre was set up in the Netherlands and rolled out to the 19 major countries in Europe. The solution centralises cash positions automatically and uses cash balances to reduce external debt and minimise interest costs. Balances from the local subsidiaries are swept on a daily basis – via cross-border cash concentration – to the non-resident accounts held in a cross-currency notional overlay with full off-set. Every day, all positions are notionally converted into a single euro position and managed by central treasury. A single person is now managing the European-wide cash position, investing the excess cash via the central euro account in overnight money market instruments and paying down external debt on a quarterly basis. The company started off by incorporating its 11 largest currency positions. Other currencies are set to be included when volumes justify.

Although a regional bank has been selected and the number of local banks has been reduced significantly, the company has kept some of its local banks. The balances held at these banks are incorporated into the overlay structure through multi-bank cash concentration. This service generates an automatic request to transfer surplus funds from or to the local bank account and into or out of the centralised multi-currency centre. For efficiency reasons, the company has set minimum thresholds to ensure that sweeps are only triggered when economically justifiable.

A multi-currency credit facility is attached to the overlay account structure. If extra funds are required, the local companies can draw upon the centralised facility. The credit facility is available in any currency that is included in the overlay. Central treasury has established credit limits for each local entity.

FIGURE 25.2   TREASURY CENTRE IN EUROPE – LIQUIDITY STRUCTURE EXAMPLE

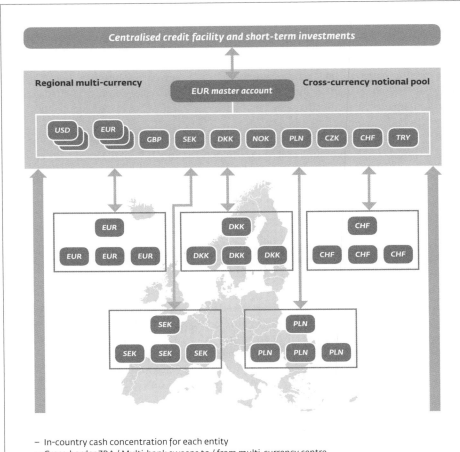

- In-country cash concentration for each entity
- Cross-border ZBA / Multi-bank sweeps to / from multi-currency centre
- Cross-currency overlay with mirror accounts per entity
- Single euro master account to manage the pool
- Short-term investments and pay down debt via the euro master account

Bank account structure with one regional bank
- Multi-currency overlay with in-country master accounts
- Cross-border sweeps for each legal entity to / from a centralised mirror or reference account (in the name of the regional treasury centre referencing the individual entity)

Multi-currency overlay structure
- Cross-currency notional pool based on full set-off without FX conversions
- 11 currencies already included (and ready for more)
- Working capital facility attached to overlay structure

Fully-automated cash concentration tools
- Cash concentration for all accounts held with the regional banks
- Multi-bank sweeping from local banks
- Flexible parameter setting to ensure efficient set-up
- Multi-currency overnight credit facility attached to the overlay structure

Cash flow management

In addition to liquidity centralisation in Europe, the company decided to increase efficiency by optimising its payment processes. To achieve this, it chose to set up a regional payment factory. The SEPA region enabled the use of uniform payment instruments, uniform formats and a simplified account structure for a considerable number of countries.

Thanks to its multi-currency centre – managed by the regional treasury team – the company optimised the availability of funds, making it a logical next step to establish a payment factory in the same location.

An integrated processing platform and secure online functionality helped the company build the payment factory and deliver the payments. After completing a pilot in three countries with relatively small business volumes, the company was able to migrate its remaining European territories to the new system within one month.

Key benefits of migrating to a payment factory

- Reduced internal costs
- Reduced bank costs due to lower prices for credit transfers and a reduction in pan-European bank accounts
- Improved transparency as a result of streamlined processes and bank account structure
- Fewer errors through improved back-office efficiencies
- Greater insight into transaction volumes and cost drivers

The implementation of both projects went relatively smoothly because of the support treasury received from senior management and the strong communication with all internal stakeholders. It took the company over seven months to roll out both the multi-currency centre and the regional payment factory. In order to win the buy-in of the local subsidiaries – an important factor in accelerating the efficiency gains of the new solutions – the company and the bank closely cooperated in educating and training the local staff.

Lessons learned from the implementation

1. **Early sign-off by tax and legal representatives is a prerequisite**
   Transfer pricing and withholding tax need to be addressed up front – there are as many legal requirements as countries in scope

2. **Ensure involvement of IT and operations**
   Technical aspects can be very time consuming

3. **Bank relationships**
   Inform and, if required, involve local banks in the early stages of the process

4. **Internal communication**
   Communicate every stage of the project to all staff involved so that issues can be identified and addressed quickly and effectively

---

25.4.4 THE RESULTS

The liquidity management solution enables the company to use consolidated currency positions to mobilise working capital with a view to paying down debt or funding other parts of the group as well as optimising group liquidity. In the first full year after implementation, the company reduced its consolidated European interest-bearing debt by EUR 45 million. The regional payment factory is functioning efficiently. The number of local bank accounts and payment instruments have been reduced. The switch to a payment factory has also helped enable more accurate reconciliation and improved service levels, and to generate associated time and cost savings. As a result of these projects, treasury exceeded the 10% cost saving target and they contributed significantly to the company's overall financial position.

25.5
Virtual cash management

25.5.1   THE COMPANY

Company

Our last case is an European tech company specialised in software services. It has two business units: one that sells software licences (mainly through direct debits (DDs)) and another that provides maintenance services for hardware and software, which are typically invoiced in arrears. The company has entities in the following countries: UK (5), FR (3), NL (3), DE (5) and CH (3). It conducts its business in GBP, EUR and CHF.

Treasury organisation

The company recently underwent a reorganisation and has centralised a number of its financial operations and responsibilities in a new central treasury department in the Netherlands. There are two FTEs working in the department. As this department was relatively new, the company did not yet have advanced TMS systems in place. A lot of management information came from centralising local procedures and processes, for which Excel was often used. Prior to the reorganisation, the company had local operations in each country as well as a lot of local bank relationships (11) and an overabundance of current accounts (70+).

25.5.2   OBJECTIVES

The company's main challenges were to optimise its cross-border positions by obtaining full visibility and full availability of cash at the central treasury level. It also wanted to better leverage its economies of scale. This meant that instead of having small volumes handled by many different banks, the company concentrated on one or two banks and negotiated better terms & conditions.

FIGURE 25.3

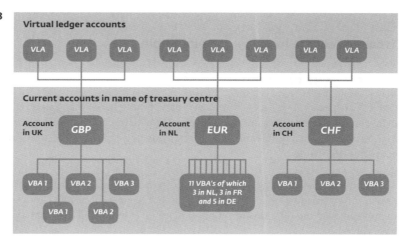

25.5.3　THE NEW STRUCTURE

The company conducted a request for proposal (RFP) process and chose two banks for its European cash management. The main drivers were the operational and counterparty risk policy, innovative cash management solutions, footprint and fit with cash requirements. It then decided to implement a virtual cash management structure at one of the banks:

- Treasury opened a current account in each of the currencies of the currency centres (a CHF account in Switzerland, a EUR account in the Netherlands and a GBP account in the UK). All these accounts were opened in the name of central treasury.

- Each of the entities received a virtual bank account (VBA) for each currency they traded in. This virtual account could be used for receivables and payables, and was connected to the current account of central treasury. Clients would pay into the IBAN of the VBA in the name of the local entity, while the funds would be booked real time to the connected current account in the name of central treasury.

- At the same time payments could be made from the VBA, connected to the local clearing in the country of the entity, while the funds would be debited from the current account in the name of central treasury.

- In order to keep track of the intercompany positions, the company used an intercompany loan administration tool provided by the bank, which was highly integrated into the virtual account solution, via virtual ledger accounts (VLA) and enabled the company to configure custom reports for internal management reporting purposes.

This solution enabled the company to achieve central visibility and availability of cash while minimising the risk of not knowing the specific positions of specific currencies at any time. The RFP also enabled the company to agree on improved terms and conditions.

25.6
Treasury centre in Asia – case example

25.6.1　THE COMPANY

Our last case example is a fragrance, flavour and luxury goods manufacturer that is privately owned and headquartered in Asia. It is a medium-sized company with 54 operating companies, 17 manufacturing sites and four research and development centres across more than 50 countries worldwide.

The company has a very decentralised management culture. This is mainly because it has grown through acquisitions. The global nature of its operations and client base has resulted in multiple banking relationships. Consequently, a complicated cash management structure has evolved.

25.6.2 OBJECTIVES

The company had an aggressive plan to grow the business in Asia and China specifically. However, with many legal entities using different processes, ERP systems and a large number of relationship banks, a variety of banking platforms and non-standardised reporting practices, the company was suffering from a lack of financial information. The strategic policy of the company was focused on two goals:

- Allow the conversion of profits into cash more quickly (ensuring a steady cash flow to fund growth initiatives)
- Provide senior management with improved information on company finances and enable them to make timely decisions

These strategic goals have been translated into three cash management goals:

- Optimise liquidity management to minimise excess funds in Asia and reduce external debt
- Automate transaction processes and improve efficiencies through improved cash flow forecasting and better control of payments, and optimise DSO by speeding up collections
- Centralise all back-office processes into a regional shared service centre

25.6.3 THE NEW STRUCTURE

Asia is a more complicated area for cash management than the Europe and the US – where an established common legal framework hastens the standardisation of regulations and payments across an entire region. Each country in Asia has its own laws and foreign exchange regulations, and treasurers must deal with this diversity. The complexity of managing cash across Asia has led to the growth of hybrid structures for organising regional treasury. As a result, the company decided to operate a split model in Asia where it would operate in-country treasury centres in the largest regulated countries and a regional treasury centre in Hong Kong for non-regulated countries. The company chose the in-country model for the regulated countries while the regional treasury centre will manage the non-regulated countries on an 'arm's length' basis. Cash in the non-regulated countries can be centralised into the regional treasury centre. However, liquidity in the regulated countries must be managed in-country and cannot be transferred to other countries due to foreign exchange regulations. The company chose Hong Kong as a treasury centre location for the following reasons:

- International financial centre with a transparent financial system
- Robust banking system
- Comprehensive tax treaties network to avoid double taxation
- No withholding tax on treasury-related payments
- No FX controls
- Proximity to mainland China and good availability of RMB services
- Highly qualified financial workforce

Liquidity management

The main regulatory constraints on cash management in Asia concern foreign exchange restrictions, the limitation on inter-company lending and the varying tax regimes in each country. To ensure that the company's liquidity management structure was legally valid, due diligence specific to this project was carried out by a qualified legal and tax firm.

Regional solution – non-regulated countries

The company decided to set up a regional USD cash pool with a regional banking partner. Bank rationalisation was an important part of the project, i.e. transferring numerous bank accounts into one bank for the region. All local entities had to migrate their accounts to the regional bank.

For each country, one local USD master account needed to be set up with the regional bank. In addition, operating companies continued to use bank accounts in local currencies with an in-country bank. All operating companies were asked to swap local currency balances into USD balances with the regional bank at regular intervals. The USD balances were included in an automated cross-border cash concentration into the master account held in Hong Kong. A multi-entity notional cash pool was set up in Hong Kong, combining non-resident accounts in the name of the local operating companies to avoid inter-company lending between the participating entities. The regional treasury team is managing the notional pool (which is often running a net surplus position). However, a USD intra-day and overnight credit facility has been attached to the notional pool in order to deal with temporary deficit positions.

Regional solution – all countries

For all countries that are restricted by local regulations and cannot participate in the USD cash pool, an interest optimisation scheme has been set up with the regional banking partner. This scheme enhances the credit interest on the local currency balances in all countries, without the requirement of sweeping the balances into the pool. So although the cash is trapped, it earns the company a higher yield. The yield is calculated by the regional bank, taking into account the overall credit position of all accounts in the region. The higher the total balances, the higher the interest the bank will pay.

FIGURE 25.4   TREASURY CENTRE IN ASIA – LIQUIDITY STRUCTURE EXAMPLE

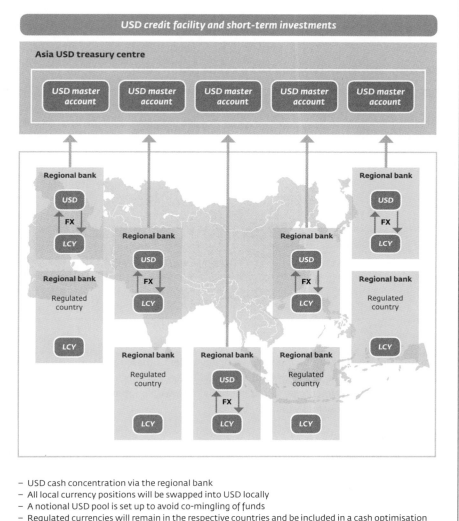

- USD cash concentration via the regional bank
- All local currency positions will be swapped into USD locally
- A notional USD pool is set up to avoid co-mingling of funds
- Regulated currencies will remain in the respective countries and be included in a cash optimisation scheme

In-country solution for China

Conventional cash and liquidity management solutions available to a treasurer in China are very limited and are restricted by what the law in China permits. A method officially approved since 2001 by the Peoples Bank of China, China's central bank, is the 'entrusted loan arrangement'. An entrusted loan is defined as a loan where the bank acts as an agent of entrusted funds from a depositor (the operating company) and on-lends the funds to a borrower (another operating company) designated by the depositor. The company in this case example decided to adopt such a structure to concentrate its rapidly growing renminbi (RMB) balances held by the subsidiaries in China. Under this arrangement, daily physical sweeps are set to sweep to a single master account.

FIGURE 25.5 MULTI-ENTRUSTED LOAN STRUCTURE – CHINA

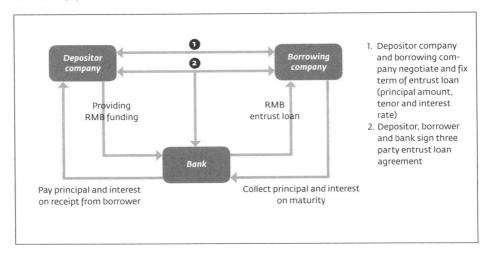

Cross-border transfers of capital are very restricted under Chinese regulations and automated cross-border sweeps are therefore not available. In light of this, the company decided to execute cross-border payments on a manual basis only, with supporting documentation to demonstrate their purpose and validity.

Cash flow management
Although the ultimate goal is to set up a regional shared service centre, the company decided to start with a regional payment factory. A phased approach was used because of the complexity of this project. The company had many legal entities using different processes, different ERP systems, different banking platforms and non-standardised reporting. Choosing a regional bank and setting up the regional treasury centre in Hong Kong accelerated the rollout of the payment factory. Because of its fragmented existing organisation, the company decided to focus on four areas:

- Standardisation
- Central control
- Visibility of cash
- Reduced expenses

Standardisation

In the past, the company made use of multiple electronic banking platforms, ERP and treasury systems. A decision was made to implement a region-wide ERP system. After implementation of this regional ERP system, the company would be able to centralise all outgoing payments into the new payment factory. The payments processes (such as batch payments, urgent payments and manual payments) would all be standardised, regardless of the country where they originated or would be routed to. The plan is that formats, workflow and security will all be standardised in order to provide substantial benefits to the business.

Central control

Without changing local responsibilities related to invoice handling and approval, the regional treasury centre is able to gain central control over outgoing payments. When and what will be paid can be controlled in real time. The timing of the submission of the payment instructions is set by the treasury centre, which will ensure close alignment with the forecasting process.

Visibility of cash

The centralisation of all outgoing payments and the centralised and real-time access to transaction information provides considerable benefits. Visibility of cash balances and cash flows can be improved significantly and the timing of the cash flows can be optimised. In combination with the regional USD cash pool, liquidity management can be centralised for the non-regulated countries – reducing in-country resources and providing an automated tool to fund deficits by using excess balances.

Reduced expenses

The company expects costs savings through:

- Lower bank fees
- Reduced cash float
- Minimised volumes of payment errors
- Reduced staff time / resources at a local level

25.6.4   THE RESULTS

The centralised liquidity structure supports the company's aggressive regional growth initiatives. From the central USD pool in Hong Kong, the company can significantly finance its expanding businesses with internally generated cash. The 'entrusted loan arrangement' in China guarantees the most efficient use of the in-country renminbi (RMB) positions and the regional cash optimisation scheme is delivering immediate results by improving the interest on all balances in local currencies. The visibility and availability of cash positions and the newly set-up payment factory are all providing senior management with improved information on company finances and are providing treasury with more control over the regional liquidity positions. A key enabler of the payment factory is the regional ERP system, which has been rolled out country by country. Although the roll-out took longer than expected, improved efficiencies and cost savings have already made the project a great success. With the regional payment factory up and running, the company is now ready for the next step towards an SSC.

Index

collection factory 177
collection product 182
collections management 104, 108
commercial paper 369, 380
company cheque 191, 210
compliance 61
confidentiality 227
constant balancing 309
control function 36
controller 34, 48
core bank 63
corporate benefit 457
corporate bond 380
corporate finance 31
corporate fraud 229
correspondent banking 268, 274, 277
cost centre 39
counter deposit 207
credit card 196, 210
credit facilities 326
credit risk 103, 107
credit terms 102
credit transfer 182, 198, 210
crisis, financial 68, 365, 538
cross-border payment 163
cross-border transaction 49
cross-border transfer 56, 159, 277
cross currency liquidity management 407
currency crisis 393
currency fluctuations 387
currency swap 401
customer-to-cash 100
cybercrime 228

D
days inventory outstanding 85, 87, 91, 361
days payable outstanding 91, 95
days payables outstanding 85, 87
days sales outstanding 84, 86, 91, 100
days working capital 84, 86, 87, 91
debit card 196, 210
decentralisation 38
delivery channel 213
deposit 367
deviation analysis 347, 353
digitalisation 520

direct debit 206, 210
direct link system 213, 217
direct method 344
discounting 147
discrepancy management 99
disintermediation 62
dispute management 96, 104, 108
documentary collection 144, 198, 210
documentary letter of credit 141, 186
draft 144
duration 366
dynamic discounting 123

E
early warning indicator 354
EBA clearing 257
EBICS 223
e-channel delivery 148
economic exposure 391
economic risk 32, 398
electronic data interchange (EDI) 219
EMIR 41
encryption 227
end-of-day balance 291
enterprise resource planning 72, 168
enterprise risk management 73
entry-level treasury management system 239
ERP system 61, 72, 74
EU interest and royalties directive 433
euro 49, 57
european treasury 558
exposure at default 377

F
fair value 472
fair value hedging 478
fair value hierarchy 473
FCF 90
finality 262
final system selection 250
financial accounting 50
financial risk 57
financial supply chain 47
fixed-term cash 363
flexible-term cash 363

Author Profiles

The editorial board

Anthony N. Birts

Anthony Birts is an in independent lecturer specialised in cash management. For many years, he was the Chief Examiner for the Certified International Cash Management programme of the Association of Corporate Treasurers (UK). In addition, as a Senior Teaching Fellow at the University of Bath's School of Management, he lectured in both the undergraduate and post-graduate programmes. Prior to joining the university, he was with Bank of America based in London. During his time at the bank Anthony fulfilled a variety of roles, initially as an account officer and finally as a Vice President in the Bank's Global Cash Management department.

Alexander Huiskes

Alexander Huiskes has worked in the financial industry for over 18 years and has held a number of positions with several international firms, including ABN Amro, RBS, EY and JP Morgan. He has fulfilled roles in the areas of Financial Markets, Product Management, Advisory and Coverage. During his career, Alexander partnered with Fortune 500 firms as well as fast growing FinTechs, developing innovative treasury solutions and executing financial transformation. Alexander earned a Master of Laws at Leiden University and his Register Treasurer qualification at the Vrije Universiteit of Amsterdam. He is a co-author and editorial board member of the third edition of the International Cash Management book 2013.

Carlo R.W. de Meijer

Carlo R.W. de Meijer is an independent Economist and Senior Researcher. Until October 2015, he worked at the Market Engagement Department of Services Payments at the Royal Bank of Scotland. During his career at ABN Amro and RBS, Carlo held various positions within financial services, including senior economist and private investment adviser. He has published many articles on a number of economic and financial topics, particularly in relation to international financial markets and European financial and monetary integration. He was also one of the editors of the International Cash Management Handbook 2013. Carlo holds a Master's degree in international economics from the University of Tilburg (1977).

Petra Plompen

Petra Plompen has been working in transaction banking since 1997. She was responsible for the implementation of euro payments market infrastructure developments within international banks, both for high-value and commercial payments. She is currently Senior Manager of Services Development and Management at EBA CLEARING.

Gary Throup

Gary Throup is Head of Treasury at Philips Lighting. With over 20 years' experience in Corporate Treasury and financial service environments, he has led global teams through change and transformation in complex and challenging environments while delivering leading and innovative solutions in Treasury. He also has extensive experience running major projects for implementation of new treasury structures, including establishing global treasury organisations for a number of corporate disentanglement and IPO projects.

Michiel Ranke

Michiel is the head of the liquidity management product team within ING's Wholesale Banking Transaction Services. He has worked in the financial industry for over 20 years and held a number of positions at different international banks. He has also led global teams focusing on business change and transformation. Michiel holds a Master's degree in monetary economics from the Erasmus University of Rotterdam.

Contributing Authors

Frank Bauling

Frank Bauling is a Principal Legal Counsel within the Payments & Cash Management Team of ING Bank's Legal Wholesale Banking department in Amsterdam. Frank advises ING's cash management Sales and Product Management departments with respect to the legal aspects of national and international cash management product offerings. Frank is an in-house lawyer with more than 30 years of experience, over 10 years of which were in the field of cash management.

Marten Bleijenberg

Marten is Director Product Management within ING's Wholesale Banking Transaction Services. He has more than 22 years of experience in product development and sales of payments and cash management solutions, with a special focus on electronic banking. Marten represents ING in the worldwide Swift community. A large part of his banking experience has been developed in ING's Central and Eastern European network

Ruud Bulkmans

Ruud is an Executive Director in EY's Financial Accounting Advisory Services practice. He joined EY in 2000 and leads the assurance services proposition for Treasuries at EY in the Netherlands. Ruud is specialised in such areas as the valuation of derivatives, hedging, processes and controls around financial instruments.

Dermot Canavan

Dermot is the Head of Trade Finance Services Product Management within ING's Wholesale Banking Transaction Services. He has over 20 years of experience in financial services having worked in sales, product management and as CAO of trade finance businesses. Prior to entering the banking sector, Dermot served as Chief Accountant of a leasing company. He is a Fellow of the Institute of Chartered Accountants. He has also contributed to and written a number of articles on trade finance which have appeared in various trade finance publications.

Paul DeCrane

Paul DeCrane is the leader of Ernst & Young's Global Treasury Services practice. Paul provides market leading consulting advice to Treasurers, CFOs, CIOs, COOs, and CROs. He leverages over 20 years of consulting and industry experience, including quantitative analysis and banking and insurance liquidity management. He is a regular presenter of thought leadership to the international community at conferences and through publications.

Robert O'Donoghue

Robert is the Global Head of Trade Solutions within ING's Wholesale Banking Transaction Services. He joined ING in 1992 and has almost 30 years of banking experience in areas such as Receivables Finance, Supply Chain Finance, tradition Trade products, balance sheet restructuring and Risk Management

Lenneke van Dijk

Lenneke van Dijk is an Executive Director within EY's tax department in Amsterdam. She is part of the global EY Treasury & Finance network and has been advising corporates and banks on the tax aspects of implementing cash management and in-house banks for more than 18 years.

Roger Disch

Roger Disch is a Partner at Ernst & Young and leads the Swiss Treasury Services practice as well as acting as a leading member of the EMEIA Treasury Services group. He provides market leading Treasury and Financial Risk Management consulting advice to corporates, insurers and banks. He is globally responsible for a multinational commodity trading company. In addition, Roger regularly presents and publishes thought leadership in Treasury.

Charles Duijmelings

After 21 years with ING, Charles has extensive experience in transaction services. He has worked both in Retail and Wholesale in various roles, leading product management teams and has managed complex strategy and change programmes. In his current position he is heading the Liquidity and Cash management team for ING Wholesale Banking Transaction Services. This includes leading the Cash Management and Virtual Cash Management product management team of ING Transaction Services across Europe.

Sven Goeggel

Sven Goeggel is a Senior Manager in the Swiss Treasury practice. He joined EY three years ago to take the lead in advising corporate and insurance clients. Sven was a Treasurer in his previous life and built up and worked for the in-house bank of a world leader in assembly and fastening material trade. Sven is specialised in the fields of cash & liquidity management and payments.

Freek de Haas

Freek de Haas is an Executive Director with EY Montesquieu, heading the EY corporate debt and treasury advisory practice for Dutch and Belgian Mid-Market Corporates and Institutions. Freek spent over 15 years in corporate banking, where he assumed several client-facing roles. Freek has advised over EUR 2.5bn in corporate debt.

Dick Hoogenberg

Dick Hoogenberg is a tax partner with EY and has worked since 1990 with multinationals in the field of treasury and (in-house) banking that are headquartered in the Netherlands and abroad. He is a frequent speaker at banking and treasury seminars.

Craig Kennedy

Craig is a Partner with EY in the London office with over 18 years of extensive treasury consulting experience. He is a member of EY's Treasury Executive Group and is a frequent speaker at treasury seminars.

Annelinda Koldewe

Annelinda heads up the Accounts & Cash Management department within ING's Wholesale Banking Transaction Services. She is responsible for developing and maintaining the product suite for Domestic, International and Virtual Cash Management, ensuring they meet the evolving needs for corporate treasurers.

Frank Koord

Frank is as a Product Manager responsible for International Cash Management products within ING's Wholesale Banking Transaction Services. He joined ING in 2003 and develops and deploys Cash & Liquidity solutions for large corporates. His earlier career consisted of financial administrative consulting and interim roles in managing financial operations activities.

Sara Lamont

Sara Lamont is a commercial Product Manager, working within ING's Wholesale Banking Transaction Services. Sara specialises in contract and documentation management, running several successful strategic improvement projects in this area. Sara's focus area is looking for new trends that can alleviate the burden of compliance and process inefficiency while improving customer experience.

Ludy Limburg

Ludy is business development manager within ING for the Treasury organisation. He is involved in various bank-wide transformation programmes as well as various industry developments where he combines Payments, Cash & (intraday) Liquidity expertise with a broad knowledge on the financial industry based on over 25 years of experience in various roles. He represents ING and the Dutch market in various industry groups (including ECB, EBA Clearing, EBF, DNB, CLS).

Leon Merkun

Leon is a Managing Director at ING's Working Capital Solutions team based in Amsterdam, with a specific focus on supply chain finance and working capital management fur multinationals. He has more than 25 years of experience in Finance & Control, Corporate Treasury, Corporate Finance, Mergers & Acquisitions and Banking.

Marc Monyek

Marc Monyek is a Senior Manager with Ernst & Young's Global Treasury Services practice and has experience in both consulting and audit. He provides leading advice to corporate CFOs and treasurers on financial risk management and currency risk management, cash flow forecasting, global cash management, cash collections and pooling, debt and investment management and accounts receivable reviews.

Alexander Odenthal

Alexander Odenthal is the Executive Director of EYs Treasury practice, leading Treasury IT services in Germany. In the past, he has worked on many different selections and implementations of treasury management systems.

Joost van Swieten

Joost is a Manager within EY's Financial Accounting & Advisory Services practice in Amsterdam, where he advises a range of financial institutions as well as corporates. He has over 10 years of experience in the area of treasury, and is specialised in financial markets, financial instruments and hedge accounting.

Martijn Valbracht

Martijn is a Director with the Corporate Clients department of ING Bank. He is part of the international Wholesale Banking network of ING. In this role, he advises international companies on their strategy on Corporate Financial Management, Capital Markets & Funding and Risk Management, as well as solutions for Trade & Export Finance, Working Capital Management and Cash & Liquidity Management. Martijn has over 15 years of consulting and banking experience.

Sean Whelan

Sean is a Senior Manager with EY in our London office. He has 22 years of industry experience and leads our Corporate Treasury risk advisory team, covering both treasury risk management and technical treasury accounting.

Evelien Witlox

Evelien is the Global Head of Product Management Payments & Cards within ING's Wholesale Banking Transaction Services with responsibility for payments, merchant acquiring and commercial cards. Evelien is an active member in the industry with a seat on the board of the Adviesraad Betaal Vereniging Nederland, which is the primary payments association in the Netherlands. She has authored a number of papers and articles on cross-border payments, omnichannel retail, instant payments and CAPS for PSD2.

Company Profiles

ING

ING is a global financial institution with a strong European base, offering banking services through its operating company ING Bank. The purpose of ING Bank is empowering people to stay a step ahead in life and in business. ING Bank's more than 51,000 employees offer retail and wholesale banking services to customers in over 40 countries.

ING Group shares are listed on the exchanges of Amsterdam (INGA AS, INGA.AS), Brussels and on the New York Stock Exchange (ADRs: ING US, ING.N).
Sustainability forms an integral part of ING's strategy, evidenced by ING's ranking as a leader in the banks industry group by Sustainalytics. ING Group shares are included in the FTSE-4Good index and in the Dow Jones Sustainability Index (Europe and World), where ING is also among the leaders in the banks industry group. For more information about ING, please visit ING.com

EY

EY is a global leader in assurance, tax, transaction and advisory services. The insights and quality services we deliver help build trust and confidence in the capital markets and in economies the world over. We develop outstanding leaders who team to deliver on our promises to all of our stakeholders. In so doing, we play a critical role in building a better working world for our people, for our clients and for our communities.

EY refers to the global organization, and may refer to one or more, of the member firms of Ernst & Young Global Limited, each of which is a separate legal entity. Ernst & Young Global Limited, a UK company limited by guarantee, does not provide services to clients. For more information about our organization, please visit ey.com.

List of Contributions

Chapter 1, The Treasury Organisation has been authored by Carlo R.W. de Meyer as a revised version of Chapter 2, The Treasury Organisation, in the third edition. That chapter was authored by Joost Bergen and partly based on an update of material in previous editions.

Chapter 2, Cash Management Responsibilities has been authored by Carlo R.W. de Meyer as a revised version of Chapter 3, Core Cash Management Responsibilities, in the third edition. That chapter was authored by Willem van Alphen and partly based on an update of material in previous editions.

Chapter 3, Treasury Transformation has been authored by Carlo R.W. de Meyer.

Chapter 4, Working Capital Management has been authored by Leon Merkun as a revised version of Chapter 4, Working Capital Management, in the third edition. That chapter was authored by Mikael Aberg, Veronica Heald and Jennifer Pinney and partly based on an update of material in previous editions.

Chapter 5, Supplier and Receivables Finance to Support Trade and Working Capital has been authored by Robert O'Donoghue partially as a revised version of Chapter 5, Trade Finance, in the third edition. That chapter was authored by David Millet and partly based on an update of material in previous editions.

Chapter 6, Trade Finance has been authored by Dermot Canavan partially as a revised version of Chapter 5, Trade Finance, in the third edition. That chapter was authored by David Millet and partly based on an update of material in previous editions.

Chapter 7, Cash Flow Management has been authored by Charles Duimelings and Martijn Valbracht as a revised version of Chapter 6, Cash Flow Management, in the third edition. That chapter was authored by Willem van Alphen and partly based on an update of material in previous editions.

Chapter 8, Transaction Types has been authored by Evelien Witlox as a revised version of Chapter 8, Transaction Types, in the third edition. That chapter was authored by Mark Richardson and partly based on an update of material in previous editions.

Chapter 9, Delivery Channels has been authored by Marten Bleijenberg as a revised version of Chapter 9, Transaction Types, in the third edition. That chapter was authored by Tino Kam and partly based on an update of material in previous editions.

Chapter 10, Treasury Management Systems has been authored by Alexander Odenthal.

Chapter 11, The Payment, Clearing and Settlement Process has been authored by Ludy Limburg as a revised version of Chapter 12, The Payment, Clearing and Settlement Process, in the third edition. That chapter was authored by Ludy Limburg and partly based on an update of material in previous editions.

Chapter 12, Cash Balances Management has been authored by Frank Koord as a revised version of Chapter 13, Cash Balances Management, in the third edition. That chapter was authored by Willem van Alphen and partly based on an update of material in previous editions.

Chapter 13, Cash Pooling Techniques has been authored by Annelinda Koldewe as a revised version of Chapter 14, Cash Pooling Techniques, in the third edition. That chapter was authored by Bert Terlien and partly based on an update of material in previous editions.

Chapter 14, Cash Flow Forecasting has been authored by Robert Disch and Sven Goeggel as a revised version of Chapter 17, Cash Flow Forecasting, in the third edition. That chapter was authored by Joost Bergen and partly based on an update of material in previous editions.

Chapter 15, Investment and Funding Management has been authored by Freek de Haas as a revised version of Chapter 16, Investment and Funding Management, in the third edition. That chapter was authored by Nick Claus and partly based on an update of material in previous editions.

Chapter 16, Forex Exchange Risk Management has been authored by Paul deCrane and Marc Monyek as a revised version of Chapter 18, Forex exchange risk management in the third edition. That chapter was authored by Lex van der Wielen and partly based on an update of material in previous editions.

Chapter 17, Cross Currency Liquidity Management has been authored by Paul deCrane and Marc Monyek as a revised version of Chapter 19, Cross Currency Liquidity Management, in the third edition. That chapter was authored by Lex van der Wielen and partly based on an update of material in previous editions.

Chapter 18, Short-term Interest Rate Management has been authored by Craig Kennedy and Séan Whelan as a revised version of Chapter 20, Short-term Interest Rate Management, in the third edition. That chapter was authored by Lex van der Wielen and partly based on an update of material in previous editions.

Chapter 19, Tax Consequences of Cash Management has been authored by Lenneke van Dijk and Dick Hoogenberg as a revised version of Chapter 21, Tax Consequences of Cash Management, in the third edition. That chapter was authored by editorial board and partly based on an update of material in previous editions.

Chapter 20, Legal Considerations has been authored by Frank Bauling partially as a revised version of chapter 15, Setting-up International Cash-Pools, in the third edition. That chapter was authored by Bert Terlien and partly based on an update of material in previous editions.

Chapter 21, Treasury Accounting and Control has been authored by Ruud Bulkmans and Joost van Swieten.

Chapter 22, Regulatory Implications has been authored by Carlo R.W. de Meijer and Sara Lamont as a revised version of Chapter 22, Regulatory Implications, in the third edition. That chapter was authored by Carlo R.W. de Meijer and partly based on an update of material in previous editions.

Chapter 23, Key Developments has been authored by Carlo R.W. de Meijer.

Chapter 24, Cash Management Structures has been authored by Alexander Huiskes partially as a revised version of Chapter 23, Regional Cash Management Structures, in the third edition. That chapter was authored by Willem van Alphen and partly based on an update of material in previous editions.

Chapter 25, Case Studies has been authored by Martijn Valbracht partially as a revised version of Chapter 23, Regional Cash Management Strucures, in the third edition. That chapter was authored by Willem van Alphen and partly based on an update of material in previous editions.